Special Interest Politics

Special Interest Politics

Gene M. Grossman and
Elhanan Helpman

The MIT Press
Cambridge, Massachusetts
London, England

This book was set in Palatino on 3B2 by Asco Typesetters, Hong Kong, and was printed and bound in the United States of America.

Library of Congress Cataloging-in-Publication Data

Grossman, Gene M.
    Special interest politics / Gene M. Grossman and Elhanan Helpman.
      p. cm.
    Includes bibliographical references and index.
    ISBN 0-262-07230-0
    1. Pressure groups. 2. Lobbying. I. Helpman, Elhanan. II. Title.
JF529 .G74   2001
328.3′8—dc21

                                         2001045287

To my parents, Alfred and Edith Grossman
G.M.G.

To Henia, Jozef, and Victor
E.H.

Contents

List of Figures   xi
Preface   xiii

1   Introduction   1
1.1   SIG Activities and Tactics   4
1.2   About This Book   14
        1.2.1   Methodology   14
        1.2.2   Organization and Content   16

I   **Voting**   39

2   Voting and Elections   41
2.1   Direct Democracy   42
        2.1.1   The Median Voter and the Agenda Setter   42
        2.1.2   Sincere Versus Strategic Voting   45
        2.1.3   Direct Democracy without Agenda Setters   45
        2.1.4   Non-Single-Peaked Preferences   48
        2.1.5   Multiple Policy Issues   50
        2.1.6   Summary   52
2.2   Representative Democracy   53
        2.2.1   The Downsian Model   54
        2.2.2   Candidates with Policy Preferences   56
        2.2.3   Endogenous Candidates   59
2.3   Electing a Legislature   64
        2.3.1   Single-Member Districts   65
        2.3.2   Proportional Representation   68

3   Groups as Voters   75
3.1   Turnout   76

3.2   Knowledge   87
3.3   Partisanship   95

II Information   101

4   Lobbying   103
    4.1   One Lobby   105
          4.1.1   The Setting   106
          4.1.2   Two States of the World   107
          4.1.3   Three States of the World   110
          4.1.4   Continuous Information   113
          4.1.5   Ex Ante Welfare   118
    4.2   Two Lobbies   120
          4.2.1   Like Bias   121
          4.2.2   Opposite Bias   130
          4.2.3   Multidimensional Information   133
    4.3   Appendix: A More General Lobbying Game   138
          4.3.1   The General Setting   139
          4.3.2   Properties of an Equilibrium   140

5   Costly Lobbying   143
    5.1   Exogenous Lobbying Costs   145
          5.1.1   Single Lobby, Dichotomous Information   145
          5.1.2   Single Lobby, Continuous Information   150
          5.1.3   Two Lobbies   152
    5.2   Endogenous Lobbying Costs   161
          5.2.1   Dichotomous Information   161
          5.2.2   Many States of Nature   164
          5.2.3   Multiple Interest Groups   168
    5.3   Access Costs   171
          5.3.1   Group with a Known Bias   172
          5.3.2   Group with an Unknown Bias   176
          5.3.3   Access Fees as Signals of SIG Preferences   180

6   Educating Voters   185
    6.1   The Election   188
          6.1.1   The Voters   188
          6.1.2   The Parties   191
          6.1.3   The Interest Group   192

6.2   Early Communication   194
      6.2.1   Party Competition and Voting   195
      6.2.2   Credible Messages   195
      6.2.3   Who Gains and Who Loses?   199
6.3   Late Communication   201
      6.3.1   Reports and Voting   202
      6.3.2   Political Competition   204
      6.3.3   Early and Late Communication   209
6.4   Endorsements   210
6.5   Educating Members   212
6.6   Appendix: SIG Leaders with a Broad Mandate   216
      6.6.1   Communication Game When SIG Leaders Have a
              Broad Mandate   217
      6.6.2   Political Competition When SIG Leaders Have a
              Broad Mandate   220
      6.6.3   A Comparison of Two Mandates   221

III Campaign Contributions   223

7   Buying Influence   225
     7.1   One-Dimensional Policy Choice   226
     7.2   The Allocation of Public Spending   233
     7.3   Multiple Policy Instruments   235
     7.4   Regulation and Protection   238
     7.5   Bargaining   243

8   Competing for Influence   247
     8.1   The Politician as Common Agent   249
     8.2   The Minimum Wage   256
     8.3   Compensating Equilibria   265
     8.4   Trade Policy   270
     8.5   Redistributive Taxation   275
     8.6   Competition for Influence: Good Thing or Bad
           Thing?   279

9   Influencing a Legislature   283
     9.1   Buying Votes   284
     9.2   A Legislature with an Agenda Setter   291
     9.3   Multiple Interest Groups   299

9.3.1   Randomized Offers   302
9.3.2   Competing for Influence at the Proposal Stage   309
9.3.3   The Scale of a Public Project   314

10 Contributions and Elections   319
10.1 Electoral Competition with Campaign Spending   321
     10.1.1 The Voters   321
     10.1.2 The Parties   324
     10.1.3 The Interest Groups   326
10.2 One Interest Group   328
     10.2.1 The Influence Motive   328
     10.2.2 A Pure Electoral Motive   331
     10.2.3 A Choice of Motives   334
10.3 Multiple Interest Groups   339

References   347
Index   357

List of Figures

2.1 Pairwise Comparison   43

2.2 Two-Stage Voting with an Extreme Outcome   47

2.3 The Policy Constructed from the Median in Each Dimension Is Not a Condorcet Winner   50

2.4 An Intermediate Policy May Not Win a Majority   51

4.1 Example with Two States   108

4.2 Partitions and Policies with Two Reports   126

4.3 Equilibrium Partitions When SIG 1 Reports First   128

4.4 Messages with Two Policy Dimensions   135

4.5 Best Response by SIG 1   136

5.1 Equilibrium Lobbying Function with a Minimum Cost of Lobbying   168

5.2 Contributions as a Function of δ 175

5.3 The SIG's Incentive to Lobby   178

5.4 Expected Utility for a SIG with Bias δ 182

6.1 Equilibrium Policies with Late Communication   206

7.1 Candidate Equilibrium   229

7.2 Optimal Contribution Functions   231

7.3 Budget Allocation   234

7.4 Bargaining Outcome   245

8.1 SIG i's Choice   254

8.2 Compensating Contribution Schedule   267

9.1 Compensation Functions for Legislators   288

9.2 The Cost of Legislation   290

9.3   Equilibrium Policy without an Agenda Setter   290

9.4   The Agenda Setter's Best Alternative   295

9.5   Equilibrium Policy with an Agenda Setter   296

9.6   The Agenda Setter's Best Alternative $\bar{p}$ When $\pi > q$ 299

9.7   Regions of Conflict and Nonconflict between the SIGs   310

9.8   Joint Welfare of SIG 1 and SIG 2   311

9.9   Conflicting SIG Tastes for a Public Project   315

Preface

Our research on special interest politics emerged from our interest in international trade policy. After years of reading and writing about optimal policies, we could not help but wonder why observed trade policies are so different from the prescriptions of the normative literature. Of course, that literature presumes the existence of a "benevolent dictator"—a species that is all too rare in the real world of economic policy making. Once we began to examine the role of special interest groups in the process of trade policy formation, we began to realize that there is little that is unique about this particular type of policy. The methods that interest groups use to affect trade outcomes are the same as the ones they use to influence a myriad of other policy decisions, including both economic issues and issues outside the economic realm.

This book reports the results of our research. It is intended as a monograph, not as a textbook. We do not attempt to survey the burgeoning literature in political economy. Rather, we focus narrowly on the role of special interest groups in the policymaking process. Readers interested in broader coverage of a wide range of topics—including, for example, monetary politics, public debt, political budget cycles, economic reform, the size of government, and comparative political systems—would do well to delve into the two excellent recent textbooks by Drazen (2000) and Persson and Tabellini (2000). The former contains a detailed, critical discussion of macroeconomic issues, while the latter is broader in its scope. Both are worthy of close examination and study.

Not only is our focus relatively narrow, but we do not attempt to provide a comprehensive review of the existing literature on special interest groups. We recognize, of course, our intellectual debt to those who have studied these groups before us, and we have tried to acknowledge the many contributions by political scientists and economists that have influenced our thinking. But we have also sought to present a relatively unified treatment of a variety of topics, while keeping the number of different models and the amount of different notation to a relative minimum. One cost of this attempt at unification is that we were unable to incorporate all of the useful ideas and insights in the literature; some points are simply too difficult to make in the context of the framework we have chosen.

This book draws on our earlier published articles, particularly in Part III on campaign contributions. But it also contains much material that is new. Some of the new material is original, such as our treatment in Chapter 6 of activities aimed at educating voters and in Chapter 9 of strategies for influencing a legislative body. Other new material is synthetic: we have tried to reformulate some of the ideas and models in the literature so as to lay bare the relationships between them. The book is targeted to an audience of professional economists and political scientists, and to graduate students embarking on careers in these fields. However, the Introduction (Chapter 1) provides a lengthy summary of the issues, methods, and results that we hope will be accessible to a wider audience.

Many debts are accumulated in the course of writing a book, and this one is no exception. Among those who generously shared their wisdom with us, or who read and commented on draft materials, are Marco Battaglini, Elchanan Ben-Porath, Tim Besley, Eddie Dekel, Avinash Dixit, Allan Drazen, Peter Eso, Torben Iverson, Ehud Menirav, John Morgan, Torsten Persson, Wolfgang Pesendorfer, Andrea Prat, Tom Romer, Ariel Rubinstein, Ken Shepsle, David Strömberg, and the participants in myriad seminars and conferences, who are too numerous to mention. Ruben Lubowski, Ronny Razin, and Taeyoon Sung provided invaluable research assistance. Ronny Razin also read the manuscript from beginning to end, finding as many of our errors in reasoning and typing as was humanly possible. We thank him warmly for these efforts.

Our research on political economy has been generously supported over the years by the U.S.-Israel Binational Science Foundation and the Canadian Institute for Advanced Research, in a series of grants to Tel Aviv University, and by the National Science Foundation, in several grants to the National Bureau of Economic Research. Many institutes and universities have hosted one or the other of us for periods ranging from a week to a month during the (long) time we were slaving over this manuscript. They include the Laboratoire d'Économie Quantitative d'Aix-Marseille de l'Université d'Aix-Marseille II, the Universita Commerciale L. Bocconi in Milan, the European University Institute in Florence, the Department of Economics at Agder University College in Kristiansand, the Indian Statistical Institute in New Delhi, the Institute for Advanced Studies in Vienna, the Suntory and Toyota International Centres for Economics and Related Disciplines (STICERD) at the London School of Economics and Political Science, the Department of Economics at the University of Sydney, the Institut d'Économie Industrielle de l'Université des Sciences Sociales de Toulouse, the Institute for International Economic Studies of the University of Stockholm, the Economic Policy Research Unit (EPRU) of the Copenhagen Business School, and the Department of Economics and Finance at the City University of Hong Kong. Visiting these diverse departments, and enjoying the hospitality there, has made our research and writing much more enjoyable.

Last, but certainly not least, there are the behind-the-scenes heroes of any book-writing project. Our families put up with our endless complaining and our too frequent absences during the many years of this research project. There are no words to express our gratitude to them.

1   Introduction

In the idealized democracy, public policy is guided by the principle of "one man, one vote." But in all real polities, special interest groups participate actively in the policymaking process. In this book, we examine the role that special interest groups play in democratic politics. We ask, From what features of the political landscape do special interest groups derive their power and influence? What determines the extent to which they are able to affect policy outcomes? And what happens when several groups with differing objectives compete for influence?

There is little consensus among social scientists about the appropriate definition of a special interest group (or SIG, for short). Some authors use the term broadly to refer to any subset of voters who have similar social or demographic characteristics, or similar beliefs, interests, and policy preferences. Others reserve the term for membership organizations that engage in political activities on behalf of their members. Here we need not limit ourselves to any one definition of a SIG. Thus, in Chapter 3 we entertain the broader definition of an interest group and discuss the ability of certain groups in society to gain favorable treatment from the government based only on their voting behavior. In that chapter, we take a SIG to be any identifiable group of voters with similar preferences on a subset of policy issues. Thereafter we focus on organizations that take political actions on behalf of a group of voters. In each chapter beginning with Chapter 4, we describe an activity that an organized group might undertake, and define a SIG to be any group that can engage in the activity. We consider the "members" of the SIG to be those individuals whose welfare the leaders take into account in deciding their actions, be they formal dues-paying members of the organization or not.

How many SIGs are there in the United States?[1] Considering how difficult it is to define such groups, it should come as no surprise that this question is nearly impossible to answer. Some authors have relied on the *Encyclopedia of Associations* for a rough tally of interest groups and a sense of their rate of proliferation. The 2000 edition of this reference work lists more than 22,000 nonprofit membership organizations in the United States that are national in scope. However, not all of these organizations are SIGs in the sense used here, inasmuch as only about an estimated one-third of them devote resources to political activities.[2] The number of organizations cited in the 1959 edition of the *Encyclopedia of Associations* was 5,843, and in the 1980 edition was 14,726. These figures suggest rapid growth in the number of organized interests, although it is impossible to know how much of this reflects the actual proliferation of groups and how much is due to the research efforts of the publishers or to changes in the criteria for inclusion in the book.

Another publication, *Washington Representatives*, lists more than 11,000 companies, associations, and public interest groups that engaged representatives in Washington, D.C., in 1999. Again, the list is much longer than in earlier years; for example, the 1979 edition of the book includes only 4,000 clients. Political action committees (PACs), which are organizations that have registered with the U.S. government under the reporting requirements of the Federal Election Campaign Act of 1974 so as to be able to contribute legally to political candidates, numbered 3,835 at the end of 1999. This represents a dramatic increase from the 608 PACs that had registered by the end of 1974 or the 2,000 that had registered by the end of 1979, although the number had already reached 4,000 by 1984 and has been fairly constant since then.[3] The overall impression that these figures give is that the number of SIGs active in national politics in the United States is by no means small, and probably continues to grow.

Special interest groups represent a highly diverse set of individuals and interests. Many but not all of the groups are organized around economic concerns. Most prominent, perhaps, are the groups repre-

1. We have made no attempt to find evidence on the number and activities of SIGs outside the United States, but casual observation would suggest that these groups are no less important to the political process in other countries.
2. Sheets (2000, p. vii) reports this figure, which derives from a study of 5,500 national associations conducted by the Hudson Institute on behalf of the American Society of Association Executives.
3. See http://www.fec.gov/press/pacchart.htm (accessed August 28, 2000).

senting business interests, such as trade associations (e.g., the Semiconductor Industry Association, American Iron and Steel Institute), peak business associations (U.S. Chamber of Commerce, National Association of Manufacturers), and the many individual corporations that maintain a political presence in Washington. Numerous groups also represent occupational interests, including labor unions (e.g., the American Postal Workers Union, American Federation of Teachers), professional associations (American Medical Association, National Bar Association), and farm groups (National Farmers Union). Nonmaterial interests also find representation in the political process. Groups have organized to represent those who share common views on a set of ideological or social issues and who wish to see those views reflected in government policy. There are, for example, groups representing different views on religion (American Jewish Congress, Christian Coalition), drug and alcohol policy (Mothers Against Drunk Driving, National Organization for the Reform of Marijuana Laws), gun control (National Rifle Association, Handgun Controls, Inc.), abortion rights (National Right to Life Organization, National Abortion and Reproductive Rights Action League), civil rights (National Association for the Advancement of Colored People), gay rights (National Gay and Lesbian Task Force), capital punishment (Citizens for Law and Order, National Coalition to Abolish the Death Penalty), and a host of others. Some groups press both economic and noneconomic policy objectives; environmental groups such as the Sierra Club and veterans groups such as the American Legion fall into this category.

Baumgartner and Leech (1998) have sorted the groups listed in the 1995 edition of the *Encyclopedia of Associations* into 18 categories, to give a sense of their breadth and distribution. First on their list are the trade, business, and commercial associations (3,973), followed by health and medical associations (2,426), public affairs associations (2,178), cultural organizations (1,938) and social welfare organizations (1,938). They also count 1,243 religious associations, 1,136 environmental and agricultural associations, and 226 labor unions. Schlozman and Tierney (1986) began instead with the list of represented clients in the 1981 edition of *Washington Representatives* and classified the interest groups a little differently. However one categorizes the different organized interests, there is no escaping the conclusion that SIGs are active in nearly all areas of government policy making.

Ever since James Madison penned his well-known concerns about
"factions" in *The Federalist Papers*, the overriding questions about the
role of SIGs in democratic politics have been normative ones. Social
scientists have debated whether special interests exert a positive or
a negative force on politics and society, and whether the activities
of SIGs collectively induce an outcome that approximates a social
optimum or whether the groups tend instead to subvert the public
interest. In contrast, most of the analysis in this book will be directed
at positive questions. We are interested in the conditions under
which SIGs can exert influence, and in identifying the determinants
of the extent of that influence. We are also interested in the different
tactics that SIGs use, and the reasons for their effectiveness or lack
thereof. Finally, we are interested in the outgrowth of competition
between special interests—which groups are most likely to prevail
when several of them seek conflicting policy objectives. Moreover,
as we elaborate further below, our intent in writing this book was
partly methodological: we would like to promote the use of certain
tools that we feel are well-suited to the analysis of political competition but that heretofore have found only limited application to special interest politics.

1.1 SIG Activities and Tactics

Interest groups engage in a variety of activities to promote their
political objectives. These have been documented in a number of
survey studies of organizations and their representatives, beginning
with Milbrath (1963) and including, more recently, Berry (1977),
Schlozman and Tierney (1986), Walker (1991), Heinz et al. (1993),
and Nownes and Freeman (1998).[4] In this section we describe some
of the groups' activities and discuss, where possible, their prevalence
and the trends in their use. This overview lays the groundwork for
subsequent chapters, in which we scrutinize the different types of
activities one by one.

   According to the survey findings, the activities undertaken by the
greatest numbers of organized interest groups are those intended
to educate and persuade lawmakers of the wisdom of the groups'
positions. Collectively, these activities comprise what is commonly
known as lobbying. Schlozman and Tierney (1986), for example, in

---

4. See Baumgartner and Leech (1998, chapter 8) for a summary of findings.

their interviews of 175 organizations with Washington representation, found that 99 percent of the groups prepare testimony for congressional or agency hearings, 98 percent meet with legislators in their offices, 95 percent have informal contacts with legislators at conventions, lunches, and the like, and 92 percent present research results or technical information to policymakers. Moreover, 36 percent of the groups indicated that direct contact with government officials was one of their three most time- and resource-consuming activities (out of a list of 27 choices), while 27 percent identified testifying at hearings and conveying research results and technical information as among their three most consuming activities. No other activities were mentioned as being critical ones as often as these three. The prevalence of lobbying activities was corroborated in the interviews of nearly 800 Washington representatives performed by Heinz et al. (1993), and in a mail-in survey of 595 representatives and 301 interest-group leaders in three state capitals, conducted by Nownes and Freeman (1998).

Journalistic accounts of lobbying activity, such as Birnbaum and Murray's (1987), H. Smith's (1988), and Birnbaum's (1992), paint a vivid picture of the pervasive involvement of representatives of special interests in nearly every phase of the legislative process. Lobbyists meet with sympathetic legislators to help plan legislative strategy, assist legislators in drafting new bills, meet with lawmakers who are on the fence to try to gain their support, broker logrolling deals between legislators, and so on. What makes lobbyists the ubiquitous force they seem to be in Washington and in other nations' capitals? The answer, provided by the journalists and corroborated in the interview studies, is clearly their access to information. Since legislators must deal with an enormous array of complex and highly technical issues, they cannot hope to master all of them using only their own resources and expertise. Interest groups are an obvious source of information for policymakers, both because the groups are already familiar with many of the technical issues from their everyday involvement in the areas where policies are to be determined and because they are prepared to undertake research to produce information that they do not initially have. According to the surveys, SIGs provide legislators with intelligence of various sorts, including technical information about the likely effects of a policy, assessments of how the legislator's home district will be affected, and information on how other legislators are likely to vote. The groups are especially valuable to those who are drafting bills, because they are usually familiar with existing laws and programs and can provide assistance in wording legislation that accords with existing statutes.[5] We can gain a sense of the scale of lobbying activity from data on the size of the Washington lobbying establishment. These data are available for recent years, thanks to the reporting requirements introduced in the Lobbying Disclosure Act of 1995. Under the provisions of that bill, lobbying firms must report an estimate, to the nearest $20,000, of their income from lobbying in every six-month period. Likewise, organizations that hire lobbyists are required to report biannually on their lobbying-related expenses in excess of $10,000. The law defines a lobbyist as anyone who spends at least 20 percent of his or her time for a particular client on lobbying activities, who has multiple contacts with legislative staff, members of Congress, or high-level executive branch officials, and who works for a client paying more than $5,000 for those services in a six-month period. All such lobbyists must register with the government, as must firms that employ in-house lobbyists if their lobbying expenses exceed $20,000 in any six-month period.

The Center for Responsive Politics (1999) has compiled data for 1997 through mid-1999 from filings by lobbyists and clients and has reported the results in *Influence, Inc.*[6] We find that 20,512 lobbyists had registered by June 15, 1999, a 37 percent increase from the 14,946 lobbyists who had done so by September 30, 1997.[7] Expenditures on federal lobbying by those who filed reports totaled $1.42 billion in 1998, an increase of nearly 13 percent from the $1.26 billion reported in 1997. The aggregate expense was spread across a wide variety of groups, with the financial, insurance, and real estate industry topping the list at $203 million, followed by the communications and electronics industry ($186 million), a miscellaneous business category

---

5. Smith (1988, p. 235) quotes Tony Coelho, a former congressman from California, on this point: "There are lobbyists who are extremely influential in the subcommittees. They know more about the subject than the staff or the committee members. The Cotton Council will be writing legislation for the cotton industry in the cotton subcommittee."
6. The report is available on the World Wide Web at http://www.opensecrets.org/pubs/lobby98/index.htm (acessed August 24, 2000).
7. These numbers are roughly in accord with the more than 17,000 lobbyists, lawyers, and government relations executives who are listed in the 1999 edition of *Washington Representatives*. That publication listed only 5,000 names in its 1979 edition, although again, it is difficult to know how much of the list's expansion reflects actual growth in the number of lobbyists and how much is due to the increased research efforts of the publishers.

($172 million), the health industry, including health professionals ($165 million), the energy and natural resource sector ($144 million), and agricultural interests ($119 million). Single-issue and ideological organizations—those organizations motivated by their views on cultural issues or by other noneconomic concerns—spent $76 million on federal lobbying in 1998, while labor unions laid out $24 million. The total amount spent on lobbying exceeds the corresponding figure for federal campaign contributions, making lobbying the most expensive as well as the most prevalent practice.

In addition to their efforts to inform and persuade legislators, many SIGs also attempt to educate the general public. Among the representatives surveyed by Schlozman and Tierney (1986), 86 percent said they provided information to the mass media, 44 percent attempted to publicize candidates' voting records, 31 percent engaged in issue advertising in the media, and 22 percent endorsed their preferred candidates for office. The scale of these activities is difficult to gauge, although the Annenberg Public Policy Center has attempted to track issue advertising by interest groups since 1994. The center monitored the broadcast media for issue advertising throughout the 1997–1998 election cycle and catalogued 423 different ads aired by 77 organizations. It estimates the total cost of these ads to have been between $275 million and $340 million.[8]

The reason for these efforts would seem to be much the same as for lobbying activities. The typical voter, even more so than the typical legislator, lacks the expertise and technical information needed to evaluate alternative policy proposals. Moreover, individuals have little personal incentive to bear the cost of researching the issues in any detail. To the extent that voters can gain information readily from the media, direct mailings, or other free sources, they will be eager to have it. For their part, the SIGs are happy to serve as educators, because by doing so they can try to shape public opinion in a way that will be sympathetic to their cause.

Interest-group leaders also devote resources to educating their own members. Of the organizations interviewed by Schlozman and Tierney (1986), 72 percent reported spending "a great deal" of time and resources on this activity, and another 20 percent reported spending "some" resources. Internal communications from the leaders to the rank and file serve to alert the latter to issues that are

---

8. See http://www.appcpenn.org/appc/reports/issueads.pdf (accessed September 7, 2000).

coming before Congress, and to inform them of how they might be affected by the policies under consideration. Communication with members typically occurs through a regular medium, such as an organizational magazine or newsletter, but direct mailings and targeted advertising also are used.

Less frequently, SIGs engage in demonstrations and protests. The protests that took place during the November 1999 Ministerial Conference of the World Trade Organization, in which more than 500 different nongovernmental organizations participated, are a case in point. These activities can be seen as yet another way that groups try to educate policymakers, group members, and the general public. Some direct information is provided by the media reports that surround the demonstrations, and by the "teach-ins" that often accompany them. But even more information may be conveyed indirectly, as the willingness of participants to bear discomfort and inconvenience signals the intensity of their feelings about the issues. Of the organizations surveyed by Schlozman and Tierney (1986), 20 percent reported engaging in some sort of protests or demonstrations. Berry (1977) and Nownes and Freeman (1996) found similar figures of 23 and 21 percent.

All of the activities we have mentioned so far involve the dissemination of information by one means or another. Another SIG tactic that may be unrelated to the groups' access to information is their giving of resources to candidates and parties. Fifty-eight percent of the organizations surveyed by Schlozman and Tierney (1986) reported making financial contributions to electoral campaigns. Another 24 percent reported that they had provided campaigns with work or personnel. Of course, campaign contributions have become a visible and widely discussed practice in recent years. Hardly a day passes without the media reporting on the role that moneyed interests are playing in the electoral process.

Campaign giving by special interest groups has long been regulated by federal law. Congress outlawed direct contributions to federal candidates by corporations and trade associations in 1907, and extended the prohibition to include labor unions in 1943. By the early 1970s, many of the unions and some other organizations had found a way to circumvent the law. They formed political action committees—stand-alone organizations that collect voluntary contributions from individuals on behalf of the groups and funnel them to the candidates and parties. The Federal Election Campaign Act of

1974 gave legal sanction to this practice, fueling an explosion in the number of PACs and in their activity. Corporate PACs grew in number from 89 in 1974 to 1,816 at the end of 1988, before falling off somewhat to 1,548 by the end of 1999.[9] "Nonconnected" PACs, which did not exist before 1977, numbered 1,115 in 1988 and 972 at the end of 1999.[10] The 201 labor PACs already in existence in 1974 grew only modestly, to a peak of 394 in 1984, before settling at 318 in 1999. And while the act also introduced limits on the size of PAC gifts ($5,000 to any candidate per election[11] and $15,000 to a national political party per calendar year from any PAC that has at least 50 contributors and contributes to at least five candidates), the total volume of PAC giving grew by leaps and bounds.

In 1973–1974, PACs gave a total of $12.5 million to congressional candidates.[12] By 1977–1978, this figure had almost tripled, to $34.1 million.[13] It tripled again, to $105.3 million, by 1983–1984, and continued to escalate rapidly to $151.1 million in 1987–1988, $179.4 million in 1991–1992, and $206.8 million in the 1997–1998 election cycle. Of this last amount, corporate PACs accounted for $78 million, labor PACs for $45 million, and nonconnected PACs for $28 million. The monies from the PACs, which go overwhelmingly to incumbent candidates (78 percent in 1997–1998), represented 30 percent of total receipts by congressional candidates in 1997–1998.

Since the early 1980s, SIGs have developed new methods for circumventing the limitations on their giving to federal candidates and national parties. The loophole derives from differences between state and federal laws. Most states do not prohibit gifts to political parties from corporations and labor unions. Many do not have any limits whatsoever on the size of campaign contributions by PACs, while others have limits that are more lenient than those imposed by the federal law. In an Advisory Opinion issued by the Federal Election Committee in 1978 and affirmed in several legal cases since then,

9. All data on the numbers of PACs comes from the Federal Election Committee. See http://www/fec.gov/press/pacchart.htm (accessed August 28, 2000).

10. Nonconnected PACs are those with no parent organization. They are founded by one or more political entrepreneurs, and may solicit contributions from any American citizens. In practice they represent a diverse set of (mostly) ideological interests.

11. Federal law treats the primaries and general elections as separate elections, so a PAC can, in effect, give $10,000 to a candidate in a single election cycle.

12. See Corrado et al. (1997).

13. This figure and all subsequent data on PAC contributions are from the Federal Election Committee. See http://www.fec.gov/press/pacye98.htm (accessed August 28, 2000) and http://www.fec.gov/press/paccon98.htm (accessed August 28, 2000).

the Federal Election Campaign Act of 1974 has been interpreted to allow the national parties to use funds collected at the state level and subject to state limits to defray a share of party administrative costs, the cost of voter targeting and turnout programs, the cost of issue advocacy ads, and other expenses, so long as the spending is not (obviously) directed to benefit a single federal candidate. The ruling gave birth to so-called "soft money" finance, whereby national parties can raise unlimited amounts from SIGs, and redistribute the proceeds to the state party organizations in states where electoral needs are perceived to be great. The state organizations can spend the funds in a way that generally benefits the party's congressional and presidential candidates (for example, by issuing advertisements that press the party's policy themes), as well as on overhead expenses that would otherwise have to be paid with funds raised subject to the federal restrictions.

Only since 1991 has the Federal Election Committee required disclosure of soft money contributions, and then only those donated to the national parties. According to Corrado et al. (1997, p. 173), best estimates place total soft money spending by Republicans and Democrats at $19.1 million in the 1979–1980 election cycle and $21.6 million in the 1983–1984 cycle. Since then the collection of soft money has exploded, with the national committees of the two major parties reporting receipts of $101.7 million in 1993–1994, $262.1 in 1995–1996, and $224.4 million in 1997–1998.[14] By June 2000, the national parties had already raised more than $256 million in soft money for the 2000 elections.[15] The figures for 1999 show business groups and corporations to be the largest contributors of soft money, with donations totaling $80.7 million. The national parties received $6.9 million in soft money from labor groups in 1999, and $1.6 million each from ideological groups and from other organizations (mostly single-issue groups such as the National Rifle Association).[16]

What do the special interests buy with their hard and soft money? This question has been much debated by social scientists and the policy community, without a consensus having been reached. Some

---

14. See http://commoncause.org/publications/campaign_finance_stats_facts.html (accessed August 29, 2000).

15. See http://www.commoncause.org/publications/july00/072500.htm (accessed August 29, 2000).

16. See http://www.commoncause.org/soft_money/study99/chart1.htm (accessed August 29, 2000).

have argued that contributions buy access—a chance for a lobbyist to meet with a lawmaker to present his positions. Many lobbyists are adamant that this is all they get for their donations, and some former congressmen support them in this claim. For example, former congressman Thomas Downey of New York asserts that "money doesn't buy ... a position. But it will definitely buy you some access so you can make your case" (Schram, 1995, p. 63). Former Senate majority leader George Mitchell of Maine concurs: "I think it gives them the opportunity to gain access and present their views in a way that might otherwise not be the case" (ibid, p. 62). This view is also prevalent in the writings of some political scientists, such as Truman (1951), Milbrath (1963), and Hansen (1991).

When access must be purchased, it may be because the legislators view their time as a scarce resource. As Congressman Downey put it, "It is difficult to see members of Congress. Not because they hide themselves from you, but because they are very busy, between committee work and traveling back and forth from their districts, maintaining their office appointments and seeing their constituents" (Schram, 1995, p. 63). In such circumstances, legislators may allocate the slots in their schedules at least partly on the basis of campaign contributions.

But there is a logical difficulty with this argument. If SIGs are willing to pay for access, it must be that they see some prospect for convincing the legislator with their arguments. This means that they hold or hope to acquire information that might persuade the legislator to support their goals. But if interest groups have information that might be valuable to the policymaker, he or she ought to grant visits to the groups that are likely to provide the most useful information. Money can play a role in allocating appointments only if it signals to the legislator something about the value of what the group has to say, or if legislators value the funds as a potential source for campaign spending, apart from their wish to put a price on their time.

Campaign contributions might also buy credibility. In many situations, a group's claims—about, for example, the intensity of its members' feelings on an issue or the likely adverse effects of some proposed legislation—may not be fully credible. A legislator may lack the means to verify a group's assertions, in which case the group may be tempted to exaggerate. If a group puts up money to back its words, it may signal to the legislator that its members indeed have strong preferences or that the prospective threat from the proposed policy indeed is great.

A third possibility, and the most invidious, is that contributions buy influence. This, of course, is the view of many social scientists, politicians, and media persons, and it has spawned popular demands for campaign finance reform. Influence can come at many stages in the legislative process. "The payoff may be as obvious and overt as a floor vote in favor of the contributor's desired tax loophole or appropriation," writes William Proxmire, a former senator from Wisconsin (Stern, 1992, p. xii). But this is not the only possibility. In continuing his observation, Proxmire notes that "it may be more subtle. The payoff may come in a floor speech not delivered. It may take the form of a bill pigeon-holed in subcommittee,... or of an amendment not offered...." Special interest groups might also reap their returns in the fine details of legislation—in, for example, the exclusions to a trade agreement, the exceptions to an environmental regulation, the special deductions allowed under a new tax law, or the formulas adopted for apportioning federal aid to municipalities. Even contributions given only to boost the prospects for a preferred candidate can be seen as buying a kind of influence, as they can affect the composition of the legislature and thereby the policy outcomes.

Documenting that money affects policy outcomes has been no easy task. After all, it is difficult to know what a bill would have looked like absent the net effect of all contributions. Even if we focus on roll-call votes, as many researchers have done, the effort is confounded by the counterfactual: how would a legislator have voted absent the contributions? Perhaps a representative's vote on a bill was dictated by a concern for jobs in his district, which happen to be associated with the economic health of a contributor such as a large corporation. Or perhaps the legislator was simply following the directives of party leaders. To address this problem, variables can be introduced to control for the effect on constituents' welfare and other possible determinants of a legislator's voting behavior. For example, Baldwin and Magee (2000) explain how legislators voted on several trade bills with information about the industry composition of their districts, the demographic and educational characteristics of their constituents, the legislator's ideological stance as reflected in his ratings with several political rating organizations, and the legislator's party affiliation. After holding all these influences constant, they found that the probability of a vote in favor of trade liberalization increased with the amount of contributions that a legislator received from business interests and fell with the amount collected from labor unions.[17] More indirect evidence about groups' motives in providing campaign contributions can be found in the preponderance of donations that go to incumbent legislators, in the frequency with which many SIGs contribute to both political parties, in the timing of contributions, and in the tilting of an industry's gifts to members of subcommittees that deal with issues and regulations of concern to the industry.[18]

Finally, note that the link between a contribution and a legislator's actions need not be made explicit. Indeed, most elected officials would rankle at the suggestion that legislative favors are being provided in exchange for campaign gifts. But, from repeated interaction with a lobbyist, a legislator may come to recognize when such a link exists, and may learn to interpret the lobbyist's code words that indicate how important an issue is to the group. As former congressman Tim Penny of Minnesota succinctly put it, "There's no tit for tat in this business, no check for a vote. But nonetheless, the influence is there. Candidates know where their money is coming from" (Schram, 1995, p. 16).

17. The Baldwin and Magee study is just one example of an entire genre of research. R. A. Smith (1995) cites more than 35 studies published between 1980 and 1992 that attempted to explain roll-call votes in the U.S. Congress by campaign contributions from interested parties and by various indicators of a congressperson's ideology and constituency. A positive influence of SIG contributions on voting behavior has been found, for example, by Welch (1982), Feldstein and Melnick (1984), Saltzman (1987), Langbein and Lotwis (1990), Durden, Shogren, and Silberman (1991), and Fleisher (1993) for a diverse group of policy issues, including dairy price supports, hospital legislation, labor law, gun control, strip-mining regulation, and defense spending. But, as Smith points out, some researchers, such as Chappell (1981), Owens (1986), and Vesenka (1989), found little or no influence of campaign contributions on roll-call votes on cargo preferences and agricultural legislation, while others, such as Kau, Keenan, and Rubin (1982), Johnson (1985), and Evans (1986), found that the influence of contributions varied across issues, and even across votes within a single policy area.
18. Stratmann (1998) found a significant increase in campaign giving by agricultural PACs in the weeks immediately preceding a vote on a farm subsidy bills. But see also Bronars and Lott (1997), who found no significant change in the way members of congress vote in their last congressional term before retirement, even though their contribution receipts fall dramatically. Munger (1989), Loucks (1996), Stratmann and Krozner (1998), and Thompson (2000a) have compared the pattern of PAC giving by different industries. Thompson, for example, found a significant increase in the share of gifts that came from industries under the jurisdiction of a Congress member's committees during his first bid for reelection compared to the share he received from those industries in his initial election bid (when his committee assignments were not yet known).

1.2 About This Book

1.2.1 Methodology

It is important for the reader to understand what this book attempts to do and what it does not. The book is designed to provide tools for analyzing the interactions between voters, interest groups, and politicians. With these tools, we aim to shed light on the mechanisms by which SIG activities affect policy outcomes in modern democracies. We do not, however, describe in detail the policymaking process of a particular country, nor do we capture the full richness and complexity of these processes. In other words, we seek to portray the key tensions and conflicts that are bound to be present in any democratic political system, without tying ourselves to a particular set of political institutions.

There are several assumptions that are fundamental to our approach. The first assumption is that individuals, groups, and parties act in their own interest, and that their behavior is characterized by an absence of systematic mistakes. The assumption that actors pursue their self-interest excludes neither altruistic behavior on the part of individuals nor statesmanship on the part of politicians. Individuals do show concern about the welfare of others when they vote for candidates who support income redistribution. Most politicians do derive pleasure from pursuing programs that they perceive as beneficial to society. Rather, our assumption implies only that behavior is predicated on the attempt to maximize a well-defined objective function. We are agnostic about individuals' and politicians' objectives. But we assume that preferences can be specified in advance and that agents take political actions that help to achieve their preferred outcomes.

Nor does the absence of systematic mistakes mean that individuals, politicians, and groups are infallible calculating machines. Identifying a best action may involve complex computations and require that subtle inferences be drawn from observable variables. Voters are not trained to carry out these computations, nor do they have much incentive to invest time and effort in acquiring these skills. Even interest groups and politicians, who face political decisions every day and have ample reason to learn to respond well, may find the type of analysis we impute to them difficult to carry out. So, mistakes will be made, and not every outcome will be exactly as we predict. Our assumption that there are no systematic mistakes means only that actors will not miscalculate in the same way every time they confront a similar set of circumstances. The subjects in our models are not systematically myopic, systematically gullible, or systematically naive about the response of others. So long as this description of political actors accords with reality, our models can be used to identify channels of policy influence and tendencies for political outcomes.

A second key assumption is that political outcomes can be identified with the game-theoretic concept of an equilibrium. Equilibrium means several things here. First, it means that political actors recognize that they operate in a strategic environment and forecast how others will respond to their actions. This seems a reasonable assumption, since politics inherently involves strategic interaction and the players know well that they are in competition with one another. An equilibrium with strategic interaction has the property that each player's action is an optimal response to the actions taken by the others. Second, equilibrium means that in a game with several stages, actors are forward-looking and recognize that their current choices will affect the conditions, and outcomes, in subsequent stages of the game. Third, equilibrium means that in a game in which players are imperfectly informed, they update their beliefs using a coherent interpretation of what they observe. For example, if a politician is unsure about a rival's preferences, and he observes the rival take an action that would only be taken if the preferences were a certain way, then he must impute these preferences to his rival in subsequent stages of the game.[19]

The combined assumptions of optimizing behavior and equilibrium responses allow us to analyze special interest politics in a consistent way. Specifically, we can investigate how the different stages of political competition interrelate. Interest groups compete with one another to influence and persuade politicians and voters. Politicians compete with one another to be elected. Voters compete with other voters to elect their favorite candidates. But each set of players must consider the incentives and constraints facing the others. Special interest groups must consider the competition between political parties to forecast how they will respond to information or campaign con-

---

19. Those readers familiar with game theory will recognize the three features of equilibrium as being the conditions for a perfect Bayesian equilibrium.

tributions. The parties must consider how their positions will affect their appeal to voters, on the one hand, and to PAC contributors on the other. These interactions between the players are complex. Analytical models such as those we develop are needed to ensure mutual consistency of our assumptions.

Another notable feature of our approach is the recurrent use of a progression from the simple to the more complex. For example, when we analyze lobbying, we begin with a single interest group that tries to distinguish between two possible states of the policy environment. Then we introduce a third state, then many states. Only when these simpler settings are clear do we introduce competition between informants. Similarly, when we analyze campaign giving as a tool for influence, we begin with a single interest group and a single policymaker. We proceed to add additional SIGs, to allow for a legislature with several independent politicians, and to introduce competition between rival political parties.

Our mode of inquiry is theoretical. We aim to provide an analytical framework that can be used to study a wide range of policy issues, both economic and noneconomic. But we make no attempt to explain particular policy outcomes, such as the high level of protection afforded to agricultural groups in the European Union or the many policy triumphs of the National Rifle Association in the United States. We do offer some examples of our models in action, with discussion of such problems as the choice of a minimum wage, the allocation of public goods, and the structure of trade protection. In each of these cases, however, our approach again is analytical, serving primarily to demonstrate how the theory can be tailored to specific applications rather than to test its empirical validity. We hope that our readers will be able to apply the tools developed in this book to a variety of policy issues, and, in the process, will introduce the institutional details that are most relevant to their particular context. We also hope that our theory will inspire empirical testing and measurement, as in the recent studies by Goldberg and Maggi (1999) and Gawande and Bandyopadhyay (2000) on the structure of trade protection in the United States.

1.2.2 Organization and Content

The book is divided into three parts. Part I focuses on voting and elections. We first conduct a selective review of the voting literature to provide benchmarks for the subsequent discussion (Chapter 2) and then address reasons why certain groups of voters, even if not organized into formal associations, may fare especially well in democratic politics (Chapter 3). In Part II we examine the use of information as a tool for political influence. Specifically, we study how organized interest groups might use their superior knowledge of the policy environment to wage lobbying campaigns aimed at policymakers (Chapters 4 and 5) and the voting public (Chapter 6). Part III deals with campaign finances. Here we consider how SIGs might use their campaign giving to influence the policy choices of a unified policymaking body (Chapters 7 and 8), of a legislative body comprising elected representatives with disparate objectives (Chapter 9), and of political parties engaged in electoral competition (Chapter 10). The remainder of this chapter provides additional detail about the content of the book and is intended as a nontechnical summary of the material that follows.

Part I: Voting and Elections
Part I begins with a review of the literature on voting and elections. Although this is an enormous literature, our goals in reviewing it are modest. We aim to provide some benchmarks against which to gauge the influence of interest groups. That is, we need a sense of what policies would emerge in the absence of group politics in order to assess the biases that SIGs introduce.

We begin with direct democracy, a setting in which voters choose directly among a set of policy options. A well-known result is the median voter theorem. It states that if there is a single policy issue (such as the height of a tax or the size of a quota) and an odd number of voters with single-peaked preferences,[20] then there is a unique policy—the policy most preferred by the median voter—that can defeat every alternative in a pairwise contest. The median voter theorem has often been interpreted to mean that the median voter's favorite policy will carry the day in any democratic process. But the inference is unwarranted, because the theorem does not specify a voting procedure and thus does not identify the equilibrium of any voting game.

---

20. A voter's preferences are single-peaked if he has a unique favorite policy and if he considers alternatives to be less and less desirable the more they fall short of or exceed his ideal.

Most voting procedures assign a role to agenda setters. These are individuals who designate policies to appear on the ballot. The outcome in a direct democracy will depend on how these individuals are chosen and on whether the voting procedures call for plurality rule (the winner being the option that receives the most votes) or a series of run-off elections. It might also matter whether individuals vote "sincerely" for the option they prefer most or "strategically," with an eye toward the likely voting behavior of others. A strategic voter may eschew his favorite policy, either because he does not expect that option to receive enough support from other voters or because he foresees a sequence of run-off votes in which another well-liked alternative will have a better chance down the line if a strong competitor is eliminated early on. We conclude that while the median voter's favorite policy is a conceivable outcome in a direct democracy, its emergence from a well-specified voting process is by no means assured.

Most democratic societies operate not by direct democracy but by electing representatives and delegating to them the authority to make policy decisions. The simplest model of representative democracy was formulated by Downs (1957). In the Downsian model there are two candidates, each of whom cares only about winning the election. The candidates announce positions on a single policy issue and are committed to carry out their promises in case they are elected. As long as voters' preferences are single-peaked, there is a unique equilibrium in this model. Namely, both candidates announce the position most preferred by the median voter. This result can be extended to include situations in which the candidates have personal preferences over the policy alternatives, provided that each candidate has at least some taste for the spoils of office. The Downsian model gives us a firmer basis for considering the median voter's ideal policy as a benchmark outcome, although other outcomes can arise when the candidates are uncertain about the distribution of tastes in the voting population, when a number of issues are to be settled by a single election, and when campaigning is costly and potential candidates must decide whether or not to throw their hats into the ring.

The final part of Chapter 2 discusses legislative elections. One stylized electoral system has separate contests in an odd number of geographic regions or districts. We consider an election in which each district elects one representative. If the candidates belong to one

of two political parties, and if each party announces a single platform for all of its candidates with the aim of maximizing its chance
of winning a majority of seats, then both parties will announce the
policy most preferred by the median voter in the median district. If
instead the platforms are chosen by the candidates themselves, and if
these individuals care about their own electoral fortunes rather than
(or in addition to) those of their party, then there will be a conflict of
interests in each party. The outcome in this case will depend on the
procedures used for aggregating the disparate objectives.

Another stylized electoral system has a single national contest,
with representation in the legislature granted to each party in proportion to its share of the aggregate vote. We study in detail a model
in which there are two political parties and two types of issues to
be decided in the election. For one set of issues the parties have
"fixed" positions, reflecting perhaps their ideological beliefs or the
positions they have staked out in previous elections. On the remaining, "pliable" issues, the parties choose their positions to maximize
their chances of capturing a majority. Voters care about both sets of
issues and have heterogeneous tastes. We assume that the parties are
uncertain about the distribution of voter tastes on the fixed issues at
the time they must announce their positions on the pliable issues.
Each party is committed to carry out its complete platform, if elected.
This model yields a strong prediction; the unique equilibrium has
each party announcing the pliable positions that would maximize
the welfare of the *average* voter.

In Chapter 3 we introduce interest groups into our discussion of
electoral politics. At this stage the groups are not organized in any
way. Rather, we consider outcomes that can arise in elections with
distinguishable groups of voters who share similar preferences on
some issues. We are interested in the reasons why certain groups
(demographic, socioeconomic, religious, or other types) fare especially well in electoral politics while others do not. Our benchmark
equilibrium is one in which the policies maximize the welfare of the
average (or perhaps the median) voter.

The first part of Chapter 3 deals with voter participation. Obviously, election-seeking political parties and candidates will cater
more to groups whose members are more likely to turn up at the
polls. Thus, we examine the determinants of voter turnout and
why some groups have higher participation rates than others. Voter
turnout is difficult to explain using standard cost-benefit reasoning,

because the typical voter is quite unlikely to cast the deciding vote in an election with many voters. With little to gain from voting, even a small cost of casting a ballot should be enough to deter participation by most individuals. We review arguments that suggest a strategic motive for participation: citizens might randomize their decision of whether to vote or not, because it would not be optimal for an individual to refrain from voting if he expected all others to do likewise. We conclude, however, that such reasoning does not resolve the paradox of why people choose to vote.

We believe that participation in elections is best understood as a social norm. A social norm is an action that an individual undertakes for the good of the community, because failure to behave in the manner expected of him would invoke sanctions from his fellow citizens. Some have argued that society as a whole punishes those who fail to vote, because high participation is needed to lend legitimacy to the democratic process. While this may be true to some extent, we argue that individuals have little reason to support participation by those who would vote differently from themselves. Rather, enforcement of a voting norm is more likely to come at the level of a social or interest group, where members share a common interest in having their colleagues turn out to vote, and where they also have an opportunity to observe violations of the norm and to impose penalties.

If group norms are the basis for voter participation, then turnout should be highest in groups that are best able to enforce the norms. Frequent interaction among group members facilitates enforcement of a norm, both because individuals are more likely to know whether a fellow member has voted—and, if not, whether he has a valid reason for failing to do so—and also because there are more opportunities to reward those who conform to the norm and punish those who do not. Also, enforcement is more effective when group members have more at stake in their interpersonal exchanges. In short, groups with frequent and intensive interaction are more likely to have high turnout than those with sporadic and casual exchanges. Many labor unions fit the bill as groups in which social norms are readily enforceable, and turnout rates indeed are high among union members.

In Section 3.2 of Chapter 3 we show how knowledge can be a basis for group success or failure in electoral politics. Voters need to understand the technical aspects of policy issues and to know the candidates' positions on the issues in order to cast their votes in the way that best serves their interests. But individual voters have little incentive to collect the information needed for optimal voting. Some groups share information that members can use to pursue their common cause. Other groups are better informed merely as a result of their generally superior education, or because their members gain valuable information in the course of performing their daily activities. We investigate whether differences across groups in understanding of the policy issues and differences in knowledge about the candidates' positions translate into biased policy outcomes.

First we consider a legislative election in which some voters do not understand the link between the level of a pliable policy variable and their own well-being. Two political parties are distinguished by their positions on a set of fixed policy issues. Two groups of voters are distinguished by their most-preferred pliable policies and by the fractions of the voters in each group who are well-informed. We show that, in equilibrium, each party announces a pliable position that is the weighted average of the favorite positions of the well-informed voters and the positions that the uninformed voters perceive to be their expected ideal policies. If the uninformed voters have conservative expectations, in the sense that each places a lot of weight on the likelihood that the best policy level for him is a moderate one, then an increase in the share of informed voters in any group will drive the policy outcome closer to the group's ideal. However, if the uninformed voters in a group believe (wrongly) that their ideal policy is likely to be quite extreme, then an increase in the share of the group's well-informed voters may work to the group's detriment. This is because uninformed voters who view their ideal pliable policy as likely to be extreme will be very responsive to a party that caters to their perceived interest, and so the parties may announce positions that serve the group's actual interests quite well in order to woo these uninformed and ill-informed voters. In contrast, when voters understand the technical issues but some in each group observe the parties' pliable positions imperfectly, the policy outcome must be biased in favor of the group that has relatively more well-informed voters. Any increase in the share of voters in a group who know the parties' positions will result in a pliable policy more to the group's liking.

The final section of Chapter 3 deals with differences in partisanship. A partisan in our model is one who has a strong preference for the fixed positions of a particular party. Such an individual is unlikely to be influenced in his voting by the parties' pliable positions. We assume that the members of an interest group share the same views on the pliable issue (and have no uncertainty about their ideal policy) but differ in their opinions about the parties' fixed positions. A group with a large number of partisans is one that has many voters with a strong preference for the fixed positions of one party or the other. A group with relatively few partisans has many members who do not see much difference between the parties' fixed positions or who view the parties' positions as (almost) equally desirable or undesirable.

In this setting, the parties again announce identical pliable positions, and the outcome again is a weighted average of the ideal policies for the different groups. But this time the weights measure the number of political moderates in each group. That is, if a group has a large number of voters who are indifferent between the fixed positions of the two parties, its interests will receive a large weight in the outcome of the pliable issue. If a group instead has many partisans, its concerns about the pliable issue will be largely ignored. The reason is that the parties compete for the votes of "swing voters" who respond to the incentives offered to them. The parties will not cater to a group with many partisans, because one party suspects that it cannot win many votes among such group members no matter how close its pliable position is to what the group desires, while the other suspects that its share of votes in the group is safe even if it takes a position on the pliable issue that is far from the group's ideal.

Part II: Information
In Part II we begin to study the practices of *organized* special interest groups. Here we take up activities that involve the dissemination of information. Many SIGs are well placed to deal in information, because their members gain knowledge about issues of concern to the group in the course of conducting their everyday business, and because groups frequently collect information that bears on their members' interests.

In Chapters 4 and 5 we focus on lobbying activities. These are things that SIGs say and do to persuade policymakers that the group's preferred policies would also serve the policymakers' own political objectives. In Chapter 4 we examine lobbying that imposes little cost on the interest group. Here we think of experts who pay visits to a legislator and her assistants or who submit briefs for their consideration. Such lobbying, which we regard as "cheap talk," must be persuasive solely on the basis of the arguments that are made. Chapter 5 considers more costly forms of lobbying, such as advertising campaigns and public demonstrations. These too can be persuasive based on their content, but they may gain additional credibility from the fact that a group was willing to bear an avoidable expense in order to make its case. In the jargon of the economics literature, costly lobbying can serve as a "signal."

Our starting point for discussing lobbying is the assumption that an interest group has some expertise that bears on a policymaker's decision. An environmental group, for example, may know the costs and benefits of scrubber devices, knowledge that would be valuable to a policymaker in establishing an environmental standard. Two important considerations impede the group's ability to share its policy-relevant information. First, the group and the policymaker typically do not share exactly the same objectives. Given the realities about costs and benefits, for example, an environmental group might prefer a stricter environmental standard than would a fully informed politician. Second, the policymaker often will not be able to independently verify a lobbyist's assertions. Since we assume that policymakers are not gullible, their inability to verify what they hear creates a credibility problem for the lobbyist. We take it that policymakers accept at face value only those assertions that a lobbyist has reason to make truthfully; otherwise, they discount the claims appropriately in recognition of the group's bias.[21]

We study a situation in which a SIG has some specific bit of information about the policy environment, as summarized by the variable θ. The policymaker does not know the precise value of θ but has prior beliefs about the relative likelihood of different values. A lobbyist, who knows θ, can make a claim about it, which may cause the policymaker to update her beliefs. If the policymaker knew the precise value of θ, she would set the policy to match it. The mem-

---

21. Legislators and their staffs seem well aware of the need to filter information received from lobbyists. For example, Schlozman and Tierney (1986, p. 298) cite Fallows (1980, p. 103), who quotes a congressional staffer as follows:

Everybody has a vested interest, and it's reflected in what they're telling you. But I honestly find it easier to deal with information when you know there's a vested interest, because you can interpret that information according to the bias, which is easier in some cases than testing the accuracy of the data itself.

bers of the SIG covet a different policy of $\theta + \delta$, when the objective conditions are those represented by θ. Thus, δ measures the degree of conflict in the relationship. As an example, we may think of the policy variable as being the rate for a taxi ride and θ as measuring the demand for taxi services. The interest group might represent the interests of taxicab drivers. Both the policymaker and the drivers prefer a higher rate the greater is demand, but for any given level of demand the ideal rate for the drivers is higher.

We begin with a case in which θ can take on one of two different values, say "high" and "low." In this setting, informative lobbying is possible if and only if the bias in the group's preferences (as measured by the parameter δ) is not too large. For large values of δ, the lobbyist's claims can never be trusted, because he would always prefer to report "high" no matter what the truth might be.

When θ can take on three different values, the requirements for full disclosure are more stringent: in order for the lobbyist to be able to credibly distinguish among "high," "medium," and "low" values of θ, the bias in the group's preferences must be small relative to the distance between any two of these values. However, if the lobbyist lacks full credibility, he may nonetheless be able to make statements that the policymaker would find believable. We show that in situations where the lobbyist cannot credibly distinguish between, say, low values of θ and medium values of θ, he may be able to advise the policymaker whether θ is "reasonably low" or "quite high." The policymaker would interpret the first statement to mean that θ has either the lowest value or the intermediate value—with no new information about which of these two is more likely—and the second statement to mean that θ has the highest value. In other words, coarse statements that convey some information may be credible even when more detailed reports are not.

After discussing the cases with two and three possible values of θ, we turn to a setting in which θ is a continuous variable. In such an environment, it is never possible for the lobbyist to disclose the exact state of the policy environment. If the lobbyist anticipates that the policymaker would believe his very precise claims (e.g., that "$\theta = 1.36$"), then he always has an incentive to exaggerate. The requirement that all statements be credible limits the detail that can be communicated in any lobbying report. In fact, Crawford and Sobel (1982) have shown that all equilibria must be "partition equilibria," in which the lobbyist places θ into one of a finite number of ranges of values. The end points of these ranges are determined endogenously, so that the lobbyist is indifferent between reporting the higher range and the lower range when θ falls on the boundary between two ranges. The smaller the bias in the SIG's preferences relative to those of the policymaker, the larger is the maximum number of ranges that can be credibly distinguished. Thus, the lobbyist for a group whose interests are similar to those of the policymaker will be able to provide a more precise report about the policy environment than one whose interests are very different.

In Section 4.2 we consider lobbying by two groups with different preferences. We suppose that each SIG knows the value of θ, and concentrate on the case in which each lobbyist makes his report privately and confidentially. This is a fundamentally different situation than with only one lobbying group, because the policymaker can possibly use each group as a check on the claims of the other.

Two groups may have either "like biases" or "opposite biases," relative to the preferences of the policymaker. A like bias means that both groups prefer either larger policy levels than the policymaker or smaller policy levels than the policymaker for every value of θ, although the extent of their biases may differ. For example, the Environmental Defense and Greenpeace have like biases with respect to most environmental policy issues, although Greenpeace is undoubtedly the more extreme. An opposite bias means that one group would prefer a larger policy level than the policymaker and the other a smaller level for any given objective conditions. Environmental Defense and the Chemical Producers and Distributors Association are often oppositely biased on issues to do with hazardous waste disposal. The outcome of lobbying is quite different in these alternative cases.

With a pair of like-biased groups, all lobbying equilibria are partition equilibria. Moreover, no equilibrium exists in which more information is conveyed to the policymaker than in the most informative equilibrium with lobbying by only the more moderate of the two groups. In other words, the addition of a second, more extreme lobby does not improve the prospects for advising the policymaker. In contrast, with a pair of oppositely biased groups, it is possible to have precise reporting of θ for a range of values of θ—although not for all values. Each group has an incentive to report truthfully about θ when it falls in a certain range, because it knows that the other group would contradict any of its attempts to exaggerate. Paradoxically, a group may fare better if there is an oppositely biased group around to serve as its foil than it would if other lobby groups would invariably affirm its claims. An opposing lobby can give credibility to a lobbyist, whereas a more extreme group on the same side of the issue can never do so.

When lobbying is costly—as it may be because legal representation and advertising are expensive, or because the policymaker insists on a campaign contribution before being willing to grant access to an interest group—some of the calculus changes. On the one hand, lobbying costs reduce a group's incentive to provide information to the policymaker. On the other hand, they may enhance the group's credibility when it chooses to do so.

We distinguish three types of lobbying costs in Chapter 5: those that are outside the interest group's control and are independent of the content of its message; those that the group may vary at its discretion to signal what it knows or the intensity of its feelings; and those that are imposed by the policymaker herself as a condition for allowing a meeting to take place. We refer to these as *exogenous costs*, *endogenous costs*, and *access costs*, respectively.

When lobbying costs are exogenous, their impact on a group's ability to convey information depends on their size. Modest lobbying costs do not affect a group's ability to distinguish among a small number of values of θ, whereas large costs can deter lobbying entirely. An interesting situation arises when the costs of lobbying are neither very small nor very large, but somewhere in between. Consider a setting in which a lobbyist could not distinguish between two values of θ with cheap talk, because he would have an incentive to report "high" no matter what the true value of θ happened to be. If lobbying is moderately costly, it might not pay for the group to incur these costs when θ is low, even if by doing so it could fool the policymaker into believing otherwise. But the SIG might find it worthwhile to bear the moderate lobbying cost if θ actually were high, since a low level of the policy would be especially damaging to the group's members in such circumstances. In this case, the mere act of lobbying conveys a message to the policymaker, quite aside from anything that the lobbyist might say.

When θ is a continuous variable, then even a small cost of lobbying will have some effect. For a range of values of θ near the minimum value, the SIG will choose to forgo the opportunity to present its case. The policymaker will infer from this that conditions do not warrant the effort, and will set the policy at a relatively low level. For higher values of θ, the SIG will incur the lobbying expense, and then provide a report that places the variable θ into one of a number of ranges. In other words, the outcome with costly lobbying is a partition equilibrium, but one in which the act of lobbying or not serves as one of the possible messages. In general, the interest group can convey more information when lobbying is somewhat costly than when it is free. When more than one interest group has expertise on a policy issue, the number of groups that choose to lobby can provide additional information to the policymaker.

Once we recognize that the act of lobbying can serve as a signal, we can appreciate why an interest group might spend more than is absolutely necessary on its lobbying campaign. The interest group might assume that by spending more, it can convince the policymaker of the legitimacy of its claims. Indeed, the policymaker might expect the group to spend relatively little on lobbying when θ is small (since the group's members have relatively little to gain from a high level of policy in such circumstances) and to spend more lavishly the larger is θ. We show in Section 5.2 how a "lobbying schedule" can be constructed such that each level of spending indicates a different value for θ. If the policymaker expects the group to spend on lobbying according to the schedule, then it will in fact be optimal for the group to do so. With endogenous lobbying costs, variations in the group's outlays can provide enough information that the lobbyist's words become superfluous.

We go on to discuss whether endogenous lobbying costs permit full disclosure of the group's information, and whether the group benefits from being able to communicate in this way. If there is no minimum cost of lobbying that is needed to collect and disseminate the information, then an equilibrium does exist in which the policymaker can infer the exact value of θ from the size of the lobbying campaign. However, if the SIG must spend at least some minimum amount to prepare and present its case, then there will be a range of relatively low values of θ for which the group will be unwilling to bear the expense, and so the policymaker will have no means to distinguish these values. The ability to communicate by endogenous lobbying can be a mixed blessing for the interest group; in some situations, the members of an interest group may fare worse when they are expected to pay for lobbying than they would if there were no possibility of lobbying at all.

Why might a policymaker impose an access fee, if she knows that lobbyists hold information that would be valuable to her? In Section 5.3 we explore three different reasons. First, the policymaker might regard her time as a scarce resource, in which case she will want to make sure that the value of the information is at least equal to the opportunity cost of the time. Second, the policymaker may value campaign contributions in their own right and be willing to trade off a loss of information for the possibility of raising needed campaign funds. Third, the policymaker might use an access fee as a screening device, in situations where she is unsure about the extent of an interest group's bias.

We suppose that the SIG must secure its visitation privileges well before it knows what specific policy issues will appear on the policymaking agenda. At this stage, the SIG may have little or no informational advantage vis-à-vis the policymaker. We capture this by assuming that the SIG buys access, if at all, before it knows the precise value of θ. We first consider the case in which the group's bias is known to the policymaker. She sets an access fee as a function of a group's bias, in order to balance her needs for information and revenue, and to conserve her valuable time. The SIG that has the smallest bias is charged the most, and the fee declines with δ to some minimum, positive level. A group that has a large bias is denied access altogether.

Next we look at a setting in which the policymaker is unsure about the extent of a group's bias. In this case the access fee is used to screen potential advisers as well as to raise revenue. The optimal fee depends on the weight that the policymaker attaches to campaign funds relative to making the best policy decision and the opportunity cost of her time. Interestingly, a given fee will be paid by the group if its bias is quite small or quite large, but not if it falls in an intermediate range. Thus, the policymaker may receive advice in equilibrium from a group that almost shares her preferences or one that advocates an extreme position, without her knowing which is the case. If the policymaker allows the group to choose the size of its contribution in order to signal the extent of its bias, she will be able to infer some information about what type of group she is hearing from. However, it will be impossible for her to surmise the precise bias of a group from the size of the tribute it chooses to pay.

In Chapter 6 we shift our focus from educational activities aimed at the policymaker to those aimed at voters. Many interest groups attempt to educate voters in an effort to woo them to their side of an issue. Voters may be keen to learn from the groups, because it would be costly for them to conduct the research on their own. But, like policymakers, voters must be wary of their sources, lest they be fed biased and misleading information.

We develop a model of a legislative election similar to the one in Chapter 3. We assume that all voters initially are uncertain of the relationship between the policy level and their own welfare. Members of the interest group share a common interest in a pliable policy issue; other voters do not. The central organization of the SIG has knowledge about the issue that pinpoints the ideal policy level for its members. This information may or may not help to identify the ideal policy for other voters. We give the group an opportunity to publicize a statement about the policy environment.

We first consider a case in which the group can issue its statement before the parties have adopted their positions on the pliable issue. Such early communication allows voters to update their beliefs about what policies would suit them personally. Following the report, the parties will cater to voters whose understanding of the issues has been cultivated by the interest group. Anticipating this, the SIG may wish to mislead the public, so that the subsequent competition delivers something close to the members' ideal policy. But we assume that voters are not gullible, which means that the SIG faces a credibility problem. Again, the outcome must be a partition equilibrium in which the SIG makes only coarse statements about the policy environment. The precision of these statements reflects the degree to which its information is relevant to the concerns of the average voter, the bias in the group members' preferences relative to those of nonmembers, and the fraction of SIG members in the voting population.

When the SIG can issue its statement closer to election time, it will use its message for a different purpose. Once the parties have taken positions on the pliable issue, the group will attempt to steer voters to the party whose position it prefers. Here the credibility problem facing the organization becomes especially severe. Voters will recognize that the SIG has an incentive to paint the policy environment in a way that casts its preferred party in as favorable a light as possible. Since the organization's late statements will always be immoderate, voters will discount them accordingly. The only information that a group can be trusted to provide once the parties' positions are well-known is an indication of which party has a pliable position closer to the members' ideal level.

Next we examine the political competition that occurs in anticipation of a late message from the interest group. Paradoxically, the group's inability to provide detailed information works to its members' benefit. The parties anticipate that once they announce their positions, the group will issue an extreme statement about the policy environment. Even with the appropriate discounting, the statement will shift more voters to the party whose position is closer to the group's ideal than would a more refined statement. Thus, the parties have a greater incentive to cater to the members' true interests when they anticipate a coarse statement than they would if they expected voters to become better informed. We show that SIG members fare well when their organization can conduct issue advertising late in the political contest. In fact, for a range of values of θ, the group's members attain their ideal pliable policy.

In the final sections of Chapter 6 we describe two additional methods that SIGs commonly use to provide information to segments of the public. Section 6.4 deals with political endorsements. These are simple communiqués that announce a group's preferred outcome in an election. We show that endorsements have much the same effect as late pronouncements about the policy environment—both serve to identify the party that has a position closer to the members' ideal policy level. Section 6.5 examines the information that organizations provide to their members in newsletters, trade magazines, targeted mailings, and the like. We argue that SIGs face a credibility problem even in their attempts to educate their own rank-and-file members. The informational content of messages delivered privately to members can be studied using much the same methods as for other, more public statements.

Part III: Campaign Contributions
Special interest groups derive much political power from their specialized knowledge of policy issues. But many groups also deal in another currency besides information. Interest groups have become an ever more important source of the money and other resources that politicians need to wage their political campaigns. We have already observed that SIGs may contribute to policymakers to gain an opportunity to plead their cases. In the last part of the book, we study

more direct channels by which money from SIGs affects the policy-making process.

In Chapter 7 we begin to investigate the possible exchange of money for influence. We consider a policymaker who is concerned about her constituents, but who also needs campaign resources. Such a politician might well regard an interest group with a stake in her policy decisions as a potential source of campaign financing. We do not necessarily envision the policymaker as overtly peddling her influence, nor do we see the interest group as making explicit conditional offers. Rather, we imagine that the SIG develops a reputation for supporting its political allies, and that the policymaker realizes that her actions will affect the group's readiness to contribute.

We aim to illuminate the trade-offs inherent in such a relationship between a policymaker and an interest group, and the policy choices to which it might lead. To this end, we introduce the fictitious construct of a "contribution schedule." This schedule relates a level of campaign giving to every policy option. If the policymaker believes the group will contribute according to such a schedule, she will choose the policy to maximize her political welfare in view of the implications for both her constituents' well-being and her campaign receipts. An equilibrium comprises a contribution schedule that is optimal for the interest group in light of the anticipated behavior of the policymaker and a policy that is a best response by the politician to the group's implicit offer.

With one interest group and one dimension of policy, there are many contribution schedules that support an equilibrium outcome. But no matter which of these schedules the policymaker expects will guide the SIG's behavior, the equilibrium combination of policy and contribution is always the same. The outcome is the one that maximizes the group's welfare subject to the constraint that the policymaker is no worse off than she would be if she were to have her favorite policy but no contributions from the interest group. This equilibrium is jointly efficient for the politician and the interest group—the policy and contribution could not be changed in such a way as to benefit one side without harming the other.

The efficiency property remains when there are several dimensions of policy choice. It also remains when the policymaker bargains with a representative of the SIG over the size of the contribution and the policy to be enacted. We illustrate the predictions of the theory in

applications to the allocation of public spending and the joint determination of an emissions tax and an import tariff.

In Chapter 8 we study the competition for influence among several
interest groups with differing policy objectives. Each group confronts
the policymaker with a contribution schedule that associates a gift
from the group with every possible level of the policy instrument.
The policymaker sets the policy with an eye toward her constituents'
well-being and her aggregate receipts from the various contributors.
In an equilibrium, each group's schedule is optimal for its members
given the bids expected from the others and the policymaker's anticipated response. This relationship between the policymaker and the
various groups is one of "common agency," inasmuch as the policymaker acts as a common agent for the groups by setting a policy
that simultaneously affects all of their well-being.

When several interest groups vie for policy influence, the policy
outcome is not uniquely determined. Every group has some latitude
in designing the shape of its contribution schedule, yet the choices
made by each affect the incentives facing the others. However, when
all of the contribution offers vary continuously and smoothly as a
function of the policy level, the various equilibria share some common properties. Most notably, the political equilibrium often will be
jointly efficient for the policymaker and the collection of interest
groups; that is, it will not be possible to find a different set of contributions and a different policy choice with the property that at least
one SIG or the policymaker is made better off relative to the equilibrium without another group or the policymaker being made worse
off.

Section 8.2 of Chapter 8 provides a detailed application of the
model to the determination of a legal minimum wage. We assume
that there are two industries—textiles and pharmaceuticals—and
many workers with different skill levels. One organized SIG represents the interests of the owners of textile firms, while another SIG
represents the interests of a group of relatively highly skilled workers.
These groups use their campaign giving to influence a policymaker
who values campaign receipts and aggregate welfare. We show that
if the textile industry is large and the labor union is small, there can
be no binding minimum wage in the political equilibrium. However,
if the skill-adjusted supply of labor by the union exceeds the skill-
adjusted demand for labor by the textiles industry at the wages that
ensure full employment, and if the policymaker puts a sufficiently

large weight on campaign finances in her political objective function, then the combined bids for influence by the two groups will result in a binding minimum wage. The greater the wage sensitivity of labor demand and the more skewed the distribution of union membership toward high-skill workers, the greater the minimum wage rate is likely to be.

In Section 8.3 we identify a particular type of equilibrium that arises when all groups resort to "compensating" contribution schedules. Compensating schedules have the property that the difference in a group's positive bids for any two policies compensates the group exactly for its different evaluation of the two options. We show first that, no matter what type of contribution schedules a given group's rivals are expected to follow, the group can always respond with a compensating contribution schedule at no extra cost to itself. Thus, the groups bear no burden from restricting their attention to compensating schedules. Moreover, the equilibria supported by compensating schedules are "coalition-proof"; that is, they remain as equilibria when the groups have an opportunity to engage in nonbinding communication before the play of the game. Most important, all of the equilibria that result when all SIGs use compensating schedules are jointly efficient for the groups and the policymaker. By using such schedules, the groups can avoid outcomes that leave unexploited gains in their political relationship with the policymaker.

We apply the notion of a compensating equilibrium—an equilibrium that arises when all groups use compensating contribution schedules—to two policy problems. First we study in Section 8.4 the outcome of bids for influence over a small country's trade policy. Organized groups represent the interests of workers and capital owners. If every citizen is represented by one of these groups, then any set of equilibrium policies induces the same allocation of resources as would result from a policy of free trade. Although this allocation is efficient for the small country, there is no presumption that the population fares well in the associated political equilibrium. In our setting, the labor SIG bids for a protective tariff that would be harmful to the interests of capital owners, while the capital SIG bids for an export subsidy that would be harmful to labor. Thus, the outcome with offsetting policies represents something of a political stalemate. However, the groups may contribute handsomely to achieve this outcome, because each must ward off the damaging policies that would result were it to refrain from contributing. It follows that the influence game leaves all citizens worse off than they would be if campaign contributions were prohibited.

Next we discuss redistributive taxation. We show that if the policymaker's objective is an increasing function of the level of welfare of every citizen, then a compensating equilibrium has a striking property. Not only must such an equilibrium be efficient for the policymaker and the organized interest groups, but in this case it must be efficient for the polity as a whole. This means that the vast array of results that have been derived in the normative literature on efficient taxation can be seen as positive predictions about political outcomes under certain conditions.

In Chapter 9 we turn from groups' efforts to influence a single policymaker to their attempts to influence a legislative body. The discussion in Chapters 7 and 8 might apply to legislative decision making if a single party controls the legislature and party discipline is strict. Then it will be enough for the groups to curry favor with the ruling party to achieve their desired outcomes. But if party discipline is relatively weak and legislators pursue their own political objectives, then the interest groups face a more subtle problem. They must decide which legislators to target, how much support to offer them, and whether to seek influence with those who are in positions to draft and amend legislation, in addition to (or instead of) those who will vote on the bill. The optimal strategies will depend on the details of the institutional setting.

We begin with an institutional setting that is simple and analytically convenient, if not an accurate depiction of any real polity. We suppose that there is a single interest group and a legislature comprising three members. The group proposes a policy level and offers contributions to some or all of the legislators in order to encourage their support. Then the legislature votes on the group's proposal, which passes if at least two members vote in favor. Otherwise, a status quo policy is invoked.

In this context, we investigate what bill the group will propose and how it will go about ensuring its passage. We construct a schedule that gives the minimum cost of passage of every conceivable policy level. These costs are the amount the SIG would have to pay for the support of the two legislators who are most favorably disposed to the given various proposals. For some possible policies and legislators the required payment will be zero, because the politicians prefer these policies to the status quo. For other policies it may be necessary for the SIG to buy one or two votes in order to engineer the bill's passage. Once the schedule has been constructed, the group chooses the option that maximizes its welfare in light of the relative costs. In the equilibrium, the group achieves a "minimum winning coalition": it offers contributions to at most two of the three legislators, who turn out to be those whose preferences are most similar to its own.

The simple model provides some useful insights, but it grants too much power to the interest group. Not only can the SIG use the resources at its disposal to guide the legislators' voting behavior, but it somehow can choose the proposal that stands as the sole alternative to the status quo. In reality, proposal-making authority often resides with a legislative "agenda setter"—one or more legislators who have the authority to draft legislation in areas of their jurisdiction. Accordingly, in Section 9.2 we turn to a model in which one of the legislators has agenda-setting authority and the other two are floor members. For simplicity, we adopt a "closed rule" under which amendments to the proposed legislation are not allowed.

We investigate a game with the following sequence of moves. First, the SIG designs a contribution schedule to offer to the agenda setter, which associates a campaign gift with every proposal he might make. Next, the agenda setter drafts a bill, which stands in opposition to a given status quo. Then the SIG offers contributions to one or both of the remaining legislators, which may be conditional on their support for the bill or conditional on their voting for its defeat. Finally, the legislature votes on the proposal.

The analysis yields some interesting predictions. For example, the SIG may contribute to the agenda setter even if its members' preferences are rather different from his. Moreover, the size of the contribution to the agenda setter may well exceed the amount the group gives to legislators who are more naturally sympathetic to its cause. These predictions are in keeping with evidence for the United States, which suggests that congressmen receive especially large contributions from groups that have stakes in the policy areas under the control of committees on which they serve. Also, the SIG may contribute positively in circumstances where the status quo prevails in equilibrium. Here the influence of the SIG is to be found in its ability to block legislation that would harm its members. The equilibrium may even give rise to a new policy that the group likes less well than the status quo; the outcome might have been still worse but for the group's influence.

In the last section of Chapter 9 we study competition for influence in a setting with legislative policy making. The model is the same as in Section 9.2, except that two SIGs can contribute to the agenda setter to influence his proposal. Later, these same groups make offers to the floor members in efforts to gain their votes. The most interesting case arises when the groups wish to pull the policymakers in opposite directions relative to the status quo. In this situation the SIGs may randomize their bids, so that neither side is sure how much the other will contribute or to whom. A group that fails to vary its offers leaves itself open to being slightly outbid by its rival, or to having its rival target the legislators that the group itself has chosen to ignore.

In the resulting equilibrium, the policy outcome also is random. The agenda setter proposes a bill that one group supports and the other opposes. Then the groups choose among their various possible offers. One group bids for an additional vote (together with the agenda setter's) to pass the legislation. The other seeks two votes against the bill. Depending on how this all turns out, the proposal may succeed or fail. Contrary to our other findings, there is no presumption here that the outcome will be jointly efficient for the interest groups and the legislators.

Chapters 7, 8, and 9 treat a policymaker's motivations in reduced form. We ascribe to her a welfare function that includes voters' well-being and campaign resources as distinct arguments, but we do not explicitly consider the electoral considerations that give rise to an objective function with this form. While useful for many purposes, this reduced-form approach suffers from at least two shortcomings. First, it does not allow us to analyze the determinants of the policymaker's trade-off between aggregate welfare and contributions. Second, it does not permit us to entertain the possibility that SIGs contribute to their favorite candidates not to extract favors, but rather to bolster the candidates' chances of being elected.

In Chapter 10 we address these shortcomings by incorporating campaign giving into a model of electoral competition between two political parties. The parties compete for votes by adopting positions on a set of pliable issues and by spending on their campaigns. There are two types of voters, those who cast their ballots solely on the basis of comparing the parties' platforms and those who are susceptible to campaign advertising and the like. By catering to special interests, the parties lose some support among the former type of voters, but they can raise funds that allow them to woo the latter. This trade-off guides their positioning on the issues.

First we consider a single interest group that contributes only to influence the parties' positions. We hypothesize that the SIG gives exactly what is needed to exert its influence but nothing more. Under this restriction, the group contributes to both political parties. It gives the larger donation to the party that it sees as more likely to win the election. But it also gives to the underdog, in case that party should emerge victorious. The asymmetric pattern of contributions gives rise to divergent platforms; in particular, the party that initially has the more popular fixed positions adopts pliable positions that are more to the group members' liking. The influence of the SIG over the parties' pliable positions is greater the more diverse are the opinions of the strategic voters about the parties' fixed positions, the greater is the fraction of impressionable voters, and the more effective is campaign spending in winning their votes.

Next we consider a pure electoral motive for campaign giving. We assume for a moment that the SIG can contribute to the parties only after they have announced their pliable positions, when there is no opportunity for the SIG to influence the parties' choices. The only reason the SIG might have for giving at that time would be to alter the election odds. An electorally motivated SIG never contributes to both parties; rather, it concentrates its largesse on the party whose pliable positions it prefers. The electoral motive is more likely to operate when there is a significant difference in the group's evaluation of the two pliable platforms. However, when the parties set their positions in anticipation of the group's contributions, their pliable platforms tend to converge. This means that the SIG may find that it lacks any incentive to contribute to either party when the time comes for it to make that decision.

Finally, we allow the interest group to give for either of the two reasons—to influence a party's platform or to further its electoral prospects. Here we assume the SIG offers its contributions before the parties take their pliable positions, but we do not insist that the gifts be the minimal amounts to exert influence. Interestingly, the influence motive and the electoral motive can interact. The SIG buys greater influence with the party that has the better ex ante chance to win the election. As a result, this party chooses a position more to the group's liking. But now the parties' pliable positions indeed are indifferent, and the SIG may wish to make further unconditional contributions to the ex ante favorite so as to improve its chances of being elected. The electoral motive for campaign giving is more likely to operate—in concert with the influence motive—the greater the fraction of impressionable voters in the total electorate, and the more susceptible these voters are to campaign activities.

The final section of Chapter 10 deals with competition between interest groups in the context of an electoral contest. When several interest groups favor the same political party, each faces a free-rider problem in contemplating its electorally motivated giving. That is, while each would like to see its favorite party win the election, each would also like to have other groups foot the campaign bill. Typically, at most one of the interest groups that prefer a given party will contribute more than is necessary to exert its influence on the party's platform. Moreover, as the number of interest groups increases (and the size of each one shrinks), it becomes less and less likely that any one of them will have adequate incentives to give to a party to further its electoral cause.

With influence-motivated giving by more than one interest group, there is the interesting possibility of a self-fulfilling prophecy. Each group would like to buy greater influence from the party that it regards as more likely to win the election. But the parties' chances of winning depend not only on their popularity, but also on their ability to raise campaign resources. If all groups expect that one party will receive a greater share of the campaign contributions than the other, they all will be justified in giving more to the better financed party. There can be many equilibria of the giving game, each with different electoral prospects for the two parties. Given a party's probability of winning the election, it chooses a pliable platform that maximizes a weighted sum of the welfare of strategic voters and the welfare of interest-group members; the weights reflect the effectiveness of campaign spending, the diversity of opinions on the parties' fixed positions, and the probabilities of an electoral victory by each side.

I   Voting

2   Voting and Elections

Voting is the most basic political activity in a democratic society. Modern democracies grant suffrage to all citizens who meet minimal requirements of age, mental health, intellectual capacity, and freedom from incarceration for criminal activity. Indeed, many nations consider participation in the electoral process to be a responsibility as well as a right, and impose sanctions on those who fail to vote.

The democratic credo of "one man, one vote" is meant to enforce the "will of the majority." With universal suffrage, it is hoped, society will not enact policies that benefit the few at the expense of the many. But does it work? Do the policies that emerge from electoral competition always serve the common good? Or might small groups sometimes succeed in tilting the political process in their own direction? In this chapter and the next, we will attempt to answer these questions by examining the policies that emerge from electoral competition under different voting conditions. For the time being, we will take a broad view of a special interest group as being any identifiable group of citizens who share similar policy preferences. We postpone discussion of *organized* interest groups and their political activities until Chapter 4.

In the present chapter we review the literature on voting outcomes in situations of direct democracy and representative democracy. This is a vast literature, and our goals in surveying it are modest.[1] We hope to introduce some of the central ideas and to build a base on which the modeling in the remainder of the book can rest. The substantive analysis of whether voting outcomes might favor specific groups is deferred until Chapter 3. There we identify a number of rea-

---

1. More thorough surveys of the literature on voting can be found in Calvert (1986), Coughlin (1990), and Osborne (1995).

sons why elections with "one man, one vote" might yield outcomes
that do not weigh all citizens equally.

2.1   Direct Democracy

We begin with the simplest possible political environment—the setting of direct democracy, in which the members of society vote directly on policy options. Of course, direct democracy is impractical
as a political institution, except perhaps in small polities facing few
policy decisions. But direct democracy is where the political ideal
ought to work the best. By considering it briefly, we can establish a
benchmark against which to compare other institutions and outcomes.

To begin, we suppose that society faces only a single policy decision. It must choose some action (or "policy") p from among a set of
feasible alternatives. The feasible actions will be associated with the
points on a segment of the real line; that is, the policy can be any
number between (and including) p_{min} and p_{max}. We shall describe an
individual's preferences over these various alternatives by the utility
function $u_i(\cdot)$, where $u_i(p)$ tells us, for every value of p, the satisfaction that would be experienced by individual i were policy p to
be enacted. We suppose that every citizen has a unique favorite
among the set of feasible policies, and that an individual's well-being
increases monotonically as her ideal is approached from above or
from below. This property of the utility function is known as "single-
peakedness." Technically speaking, we assume $u_i'(p) > 0$ for all $p < \pi_i$
and $u_i'(p) < 0$ for all $p > \pi_i$, where π_i denotes the unique favorite
policy of individual i.

2.1.1   The Median Voter and the Agenda Setter

It is straightforward to prove the well-known median voter theorem.
Let N be the number of voters, and suppose that N is odd (to avoid
the technical details that arise from the possibility of tie votes). Now
order the individuals so that voter 1 is the one with the smallest
favorite policy, voter N is the one with the largest favorite policy,
and $\pi_1 \leq \pi_2 \leq \cdots \leq \pi_N$. Then there is a unique policy proposal that
can defeat every alternative in a pairwise comparison. This is the
policy most preferred by the voter with index $m = (N+1)/2$, namely
the *median* voter.

The theorem follows almost immediately from the single-peakedness property. In figure 2.1 we show the utility curves for three

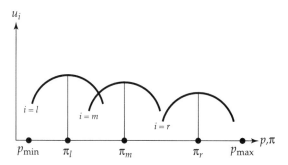

Figure 2.1
Pairwise Comparison

voters, voter l, who has a favorite policy $\pi_l < \pi_m$, voter m, the median voter, and voter r, who has a favorite policy $\pi_r > \pi_m$. As the figure indicates, the median voter, and all voters like voter l who have indexes less than m, prefer π_m to any policy $p > \pi_m$. So these high values of p are defeated in pairwise comparisons with π_m. Similarly, the median voter and all voters like voter r who have indexes greater than m prefer π_m to any policy $p < \pi_m$. So these low values of p are defeated as well. A policy such as π_m that is preferred by a majority of citizens to every feasible alternative is known as a *Condorcet winner*.

Does the median voter theorem imply that the median voter's favorite policy will necessarily emerge from any process of direct democracy? Not at all. We have said nothing as yet about the procedure by which the voting is to be carried out. One possibility is that voters are asked to write down any proposal from the list of feasible alternatives, with the winner being the proposal that receives the most votes. This is known as "plurality rule." Alternatively, the political rules might call for a sequence of one or more runoff votes among alternatives that receive the most votes in a first and subsequent rounds. Yet another possibility is that some citizen or citizens are designated to nominate proposals for the ballot. Then a vote or sequence of votes is held among the alternatives named by the "agenda setters."[2] The equilibrium outcome in a direct democracy depends on the rules of the voting game.

It is easy to see that not all voting procedures deliver the median voter's favorite policy as a unique equilibrium outcome. Suppose, for example, that the rules call for two individuals to be selected at

---

2. See, for example, Romer and Rosenthal (1979) and Baron and Ferejohn (1989).

random to serve as agenda setters, and that a coin toss determines which of the two proposes first. Let it happen that citizen a, who has a favorite policy π_a, is selected to make the first nomination, and that citizen b, who has an ideal policy π_b, is chosen to follow suit. By the time citizen b gets a chance to make her proposal, citizen a will have nominated some policy, say p^a. Then, if $\pi_b < p^a \leq \pi_m$ or if $\pi_b > p^a \geq \pi_m$, there is no alternative among the policies that citizen b prefers to p^a that can defeat the previously nominated proposal. In such circumstances, citizen b might as well designate her favorite policy, or else any other policy that will surely lose to p^a. If it happens instead that $p^a < \pi_b \leq \pi_m$ or that $p^a > \pi_b \geq \pi_m$, then citizen b can propose π_b, and rest secure in the knowledge that her own favorite policy will carry the day. Finally, if $p^a < \pi_m < \pi_b$ or if $p^a > \pi_m > \pi_b$, then citizen b should name her own ideal if that policy is preferred by the median voter to p^a, or else the policy that is closest to π_b among those that the median voter prefers to p^a.[3]

Knowing how citizen b will respond to any initial nomination, we can now examine the incentives facing citizen a. She certainly should name her own ideal policy π_a if $\pi_b < \pi_a \leq \pi_m$ or if $\pi_b > \pi_a \geq \pi_m$. By doing so, she guarantees her favorite outcome. Citizen a might as well nominate her own favorite policy if $\pi_a < \pi_b \leq \pi_m$ or if $\pi_a > \pi_b \geq \pi_m$. In this situation, she has no way to induce a better outcome for herself than the anticipated choice of π_b. Note that the political process does not deliver the median voter's favorite choice as a policy outcome in any of these cases. The policy π_m emerges in equilibrium only if the favorites of the two proposers happen to lie on opposite sides of π_m. Then, were citizen a to propose any policy that she preferred to π_m, citizen b would counter with a proposal that would defeat the first-mover's choice and that would be worse for citizen a than π_m. Foreseeing this eventuality, citizen a will recognize the futility of proposing anything different from the median voter's ideal.[4]

---

3. There is a technical difficulty here, inasmuch as there is no single policy among the continuum of alternatives that the median voter prefers to p^a that is "closest" to π_b. This technicality is not of substantive importance. We may say that b chooses the policy that leaves the median voter indifferent between the two proposals but that the median voter nonetheless votes for π_b in the pairwise comparison.

4. These conclusions do not require that the proposals be made sequentially, as described here. Osborne (1995, p. 270) has shown that the policy outcome in a Nash equilibrium of simultaneous proposals coincides with the median voter's ideal when the two agenda setters (he calls them "candidates") have favorites that lie on opposite sides of π_m, but will do so only by chance if their favorites happen to lie on the same side of π_m.

2.1.2   Sincere Versus Strategic Voting

In the preceding discussion we implicitly assumed that citizens auto-matically vote for their favorite alternative from among those listed on the ballot. This behavior has been termed *sincere voting* in the lit-erature on elections. When the ballot offers only two alternatives and majority rule determines the outcome, sincere voting is the only sensible action. In the jargon of game theory, such behavior is a "weakly dominant strategy"; that is, it might possibly further a voter's interests and it can never harm them. The voter gains from voting sincerely in those (perhaps rare) situations in which her own vote makes the difference in the election. Then, by voting in this manner, she induces her favorite outcome instead of the less-preferred alter-native. In all other situations in which the voter's ballot is not deci-sive, the manner in which she casts it has no bearing on the ultimate outcome.

But the matter is not nearly so straightforward when the ballot contains more than two choices. A voter who suspects that her favorite alternative will receive little support from others might be reluctant to vote for it lest her vote be "wasted." She might vote instead for a less-favored alternative that she perceives as having a reasonable chance to win. But how will she know which alternatives have decent prospects for victory? To form a view on this, she must assess the likely voting behavior of all other voters. When voters consider how others are likely to vote in deciding how to do so themselves, they engage in what has been called *strategic voting*. A strategic voter casts her vote to maximize her (expected) utility, given her conjecture of how others will behave. If all voters vote strategically and their expectations about one another are fulfilled, the outcome is a *Nash equilibrium* of the voting game.

2.1.3   Direct Democracy without Agenda Setters

Let us return to our discussion of direct democracy and consider what happens when there are no agenda setters. Suppose that the ballot lists all of the feasible policy options, or that voters have the opportunity to write in any policy level they wish. With strategic voting and simple plurality rule, the median voter's most-preferred policy can always emerge as an equilibrium outcome. Let all voters anticipate that only two alternatives will tally positive vote shares.

Suppose one of these is π_m, and the other is some alternative $\hat{p}$ that is greater than π_m. Then voting for π_m weakly dominates voting for $\hat{p}$ for all voters with indexes less than or equal to m. Moreover, these voters do not prefer to vote for any other alternative, given their beliefs. The support of the voters with indexes less than or equal to m is enough to ensure that π_m is adopted.

But many other policies also can be supported as equilibrium outcomes. Consider an arbitrary pair of alternatives, p^a and p^b, with the sole restriction that neither alternative is equal to p_{min} or p_{max}. We will refer to such nonextreme options as "interior policies." Suppose that all voters expect that only p^a and p^b will receive electoral support from others. Then it is a rational, strategic response for each voter to cast her vote for the one of these alternatives that she prefers. Whichever of the pair has greater support in the voting population at large will end up as the winning policy. From this logic we can see that any interior policy can emerge as an equilibrium outcome. Since every such policy is preferred by a majority of voters to at least one other option, any one can be a winner if it happens to be pitted (in voters' minds) against the right alternative.

Evidently, the theory of strategic voting has little predictive power when a direct democracy operates with no agenda setters and simple plurality rule. Everything depends on what expectations voters have about how others will behave. Unfortunately, nothing in the theory dictates what these expectations should be. By contrast, a theory of sincere voting offers a stronger (albeit trivial) prediction under plurality rule. If every citizen casts her ballot for her favorite alternative without giving any thought to how others might vote, then the outcome will be the policy favored by the modal voter.

A system with runoff elections might seem to offer a better chance to the median voter's favorite policy, but in fact such a system does not ensure that π_m will emerge as a unique equilibrium. If, for example, the voting procedure calls for a runoff election between the top two vote-getters in an initial round of balloting, it is still true that any interior policy can emerge as an equilibrium outcome with strategic voting. Voters need only expect that others will concentrate on some p^a and p^b in the initial round to justify restricting their own attention to this (arbitrary) pair of alternatives. Then all of those who prefer p^a to p^b will cast their ballots for p^a in both rounds of voting, and those who prefer p^b to p^a will vote each time for p^b. The more popular of the two is implemented as an equilibrium.

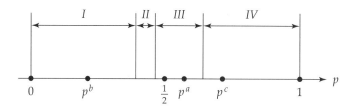

Figure 2.2
Two-Stage Voting with an Extreme Outcome

Nor does a procedure that calls for a sequence of pairwise comparisons—even one that eventually introduces every option into the contest—necessarily select the median voter's favorite policy as the unique equilibrium. In order for a procedure that introduces all options to be feasible, there must be a finite number of alternatives. Consider an election with three options, where the procedure calls for an initial vote between p^a and p^b and a subsequent contest between p^c and the first-round winner. For the purposes of this example, let there be a continuum of voters with symmetric utility functions, where the voter i has an ideal policy π_i. The parameter π_i is uniformly distributed in the voting population on values between 0 and 1. Let p^a be the proposal favored by the median voter, and let $p^b < p^a < p^c$, as depicted in figure 2.2.

A strategy for each voter dictates how she will vote in the initial contest and how she will vote in each of the possible second-round pairings. The figure shows four sets of voters, labeled I, II, III, and IV. Set I consists of voters with ideal points between 0 and $\frac{1}{2}(p^a + p^b)$, set II consists of voters with ideal points between $\frac{1}{2}(p^a + p^b)$ and $\frac{1}{2}(p^b + p^c)$, set III consists of voters with ideal points between $\frac{1}{2}(p^b + p^c)$ and $\frac{1}{2}(p^a + p^c)$, and set IV consists of the remaining voters. Now consider the following strategies for the various groups of voters. Voters in set I vote for p^b in the first election, and for the winner of that election in the subsequent runoff against p^c. Voters in set II vote instead for p^a in the first round, but also for the winner of that contest in the comparison with p^c. Those in set III vote for p^a whenever they have the opportunity to do so, and for p^c over p^b if that contest arises. Finally, those in set IV vote for p^b in the first election and for p^c in the second election, no matter what the alternative is then.

With the three options located as shown in the figure, p^b defeats p^a in the first contest, only to lose to p^c in the second round. The indi-

cated strategies are individually rational for the various voters, because no single voter could induce a different outcome by changing
her strategy, nor is any voter being asked to adopt a strategy that is
weakly dominated.[5] Thus, the policy p^c can emerge as an equilibrium
outcome, even though it is not the option preferred by the median
voter.

The possible emergence of option p^c as an equilibrium outcome
reflects the coordinated play of the members of set IV. Although
these voters prefer p^a to p^b in a pairwise comparison, they vote for
p^b over p^a in order to knock the latter out of the competition. This
allows their favorite option to triumph. Notice that the voters in set
I collectively could thwart this effort—which leaves them with their
least-preferred alternative—by voting as a block for option p^a in the
initial election. But to do so would require them to change their
strategies together, and they have no guarantee that the necessary
coordination will occur. Although the model gives no reason to predict that members of set IV would achieve coordination while those
in set I would fail to do so, neither can this outcome be ruled out by
appeal to individual rationality.

Once again, the theory of sincere voting points to a different conclusion. If all voters were to vote sincerely and if each option was
introduced in a sequence of pairwise comparisons, the median
voter's favorite policy would necessarily emerge victorious. Since
more than half of the voters prefer this policy to any alternative, π_m
would defeat the standing champion as soon as it entered the race,
and it would go on to defeat every subsequent contender in turn.

2.1.4 Non-Single-Peaked Preferences

We have so far maintained the assumption that all citizens' preferences are single-peaked. This assumption seems quite natural for
many applications, such as those that arise frequently in the study
of economic policy. In any analysis of tax policy, for example, each
individual may have a unique favorite tax rate and may regard
higher rates and lower rates as inferior, the more so the more they
differ from her perceived optimum. Similarly, in problems having to
do with the purchase of public goods, individuals may have favorite

---

5. That is, no voter's strategy is such that another strategy would yield a better (or not
worse) outcome no matter how the others happened to vote.

levels of provision that depend on the social cost of the good and their own taste for it. Higher and lower levels of supply yield lower utility, and increasingly so the greater the deviation from the most-preferred level.

But in other applications the notion of "more" and "less" may not be so apparent. Society may face a choice, for example, between a system of public health, a system of private health, and a system of private provision with public insurance. Call the alternatives p^a, p^b, and p^c, respectively. Then it would be perfectly reasonable for citizens to differ in their views of which is best, and also in their views of which is second best. Consider a society with three voters (or three types of voters) whose preferences over the three alternatives happen to be

$$u_1(p^a) > u_1(p^b) > u_1(p^c),$$

$$u_2(p^b) > u_2(p^c) > u_2(p^a),$$

$$u_3(p^c) > u_3(p^a) > u_3(p^b).$$

Then it is apparent that none of the three policies is preferred by a majority of voters to each of the other alternatives. A majority prefers public health to private health, a (different) majority prefers private health to public insurance, and a (still different) majority prefers public insurance to public health. In short, the absence of single-peakedness in preferences can mean the nonexistence of any Condorcet winner.

In such situations, the order in which options are introduced becomes important to the outcome. With sincere voting, for example, p^c will be selected if p^a and p^b are paired first, with the winner taking on p^c. But p^a will emerge victorious if the initial vote pairs p^b and p^c, while p^a waits in the wings. With strategic voting, the problem is even more difficult, and in either case some procedures (such as one that allows any citizen to call for a vote between any feasible option and the prevailing status quo) may have no equilibrium at all.

It is beyond our scope to discuss the various proposals that voting theorists have offered to deal with the problems arising from non-single-peaked preferences in direct democracy. Suffice it to say that there are no simple answers. The interested reader is referred to Hinich and Munger (1997).

2.1.5   Multiple Policy Issues

The other restrictive assumption that we have imposed concerns the
dimensionality of the policy choice. Obviously, many policy decisions have more than a single dimension. Health policy is a good
example. The choice facing society is more than the choice between
public provision and private provision, or between various mixes of
the two. There are also the questions of how many clinics should
operate, where they should be located, what services they should
provide, what fees they should charge, and so on. Citizens may have
different preferences over the various components of a health policy
package, and all of these components must be jointly determined in
the political process.

Like multipeaked preferences, multiple dimensions of policy also
create problems for direct democracy. With several dimensions of
policy, it may not be clear who the median voter is. Consider figure
2.3. Here we depict a social choice with two dimensions of policy, p_1
and p_2, and three voters. The utility function of voter i is $u_i(\mathbf{p})$, where
$\mathbf{p} = (p_1, p_2)$ is the policy vector. The figure shows the favorite policy
combinations for the three voters, $\boldsymbol{\pi}_i = (\pi_{i1}, \pi_{i2})$, and a representative
indifference curve for each one. In the situation depicted, voter 1 has

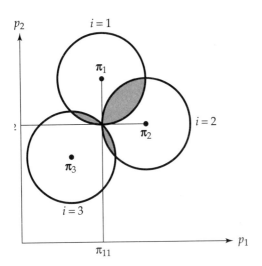

Figure 2.3
The Policy Constructed from the Median in Each Dimension Is Not a Condorcet
Winner

the median ideal point along the p_1-dimension, whereas voter 2 has the median ideal point along the p_2-dimension.

One might be tempted to focus on the median position along each dimension. For the case illustrated in the figure, this would be the point (π_{11}, π_{22}). But it is clear that this policy combination is not a Condorcet winner. All of the combinations in the shaded "clover" are preferred by a majority of voters to the proposal (π_{11}, π_{22}).

Even when the identity of the median voter is clear, there are dim prospects for her favorite to be able to defeat every possible alternative. Figure 2.4 highlights the problem. Here voter 2 is the median voter, as her favorite policy combination is the centermost along each dimension. But π_2 will be defeated in a pairwise comparison by all policy pairs in the shaded region; these pairs are preferred by both voter 1 and voter 3 to the median voter's ideal. Only if the indifference curves of voter 1 and voter 3 happen to be tangent at π_2 can we characterize this combination of policies as a Condorcet winner.

Are there any other points that command majority support against all feasible alternatives? Plott (1967) and McKelvey and Wendell (1976) have shown that such points exist only under exceptional conditions. In particular, the voters' preferences must be smooth, convex, and distributed in a precisely symmetric fashion. Typically, a Condorcet winner will not exist, leaving the outcome of the democratic

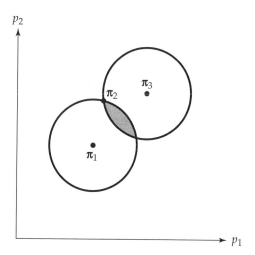

Figure 2.4
An Intermediate Policy May Not Win a Majority

process still in question. Some authors have suggested possible solutions. For example, Shepsle and Weingast (1981) argue that institutions will arise to restrict the range of proposals that may be introduced to challenge a prevailing status quo. Perhaps the rules of the polity will allow only amendments that change a single component of policy (see Shepsle, 1979), or perhaps only alternatives that are sufficiently different from the status quo will be allowed as contenders (see Tullock, 1967). If such restrictions on the voting procedures are introduced, there may exist policy vectors that cannot be defeated by any *admissible* alternative. Shepsle and Weingast refer to this possibility as a "structure-induced equilibrium" for direct democracy. We will not pursue this idea any further.

2.1.6 Summary

Even before we introduce politicians, who may have their own agendas, and SIGs, who may seek to influence them, we find that the problem of collective decision making is hardly a trivial one. Although the median voter theorem seems a powerful result, it is frequently misunderstood and often misused. Even if we ignore the thorny issues having to do with preferences that are not single-peaked or policy issues that are not unidimensional—which call into question the very existence of a policy that could defeat all alternatives in a set of pairwise votes—we must be careful about what the theorem predicts about policy outcomes. The median voter theorem makes no reference to any particular procedure for policy making, nor does it reveal the median voter's ideal to be an equilibrium of any well-specified game. As we have seen, if a median voter can be identified and a favorite policy attached to her, then this policy often emerges as one possible equilibrium outcome, once a procedure for proposal making and a sequence of votes has been described. But only in special cases will such an equilibrium be unique. Strategic behavior on the part of either agenda setters or voters can generate outcomes that deviate from the median voter's ideal. Moreover, such behavior is fully in line with individual utility maximization, even when citizens know and understand everything there is to know about their political environment.

The problems of prediction will not disappear as we proceed to more complex environments that include politicians and interest groups as additional actors. Unfortunately, we can offer no comprehensive solution to these problems. Our approach, somewhat akin to what has been suggested by Shepsle and Weingast, will be to examine institutional environments in which the problems of existence are not so severe. And where there may be multiple political equilibria, we will endeavor to point out the various possibilities and to indicate the ones that seem most compelling to us.

2.2 Representative Democracy

As we noted before, direct democracy is unwieldy as a method of governance. Most democratic societies operate instead by electing a small group of policymakers. In a representative democracy, the citizens elect a subset of their number and endow them with the authority to make policy decisions on their behalf. There are, of course, many different forms of representative democracy. Sometimes a single executive makes the policy choices. More often a group of individuals, representing perhaps different geographic regions or other types of constituencies, has this job. In some systems the legislature has final authority to make and revoke policy decisions, while in others such power is split between the legislature and an executive. Also, in some polities decisions are made centrally and the policies apply to all of the citizens, whereas in other polities only some decisions are made in the center, with others left to local bodies whose mandate to enforce policies is geographically limited.

Even within these broad classes there are finer distinctions of different forms of government. What rules are used to elect the legislators? How long do the representatives serve? Who has authority to propose legislation? How does the legislative body conduct its business? The answers to these questions and many others surely affect the policy process and outcomes.

Nonetheless, we shall abstract from much of this institutional detail. Although we do not deny the importance of political institutions, they are not the main focus of our interest here. Accordingly, we shall describe highly stylized governments, with components that may not match closely the institutional arrangements in any particular country or municipality. But the forces we describe in this book are quite general and will be present in many, if not all, forms of government.

2.2.1 The Downsian Model

The simplest model of representative democracy was formulated by
Downs (1957), who built on the foundation provided by Hotelling
(1929). We imagine first that a unidimensional policy decision must
be taken by a single representative of society. There are two members of society who would like to act in this capacity. These two are
the "politicians"; here they are the only candidates for office. The
winner will be the one who captures a majority of votes in a single
electoral contest.

One must ask, first, what reason these candidates have for seeking
political office. Are they, like other members of society, concerned
about the policy outcome? Or do they covet the job as decision
maker per se? Or do they perhaps seek the position as a stepping
stone to higher office? In practice, career politicians probably have all
of these motivations (and more), but to begin, we assume that the
candidates care only about winning the election at hand. Technically,
each politician's utility is assumed to be strictly higher when he
holds office than when he does not, no matter what policy decision
applies. The utility from holding office might come in the form of a
high income from the job, or from the "ego rents" associated with
being in a position of power.

A second critical assumption of the simplest Downsian model
concerns the candidates' policy pronouncements. We assume that
when the candidates announce policy positions during the course of
the campaign, they are able to commit to carrying out their promises
if elected. It may be hard to envision how such commitments would
be possible in a one-shot election, so voters might be suspicious of
campaign promises unless the politicians literally are indifferent
between the alternative policy outcomes. However, politicians might
have an incentive to carry through on their promises if they intend to
compete in more than one election and if they care about their reputation for telling the truth. The one-shot election with policy commitment can be viewed as a kind of analytical shorthand for a
repeated political game in which politicians value their reputations.

Now we are ready to analyze the following political contest. First,
the candidates simultaneously announce their policy positions, p^A
and p^B. Then the voters with single-peaked utility functions cast
their votes for one candidate or the other. Finally, the candidate with
the most votes assumes office and implements his campaign plat-

form. In case both candidates announce the same policy, we assume
that each wins with a probability of one-half. We seek a Nash equilibrium in the two campaign announcements, as well as the identity
of the winning candidate and the implications for the policy outcome.

This game has a unique Nash equilibrium in which each candidate
announces the policy π_m that is the favorite of the median voter. To
verify that this is an equilibrium, we must show that neither politician has any incentive to act differently. With the indicated strategies, the platforms coincide, and each politician wins the election
with a probability of one-half. But if one politician were to announce
a different platform, more than half of the voters would prefer π_m to
any that the deviant might announce. Thus, the politician who
altered his strategy would lose the election for sure. It follows that
neither politician has any incentive to deviate.

It is also easy to see that this equilibrium is unique. Suppose, to the
contrary, that the politicians were intending to announce some other
pair of platforms besides $p^A = p^B = \pi_m$. If these other platforms were
the same, then either candidate could improve his lot by announcing
π_m instead, which would guarantee an electoral success. If the platforms were different, then at least one of the candidates could gain
by changing to π_m. In short, it is a weakly dominant strategy for each
politician to announce the median voter's favorite policy. This policy,
then, is the unique outcome of the political game.

Notice that the indeterminacies of direct democracy do not arise
here. By limiting the competition to two candidates, we have eliminated the scope for strategic voting. And by giving the agenda
setters electoral rather than policy motives, we have ensured their
convergence to the Condorcet winner. The strong predictions of the
Downsian model no doubt account for much of its appeal.

Still, some of the ambiguities we encountered with direct democracy remain. Take the case in which voters' preferences are not
single-peaked. Suppose, for example, that there are three policy
alternatives, with one-third of the voters preferring p^a to p^b and p^b to
p^c, another third preferring p^b to p^c and p^c to p^a, and the remaining
third preferring p^c to p^a and p^a to p^b. This situation leaves the two
candidates in a quandary. If candidate A expects his rival to announce
platform p^a, then his best response is to announce p^c himself. If he
expects p^c from his rival, then he will want to announce p^b. And if he
expects p^b from his rival, then he will wish to offer p^a. But candidate
B has the same incentives. In the situation described, there is no pair

of policies that are mutual best responses, and thus no (pure-strategy) Nash equilibrium exists.[6]

Similarly, if the policy space is multidimensional, a pure-strategy equilibrium may fail to exist. In fact, the competition between office-seeking candidates admits a pure-strategy equilibrium if and only if the policy space has a Condorcet winner.[7] By definition, such a policy vector can defeat any alternative in a pairwise comparison. If it exists, then it is a weakly dominant strategy for each candidate to announce this vector as his platform. And if no Condorcet winner exists, then, given any policy announcement by one candidate, the other can find a response that defeats it. As we noted earlier, with multiple policy issues the conditions for the existence of a Condorcet winner are rather stringent, and so the simplest Downsian model is likely to have little predictive power.[8]

2.2.2 Candidates with Policy Preferences

Now suppose that the candidates care not only about winning the election, but also about the policy outcome. Let the politicians have the utility functions $G^j = u^j(p) + I^j$, $j = A, B$, where p once again is a scalar policy variable and I^j takes the value zero if candidate j loses the election and the (non-negative) value γ^j if he wins. We assume here that the candidates, like the voters, have single-peaked policy preferences and that they are able to commit themselves to carry out their campaign announcements.

Surprisingly, perhaps, the introduction of policy concerns does not change the politicians' behavior, provided that they give some positive weight (however small) to the spoils of office. Consider first the case in which the politicians' favorite policies lie on the opposite sides of the median voter's ideal, as, for example, when $\pi^A < \pi_m < \pi^B$. For any announcement p^B that candidate A anticipates from his rival, his best response is to counter with a proposal as close to π^A as possible that defeats p^B for sure. Such a platform ensures the candi-

---

6. A pure-strategy equilibrium is one in which each player pursues a certain strategy with probability one. A mixed-strategy equilibrium arises when one of the players randomizes among two or more actions. We will consider some examples of mixed-strategy equilibria later in the book.

7. Kramer (1978) discusses the conditions for the existence of a mixed-strategy equilibrium with two candidates and a multidimensional policy space.

8. This model also breaks down when there are more than two candidates. See Sutton (1998, pp. 42–44) for a clear discussion of this point.

date of at least as good a policy outcome (from his own perspective) as any achievable alternative, and also delivers the welfare component γ^A associated with electoral success.[9] Each politician always has an incentive to shade the other's platform a bit more toward the center, and thus each is driven inextricably to the median voter's ideal.

Now consider the case in which the two politicians' favorites lie on the same side of π_m, as, for example, when $\pi^A < \pi^B < \pi_m$. In this case, each candidate would prefer to win the election for sure with a policy announcement slightly closer to π_m than his rival's proposal rather than lose it for sure with a proposal (that would not be implemented) closer to his own favorite, or to leave the matter to chance with a platform identical to that of his rival. Again, the process drives the politicians to the center of the policy space.

Moreover, even when neither politician cherishes power per se (that is, $\gamma^j = 0$ for $j = A, B$), the pull toward the center is still rather strong. If the pair of politicians come from opposite sides of the political spectrum (that is, $\pi^A \leq \pi_m \leq \pi^B$), the unique Nash equilibrium again has both locating at the median voter's bliss point. Neither can choose a policy closer to his own ideal, for then the other would respond with one preferred by a majority of voters that the first would regard as even worse than π_m. Only if the politicians happen to share relatively similar political biases might the policy outcome depart from the median voter's ideal. For example, if $\pi^A \geq \pi^B > \pi_m$, then there is an equilibrium in which candidate B announces his favorite policy and candidate A adopts any position greater than or equal to π^B. In this situation, there are also equilibria in which the two candidates announce identical platforms between π^B and π_m, including one in which both candidates announce π_m.

The Downsian model (with or without policy-motivated candidates) seems to capture well the pressures for policy convergence in electoral politics. Moreover, it gives pride of place to the median voter's favorite policy. Any departure from this position can be very costly to a candidate, because it leaves an opening for a rival to

9. Technically speaking, with a continuous policy variable p, the best response to an arbitrary p^B may not be well-defined. For every policy $p^A < \pi_m$ that the median voter prefers to p^B, there may be another slightly closer to p^A that the median voter also prefers. However, nothing in our analysis hinges on this "closed-set" problem. We do know that candidate A would never go so far as to announce the policy that leaves the median voter indifferent between p^A and p^B, because that announcement would deliver the spoils of office only by chance, and it would yield lower expected "policy welfare" as well.

choose a more popular platform that would spell his own electoral defeat. But the model may overstate the tendency toward convergence, as can be seen in the following two variants of the basic setting.

First, let the candidates be uncertain about the exact distribution of tastes in the voting population. Suppose that each holds some prior belief about the median voter's bliss point but does not know where this point is for sure.[10] A candidate's objective is to maximize expected utility, which includes a concern for the policy outcome as well as (perhaps) a taste for the spoils of office. Then, if the utility component from holding office is not too large, the campaign platforms of politicians with different tastes must diverge. To see this, suppose candidate B anticipates that his rival will announce some position p^A different from his own ideal of π^B. If candidate B were to announce p^A as his own platform, the policy outcome would be p^A for sure. Candidate B can achieve what he regards as a better expected policy outcome by announcing a position a bit closer to π^B. At worst, he would lose the election, and then the outcome anyway would be p^A. And there is some chance that the median voter and a majority of others will prefer his position closer to π^B, in which case he would attain a policy outcome more to his liking. Of course, the announcement might hinder his electoral prospects. But as long as the candidate does not put too much weight on being in office, he will prefer to distance himself from his rival.

Alternatively, let the candidates know the tastes of the voters (and vice versa), but suppose they cannot commit themselves to carry out their campaign pledges. In the extreme, the platforms might be seen as empty promises. A politician with preferences $G^j = u^j(p) + I^j$ might be expected to enact the policy $p = \pi^j$ that maximizes $u^j(p)$, despite his having a taste for the spoils of office that would inspire efforts to convince voters otherwise. Surely, this will be his course of action if the election is a one-shot affair and if the politician cares nothing about keeping his word. In the event, a competition between two arbitrary candidates leaves the electorate with a choice between their particular favorites. The democratic process chooses whichever of the two happens to command greater support. There is greater

---

10. See Roemer (1994). Wittman (1983) examines a similar model, but he takes each candidate's probability of being elected to be a continuous function of the pair of platform positions without linking the function to any explicit source of underlying uncertainty.

scope for convergence toward the median voter's ideal point if the contest is a repeated one, but full convergence requires a low discount rate and a high ongoing probability that there will be at least one more election (see Alesina, 1988).

2.2.3   Endogenous Candidates

The foregoing discussion suggests an obvious question. Which individuals will run for political office, if doing so is costly? We can analyze this issue using a multistage model of political entry, electoral competition, and voting. Let citizen i have the utility function $u_i(p) + I_i$, where I_i equals zero if citizen i is not in office and $\gamma > 0$ if he is. γ now is the common value of being in office to all individuals. For the time being, take p to be a scalar (i.e., a unidimensional policy issue) and $u_i(\cdot)$ to be single-peaked and strictly concave function for all i. The cost of conducting a political campaign is e.

Office Seekers with Policy Commitment
Consider first the case in which politicians are primarily concerned about gaining office. This case arises when both γ and e, as well as the difference between them, are large relative to $u_i(p)$. Let the citizens simultaneously announce their entry decisions and policy platforms, as in Feddersen et al. (1990). They do so with the knowledge that the winning candidate will be the one capturing the most votes and that a tie will generate a random choice among the maximum vote-getters, with each being selected with equal probability. Policy announcements are taken by voters at face value, because candidates can commit to carry out their promises. Finally, in the election stage, voters cast their ballots strategically to maximize their (expected) utilities, but are precluded from randomizing their choices.

   If politicians care mostly about being in office, then all entrants must locate at the median voter's ideal policy. Here we will only sketch the argument, leaving the interested reader to consult Feddersen et al. (1990) for the details. Notice first that, since e is large relative to $u_i(p)$, no citizen will enter the race solely to influence the policy outcome. If an entrant foresees that he will lose for sure, the influence he can have on the choice of p cannot justify the cost of his candidacy. Accordingly, an individual will enter the contest only if he has some prospect of winning. It follows that all entrants receive the same number of votes in equilibrium.

There are several possible configurations of candidate positions
to consider. First, suppose that there are several candidates who
announce policies at the median voter's ideal, and one or more candidates who announce something different. Then one of the voters
who prefers π_m to any of the available alternatives could switch her
vote from her intended choice to another running on the same platform and ensure the latter's victory. This would be advantageous
to her, which means that the opportunity could not exist. Second,
suppose there is only one candidate at π_m and one other with some
alternative platform. Then the two could not attract an equal number
of votes, as would be necessary for each to have a chance at victory,
because a majority of voters prefers π_m to any alternative. Third,
suppose there is one or more candidates located at a single point
away from the median voter's ideal position and no other candidates
in the race. Then the citizen with the median ideal point could enter
the race with an announcement of π_m and could defeat the original
entrant(s). If $\gamma - e > 0$, as it must be for any individual to see a
candidacy as worthwhile, it would pay for this citizen to throw her
hat into the ring. Fourth, suppose there is one candidate running on
the π_m platform, and several others located at other points. If two or
more of these other candidates are located at the same alternative
point, then a voter who likes their common position could alter her
vote and decide the election to her own advantage. If the others are
located at distinct points, then there must be some smallest alternative p^j and some largest alternative p^k, with the property that either
$p^j < \pi_m \leq Ep < p^k$ or $p^j < Ep \leq \pi_m < p^k$, where Ep is the expected
policy outcome. Take, for example, the first of these possibilities.
Since strategic voters vote sincerely here and all have strictly concave
utility functions, an individual who votes for the candidate at p^j
must like this outcome at least as much as π_m, which in turn she must
strictly prefer to the lottery between all the available positions. This
voter could switch her vote from the candidate with platform p^j to
the one with platform π_m, ensure the victory of the latter candidate,
and thereby improve her expected well-being. By a similar argument,
there can be no three or more candidates with distinct policy positions, none of which is located at π_m.

This leaves only two possibilities. Either there are two candidates,
each with an equally popular position away from the median voter's
ideal, or all candidates are located at π_m. But in the former case, one
of the entrants would have an incentive to locate instead at π_m. By

doing so, he would ensure for himself electoral victory, which by
assumption is worth more to him than any loss he might suffer from
the change in policy. So all entrants (however many there are) locate
at the median voter's ideal point. Each such entrant receives the
same number of votes. Then, if the number of entrants is N_e, each has
a $1/N_e$ chance of being elected to office. To be consistent with rational
foresight, the expected payoff from running, γ/N_e, must equal or
exceed the cost of candidacy, e. This puts an upper limit on the
number of possible candidates.

As Feddersen et al. (1990) themselves point out, the equilibrium
with endogenous entry requires a great deal of coordination among
the voters. Each entering candidate must expect to receive exactly the
same number of votes in equilibrium, despite the fact that their
platforms are indistinguishable and that voters do not communicate.
Also, potential entrants must anticipate defeat, which implies that
voters who split their votes among winning candidates in equilibrium would flock en masse to a single candidate were they to be
called upon to defeat a less desirable alternative (Shepsle, 1991, p. 76).
These features of the model are disturbing, especially since the strong
characterization result is not robust to the introduction of voters who
are imperfectly informed about other voters' tastes or to voters who
randomize. Still, it is intriguing that the median voter's ideal emerges
as the unique equilibrium outcome in a model with strategic voting
and endogenous candidacy, in the light of the inevitable ambiguity
about policy that is present in models of direct democracy.

Lack of Policy Commitment
Different outcomes are possible when candidates cannot commit to
carry out their campaign promises. This setting has been studied in
depth by Besley and Coate (1997) and Osborne and Slivinski (1996).[11]

We follow Besley and Coate (1997) and allow the issue space to be
multidimensional, so that **p** represents a vector of policy choices.
Each citizen has (perhaps) a taste for office $\gamma \geq 0$, but also a real
concern for the policy outcome. In fact, since policy commitments

---

11. There are some differences between the models in these two papers. Osborne and
Slivinski restrict attention to the case of sincere voting and to a unidimensional policy
issue with single-peaked preferences. They compare outcomes under plurality rule and
a runoff system that pairs the two leading vote-getters in an initial round of voting.
Besley and Coate allow strategic voting and an arbitrary policy space, but examine
only plurality rule.

are infeasible, the citizens' policy preferences dictate their actions in case they are elected. If citizen i with utility function $u_i(\mathbf{p}) + I_i$ runs for office and wins, she enacts the policy vector $\boldsymbol{\pi}^i$ that maximizes $u_i(\mathbf{p})$. We assume that each individual has a unique favorite and that this favorite is known to all voters.

Citizens initially face a choice of whether to enter the race or not. They know that the winner will be the one receiving the most votes or, if several candidates tie for most votes, one selected at random from among the leading candidates. Later, as voters, the same citizens cast their ballots strategically, seeking to maximize their expected utilities. An equilibrium must be sequentially rational, which means that the Nash equilibrium at the entry stage must rationally anticipate the subsequent (equilibrium) actions in the voting phase. Finally, it is assumed that the polity resorts to some status quo policy vector $\mathbf{q}$ in the event that no candidate is willing to stand for office.

We describe some examples of pure-strategy equilibria in this two-stage game. Although the existence of such equilibrium is not guaranteed, there are many circumstances where existence is not a problem, in contrast to the Downsian world with multidimensional policy and an exogenous list of candidates.[12]

Besley and Coate show that there can be multiple equilibria, including equilibria with different numbers of candidates. The number of candidates can be one, two, or more than two, and each of these types of equilibria has different properties. Consider first the possibility that there is a single candidate i who runs for office unopposed. This individual must fare better by standing for election than not, which implies $u_i(\boldsymbol{\pi}^i) + \gamma - e \geq u_i(\mathbf{q})$. Moreover, it must not pay for another citizen to enter the race. Were another citizen to enter the race, voters would face a choice between two alternative policy vectors. In the event, they would vote for the candidate whose favorite policy they preferred. So any citizen with an ideal point preferred by a majority of voters to that of citizen i could defeat the assumed sole entrant. Entry would be profitable for that citizen, provided her policy choice would be rather different than $\boldsymbol{\pi}^i$ and that the costs of campaigning are not too large. It follows that, if campaign costs are small ($e \approx 0$), only citizens whose favorite policy is a Condorcet winner can be candidates in an uncontested election. In a

---

12. See Besley and Coate (1997), who also point out that a subgame perfect equilibrium is guaranteed to exist if citizens are permitted mixed strategies in their entry decisions.

setting with a single policy issue, this can only be the median citizen. In an election with many policy issues, no such equilibrium with a single candidate is likely to exist.

Next consider equilibria with exactly two candidates, i and j. In such an equilibrium, voting is sincere. So each candidate captures the votes of all those who prefer her ideal point to that of her rival. Moreover, as was the case with policy commitment, the candidates must receive an equal number of votes. Otherwise, the sure loser would have no reason to enter the race. Finally, each candidate must prefer to enter the race than to stay on the sideline, which requires

$$\tfrac{1}{2}[u_i(\boldsymbol{\pi}^i) - u_i(\boldsymbol{\pi}^j) + \gamma] \geq e$$

and

$$\tfrac{1}{2}[u_j(\boldsymbol{\pi}^j) - u_j(\boldsymbol{\pi}^i) + \gamma] \geq e.$$

Notice that, for existence, we need not worry about the prospects of entry by a third candidate, because such a candidate could be deterred by the (rational) expectation that voters would not "waste" their votes on her.[13] All we need for the existence of an equilibrium of this sort is a pair of policies that are equally popular and a cost of entry that is not too large. Thus, equilibria with exactly two candidates are likely to exist in many situations.

Perhaps the most interesting possibility is that of an equilibrium with three or more candidates, some of whom enter the race knowing that they have no chance to be elected. Consider, for example, the following possible configuration. Citizens i, j, and k enter as candidates, and citizen i captures a majority of the votes. Since citizen i is elected, the policy outcome is $\boldsymbol{\pi}^i$. Citizen j is willing to run, because she fears that citizen k could defeat citizen i in a two-person election, and $u_j(\boldsymbol{\pi}^i) - e \geq u_j(\boldsymbol{\pi}^k)$. Similarly, citizen k is willing to run, because $u_k(\boldsymbol{\pi}^i) - e \geq u_k(\boldsymbol{\pi}^j)$ and citizen k fears that citizen j would defeat citizen i. In short, the two candidates j and k enter as mutual "spoilers," each competing to ensure that the other does not end up victorious. Nothing precludes such a possibility as an equilibrium outcome. There could also be more spoilers than two in the race, as well as more than a single candidate who has a real chance of being elected.

---

13. Suppose candidate k were to enter, and consider a voter l whose preferences were such that $u_l(\boldsymbol{\pi}^k) > u_l(\boldsymbol{\pi}^i) > u_l(\boldsymbol{\pi}^j)$. Such a voter would throw her support behind k if she could be sure that enough others would do likewise. But otherwise she would fear that her vote for k instead of i would cause candidate j to win the election, which of course would lower her utility.

The model of endogenous candidates without policy commitment yields a rich set of possible outcomes. Unlike the Downsian model, it raises few questions about the existence of equilibrium, nor does it point to the median voter's preferred policy as an inevitable outcome. A drawback may be that there are often multiple equilibria, and the theory gives no basis for choosing between them. More important, perhaps, is the observation that campaign promises often do have meaning, especially if made by political parties that are long-lived and have reason to invest in their reputations.

2.3 Electing a Legislature

In the last section we considered the election of an individual lawmaker who has unilateral authority to set policy. In reality, of course, societies often elect a number of representatives to constitute a legislative body. Policymaking authority then rests with the body. Legislatures may comprise representatives of different constituencies or different regions, or the composition of the legislature may reflect the relative popularity of various political viewpoints in the population as a whole. Since the legislature may include members with different preferences and different agendas, it needs rules to guide its collective decision making, just as the society at large does.

Models of legislative elections typically assume the existence of political parties. These parties are coalitions of individuals who abide by some set of rules for coordinating their election strategies and perhaps their behavior within the legislature. It would be better, of course, to derive the existence of political parties as part of the theory, and to determine their composition endogenously. But modeling coalition formation is notoriously difficult, and so we follow tradition in taking the set of political parties as exogenously given.

Moreover, we will often find it convenient to assume that the parties have their own preferences and objectives, without addressing how these preferences are derived from those of the individual party members. A party's objective might be, for example, to maximize its probability of winning a majority of seats, to maximize the size of its legislative delegation, or to implement a set of policies consistent with the members' own preferences. Again, a more complete theory would be preferable, but is beyond our scope.

There seem to be almost as many different methods for electing legislatures, and rules for their operation, as there are political jurisdictions in the world. It is impossible for us to consider the many different variants that exist. Instead, we will discuss two stylized alternatives: a system of single-member districts and a system of strict proportional representation.

2.3.1 Single-Member Districts

Consider the election of a legislature comprising members from distinct geographic regions, or "districts." Each district elects a single representative. The various seats in the legislature are contested by two political parties, each of which has as its objective to maximize its chance of winning a majority of the seats. The candidates endorse their party's common platform, even though tastes are not the same in all districts. We take the policy space to be unidimensional, at least for the time being. Each party is committed to carry out its campaign promises in the event that it captures a majority of seats.

Let $\pi_m(i)$ be the favorite policy of the median voter in district i, for $i = 1, 2, \ldots, D$, where D is an odd number. We can order the districts so that these median ideal points are nondecreasing; that is, $\pi_m(1) \leq \pi_m(2) \leq \cdots \leq \pi_m(D)$. To capture a majority in the legislature, the parties must target the median district, which has an index of $D_m = (D+1)/2$. If, for example, party B were to adopt some position p^B greater than $\pi_m(D_m)$, party A could counter with a policy between p^B and $\pi_m(D_m)$, and its candidate would defeat her rival in district D_m. Not only that, but a majority of voters would prefer the platform of party A to that of party B in (at least) all of the districts labeled $1, 2, \ldots, D_m$. By adopting a policy different from the "median of the medians," party B leaves itself open to sure defeat. The unique Nash equilibrium has the two parties converging on $p = \pi_m(D_m)$, namely, the policy preferred by the median voter in the median district.

What if the platforms are chosen by the candidates themselves, rather than by central authorities that pursue the overall objectives of the parties? In this case, the outcome depends on the preferences of the individual candidates. Suppose, for example, that each candidate would rather see her own party win a majority with probability one-half and have a one-half probability of winning herself, than have her own victory ensured while her party loses in the process. With this restriction on the politicians' preferences, the Nash equilibrium has unanimous agreement among all candidates in each of the parties. Each party's candidates agree on the platform $\pi_m(D_m)$, recognizing that any other platform would spell sure defeat for their party (see Hinich and Ordeshook, 1974).

If the candidates care instead only about their own electoral fortunes, there will be a conflict of interests within each party. Each candidate has a most-preferred platform, which is the favorite policy of the median voter in the district she hopes to represent. Now the question is, How does the party select its platform when the various candidates have different preferences? If the candidates were to hold a party congress and somehow converge on a Condorcet winner among the potential platforms, then the outcome again would be identical platforms of $p^A = p^B = \pi_m(D_m)$. But notice that the party congress is akin to direct democracy, so it is not clear that the participants would select the Condorcet winner. Another possibility, which has been examined by Austen-Smith (1984), is that each candidate makes a proposal to the party congress, and that the platform is some (arbitrary) aggregation of the suggestions of the various participants. In this case, if the platform is sensitive to the suggestions of every candidate (in the sense that, when a candidate alters her suggestion in some direction, the platform moves at least minimally in the same direction), then there can be no equilibrium in which the parties both announce $\pi_m(D_m)$. To see this, consider the incentives facing the candidate of party A in district 1. If she expects the other party to announce a platform of $\pi_m(D_m)$ and she expects the other candidates in her own party to announce a certain set of proposals, she prefers to announce a proposal that leaves her party's platform a bit below $\pi_m(D_m)$ to one that leaves the platform equal to $\pi_m(D_m)$. Although the former announcement would doom her party to an overall defeat, it would ensure her own electoral success. Unfortunately, the procedure studied by Austen-Smith (1984) admits no equilibrium whatsoever. The candidates inevitably pursue goals that are mutually inconsistent.[14]

---

14. Ansolabehere and Snyder (1996) study a related problem. They assume that a party's platform in any election is the Condorcet winner among the most preferred positions of its sitting legislators. The legislators care foremost about winning their own race, but conditional on so doing may prefer also to be in the majority party. Their model differs from the one described here inasmuch as the district elections are determined not only by the candidates' positions, but also by a national shock (realized after the positions are set) to the parties' relative popularity. In this setting the parties have divergent positions in each election, as one caters to those districts that have a median voter who favors a low value of the policy and the other caters to districts at the other end of the political spectrum.

Another possibility is that the candidates care most about the policy outcome, rather than about their own electoral prospects or those of their party. With policy-motivated politicians, the platforms again are driven toward the favorite policy of the median voter in the median district. Suppose, for example, that the candidates from party A have a favorite of $\pi^A < \pi_m(D_m)$, while those of party B favor $\pi^B > \pi_m(D_m)$. If party A were to announce a platform p^A different from $\pi_m(D_m)$ and closer to π^A, then party B would counter with one that is greater than $\pi_m(D_m)$ and that is preferred by a majority of the voters in a majority of the districts. This would lead to a bad outcome for party A, and so it prefers to adopt a position of $\pi_m(D_m)$. The same is true for party B.

Alternatively, if π^A and π^B happen to lie on the same side of $\pi_m(D_m)$, then as long as the candidates care only about the policy outcome there will be equilibria in which the parties announce the same platform, which both prefer to $\pi_m(D_m)$. But, as was the case with the election of a single policymaker, these equilibria disappear as soon as the politicians have some (possibly small) desire to see their own party in power.

We have assumed thus far that all candidates from a party must run on a common platform. But often candidates adopt their own positions, which may differ from those of their party, in order to appeal to local voters. In such circumstances, voters must forecast how the legislative deliberations will unfold, since the differing campaign promises of the victorious candidates cannot all be fulfilled. Rather than divert our attention to the details of legislative decision making—an interesting topic, to be sure, but one that would take us too far afield—let us simply assume that the legislature settles on some policy that aggregates the announced positions of elected representatives from the majority party. We suppose that each such position has at least some small influence on the compromise outcome. Implicitly, we are assuming that each legislator is committed to "fight for" the policy position she has previously endorsed, and that policies are set by the majority party after a negotiation among delegation members.

Osborne (1995) has studied this problem and shown that the outcomes are rather similar to some we have already seen. If candidates care more about their party's fortunes than their own—in particular, if they would prefer to see their party in the majority with probability one-half and themselves in office with the same probability, compared to a situation in which they manage to win themselves but their party goes down to sure defeat—then the unique equilibrium has each candidate announcing the favorite policy of the median voter in the median district. The same is true if the politicians care primarily about the policy outcome, and if their respective most-preferred policies lie on opposite sides of $\pi_m(D_m)$. But if the politicians care mostly about their own personal prospects, then incentives will exist for some candidates to take rather extreme policy positions, and there is likely to be a difficulty in finding any equilibrium set of individual platforms.

2.3.2 *Proportional Representation*

In some electoral systems the composition of the legislature is not the result of a collection of district races, but rather is determined by the aggregate popularity of the parties. For example, in a party-list system, each party submits an ordered list of candidates to an election committee, and voters cast their ballots for one list or another. A prescribed formula translates the distribution of votes into an allocation of seats in the legislature. The simplest such formula imposes strict proportional representation; that is, the size of each party's delegation is proportional to its share in the aggregate vote. More complex schemes may include thresholds of exclusion (a minimum proportion of votes needed for any representation in the legislature), preference voting (voters rank candidates by preference, and votes for eliminated candidates are reallocated to second choices), and other provisions.

Let us examine the competition between two political parties when seats are awarded by strict proportional representation.[15] Again we must distinguish the electoral setting by the number of issues to be settled, by the objectives of the parties, and by the procedures that the legislature uses to determine policy. The simplest case involves a single issue and strict majority rule in the legislature. In this setting, voters cast their votes for the party whose platform they prefer, no matter whether their motivations are strategic or sincere.

Suppose the parties seek to maximize the sizes of their respective delegations, which is equivalent here to maximizing their shares of the aggregate vote. Such an objective might reflect a party's desire to

---

15. See Cox (1997) for a detailed discussion of other electoral systems.

spread the spoils of office to as many active members as possible. The unique equilibrium, then, is for each party to adopt the platform favored by the median voter. By announcing π_m as its platform, each party assures itself of one-half of the seats. Neither party wishes to deviate from this position, because it would forfeit seats to its rival by doing so. And no other pair of platforms can form an equilibrium, because when one party locates away from π_m, the other has an incentive to locate between its position and the median voter's ideal policy.

If the parties instead seek to maximize their chances of winning a majority, the conclusion is the same. When one party locates at π_m, the other has no chance of winning a majority unless it also locates there. The equilibrium positions converge on this position. Even if the parties have policy objectives, their positions will converge on π_m provided they also see some value in having a legislative presence or in being themselves in a majority.

What if there are many issues to be decided by the legislature? This is, of course, the most common situation, and one that we shall want to examine later in the book. We have already seen that, with multiple policy dimensions, a political equilibrium may fail to exist even when a single elected official makes all of the decisions. The problem of nonexistence of an equilibrium does not disappear with the introduction of political parties and multiseat legislatures. If anything, it becomes more severe. Rather than rehearse the reasons why an equilibrium may fail to exist in the general case, we devote our attention to a special case where an equilibrium often can be found. The special case is one to which we will return frequently in the chapters to come. Therefore, we will develop the model in somewhat more detail.

We consider an election in which the parties perceive flexibility along only a subset of policy dimensions. That is, we divide the set of policy issues into two groups. For one set of issues, the parties' positions are taken to be *fixed*. For the other set, they are *pliable*. The fixed positions might reflect the parties' leanings on issues about which feelings are so strong that any promise to betray ideology would not be credible. Or the rigid positions might remain from the past, if a party fears that any reversal from its pronouncements in earlier elections would damage its reputation. On the pliable issues, the parties have no inviolable preferences and no inherited positions. They choose their platforms to further their political objectives, whatever they happen to be. In short, we introduce some exogenous differences between the parties (specifically, in their fixed platforms) to help ensure the existence of an equilibrium, and then focus on the competition that determines the remaining positions and the outcome of the election.

For simplicity, we take voters' utilities to be additive in the components reflecting their preferences over the fixed and pliable policy dimensions. Voter i experiences utility $u_i(\mathbf{p}^A) + v_i^A$ when the vector of party A's pliable policies is $\mathbf{p}^A$ and the fixed policy outcomes correspond to the fixed positions of party A. The same voter attains welfare $u_i(\mathbf{p}^B) + v_i^B$ when the outcomes correspond instead to the positions of party B. We assume that $u_i(\cdot)$ is strictly concave.

Suppose the legislature operates by majority rule. Then it will be a weakly dominant strategy for each voter to vote for the party whose package of positions (fixed and pliable) she prefers. Voter i casts her ballot for the list of party A if $u_i(\mathbf{p}^A) + v_i^A > u_i(\mathbf{p}^B) + v_i^B$, or equivalently, if

$$u_i(\mathbf{p}^A) - u_i(\mathbf{p}^B) > v_i, \tag{2.1}$$

where $v_i = v_i^B - v_i^A$ measures the individual's preference for the fixed positions of party B over those of party A. Inequality (2.1) says that voter i should vote for party A if her relative preference for that party's pliable positions (positive or negative) exceeds her preference (again, positive or negative) for the fixed positions of its rival. If the inequality runs in the opposite direction, then voter i votes for party B. Finally, if the two sides of (2.1) are equal, then the voter abstains, or perhaps casts her vote at random.

We assume a continuum of voters with diverse tastes. This assumption facilitates the analysis and provides a good approximation to situations where the actual number of voters is large.[16] A continuous electorate can be characterized by a distribution of the relative preference variable, v_i. For simplicity, we take v_i to be uniformly distributed in the range extending from $(-1 + 2b)/2f$ to $(1 + 2b)/2f$.[17]

---

16. With a continuum of voters and diverse tastes, the fraction of voters that is indifferent between the two parties is negligible. Therefore, it does not matter how these individuals cast their votes.

17. Our discussion in this chapter and the next could be conducted with a more general distribution function for v_i. We choose the uniform distribution because this specification will prove more convenient for the subsequent analysis. An early example of the type of model that we develop here appeared in the empirical study of presidential elections by Fair (1978). He also assumed a uniform distribution for v_i.

The parameter f, which represents the density, measures (inversely) the diversity of preferences in the voting population, while the parameter b measures the extent to which the fixed positions of party B are more popular on the whole. If, for example, the parties adopt common positions on the pliable issues, then party B wins a majority if $b > 0$ and party A wins a majority if $b < 0$. In fact, under this distributional assumption, it is possible to write an exact expression for the vote shares. The fraction of votes that goes to party A is given by

$$s = \tfrac{1}{2} - b + f[u(\mathbf{p}^A) - u(\mathbf{p}^B)], \tag{2.2}$$

where $u(\mathbf{p})$ is the average value of $u_i(\mathbf{p})$ in the population of voters. We assume that preferences for the fixed polices are sufficiently dispersed (i.e., that f is sufficiently small), so that the vote share s falls between zero and one for all feasible $\mathbf{p}^A$ and $\mathbf{p}^B$. In words, this assumption says that no matter what the pliable positions are, there are some voters who so much prefer the fixed platform of party A and others who so much prefer the fixed platform of party B that each party inevitably attracts a positive number of votes.

We now assume that the parties have imperfect information about voters' preferences. In particular, when the parties must announce their pliable policy positions, they remain uncertain about which set of fixed positions will prove to be the more popular.[18] In other words, the parties do not know the precise value of b but rather regard this aggregate popularity measure as the realization of some random variable, $\tilde{b}$. The parties share a common belief prior about the distribution of the random variable.

Each party chooses its pliable position to maximize its objective function. It may wish either to maximize the expected size of its legislative delegation or to maximize the probability that it will win a majority. We will see that both of these alternative objective functions imply the same equilibrium platforms.

If the objective is to maximize the expected size of delegation, then party A chooses $\mathbf{p}^A$ to maximize Es while party B chooses $\mathbf{p}^B$ to maximize $1 - Es$. In view of (2.2), this means that they seek to maximize and minimize $u(\mathbf{p}^A) - u(\mathbf{p}^B)$, respectively. In a Nash equilibrium, party A chooses the pliable platform that maximizes $u(\mathbf{p}^A)$, or in other words, the pliable platform that maximizes *average voter*

---

18. Ansolabehere and Snyder (1996) allude to an unresolved "valence" issue as the source of uncertainty over the relative popularity of the two parties.

welfare. Party B chooses the platform to maximize $u(\mathbf{p}^B)$, so it too sets its pliable platform to maximize average welfare. We see that the pliable platforms converge, but this time not to the policy vector—if one even exists—that is preferred by the median voter. Rather, the parties maximize their (expected) appeal by catering to the average voter.

If each party's objective instead is to maximize the probability of its winning a majority, then party A seeks to maximize the probability that $s > \frac{1}{2}$, while party B seeks to maximize the probability that $s < \frac{1}{2}$. But it follows from (2.2) that $s > \frac{1}{2}$ if and only if

$$b < f[u(\mathbf{p}^A) - u(\mathbf{p}^B)].$$

So party A seeks to maximize the probability that $b < f[u(\mathbf{p}^A) - u(\mathbf{p}^B)]$, which it does by choosing the platform that maximizes $u(\mathbf{p}^A)$. Similarly, party B seeks to maximize the probability that $b > f[u(\mathbf{p}^A) - u(\mathbf{p}^B)]$, which it does by maximizing $u(\mathbf{p}^B)$. Again, the parties choose a common pliable platform, namely the policies that maximize the welfare of the average voter.[19]

In this chapter, we have surveyed the literature on voting and elections. Our key assumption has been that citizens vote to promote their interests in public policy. Importantly, we impose no restrictions on how those interests might be perceived, for example whether citizens are selfish or altruistic, or whether politicians are motivated by social conscience or a lust for power.

Policy outcomes depend on the rules of the game. With some procedures for voting and policy determination, the outcome is a policy that serves well the interests of the median or average voter. But this need not be the case if, for example, the system gives undue power to an agenda setter with idiosyncratic tastes, or if political entry costs are high and actual entrants happen to be citizens with extreme policy preferences. In order to judge the influence of special interests—which is our main task in the coming chapters—it will be important to bear this lesson in mind. We will want to judge outcomes not against some hypothetical ideal, but against what they

---

19. Lindbeck and Weibull (1987) derive a similar result for the case where the parties have no uncertainty about aggregate popularity (they know b), but only about the tastes of individual voters. They show that if the population is large but finite and if each party aims to maximize its probability of winning a majority, then the platforms converge to the vector that maximizes $u(\mathbf{p})$.

would have been in the same political environment but for the actions of the interest groups. Our first example of this comes in the next chapter. There we take a broad view of a special interest group as any identifiable subgroup in the voting population. We incorporate SIGs into the model of representative democracy with legislative decision making and proportional representation, which in their absence predicts the emergence of pliable policies that are best for the average voter. We ask, will political parties still cater to the average voter when the electorate comprises groups with different ideological leanings, different voter turnout rates, and differential access to information about the parties' positions or the effects of policy?

3   Groups as Voters

As we noted in Chapter 1, there is little consensus among social scientists about the proper definition of a special interest group. Some political scientists reserve the term for membership organizations that undertake political activities on behalf of their members. They ask whether the ability to undertake these activities gives undue influence to the organized groups. This certainly is an important question, and one that will occupy us for much of the remainder of this book. But here we wish to entertain a broader notion of a SIG. An interest group may be considered "special" if its members covet policies that would not be considered desirable by the average citizen. Thus, any minority group of citizens that shares identifiable characteristics and similar concerns on some set of issues might be termed a SIG.

With this definition, the members of a profession comprise a SIG, because they share similar aims in regard to policies that affect their vocation. Similarly, those who work in a particular industry have common tastes for certain regulatory and trade policies. Retired persons form a SIG, because their goals for health policy and social security differ from those of the average voter. So also do Hispanics, Catholics, and other ethnic, religious, or social groups, because they seek particular laws and provisions consistent with their personal beliefs and well-being. Even environmentalists may be considered to represent a special interest, to the extent that their concerns for the environment exceed those of the average citizen.

In the democratic ideal, the preferences of all citizens are weighed equally. Thus, we might hope for policies that serve the general interest, which can be identified with the preferences of the median or the average voter. We saw in Chapter 2 that the electoral process does not inevitably yield the median or average voter's favorite policy as a unique equilibrium outcome. But we also saw that political competition does typically put pressure on candidates and political parties to cater to the general interest. Since we had no "groups" in the models of the last chapter, we could not ask whether policy outcomes might systematically favor certain types of voters over to others. That is the question to which we now turn.

In this chapter we identify three potential sources of policy bias in the electoral process. Certain SIGs may fare especially well in a voting equilibrium owing to their high voter participation rates, their access to information, or their centrist ideological leanings. We take up each of these potential sources of policy bias in turn.

3.1 Turnout

Voter participation is far from universal in countries that lack mandatory voting laws. In the United States, for example, turnout rates in federal elections have averaged 55.5 percent since 1960 in years with a presidential election, and only 41.0 percent in years with a congressional election but no presidential contest.[1] Moreover, voting rates vary widely across demographic and socioeconomic groups. For example, voter turnout in the 1996 U.S. federal election was 56 percent among eligible white voters, 50.6 percent among blacks, and only 26.7 percent among Hispanics.

We might ask, why do citizens forgo their opportunity to vote? But this question has proved less difficult to answer than its opposite: Why are so many individuals willing to vote? After all, it takes time and effort for an individual to visit the polling place. And many elections are decided by margins of tens or even hundreds of thousands of votes. The paradox in voting is not the failure of universal participation, but rather the choice by a reasonably high percentage of eligible voters to bear the cost of voting.

Voting theorists since Downs (1957), Tullock (1967), and Riker and Ordeshook (1968) have attempted to resolve this paradox.[2] They

---

1. See http://www.fec.gov/pages/htmlto5.htm (accessed September 14, 2000) for the data from which these calculations were made. In other countries, turnout rates are higher. In Canada, for example, the turnout rate was 73 percent in 1993 during a prime ministerial election and 67 percent in 1997 during a general election; see http://www.fec.gov/pages/Internat.htm (accessed September 14, 2000).
2. Aldrich (1993) provides a nice overview of the theoretical literature on voter turnout. His own view is that participation is a marginal decision for most voters, with low costs and low benefits. He thus regards the paradox of voting as a minor anomaly, but argues that the marginality of the decision means that small changes in perceived costs and benefits of voting can have large effects on turnout.

have developed a "calculus of voting" based on a simple cost-benefit comparison. They begin with the assumption that individual i will opt to vote if and only if

$$E_i u_i(\tilde{\mathbf{p}}) - E_{-i} u_i(\tilde{\mathbf{p}}) \geq \kappa_i. \tag{3.1}$$

Here $\mathbf{p}$ is a policy vector that will be determined by some election. Individual i may be uncertain about the outcome of the election, and so may regard vector $\mathbf{p}$ as the realization of a random vector, $\tilde{\mathbf{p}}$. The individual has beliefs about who is likely to win, which are reflected in a prior distribution for $\tilde{\mathbf{p}}$. Presumably these priors differ somewhat depending on whether or not the individual herself participates, because her own ballot would add one more vote to the side that she supports. The first term on the left-hand side of (3.1) is the voter's evaluation of the expected outcome using the probabilities that apply when she opts to participate. The second term gives her evaluation of the expected outcome using the probabilities that apply when she refrains. Thus, the entire left-hand side is the perceived benefit to voter i from exercising her vote. By voting, she alters the distribution of possible policy outcomes, and presumably improves the prospect for the outcomes she prefers. The voter compares this benefit to her personal cost of voting, which is represented by the term κ_i.

If $\kappa_i > 0$, voting can be justified only when an individual perceives some chance of making a difference to the policy outcome. If, for example, the individual perceives no uncertainty as to who will win the election, she will never choose to vote when the cost of doing so is positive. Similarly, if she anticipates that the different candidates would implement the same policies, she has no reason to bear a cost to support one over another. The paradox of voting refers to the observation that, with a reasonably large number of voters, the likelihood that a particular individual will be decisive in any election appears to be quite small. And competitive pressures often cause platforms to converge. It follows that the distribution of $\mathbf{p}$ is not affected very much by voter i's choice of whether to participate or not. In other words, the left-hand side of (3.1) ought to be very close to zero in most elections. Any positive cost of voting ought to be enough to make citizens refrain.

Ledyard (1982, 1984) proposed a resolution to the paradox that relies on strategic reasoning. Suppose individuals make simultaneous, independent, and private decisions about whether or not to vote, and consider the Nash equilibrium of a participation game. In such a game, with a finite number of voters, it cannot be an equilibrium outcome for all citizens to decide never to vote. For if every potential voter but one behaved this way, it would quite likely be optimal for the remaining one to exercise her vote. The sole participant's vote would surely be decisive, and so she could choose her favorite policy option at a cost of κ_i. In a game of strategic participation decisions, a Nash equilibrium must have at least some citizens opting to vote at least some of the time.

Ledyard's analysis, and subsequent research by Palfrey and Rosenthal (1983), showed that an equilibrium in pure strategies (in which every voter either surely votes or surely refrains) typically fails to exist. These authors focused instead on mixed-strategy equilibria, that is, equilibria in which every individual chooses randomly whether or not to participate. Such a game typically admits two types of equilibria. In one type, every voter chooses a probability of voting that is neither zero nor one. In the other type, a subset of voters randomize, while the remainder either head to the polls for sure or surely stay at home. Let us consider each of these possibilities in turn.

Imagine an election with two possible sets of policy outcomes, $\mathbf{p}^A$ and $\mathbf{p}^B$, in which every individual has the same voting cost κ. Also, for every eligible voter i, either $u_i(\mathbf{p}^A) - u_i(\mathbf{p}^B) = 1$ or $u_i(\mathbf{p}^A) - u_i(\mathbf{p}^B) = -1$; that is, individuals either prefer $\mathbf{p}^A$ to $\mathbf{p}^B$ by a monetary equivalent of 1, or they prefer $\mathbf{p}^B$ to $\mathbf{p}^A$ by this same amount. Let the number of voters who prefer policy vector $\mathbf{p}^A$ be N_A and the number who prefer policy vector $\mathbf{p}^B$ be N_B. If the election ends in a tie, then a coin toss determines the outcome.

In this election, all citizens favoring option $\mathbf{p}^A$ face similar incentives, as do all citizens favoring $\mathbf{p}^B$. It may seem plausible, therefore, to suppose that citizens within each group behave similarly. Since no pure-strategy equilibrium exists, the only candidate for a symmetric equilibrium would be one in which every citizen favoring policy $\mathbf{p}^A$ votes with some common probability ϕ_A and every citizen favoring policy $\mathbf{p}^B$ votes with a common probability ϕ_B.

What would the values of ϕ_A and ϕ_B have to be? Each citizen might reason as follows. Her vote will make a difference to the outcome in two situations: first, if the votes on either side not counting her own happen to be equal; and second, if one more voter from the opposition camp turns out for the election than the number from her own side, excluding herself. In each of these scenarios the individual's choice to exercise her vote would improve the prospects for her preferred outcome by one-half (from 50 percent to one, or from zero to 50 percent). The citizen will surely vote if the probabilities of these two scenarios arising are such that the expected gain exceeds κ. And she will surely refrain if the expected gain falls short of κ. In a symmetric equilibrium, the probability of voting can be neither zero nor one, so it must be that the expected gain from voting exactly equals κ. But the expected gain depends on how likely the two scenarios are, and therefore on the voting probabilities used by others. It remains to find values of ϕ_A and ϕ_B such that every individual regards the voting decision as a matter of indifference.

It is complicated to calculate the values of ϕ_A and ϕ_B that render this indifference, and the details are not important. The results do have an important implication, however. As the electorate grows large, the values of ϕ_A and ϕ_B that generate indifference typically approach zero (see Palfrey and Rosenthal, 1983). In other words, the chance that any single vote will make the difference in the election becomes negligibly small unless each citizen votes with only a tiny probability. Moreover, the expected participation rate (i.e., the fraction of eligible voters who exercise their vote) also approaches zero as the electorate grows large. The only exception to this rule arises when the two groups happen to be of exactly equal size. Then there exists a symmetric equilibrium in which everyone votes with probability close to one, as well as a second equilibrium in which everyone votes with probability close to zero. But this hardly resolves the paradox of voting, inasmuch as a high turnout rate requires opposing interests of exactly equal numbers, and even then it arises as only one of two possible equilibrium outcomes.

Expected turnout need not be small, however, in an *asymmetric* equilibrium of the same participation game. In particular, this is true when citizens on the minority side turn out randomly, while some on the majority side vote for sure and others surely refrain. In fact, in the electoral setting just described there are many such equilibria, and some have expected turnout rates as high as $2 \min\{N_A, N_B\}/(N_A + N_B)$ in an election with many voters.

To see how these equilibria work, consider the case in which $N_A > N_B$ and suppose that exactly N_B members of the majority side (who prefer policy vector $\mathbf{p}^A$) opt to vote for sure, while the remaining $N_A - N_B$ members of this side elect surely to stay at home.

Suppose also that members of the minority participate with some common probability ϕ. A citizen in the minority camp reasons that, absent her own participation, the probability that all $N_B - 1$ other supporters of policy vector $\mathbf{p}^B$ will turn up to vote is ϕ^{N_B-1}. In the event, her decision to participate would generate a coin toss instead of a sure defeat for her preferred policy vector, $\mathbf{p}^B$. The expected benefit from voting is one-half in this scenario. This is the only situation in which the individual's vote could matter, and so it follows that the expected benefit from voting for an individual in the minority group, if others pursue the hypothesized strategies, is $\phi^{N_B-1}/2$. This individual, and all others like her, will be indifferent between voting and not voting if $\phi^{N_B-1}/2 = \kappa$, or $\phi = (2\kappa)^{1/(N_B-1)}$.

We turn now to the incentives facing a citizen on the majority side. A typical member of the majority perceives a probability ϕ^{N_B} that all N_B minority-side voters will turn up at the polls. If this happens, and if one of the majority voters who is "supposed to vote" fails to do so, her side will suffer a sure defeat rather than achieving a tie. Also, with probability $N_B(1 - \phi)\phi^{N_B-1}$ exactly $N_B - 1$ voters on the minority side will turn out to vote. In this case, a less than full turnout by the presumed majority-side participants results in a tie instead of a win. So a decision to stay at home by a typical one of the N_B majority voters who are expected to vote causes a utility loss to this individual of one-half, with probability $\phi^{N_B} + N_B(1 - \phi)\phi^{N_B-1}$. Of course, the same decision saves the individual the voting cost κ. But $[\phi^{N_B} + N_B(1 - \phi)\phi^{N_B-1}]/2 \geq \phi^{N_B-1}/2 = \kappa$.[3] It follows that the majority-side citizens whom we have been designating as willing participants indeed prefer to exercise their votes.

What about those on the majority side who, we have hypothesized, opt not to vote? A typical such individual could swing the election by voting in situations where otherwise it would end in a tie. The probability of this occurrence in the hypothesized equilibrium is ϕ^{N_B} and the associated expected benefit is $\phi^{N_B}/2$. Since this falls short of the cost of voting, κ, these individuals indeed prefer to refrain.

The turnout rate in the equilibrium just described can be substantial. Indeed, as the number on the minority side grows large, the expected participation rate among voters on this side approaches 100 percent. Then the overall turnout is $2N_B$, which can be nearly the entire voting population, if the two sides are nearly equal in number.

---

3. The inequality follows from the fact that
$$\phi^{N_B} + N_B(1 - \phi)\phi^{N_B-1} \geq \phi^{N_B} + (1 - \phi)\phi^{N_B-1} = \phi^{N_B-1}.$$

Does the existence of this asymmetric equilibrium with potentially high participation rates resolve the voting paradox? Palfrey and Rosenthal (1985) argue that it does not. They point out that the equilibrium rests uncomfortably on the assumption that every citizen knows with certainty what others intend to do. In particular, each of the N_B members of the side favoring $\mathbf{p}^A$ who votes in the equilibrium must be confident that exactly $N_B - 1$ others on the same side will turn out at the polls, and that the remaining $N_A - N_B$ fellow supporters of $\mathbf{p}^A$ will refrain from doing so. Similarly, the $N_A - N_B$ supporters of $\mathbf{p}^A$ who do not vote in equilibrium must be sure that N_B others on their side will vote in their stead. And those who prefer $\mathbf{p}^B$ must be certain of the number of votes on the opposing side in order to justify their choice of the probability ϕ. All of this confidence seems difficult to justify in a setting in which voters act independently and have no opportunity to coordinate their actions.

An alternative approach admits uncertainty on the part of potential voters. Palfrey and Rosenthal introduce such uncertainty by assuming that an individual's cost of voting is known only to herself. Let citizen i face a personal voting cost κ_i that others regard as a draw from some probability distribution. This distribution is common to citizens who share a policy preference, but the draws for different individuals are seen as independent. If the distribution of voting costs for each group is continuous and has no mass points, then a symmetric pure-strategy equilibrium always exists. In this equilibrium, an individual who favors $\mathbf{p}^A$ exercises her vote if and only if her voting cost is less than some critical amount, κ_A, and an individual who favors $\mathbf{p}^B$ votes if and only if her cost is less than some κ_B. The values of κ_A and κ_B are such that these strategies are optimal for every individual, given that others pursue them as well.

The symmetric equilibrium studied by Palfrey and Rosenthal has one notable property. Suppose that the maximum possible value for κ_i exceeds one, and that the minimum possible value is less than or equal to zero. A maximum value of κ_i greater than one means that it is a dominant strategy for some citizens to refrain from voting.[4] Similarly, a minimum value of κ_i less than or equal to zero means that it is a dominant strategy for some citizens to exercise their vote. With some citizens who surely vote and others who surely do not,

---

4. Recall that voters perceive a utility difference between the policy options of $|u_i(p^A) - u_i(p^B)| = 1$. Thus, a voter who has $\kappa_i > 1$ will prefer to leave the decision to others.

the critical points κ_A and κ_B must approach zero as the electorate grows large.

The Palfrey-Rosenthal result carries strong implications about who votes in elections with many eligible voters. Turnout is limited to those who perceive a zero or negative cost of voting. This raises the obvious question: How can the cost of voting be zero or negative, when it clearly requires time and effort for citizens to turn up at the polls?

One possible answer has been suggested by Riker and Ordeshook (1968, 1973). They argue that the act of voting itself provides consumption benefits to some and that these benefits might outweigh the time and resource costs of voting. The consumption benefits may reflect some personal satisfaction that individuals gain from affirming their allegiance to the democratic system. Or it may be that some citizens simply enjoy taking part in the electoral process. In any case, if voting provides positive utility to a large enough fraction of the population, then high turnout rates are no longer a paradox.

While it may be correct, as Riker and Ordeshook assume, that some citizens vote because they enjoy doing so, this explanation of turnout offers little in the way of predictive power. In particular, their assumption cannot help us to understand why participation rates vary across demographic or interest groups, unless we know what determines the taste for voting. For our purposes, the voting-as-consumption approach leads to a dead end.

A negative voting cost may alternatively be interpreted as a distaste for not voting. Individuals may perceive a cost from not voting if participating in elections becomes a social norm. A social norm is an action that individuals undertake because it is expected of them, and because the community imposes sanctions on those who fail to conform (see, e.g., Elster, 1989). By enforcing social norms on its members, communities can encourage cooperative behavior that benefits the society as a whole even as it imposes immediate costs on those who follow the norm.

Kandori (1992) has studied social norms from the perspective of repeated-game theory. It is well known that, in repeated play of a game between the same two players, an outcome that is efficient for the pair can be supported as an equilibrium even when each player would benefit in the short run from behaving selfishly. To support such an equilibrium, each player must stand ready to punish miscreancy by withholding her own subsequent cooperation. The efficient outcome also requires that the pair be sufficiently patient, so that each prefers the long-run gains from cooperation to the short-run gains of defection. Kandori has extended this logic to games involving randomly matched players from the same "community." Suppose players are paired at random to play a repeated two-person game, and that the players in a given pair encounter one another only infrequently. Suppose further that the joint payoff in each play is highest when both players cooperate, but each player can benefit in a single play by acting noncooperatively. An equilibrium with universal cooperation can be sustained by the community if its members are sufficiently patient, if they can observe one another's behavior in plays of the game not involving themselves, and if they are able and willing to impose sanctions on those who deviate in interactions with other members of the community. Essentially, community enforcement replaces individual enforcement, and cooperative behavior becomes the norm.

What does the social-norm perspective say about voting behavior? Several researchers have suggested that many individuals feel externally pressured to exercise their votes. For example, Knack (1992, p. 137) cites an ABC-Harvard poll conducted in 1983 in which 41 percent of regular voters checked as a reason for voting the statement that "my friends and relatives almost always vote and I'd feel uncomfortable telling them I hadn't voted." In his own econometric investigation of voter participation, Knack found that individuals are significantly more likely to vote if they are married, reside in the jurisdiction in which they vote, and attend church regularly. On the other hand, those who are newcomers to an area and those who know fewer than three of their neighbors are less likely to vote. These results suggest the possibility that voters perceive a cost of not voting, inasmuch as fellow churchgoers, neighbors, and spouses are potential enforcers of a prevailing social norm. The penalties for failure to vote presumably come in the form of disapproval in face-to-face contact and perhaps a reduced willingness to engage in gainful social exchange.

Suppose that voting is a social norm. The next questions are, who enforces the norm, against whom, and why? One possible answer to the last question is that the norm exists because voter participation is a public good. Under this hypothesis, democratic societies benefit from having high rates of participation, no matter if eligible voters are well informed about the issues or not, and no matter how the potential voters would cast their ballots. Participation can be a public good if mass involvement is needed to legitimize the democratic process, and if a lack of legitimacy creates a risk of costly revolution. If turnout per se is a public good, then the polity as a whole has an incentive to make voting a social norm. Society will inculcate the idea that voting is a civic duty, and individuals will learn to sanction those who neglect their social responsibility. But notice that such an outcome requires the value of the public good to be reasonably high. To carry out sanctions against those who would have voted on the opposite side, individuals must prefer an election with high turnout and a disappointing outcome to one with lower turnout but results that better suit their preferences. It is possible, but perhaps doubtful, that individuals in modern democracies are willing to encourage participation indiscriminately, including from those who are likely to vote differently from themselves.

Another possibility is that enforcement of the norm comes at the level of the social or interest group. All those who share an interest in a policy outcome benefit from having their fellow group members vote their common interest. Thus, voting provides external benefits to those who hold similar preferences, even if it is valueless to society as a whole. Moreover, the members of some groups may be able to observe at least imperfectly whether their fellow members undertake to vote. Recall that observation of others' behavior plays an important part in community enforcement. Finally, since the members of some groups engage in frequent social interaction, they may have ample opportunity to sanction those who disregard the voting norm. The preconditions exist for voting to become a group norm in some (interest) groups, with each member of the group expected to participate so that common electoral goals can be achieved.

Now, finally, we come to the main question for this section. If group norms are the basis of voter participation, which types of groups will have high participation rates in equilibrium, and with what consequences for policy outcomes? This question can be addressed by introducing social norms à la Kandori into a model of group participation in voting, such as those that Morton (1991, 1993), Uhlaner (1989), and Shachar and Nalebuff (1999) have developed.

The group-participation models begin with the observation that while individuals have little incentive to bear a positive voting cost in elections with many eligible voters, groups may have ample incentive to do so. The calculus of voting is different for a group than for an individual, because the group may have sufficient numbers to improve the electoral prospects of a preferred candidate where the individual does not. Building on this observation, Morton (1993), for example, has assumed that the members of a group vote when it is jointly optimal for them to do so, and that the group's leaders somehow provide the necessary incentives for the members to act in the common interest. Her model predicts that participation will be higher in elections that are expected to be close and that participation by a group will be higher the greater is its stake in the electoral outcome.[5]

But in these models it is often simply assumed that externalities within a group are internalized, without addressing how the group goes about providing the necessary incentives to members. Moreover, the authors assume that all groups participate in the election to an extent that is optimal for the group, without allowing for any variation in the ability of different groups to achieve the fully cooperative outcome. Thus, the models have little to say about biases in policy determination that may result from differential turnout rates. Here is where the social-norm perspective can contribute. It suggests that we look at a group's ability to enforce group voting norms as an indication of who might fare well in electoral politics.

The enforcement of a group voting norm requires that members interact frequently. Interaction gives the members an opportunity to reward those who conform to the norm and punish those who do not. For example, the members of a church group that convenes weekly may have greater opportunity to express their disapproval to others who fail to vote than individuals who happen to share an interest in environmental policy but who meet rarely, if at all. Moreover, enforcement is more effective the more group members have at stake in their interpersonal exchanges. When the gains from cooperating with fellow group members are great, so too is the deterrent effect of potential isolation. Finally, group enforcement requires widespread observability of the desired behavior. Thus, groups that have ready opportunity to observe the voting behavior of their fellow members will be better able to enforce a voting norm than those that do not.

All of these observations point to "social connectedness" as an important predictor of voter turnout. Individuals who are part of

---

5. See Shachar and Nalebuff (1999) for regression results that support these predictions.

groups that meet frequently and interact intensively should be more likely to vote than those who are socially isolated or who belong to loosely linked groups.

Also, voting norms may be relatively easy to enforce among certain groups of workers. Individuals who work closely together in an industry or profession are likely to share a common interest in policy outcomes. They can often observe whether or not their colleagues exercise their votes, or at least do so more readily than those with other kinds of group links. And they interact frequently in an environment where social and work-related cooperation often is fruitful, so sanctions are likely to be available and punitive. Thus, the model would predict a strong ethos of electoral participation among tightly knit work groups. Interestingly, many labor unions are known to engage in vigorous get-out-the-vote drives. Moreover, researchers have found that union membership significantly increases an individual's likelihood of voting.[6]

We should point out that the ability of an interest group to enforce a voting norm does not mean that it will demand indiscriminate participation from all of its members. The calculus of group voting still requires a comparison of individual costs and group benefits. An efficient social contract among group members will excuse those who face a high voting cost from fulfilling this duty, with a threshold that may vary from election to election. If a group can tacitly agree on a different standard for each election, it will wish to make the threshold for nonparticipation higher in cases where the group has a lot at stake and when the election is expected to be close. In all elections those who are known to face an especially high personal voting cost will escape sanctioning if they fail to vote.

Finally, we turn to the policy consequences. A high voter turnout rate among members, whatever its cause, can benefit an interest group in two fairly obvious ways. First, it can improve the electoral prospects of a group's favorite alternative among a given set of candidates and policy proposals. Second, it can alter the positions taken by the candidates. Given a list of candidates and their positions, there may be uncertainty about the election outcome if turnout is random or if the voters' preferences are unknown. Then a group that can induce its members to turn out to vote will fare better on average

---

6. See Leighley and Nagler (1992) and Filer, Kenny, and Morton (1993). The estimates in the latter paper imply, for example, that voter turnout is likely to be from 15 to 22 percent higher among union members than among otherwise similar voters.

than one that cannot. But more important than this, perhaps, is the effect of participation on the electoral competition. As we saw in Chapter 2, politicians and political parties have an incentive to cater to the policy wishes of the electorate. But the electorate here means those who are expected to turn out to vote, not those who are merely eligible to do so. In a pure Downsian setting, for example, with candidates that can commit to a single-dimensional policy position and who gain utility only (or mostly) from the perks of office, the outcome will be the policy most preferred by the median citizen *among those who perceive a nonpositive voting cost*. Groups with high participation rates will be represented disproportionately in the distribution of voters and so will attain an outcome closer to their members' ideal. Similarly, in the model of parliamentary elections with proportional representation that we described in Section 2.3.2 in Chapter 2, where political parties have fixed ideological positions but pliable positions on nonideological issues, the parties will announce pliable platforms that maximize the average utility of voters that are expected to participate in the election. Groups with high participation rates will receive greater weight in this average than those whose members tend to refrain from voting.

3.2 Knowledge

Gathering information can be costly for voters, as much as or more so than the act of voting itself. Moreover, the calculus of informing oneself is similar to the calculus of voting: a citizen who is unlikely to be the pivotal voter is also unlikely to find it worthwhile to spend much time and effort studying the issues in an election or evaluating the candidates' positions. And whereas some groups might wish their fellow members would become fluent on the issues as a matter of social responsibility, it may be difficult for groups to enforce such behavior as a social norm, inasmuch as the act of educating oneself often is not readily observable to others. Individuals often cannot readily observe whether others have educated themselves or not. Accordingly, we would not expect all citizens to be fully informed about the issues in an election. Knowledge may be concentrated in those who have relatively easy access to information, or who enjoy the process of studying the issues.

As we noted in Chapter 1, the collection and dissemination of information are important activities for many organized interest groups. We will study these activities in Chapters 4 through 6, where we will pay special attention to the incentives that SIGs may have to issue false or misleading statements. The possibility of misrepresentation by interest groups raises important and interesting questions about credibility, which we defer for the time being. In this section we address a simpler question that arises anytime some groups of voters are more knowledgeable than others, for whatever reason. We ask, To what extent do differences in knowledge translate into biased policy outcomes? The knowledge asymmetries that we consider here may reflect differences in the cost of acquiring information or differences in education levels. Or they may be the result of the past activities of organized groups. The media may also be the source of some knowledge differences, to the extent that they target their products and coverage to certain types of voters.[7]

Voters need several types of information to cast their votes optimally. First, they must understand the technical aspects of the policy issues. For economic policies, voters must recognize the links between the policy variables and their own material well-being. Will rent control cause a scarcity of rental housing, and if so, how severe? Will it reduce the incentives for building maintenance? Will challenges to monopoly power reduce the incentives to innovate? Discourage efficient mergers? Similarly, on social issues, voters must know how changes in the policy instruments will affect the outcomes of concern to them. Will the decriminalization of drug possession increase or reduce drug usage and the prevalence of other types of criminal activity? Will school busing alleviate or exacerbate ethnic prejudices? How will gun control affect the frequency and severity of violent crime?

Second, voters must know the positions of the candidates on the issues, and how committed they are to carrying them out. They must also assess whether the candidates have the requisite skills to be effective policymakers. Two politicians with identical positions might nonetheless deliver different outcomes if they are not equally

---

7. See, for example, Strömberg (1998), who has combined a model of electoral politics with a model of endogenous news coverage by profit-maximizing news media. Strömberg shows that if the newspapers have a relatively fixed amount of space, they will target their coverage to appeal to voters with certain demographic and socioeconomic characteristics (such as high income or high receptiveness to advertising). Then these voters may become better informed about their policy interests than others who are less profitable customers for the newspaper.

adept at evaluating new contingencies, identifying talented advisers, forging legislative coalitions, and so on.

We begin our discussion by supposing that voters differ in their understanding of the technical aspects of a policy issue. In particular, some voters are better able than others to assess which levels of a policy instrument best serve their personal interests. To examine the implications of this for electoral politics, we adapt the model that we described in Section 2.3.2. In the model there are two political parties, A and B, that vie for seats in a legislature. Seats are awarded in proportion to shares of the aggregate vote. The legislature will be called on to resolve two policy issues. On one issue the parties have fixed positions. On the other, their positions are flexible. The parties take positions p^A and p^B on the latter issue in order to maximize their chances of capturing a majority. After the election, the majority party implements its announced positions on both issues.

Voters belong to one of two groups. The members of each group share a common interest in the outcome of the pliable policy issue but hold disparate views about the parties' fixed positions. We assume that the distribution of opinions about the fixed positions is the same in both groups. (We will examine the implications of varying degrees of partisanship in Section 3.3.) Let π_1 denote the ideal pliable policy for members of group 1 and let π_2 denote the ideal policy for members of group 2. The utility of voter i in group j is given by

$$u_{ij} = -(p^k - \pi_j)^2 + v_i^k,$$

where k is the identify of the party that wins the election (either A or B) and v_i^k is the voter's assessment of party k's fixed position. With this utility function, the well-being of any voter depends on how close the pliable policy outcome is to the group's common ideal policy, and on the voter's personal evaluation of the winning party's fixed position. Again, we let v_i represent the relative preference of a voter i for the fixed position of party B; that is, $v_i = v_i^B - v_i^A$. We assume that v_i is the realization of a random variable that is uniformly distributed in the range from $(-1 + 2b)/2f$ to $(1 + 2b)/2f$, where f is the density of the uniform distribution.

Now we introduce imperfect information about the pliable policy issue. We assume that some voters do not fully understand the link between the policy variable p and their own welfare. For example, a voter may know that she covets a high standard of living, but unless she has taken the time to examine the relevant research in labor economics, she may not know what level of the minimum wage would give her the highest expected income. Similarly, a voter may know that she wants to minimize her exposure to burglary and other personal crimes, but unless she has studied research in criminology, she may not know the relationship between federal sentencing guidelines and the risks faced by members of her socioeconomic group.

We let ζ_j be the fraction of voters in interest group j that are well-informed. These well-informed voters know the precise value of their group's ideal policy, π_j. The remaining members of group j do not know what policy level is best for them. Since they do not know π_j, they must form some beliefs about their ideal policy. We describe these beliefs by treating π_j as if it were the realization of a random variable, $\tilde{\pi}_j$. The probability distribution for $\tilde{\pi}_j$ gives, for each possible level of the policy variable p, the voter's subjective assessment of the likelihood that $\tilde{\pi}_j$ has that value. We assume that all uninformed members of group j hold the same beliefs about the group's ideal, and use $\bar{\pi}_j$ to denote the mean value of the random variable $\tilde{\pi}_j$.

Now consider the voting decision. It is a weakly dominant strategy for each voter to vote for the party that she perceives as offering the most desirable package of policies. For a fully informed voter, the calculus is the same as in Section 2.3.2. A voter i in group j votes for party A if and only if $-(p^A - \pi_j)^2 + v_i^A \geq -(p^B - \pi_j)^2 + v_i^B$; that is, if and only if

$$v_i \leq 2(\bar{p} - \pi_j)(p^B - p^A), \tag{3.2}$$

where $\bar{p} = (p^A + p^B)/2$ is the mean of the two policy positions. Uninformed voters, in contrast, must render their decision under conditions of uncertainty.[8] A voter i in group j compares the utility she expects to achieve if party A wins the election to the utility she expects to achieve if party B wins the election. That is, she compares $-E(p^A - \tilde{\pi}_j)^2 + v_i^A$ to $-E(p^B - \tilde{\pi}_j)^2 + v_i^B$, where the expectation is taken with respect to the perceived distribution of $\tilde{\pi}_j$. It follows that

---

8. In equilibrium, an uninformed voter can infer something about her group's ideal policy from the positions taken by the candidates. But since, as we shall see, the parties' equilibrium positions are the same, such an inference would not affect her voting decision. Our description of the voting strategies of uninformed voters applies "out of equilibrium," to announcements that the parties might contemplate in deciding what position to take. We assume that the uninformed voters would not update their beliefs about their ideal policy were they to see a pair of policy positions different from the equilibrium pair.

she votes for party A if and only if

$$v_i \leq 2(\bar{p} - \bar{\pi}_j)(p^B - p^A). \tag{3.3}$$

We can use the (uniform) distribution of v_i, together with conditions (3.2) and (3.3), to calculate the fraction of voters in group j that vote for party A. Let s_j represent this fraction. Then

$$s_j = \tfrac{1}{2} - b + 2f[\bar{p} - \zeta_j \pi_j - (1 - \zeta_j)\bar{\pi}_j](p^B - p^A). \tag{3.4}$$

Finally, we can calculate the fraction of the aggregate vote that goes to each party. Let ω_1 be the fraction of the electorate that belongs to group 1 and $\omega_2 = 1 - \omega_1$ the fraction that belongs to group 2. Then $s = \omega_1 s_1 + \omega_2 s_2$, which, after substituting equation (3.4), implies

$$s = \tfrac{1}{2} - b + 2f\left\{\bar{p} - \sum_{j=1}^{2} \omega_j[\zeta_j \pi_j + (1 - \zeta_j)\bar{\pi}_j]\right\}(p^B - p^A). \tag{3.5}$$

We turn to the political competition. As we discussed in Section 2.3.2, the parties choose their pliable positions at a time when they do not know which set of fixed positions will prove to be more popular. In other words, they are uncertain about the precise value of b and regard it as the realization of some random variable, $\tilde{b}$. Each party seeks to maximize the probability that it will win a majority of the votes. Thus, party A chooses p^A to maximize the probability that $s > \tfrac{1}{2}$, while party B chooses p^B to minimize this probability. It follows from the first-order conditions for these optimization problems that, for any perceived distribution of $\tilde{b}$, the parties announce the position on the pliable policy issue that best serves the perceived interests of the average voter. The equilibrium pliable policy is given by

$$p = \sum_{j=1}^{2} \omega_j[\zeta_j \pi_j + (1 - \zeta_j)\bar{\pi}_j], \tag{3.6}$$

no matter which party wins the election.

Equation (3.6) says that the equilibrium policy is a weighted average of π_1, $\bar{\pi}_1$, π_2, and $\bar{\pi}_2$, where the weights are the shares of informed members of group 1, uninformed members of group 1, informed members of group 2, and uninformed members of group 2, respectively, in the voting population. We can use this equation to investigate how differential access to information affects policy outcomes.

We associate the level of knowledge in a group with the fraction of its voters who can identify the group's ideal pliable policy.

There are several cases to consider. Suppose first that $\pi_1 > \bar{\pi}_1 \geq \bar{\pi}_2 > \pi_2$ or $\pi_2 > \bar{\pi}_2 \geq \bar{\pi}_1 > \pi_1$. In these cases, uninformed voters have "conservative expectations" in the sense that they put a lot of weight on the possibility that their ideal policy is a moderate one. In such circumstances, an increase in the share of informed voters in either group must drive the policy outcome closer to that group's ideal. Consider, for example, the effects of an increase in ζ_1. This will increase the weight on π_1 and decrease the weight on $\bar{\pi}_1$, in the formation of the equilibrium policy. Since the equilibrium policy is a weighted average of the four magnitudes, π_1, $\bar{\pi}_1$, π_2, and $\bar{\pi}_2$, putting more weight on π_1 will lead to an equilibrium outcome that is more to the group's liking when π_1 is the largest or the smallest of the four.

Now suppose instead that $\bar{\pi}_1 > \pi_1 > \pi_2$ or $\pi_2 > \pi_1 > \bar{\pi}_1$. Here, the uninformed members of group 1 believe that their ideal policy is likely to be rather extreme, whereas in truth it is more moderate. Under these circumstances, it is possible (but not inevitable) that an increase in the fraction of the group's members that are informed about the policy issue could prove detrimental to the group. The group would suffer, on the margin, from having a few more knowledgeable members if the weighted average of π_1, $\bar{\pi}_1$, π_2, and $\bar{\pi}_2$ were smaller than both π_1 and $\bar{\pi}_1$ in the case where $\bar{\pi}_1 > \pi_1$ or larger than both π_1 and $\bar{\pi}_1$ in the case where $\bar{\pi}_1 < \pi_1$. In either of these cases, the uninformed group members suspect their ideal policy of being extreme, and although they are incorrect in these beliefs, the parties must choose a more extreme pliable policy in order to woo their votes. Since the equilibrium policy is less extreme than what the informed members of group 1 would like, it helps the group on the margin to have more uninformed and, in this case, extremist voters.

A final case to consider arises when $\pi_1 = \bar{\pi}_1$ and $\pi_2 = \bar{\pi}_2$. Here, although the uninformed voters are unsure about their group's ideal policy, their beliefs are correct on average. This case could arise, for example, if uninformed voters carry out some limited research about the policy issue that allows them to make a noisy estimate of the true ideal. So long as the research is unbiased, the possible errors will have a mean of zero, and the estimates will be correct on average. In the event, equation (3.6) implies that $p = \omega_1 \pi_1 + \omega_2 \pi_2$, and an increase in ζ_1 has no effect on the equilibrium outcome. When uninformed voters hold beliefs that are correct on average, their voting behavior does not differ from that of their better informed colleagues.[9]

Let us suppose now that the citizens do understand the policy issues and know where their interests lie, but that some are uncertain about where the candidates stand on the issues. We assume that a fraction ζ_j of the voters in group j know p^A and p^B precisely, while the others observe only a noisy signal of the parties' pliable positions. This signal might come in the form of a newspaper article that gives only an indication of the parties' positions, or in a television show that is known to be not completely accurate. All voters do know the parties' fixed positions.

Under these conditions, the fully informed voters cast their ballots as we have described previously. Thus, inequality (3.2) gives the condition under which an informed voter i in group j votes for party A. As for the imperfectly informed voters, consider one such individual who is in group j. This voter i observes some signals p_{ij}^A and p_{ij}^B, where $p_{ij}^A = p^A + \varepsilon_{ij}^A$ and $p_{ij}^B = p^B + \varepsilon_{ij}^B$. Here, ε_{ij}^A is the error in her observation of party A's position and ε_{ij}^B is the error in her observation of party B's position. The voter does not know the sizes of the errors, of course, but considers ε_{ij}^A and ε_{ij}^B to be realizations of random variables $\tilde{\varepsilon}_{ij}^A$ and $\tilde{\varepsilon}_{ij}^B$ that have some perceived probability distributions. These random variables may have mean zero, but need not; that is, the voter's information source may or may not be unbiased. Also, the degree of uncertainty about the two parties' positions need not be the same.

It is tempting to think that the voter simply compares $-E(p^A + \tilde{\varepsilon}_{ij}^A - \pi_j)^2 + v_i^A$ with $-E(p^B + \tilde{\varepsilon}_{ij}^B - \pi_j)^2 + v_i^B$; that is, the expected utility under the alternative platforms, taking into account the possible errors in the observed signals. But if the voter made only this comparison, she would not be using all of the information available to her. In fact, the voter should realize that the forces of political competition will drive the parties' pliable positions together. In an equilibrium, if she observes different values for p_{ij}^A and p_{ij}^B, it must reflect the fact that she has observed the positions with error. A voter

9. This statement must be qualified, inasmuch as it relies on the particular form of the utility function that we are considering here. If the component of utility that reflects the pliable policy is something other than the square of the difference between the outcome and the ideal, then fully informed voters will not always vote the same way as others in their group who have an unbiased expectation but who are nonetheless imperfectly informed.

who uses Bayes' rule to update her beliefs will conclude, upon observing a $p_{ij}^A \neq p_{ij}^B$, that $p^A = p^B$, and that the difference in what she has heard or seen about the positions is a result of the noise in the signals.[10] But a voter who draws such a conclusion would ignore her own signals and simply vote for the party whose fixed position she prefers. In terms of our earlier notation, citizen i votes for party A if and only if $v_i \leq 0$.

Combining this observation with condition (3.2), and using what we know about the distribution of v_i, we can compute the fraction of voters in group j that vote for party A. We find

$$s_j = \tfrac{1}{2} - b + 2f\zeta_j(\bar{p} - \pi_j)(p^B - p^A).$$

Then, the overall vote share of party A can be found by weighting s_1 and s_2 by the fractions of the electorate in each interest group and summing the two, which gives

$$s = \tfrac{1}{2} - b + 2f\sum_{j=1}^{2}\omega_j\zeta_j(\bar{p} - \pi_j)(p^B - p^A).$$

Each party seeks to maximize the probability that it will win a majority. This leads to convergence in their positions as before, which is consistent with the conjectures of the imperfectly informed voters. The policy outcome that results is given by

$$p = \left(\frac{\omega_1\zeta_1}{\omega_1\zeta_1 + \omega_2\zeta_2}\right)\pi_1 + \left(\frac{\omega_2\zeta_2}{\omega_1\zeta_1 + \omega_2\zeta_2}\right)\pi_2.$$

Notice that the policy is a weighted average of the groups' ideal positions, with weights equal to a group's shares in the total number of fully informed voters. Thus, the policy outcome is the same as would occur if the less than fully informed members of each group did not vote at all.

We conclude that with imperfect information about policy positions, the policy outcome is biased in favor of the group that has relatively more fully informed members. Moreover, any increase in ζ_1 benefits the members of group 1, and any increase in ζ_2 benefits the members of group 2. The bias in the outcome results from the

---

10. This argument requires an additional assumption about the range of possible values of $\tilde{\varepsilon}_{ij}^A$ and $\tilde{\varepsilon}_{ij}^B$. Namely, there must be a positive probability that these errors are large enough to accommodate all conceivable observations of p_{ij}^A and p_{ij}^B. Without this condition, a voter who observed some very different values of p_{ij}^A and p_{ij}^B might be able to exclude the possibility that these observations were due to error. We assume that the needed condition is satisfied.

incentives facing the parties, which are to ignore completely the preferences of any voters who have less than perfect information about their positions. It cannot pay for the parties to cater to these voters, because if a party were to shift its position in the hope of attracting more of their votes, the imperfectly informed voters would ignore the overture. These voters would interpret their observed signals not as indications that the deviant party's platform is more attractive to them, but rather as noise in their reading of the party's positions.[11,12]

3.3 Partisanship

We have discussed how differences in turnout rates and in knowledge of the issues and candidates can bias policy outcomes. Now we will examine the impact of differences in partisanship. By a partisan, we mean a voter who ardently favors a certain political party. In our model, partisanship can be associated with a strong preference for one party's fixed positions over those of the other party. Groups may differ in terms of the fraction of partisans among their members, and in the strength of their partisan convictions. We will see that such differences can lead the parties to cater to some groups more than to others.

To examine the role of partisanship, we modify slightly the model of legislative elections that we used in the last section. Here, as before,

---

11. The equilibrium we have described is the unique equilibrium in which the parties use pure strategies. But there can also be mixed-strategy equilibria in which the parties randomize their choices of position, and the imperfectly informed voters do not infer that the parties must have identical pliable positions. When voters do not draw the inference that the positions must be identical, they pay some attention to their signals. Then the parties have incentive to heed these voters' preferences, at least to some extent.

12. Lohmann (1998) provides another example of a situation in which the electoral process favors groups that have access to superior information. In her model, a voter's well-being is determined by a combination of the policy that is pursued and the ability of the incumbent policymakers. Voters have limited information about the outcome in a period, and do not know the extent to which an observed outcome is due to the policy choice versus the policymakers' ability versus mere error in observation. Lohmann shows that the incumbents will shade their policies in the direction that favors the group that can more accurately monitor the outcome. The parties have an incentive to do so, because voters will attribute the observation of a favorable outcome at least partly to the incumbents' superior ability. The group that can monitor the outcome more accurately will give less weight to observation error and more weight to ability, and thus will be more favorably disposed to an incumbent that delivers a seemingly favorable outcome.

there are two political parties, two issues, and proportional representation. The parties have fixed positions on one issue, pliable positions on the other. But now we assume, as in Section 2.3.2 of Chapter 2, that voters are well informed about the policy impacts and the parties' positions. Meanwhile, we relax the assumption that the distribution of opinions about the fixed positions is the same in all groups. Following Dixit and Londregan (1996), we assume that the parties know the distributions of tastes in the various groups, and that each party has as its goal to maximize its share of the popular vote.[13]

The electorate comprises an arbitrary number of interest groups. A group is any subset of voters with a common interest in the pliable policy and with a known distribution of partisan views.[14] A member i of group j evaluates the fixed and pliable positions of party k according to the utility function $-(p^k - \pi_j)^2 + v_{ij}^k$ for $k = A, B$, where p^k is, as before, the pliable position of party k and v_{ij}^k is the contribution to the individual's welfare from the party's fixed position. We let $v_{ij} = v_{ij}^B - v_{ij}^A$ denote the voter's relative preference for the fixed position of party B, but now assume that the distribution of the v_{ij}'s varies across groups. More specifically, $F_j(v_j)$ is the fraction of voters in group j that prefer the fixed positions of party B by less than v_j. We use $f_j(v_j) = F_j'(v_j)$ to denote the density function.

With complete information, a citizen i in group j votes for party A if and only if $v_{ij} \leq 2(\bar{p} - \pi_j)(p^B - p^A)$. Thus, party A captures a fraction $F_j[2(\bar{p} - \pi_j)(p^B - p^A)]$ of the votes from group j (when the platforms are p^A and p^B), and achieves a share

$$s = \sum_j \omega_j F_j[2(\bar{p} - \pi_j)(p^B - p^A)]$$

of the aggregate vote.

---

13. It would be possible to introduce uncertainty about popularity, and to assume as we did before that the parties maximize their chance of winning a majority. But the analysis becomes complicated in that setting. We choose instead to mimic the assumptions made by Dixit and Londregan (1996), which allows us to better explicate their insights.

14. Actually, the group members need not share identical views on the pliable issue. What is important for the argument is that the parties be able to distinguish groups by their distributions of tastes on the fixed issue. When the various members of a group have different preferences with regard to the pliable issue, it is the average preference in each group that matters for the equilibrium policy.

Now consider the optimal strategies of the two parties. Party A chooses p^A to maximize s, which implies

$$\sum_j \omega_j f_j [2(\bar{p} - \pi_j)(p^B - p^A)](\pi_j - p^A) = 0. \tag{3.7}$$

Meanwhile, party B chooses p^B to maximize $1 - s$, which implies

$$\sum_j \omega_j f_j [2(\bar{p} - \pi_j)(p^B - p^A)](\pi_j - p^B) = 0. \tag{3.8}$$

Together, (3.7) and (3.8) imply $p^A = p^B = p$, and the common policy position is given by

$$p = \sum_j \left[\frac{\omega_j f_j(0)}{\sum_l \omega_l f_l(0)} \right] \pi_j. \tag{3.9}$$

Equation (3.9) reveals the policy outcome to be a weighted average of the groups' ideal policies. To interpret this equation, note that it is the same as the first-order condition for maximizing a weighted sum of the utilities of all voters, where each voter from group j receives the weight $f_j(0)$.[15] When the groups have the same distribution of partisan views, the equilibrium pliable policy is the one that maximizes the welfare of the average voter. Otherwise, the parties give more weight to voters in some groups than to those in others.

A party does not win many votes by catering to a group in which most individuals are highly partisan to its rival. Many of these voters will support the rival no matter what pliable position the party adopts. But neither does a party gain much by catering to a group in which most individuals strongly favor its own fixed positions. The party is bound to win most of these votes whether it tailors its pliable policy to the group or not. Rather, it is the groups with relatively many nonpartisans that attract the attention of both parties. We see this intuition borne out in equation (3.9), where the weight $f_j(0)$ reflects the proportion of voters in group j who are just indifferent

---

15. That is, the equilibrium outcome is the pliable policy p that maximizes $-\sum_j f_j(0)\omega_j(p - \pi_j)^2$. Coughlin, Mueller, and Murrell (1990) prove the existence of an equilibrium in a similar model, where the utility functions are not necessarily quadratic but the v_j's are all uniformly distributed. They show that in this case too, the equilibrium policies maximize a weighted average of the groups' utility levels. In their model, past policies affect current utilities. Therefore, the contenders' pliable positions do not converge unless their prior positions were also the same.

between the parties' fixed positions. Dixit and Londregan refer to these as "swing voters." The groups that have relatively many swing voters will respond most readily to the parties' strategic overtures, and thus will tend to be favored in the political process.

Who are the groups with relatively many political moderates? Dixit and Londregan (1996) propose several candidates. First, senior citizens may be such a group, because they comprise a cross section of the entire population and so are likely to be well represented in the political center. Californians are another such group. The close vote in California in many recent elections is suggestive of there being a large number of voters in the state who are nearly indifferent between the Republicans and Democrats on ideological grounds. Finally, Dixit and Londregan show that garment workers might be a swing group as well, because these workers are relatively concentrated in states with closely contested national elections. Each of these groups has fared well in redistributive politics in recent years. In contrast, redistributive politics have not been kind to urban minorities, perhaps because many of the members of this group are loyal supporters of the Democratic party, and thus are not likely to switch their votes in response to promises of favors.

Our model can also illuminate another possible bias in the policy process. Suppose that groups have the same distributions of partisan preferences but they differ in the intensity of their members' concern for the pliable issue. In some groups the members care about this issue much more than they do about the differences in the parties' fixed positions, while in other groups it is the differences in the fixed positions that matter. To capture this situation, we introduce a positive parameter α_j so that the utility function of a member i of group j is $-\alpha_j(p^k - \pi_j)^2 + v_i^k$. The larger is α_j, the greater is the relative weight that members of group j attach to the pliable issue. We assume now that the distribution $F_j(v_j)$ is the same for all j.

By familiar arguments, we find complete convergence in the pliable platforms of the two parties. The equilibrium policy is given by

$$p = \sum_j \left(\frac{\omega_j \alpha_j}{\sum_l \omega_l \alpha_l} \right) \pi_j.$$

Again, the outcome is a weighted average of the ideal points of all voters. The weights this time are greatest for the groups that care most about the pliable issue. This result is not surprising: when the parties engage in tactical politics, they cater to the voters who are most sensitive to changes in the policies that are up for grabs. Our finding reinforces the earlier one, inasmuch as it implies that political competition favors groups with relatively weak partisan preferences.

In this chapter, we have investigated several reasons why the policies that emerge after legislative elections might not be the ones that maximize the welfare of the average voter. Some voter groups may fare especially well in electoral politics because their members enforce a strict social norm of voter participation, because their members are knowledgeable about the issues and candidates, or because their number includes many nonpartisans. We have derived these conclusions without assuming that interest groups are formally organized or that they undertake political activity on behalf of their members.

The remainder of the book deals with the political activities of organized special interests. The material divides naturally into two parts. In the first part (Chapters 4 through 6) we examine the use of information as a tool for political influence. In the second part (Chapters 7 through 10) we examine the use of money and other resources for this purpose.

II   Information

4   Lobbying

In this chapter we begin to examine the activities of organized special interest groups. By an organized group we mean a body that undertakes political actions on behalf of a number of citizens. We shall refer to those who are served by a SIG as its "members," whether or not they are formal, dues-paying members of some organization.

At least since Olson (1965), social scientists have pondered the *logic of collective action*. On the one hand, individuals who have similar policy preferences have much to gain from pooling their resources to pursue common political aims. On the other hand, there is always the temptation to "free ride." This is so because those who share a group's objectives can benefit from its political efforts even if they refuse to help pay the bills. For example, the owners of a textile firm will benefit from a lobby-induced tariff on imported clothing whether or not they bear a portion of the lobbying costs. The fact that free riders cannot be excluded from political benefits raises the question of when collective political action is possible.

Clearly, some interest groups are more adept at overcoming the free-rider problem than others. U.S. dairy farmers are well organized and have long been active in encouraging restrictive quotas on competing imports. But consumers who enjoy imported cheese are poorly organized and have had little influence on the policymaking process. Some groups, like environmentalists, achieve an intermediate degree of success: an active lobby pursues the policy interests of a core of loyal supporters, while others with similar views take a free ride. A complete account of special interest politics surely would begin with a discussion of which groups manage to organize effectively. Unfortunately, theorizing about coalition formation has proved to be very difficult, so we opt for a less ambitious approach. We will take the existence of a set of organized groups as a given, and go from there.

As we noted in Chapter 1, organized SIGs undertake a variety of activities to further their political ends. Many of these activities entail the collection and dissemination of information. It is natural for interest groups to deal in information, for at least two reasons. First, the members of an interest group accumulate knowledge about certain policy issues in the course of performing their everyday activities. Take, for example, the area of health care policy. The design of good policy requires a detailed understanding of the fixed and variable costs of hospital care, the cost sharing between doctors and hospitals, the incentives doctors face in designing treatments, the number and characteristics of uninsured patients, and so on. SIGs that represent the interests of hospitals, insurance companies, and doctors will have much information of this sort from their members' regular involvement in the industry.

Second, interest groups may have an incentive to conduct research on issues of concern to their members. Information has the properties of a public good, inasmuch as the fixed costs of conducting research often far exceed the marginal cost of disseminating results to an additional user. Thus, the same research can inform many individuals for little more than it would cost for one such individual to assemble the information and use it herself. An organized group can take advantage of the economies of scale by researching issues centrally and educating its rank-and-file members. The groups also may use the information they gather to try to win over policymakers and the general public.

This chapter focuses on lobbying activities. We use this term narrowly to refer to meetings between representatives of interest groups and policymakers in which the former try to persuade the latter that their preferred positions would also serve the policymakers' interests and perhaps those of the general public. In other words, lobbying involves the transfer of information by verbal argument. The lobbyists for the AFL-CIO might argue that expanded U.S. trade with China would harm the residents of a legislator's home district and would impede the prospects for democracy in China. Or the lobbyists for the National Abortion Rights Action League might assert that late-term abortions are needed to save the lives of many women. Of course, interest groups on the opposite sides of these issues might well confront the policymakers with conflicting claims.

We assume that lobbying is potentially informative; that is, the interest groups have access to information that in principle could allow the politicians to make better policy decisions. But we also assume that the policymakers cannot easily verify the lobbyists' claims. If policymakers had exactly the same objectives as the lobbyists, then the costliness of verification would pose no problem. But the interests of a SIG and a policymaker rarely are perfectly aligned. For example, SIGs often care about the effects of policy on their own members' incomes, whereas elected representatives are accountable to broader constituencies. Whenever a policymaker has even a slightly different objective than the SIG, she must guard herself against exaggeration and misrepresentation by the lobbyist. The lobbyist, for his part, may choose to stretch the truth somewhat, but he does not wish to make outlandish statements that will simply be ignored. These considerations lead us to ask two important questions. First, what statements and arguments by the lobbyist will be persuasive? Second, what if anything can an interest group do to enhance its credibility?

In this chapter we address the first of these questions, leaving the second for Chapter 5. We analyze persuasiveness by considering the incentives facing a lobbyist. If talk is cheap and allegations are difficult to verify, then a lobbyist's claims will be persuasive only if he has an incentive to report information truthfully when he anticipates that his statements will be accepted and acted upon. We examine in detail the requirements for credibility and investigate how the transfer of information by lobbying affects the policies that result.

4.1 One Lobby

In this section we study a setting in which a single lobby has information relevant to a policymaker's decision. The information may concern the potential effects of different levels of a policy variable or the preferences of a group of voters. We consider a sequence of examples that allow us to develop this intuition. These examples differ in terms of the complexity of the information held by the SIG, but all make use of special forms for the policymaker's ex ante beliefs and the welfare functions of the policymaker and the interest group. A more general formulation of the model is discussed in the appendix to this chapter.

4.1.1 The Setting

The welfare of a policymaker depends on the level of a policy variable p and some facts about the world. The underpinnings for the welfare function are not important here; it could reflect, for example, the politician's desire to be reelected or her personal preferences over policy outcomes. The pertinent facts are described by a variable θ. Different facts imply a different ranking of the policy options by the policymaker. For example, θ might indicate the tightness of the labor market, which would affect a policymaker's evaluation of alternative interest rates. Or it might indicate the effectiveness of a scrubber device in reducing pollution, which would affect her view of the desirability of alternative environmental standards. Alternatively, the variable θ may describe something about the subjective preferences of the SIG members themselves. The group's preferences will enter the policymaker's objective function if, for example, the members are residents in the politician's district who will vote in the next election. The policymaker has an objective function $G(p, \theta) = -(p - \theta)^2$. With this objective function, she aims to set the policy level as close as possible to the value of θ.

The welfare of the members of an interest group also depends on the level of the policy instrument and the state of the world. The various group members need not hold the same preferences, although presumably they have somewhat similar aims. We do not consider how the preferences of the SIG members are aggregated. Rather, we simply endow the group's lobbyist with an objective function $U(p, \theta) = -(p - \theta - \delta)^2$ for some positive value of δ. Thus, the group has an ideal policy of $\theta + \delta$ in state of the world θ. Note that the group's ideal policy in any state exceeds the ideal for the policymaker. We refer to the difference, δ, as the "bias" in the group's preferences.

We assume that the interest group has better information about the policy environment than the policymaker. In particular, the lobbyist knows the state of the world, whereas the policymaker does not. If the policymaker were to learn nothing from the lobbyist, she would base her policy decision on some prior beliefs. To describe these beliefs, it is convenient to treat the state of the world as if it were the realization of a random variable, $\tilde{\theta}$. Then the domain of the probability distribution function for $\tilde{\theta}$ gives the values that the policymaker deems to be possible, while the density function gives the relative likelihood she ascribes to each possibility. The lobbyist knows the actual realization of $\tilde{\theta}$, which we continue to denote by θ.[1]

4.1.2 Two States of the World

The simplest case to consider has only two possible values for the variable θ. We denote these values by θ_H and θ_L, where H indicates the need for a "high" level of policy and L the need for a "low" level of policy. The policymaker initially regards the two values as equally likely. The policymaker sets $p = \theta$ when the lobbying reveals the true state of the world, and sets $p = E\tilde{\theta}$ when she remains uncertain about the state. In the latter case, the expectation is formed using her subjective, updated beliefs about the likely values of $\tilde{\theta}$.[2]

The lobbyist for the group knows the true state of the world and thus has no doubt about which policy the group members prefer. Notice that the policymaker and the SIG both prefer a higher level of the policy when $\theta = \theta_H$ than when $\theta = \theta_L$. This common preference creates the potential for informative lobbying. But the objectives of the SIG and the policymaker are never the same. The parameter δ measures the extent of their disagreement.

To investigate the conditions under which lobbying can be informative, we hypothesize that the policymaker takes the lobbyist's claims at face value. We then investigate the incentives facing the lobbyist. Consider figure 4.1, which shows the welfare of the SIG in different states. The curve labeled LL depicts the group's welfare as a function of the policy p when the state is θ_L, while the curve labeled HH depicts the group's welfare as a function of p when the state is θ_H. If the true state is θ_H and the lobbyist reports it as such, then a trusting policymaker enacts a policy of $p = \theta_H$. If the lobbyist instead reports that the state is θ_L, the policymaker sets $p = \theta_L$. Since a truthful report always results in a policy that is closer to the group's ideal than a false report, the lobbyist has no incentive to misrepresent the facts when the state is θ_H.

---

1. We can also use this formulation to describe the situation in which the SIG and the policymaker are both uncertain about the policy environment, but the policymaker is more so. To do so, we take θ to be a noisy signal of the state of the world rather than the state itself. Then the group's superior information is reflected in its precise observation of the signal, compared to the policymaker's noisy observation of it.
2. Let ζ be the policymaker's ex post subjective probability that $\theta = \theta_H$. The policymaker seeks to maximize her expected welfare, $EG = -\zeta(p - \theta_H)^2 - (1 - \zeta)(p - \theta_L)^2$. The first-order condition for this maximization implies $p = \zeta\theta_H + (1 - \zeta)\theta_L$; that is, the policymaker sets the policy equal to the expected value of θ.

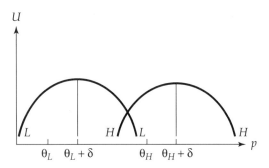

Figure 4.1
Example with Two States

If the state instead is θ_L, a truthful (and trusted) report by the lobbyist induces a policy of $p = \theta_L$. This is smaller than the group's ideal policy of $\theta_L + \delta$ in state θ_L. If the lobbyist instead claims that the state is θ_H, the policy outcome will be $p = \theta_H$. The SIG members may prefer this larger policy, but it also might be too large even for their tastes. The lobbyist will report truthfully in state θ_L if and only if the SIG members prefer $p = \theta_L$ to $p = \theta_H$; that is, if and only if $(\theta_L + \delta) - \theta_L \leq \theta_H - (\theta_L + \delta)$. Notice that this inequality is satisfied for the case depicted in figure 4.1

We can rewrite the inequality as a limitation on the size of the divergence in preferences; that is,

$$\delta \leq \frac{\theta_H - \theta_L}{2}. \tag{4.1}$$

When (4.1) is satisfied, there exists an equilibrium with informative lobbying.[3] In such an equilibrium, the lobbyist educates the policy-

---

3. Game theorists have developed the notion of a Bayesian equilibrium to describe outcomes of games with imperfect information, and the notion of a perfect Bayesian equilibrium (PBE) to select among such equilibria. In an equilibrium, beliefs are updated according to Bayes' rule, all strategies must be best responses to the strategies of rivals, and they have to satisfy subgame perfection. The latter means that players correctly anticipate subsequent incentives facing their rivals at every stage of the game. Moreover, a PBE requires that players update their beliefs using Bayes' rule even out of equilibrium, whenever that is possible. See Fudenberg and Tirole (1991, Chapter 6). In the equilibrium with truthful revelation that exists when condition (4.1) is satisfied, the policymaker updates her beliefs based on the report of the SIG. The updating causes the policymaker to attach a probability of one to the event that the state of nature is θ_H when the SIG reports it as such, and similarly for θ_L. This is consistent with Bayes' rule in the indicated equilibrium.

maker about the state of the world. The equilibrium that results is "fully revealing," because the policymaker learns the true state for all possible values of the random variable $\tilde{\theta}$.

If, in contrast, (4.1) is not satisfied, the lobbyist's report lacks credibility. The policymaker would know in such circumstances that the lobbyist had an incentive to announce the state as θ_H no matter what the true state happened to be. For this reason, his report is uninformative, and the policymaker is well justified in ignoring its content. In the event, the policymaker sets the policy $p = (\theta_L + \theta_H)/2$ that matches her prior expectation about the mean value of $\tilde{\theta}$. Evidently, the transmission of information via lobbying requires a sufficient degree of alignment between the interests of the policymaker and the interest group.

Now let us return to the case in which inequality (4.1) is satisfied. We have identified an equilibrium with informative lobbying. But that is not the only possible outcome. Indeed, there is another equilibrium in which the lobbying effort fails. To see that this is so, suppose the policymaker distrusted the lobbyist. Then she would invoke the policy $p = (\theta_L + \theta_H)/2$ no matter what report she heard. Anticipating this behavior, the lobbyist would have no incentive to report truthfully. For any parameter values, there is an equilibrium outcome in which the policymaker remains uninformed. Game theorists refer to this as a "babbling equilibrium," for it is as if the lobbyist babbles when providing his report.

Although the babbling equilibrium always exists, Farrell (1993) has argued that it is not always a reasonable prediction of what may happen in a cheap-talk game. He has proposed a stricter concept of equilibrium that sometimes rules out the uninformative outcome. Farrell's refinement is based on the idea of a supporting argument. That is, he would allow the lobbyist to accompany his report of θ with a short supporting speech. Like the report, the arguments in the speech would not be verifiable by the policymaker. But if they are nonetheless compelling, the policymaker might take them into account. Farrell suggests that a plausible equilibrium should be immune to speeches of the sort he describes.

To pursue this idea for a moment, suppose the lobbyist senses the policymaker's distrust. Let the true state be θ_L, so that the lobbyist anticipates a policy of $p = (\theta_L + \theta_H)/2$ unless he can make his case. Now imagine that he utters the following speech:

"Please believe me that the state is θ_L. You should believe me, because I would have no incentive to make this speech and have you believe me were the true state to be θ_H."

As figure 4.1 shows, θ_L is farther from $\theta_H + \delta$ than is $(\theta_L + \theta_H)/2$. So the lobbyist's claim that he would not wish to make the speech in state θ_H indeed is compelling. Now we must ask whether the lobbyist would be inclined to make the speech in state θ_L. If he did so and succeeded in convincing the policymaker, the policy outcome would be $p = \theta_L$. The SIG prefers this outcome to $p = (\theta_L + \theta_H)/2$ if and only if $\delta < (\theta_H - \theta_L)/4$. Thus, Farrell would argue that the babbling equilibrium is implausible for small values of δ, that is, for $\delta < (\theta_H - \theta_L)/4$.[4]

Farrell offers an interesting refinement of the equilibrium concept for cheap-talk games. But his proposal and others like it remain controversial.[5] Indeed, there are no equilibrium refinements that command universal support. Since it is not our aim to make strong predictions about policy outcomes, we do not take a position on which refinements are most plausible, nor do we devote much space to them in what follows.

4.1.3 Three States of the World

Now suppose there are three possible states of the policy environment. The possible values of $\tilde{\theta}$ are θ_L, θ_M, and θ_H, with $\theta_L < \theta_M < \theta_H$. Again, let the policymaker perceive the three states as equally likely. We ask: When can the lobbyist advise the policymaker of the true state?

Again, we begin by hypothesizing that the lobbyist's report will be taken at face value. Then, a report of θ_L induces a policy of θ_L, a report of θ_M induces a policy of θ_M, and a report of θ_H induces a policy of θ_H. Consider first the incentives for false reporting in state θ_L. The lobbyist has two possible false reports. He could exaggerate

---

4. Note that if $\delta < (\theta_H - \theta_L)/4$, it is always in the group's interest, and always credible, for the lobbyist to make the analogous speech about state θ_H. If $\theta = \theta_H$, the SIG prefers the outcome $p = \theta_H$ to $p = (\theta_L + \theta_H)/2$, whereas if $\theta = \theta_L$, the SIG prefers $p = (\theta_L + \theta_H)/2$ to $p = \theta_H$.

5. Farrell's proposed refinement has been criticized for its implicit assumption that the listener draws no inference from the lobbyist's failure to provide a supporting argument. See Farrell and Rabin (1996) for further discussion of equilibrium refinements in cheap-talk games.

his claim modestly and report the state as θ_M. Or he could exaggerate it dramatically and report the state as θ_H. The lobbyist prefers to report truthfully in state θ_L than to claim the state is θ_M if and only if the group's ideal point, $\theta_L + \delta$, is no closer to θ_M than it is to θ_L; that is, if and only if

$$\delta \leq \frac{\theta_M - \theta_L}{2}. \tag{4.2}$$

As for a false report of θ_H in state θ_L, this will be unattractive to the lobbyist anytime it is unattractive to report the state as θ_M. When (4.2) is satisfied, the SIG regards a policy level of θ_M as too high. Then, since $\theta_H > \theta_M$, it must consider a policy level of θ_H to be excessive as well.

Now consider the incentives for false reporting in state θ_M. The lobbyist has no incentive to report the state as θ_L when actually it is θ_M. After all, the SIG prefers a policy larger than θ_M, and the false report would induce the policymaker to choose one that is smaller than $p = \theta_M$, which is what she would choose upon hearing a truthful report. But the lobbyist might be tempted to exaggerate, because by alleging the state to be θ_H when actually it is θ_M, he induces a higher level of the policy variable than otherwise. The lobbyist is willing to eschew this temptation and report truthfully in state θ_M if and only if

$$\delta \leq \frac{\theta_H - \theta_M}{2}. \tag{4.3}$$

This inequality constitutes a second requirement for the existence of an equilibrium with full revelation.

Finally, consider the incentives for false reporting in state θ_H. In this state, the lobbyist has no incentive to report either that the state is θ_L or that it is θ_M. Each of these false reports would result in a policy level that is lower than $p = \theta_H$. And the group regards even this policy level to be less than what it desires. Thus, there is no additional restriction needed for truthful reporting in state θ_H.

The inequalities (4.2) and (4.3) constitute necessary and sufficient conditions for an equilibrium with truthful reporting. Notice that, by introducing a third possible value of $\tilde{\theta}$, we have added another restriction on the extent of disagreement between the policymaker and the interest group that is consistent with fully informative lobbying.

Now suppose that one of the conditions (4.2) or (4.3) is violated. Is the lobbyist bound to babble? Or might he be able to communicate some more-limited information to the policymaker? In fact, limited communication may still be possible, as Crawford and Sobel (1982) have emphasized in their seminal article on strategic information transmission.

Take, for example, the case in which inequality (4.3) is violated. The temptation to exaggerate in state θ_M precludes the lobbyist from revealing whether the state is "medium" or "high." But the lobbyist may nonetheless be able to distinguish this pair of states from one that requires a low level of the policy instrument. Suppose the lobbyist were to issue one of two possible reports, with the aim of making this lesser distinction. Specifically, let a report of "low" indicate that the state is θ_L and a report of "not low" indicate that the state is either θ_M or θ_H. Then a policymaker who takes the lobbyist's claims at face value sets $p = \theta_L$ when she hears that the state is "low" and $p = (\theta_M + \theta_H)/2$ when she hears otherwise. The latter policy level matches her expectation of the state of the world in situations in which she can rule out the possibility that $\theta = \theta_L$ but remains otherwise uninformed. We now must ask again whether the lobbyist has an incentive to report falsely in any of the three states.

Clearly, the lobbyist has no incentive to do so when the true state is θ_H. A false claim of "low" would induce a policy of $p = \theta_L$. This outcome is less desirable to the group than the policy $p = (\theta_M + \theta_H)/2$ that results from a truthful report of "not low." When the state is θ_M, the lobbyist also confronts a choice between the outcomes $p = (\theta_M + \theta_H)/2$ and $p = \theta_L$. A truthful report of "not low" yields the former level of policy, whereas a false report yields the latter. The lobbyist will not report falsely if and only if the former policy is at least as close to the group's ideal of $\theta_M + \delta$ than the latter, that is, if and only if $(\theta_M + \delta) - \theta_L \geq (\theta_M + \theta_H)/2 - (\theta_M + \delta)$ or

$$\delta \geq \frac{\theta_H - \theta_M}{4} - \frac{\theta_M - \theta_L}{2}. \tag{4.4}$$

Notice that condition (4.4) must be satisfied when (4.3) is violated. So, truthful reporting in state θ_M is not an issue in situations in which the lobbyist cannot credibly distinguish between θ_M and θ_H.

Finally, we must check that the lobbyist has no incentive to report falsely when the state is θ_L. In this state, a truthful report results in a policy of $p = \theta_L$, whereas a false report leads to $p = (\theta_M + \theta_H)/2$. The group prefers the former outcome if and only if $(\theta_L + \delta) - \theta_L \le (\theta_M + \theta_H)/2 - (\theta_L + \delta)$, or

$$\delta \le \frac{\theta_H - \theta_M}{4} + \frac{\theta_M - \theta_L}{2}. \tag{4.5}$$

When conditions (4.4) and (4.5) are satisfied, there exists an equilibrium with partial transmission of the interest group's knowledge. It is easy to check that (4.4) and (4.5) can be satisfied when one of (4.2) and (4.3) is violated. Suppose, for example, that $\theta_L = 0$, $\theta_M = 4$, and $\theta_H = 6$. Then (4.3) requires $\delta \le 1$, whereas (4.5) requires only that $\delta \le 5/2$. For $1 < \delta \le 5/2$, the lobbyist can credibly distinguish between a low state and others, but cannot advise the policymaker whether the state is "medium" or "high."

Suppose now that conditions (4.2) and (4.3) are satisfied, and that (4.4) and (4.5) are satisfied as well.[6] In such circumstances, there exists an equilibrium in which the lobbyist reports the precise state of the world and another equilibrium in which he (sometimes) issues a coarser report. Moreover, a third equilibrium exists in which the lobbyist babbles. Each of these reporting strategies can be justified by consistent beliefs of the policymaker. But note that the policymaker fares best in the fully revealing equilibrium.[7] So too does the SIG, at least in an ex ante sense.[8] The lobbyist and the policymaker might coordinate on this equilibrium, if each expects the other to use the language that affords both the highest ex ante welfare.

4.1.4   Continuous Information

As the number of possible states grows, full revelation becomes ever more difficult to achieve. For a lobbyist to be able to distinguish among all possible states, δ must be smaller than one-half of the dis-

---

6. When $\theta_L = 0$, $\theta_M = 4$ and $\theta_H = 6$, for example, (4.2), (4.3), (4.4), and (4.5) are satisfied for all $\delta \le 1$.

7. Expected welfare for the policymaker is $-\frac{2}{9}[(\theta_H - \theta_M)^2 + (\theta_M - \theta_L)(\theta_H - \theta_L)]$ in the babbling equilibrium, $-\frac{1}{6}(\theta_H - \theta_M)^2$ in the equilibrium with partial revelation, and 0 in the equilibrium with full revelation. Thus, the policymaker's expected welfare increases with the level of detail in the lobbyist's report.

8. By ex ante welfare, we mean the expected welfare of the group as viewed from a time before it learns the state of the world. Ex ante welfare is calculated using the prior distribution for $\tilde{\theta}$. We find that $EU = -\delta^2 - \frac{2}{9}[(\theta_H - \theta_M)^2 + (\theta_M - \theta_L)(\theta_H - \theta_L)]$ in the babbling equilibrium, $EU = -\delta^2 - \frac{1}{6}(\theta_H - \theta_M)^2$ in the equilibrium with partial revelation, and $EU = -\delta^2$ in the equilibrium with full revelation. So the group's ex ante ordering of the equilibria is the same as that of the policymaker.

tance between any two of them. But as the number of states tends to infinity—as it must, for example, when θ represents a continuous variable—this requirement becomes impossible to fulfill. An interest group that has information about a continuous variable can never communicate to the policymaker the fine details of its knowledge.

The reason for this should be clear by now. Consider two possible values of a policy-relevant variable that are close to one another. For example, the cost of building a school might be either $100 per square foot or $101 per square foot. A lobbyist for the teachers' union realizes that the policymaker will opt for a larger school if she learns that costs are lower. If the union members value space in the school more highly than the policymaker, the lobbyist will always be tempted to report the $100 figure when the actual figure is $101. A slight understatement of costs would push the policymaker toward a slightly larger school, but would never result in one being built that exceeds the teachers' preferred size. The policymaker cannot trust a claim that "costs are $100," even if the SIG has precise information of this sort.

Although the lobbyist cannot credibly distinguish between cost figures that are close to one another, it may be possible for him to advise the policymaker about ranges of costs. Suppose the lobbyist is expected to report "low" whenever costs fall between $70 and $90 per square foot and to report "high" when they fall between $90 and $110 per square foot. If the policymaker trusts such reports, she will build a school commensurate with the average cost in the indicated range. But then the lobbyist may have reason to report the range truthfully, because a misrepresentation when costs are high could lead to a bill that even the union members would regard as excessive.

What statements by the lobbyist would be credible in this situation? To answer this question, we assume that the policymaker's prior beliefs are that $\tilde{\theta}$ is uniformly distributed on the interval between θ_{min} and θ_{max}. The lobbyist knows θ, the realized value of $\tilde{\theta}$, but he does not report a precise figure, because such a report would not be credible. Instead, he indicates a range that contains the true value of θ. If the lobbyist reports that "θ is in range 1," the policymaker interprets this to mean that $\theta_{min} \leq \theta \leq \theta_1$ for some value of θ_1. If he reports that "θ is in range 2," the interpretation is that $\theta_1 \leq \theta \leq \theta_2$. Let there be n ranges in total, so that the statement "θ is in range n" means that $\theta_{n-1} \leq \theta \leq \theta_n$. We denote the ranges by

$R_1, R_2, \ldots, R_n$. Our task is to find values of $\theta_1, \theta_2, \ldots, \theta_n$ such that, if the policymaker takes the lobbyist's assertions at face value, the lobbyist has no incentive to lie.

Consider first the statement "θ is in R_1." If the policymaker treats this claim as truthful, she updates her beliefs using Bayes' rule. Then her expected value of $\tilde{\theta}$ is $(\theta_{\min} + \theta_1)/2$, and she sets the policy at this level. We must now check that the SIG prefers the outcome $p = (\theta_{\min} + \theta_1)/2$ for all values of θ that are actually in R_1 to the policy levels that would result from false claims of "θ is in R_2," "θ is in R_3," and so on. If it does not, then the policymaker should not trust the lobbyist's report.

Among values of θ in R_1, the lobbyist's greatest temptation to lie occurs when θ actually is close to θ_1. These highest values of θ are the ones for which the group's preferred policy is the largest. If the lobbyist does not wish to exaggerate his claim when θ is very close to θ_1, he will not wish to do so for smaller values of θ. Moreover, if the lobbyist has no incentive to make the false statement "θ is in R_2" when $\theta \leq \theta_1$, it is because that claim would generate a policy that exceeds the group's preferred policy given the true value of θ. Then, further exaggeration (such as "θ is in R_3") would generate even greater overshooting of the group's desired outcome. It follows that the only false statement we need investigate is the claim "θ is in R_2" when actually θ is at the upper end of R_1.

We now ask, for what values of θ_1, θ_2, and δ does the SIG prefer to tell the truth in this situation? A false claim of "θ is in R_2" causes the policymaker to update her beliefs so that $E\tilde{\theta} = (\theta_1 + \theta_2)/2$. Thus, the false claim yields a policy level of $p = (\theta_1 + \theta_2)/2$. If the lobbyist is not tempted to make this false claim when θ is a bit less than θ_1, it means that this policy level exceeds the group's ideal of almost $\theta_1 + \delta$ by at least as much as the policy that results from truthful reporting falls short of this ideal. In symbols, credibility requires $(\theta_1 + \theta_2)/2 - (\theta_1 + \delta) \geq (\theta_1 + \delta) - (\theta_{\min} + \theta_1)/2$, or

$$\theta_2 \geq 2\theta_1 + 4\delta - \theta_{\min}. \tag{4.6}$$

Now suppose that θ actually is in R_2. There are two things to check here. First, the lobbyist must not wish to understate the truth (by claiming that θ is in R_1) when θ is at the lower end of the range. Second, he must not wish to overstate the truth (by claiming that θ is in R_3 or beyond) when θ is at the upper end of the range. For values of θ in R_2, truthful reporting generates a policy of $p = (\theta_1 + \theta_2)/2$. A false report that θ is in R_1 would induce a policy of $p = (\theta_{\min} + \theta_1)/2$. The SIG prefers the former outcome to the latter when θ is near θ_1 if and only if $(\theta_1 + \delta) - (\theta_{\min} + \theta_1)/2 \geq (\theta_1 + \theta_2)/2 - (\theta_1 + \delta)$, or

$$\theta_2 \leq 2\theta_1 + 4\delta - \theta_{\min}.$$

Notice that this inequality is the opposite of (4.6). Therefore, both can be satisfied if and only if

$$\theta_2 = 2\theta_1 + 4\delta - \theta_{\min}. \tag{4.7}$$

At the upper end of R_2, the temptation is to exaggerate by claiming that "θ is in R_3." By arguments analogous to those above, truthful reporting when the actual value of θ is near θ_2 requires

$$\theta_3 \geq 2\theta_2 + 4\delta - \theta_1.$$

But truthful reporting for values of θ at the lower end of R_3 requires a similar inequality running in the opposite direction. So, we need $\theta_3 = 2\theta_2 + 4\delta - \theta_1$. More generally, a series of requirements for credibility are that

$$\theta_j = 2\theta_{j-1} + 4\delta - \theta_{j-2} \tag{4.8}$$

for all values of j from 2 through n, where $\theta_0 = \theta_{\min}$ is the initial condition.

Finally, consider values of θ in R_n. Here there is no possibility for the lobbyist to claim an even higher range for θ, because the policymaker knows the maximum value in the distribution of $\tilde{\theta}$. But then the topmost value of θ in R_n must coincide with the greatest possible value of $\tilde{\theta}$, or

$$\theta_n = \theta_{\max}. \tag{4.9}$$

If values of $\theta_1, \ldots, \theta_n$ can be found that satisfy (4.7), (4.8), and (4.9) and that have $\theta_{\min} < \theta_1 < \theta_2 < \cdots < \theta_n$, then these values describe the credible messages in a lobbying equilibrium. Notice that, if $\theta_1 > \theta_{\min}$ and (4.7) is satisfied, this implies $\theta_2 > \theta_1$. This inequality and (4.8) ensures $\theta_3 > \theta_2$. Then $\theta_4 > \theta_3$, and so on. Therefore, the procedure for finding an equilibrium is to solve the n linear equations in (4.8) and (4.9), and then verify that $\theta_1 > \theta_{\min}$.

It will not be possible to have an arbitrarily large number of ranges in a lobbying equilibrium, because information transmission is limited by the degree of similarity in the interests of the policymaker and the SIG. There must be a largest possible number of ranges that depends on δ and the other parameters. To see how this works, consider an example with $\theta_{\min} = 0$ and $\theta_{\max} = 24$. Then, if $\delta > 6$, the only equilibrium has $n = 1$. In this equilibrium, the lobbyist reports that "θ is between $\theta_{\min}$ and $\theta_{\max}$" and the policymaker sets $p = 12$. Of course, the policymaker learns nothing from such a report, so the unique outcome is none other than the babbling equilibrium. To see that informative lobbying is not possible with $\delta > 6$, note that equations (4.8) and (4.9) require, for $n = 2$, that $\theta_1 = 12 - 2\delta$ and $\theta_2 = 24$. But then $\delta > 6$ implies $\theta_1 < 0$, which is impossible because θ_1 must be at least as large as $\theta_{\min}$. With a large divergence in interests between the policymaker and the lobbyist, the lobbyist is unable to share any of his knowledge.

Now suppose instead that $\delta = 4$. Then the lobbyist can credibly claim that "θ is in the range from 0 to 4" or "θ is in the range from 4 to 24." In this case, when θ actually is a bit less than 4, a truthful report induces a policy of $p = 2$, which falls short of the group's ideal by a bit less than 6. A false report induces $p = 14$, which exceeds the group's ideal by a bit more than 6. So, the lobbyist has no incentive to claim that "θ is in R_2" when actually it is in R_1. And when the actual value of θ is a bit more than 4, the lobbyist similarly has no incentive to claim that "θ is in R_1." In this case, a lobbying equilibrium exists with two alternative reports. We shall refer to this as a 2-partition equilibrium.

It is possible to derive an explicit solution for θ_j from (4.8) and (4.9).[9] It will be useful to have this solution for some of our later discussions. We note that (4.8) and (4.9) are satisfied when

$$\theta_j = \left(\frac{j}{n}\right)\theta_{\max} + \left(\frac{n-j}{n}\right)\theta_{\min} - 2j(n-j)\delta \qquad (4.10)$$

for all values of j between 1 and n. An equilibrium further requires that $\theta_1 > \theta_{\min}$. By applying the formula in (4.10) with $j = 1$, we see that $\theta_1 > \theta_{\min}$ if and only if

$$2n(n-1)\delta < \theta_{\max} - \theta_{\min}. \qquad (4.11)$$

Inequality (4.11) is a necessary and sufficient condition for the existence of a lobbying equilibrium with n different reports. By

9. Equation (4.8) constitutes a second-order, linear difference equation for θ_j, which must be solved subject to the initial condition, $\theta_0 = \theta_{\min}$, and the terminal condition, $\theta_n = \theta_{\max}$.

inspecting this inequality, we can draw the following conclusions. First, an equilibrium with $n = 1$ always exists; this is the babbling equilibrium. Second, if an equilibrium with n reports exists, then an equilibrium with k reports also exists, for all $k < n$. This follows from the fact that the left-hand side of the inequality increases with n, so that if the inequality is satisfied for some integer n, it will also be satisfied for all smaller integers. Finally, the smaller is δ, the larger is the maximum number of feasible partitions. This confirms our intuition that the prospects for information transmission improve when the preferences of the SIG and the policymaker become more similar.

4.1.5 Ex Ante Welfare

We have seen by now that more than one equilibrium may exist in the lobbying game. For example, there always exists a babbling equilibrium, and if $\delta < (\theta_{max} - \theta_{min})/4$, there also exists an informative equilibrium in which the lobbyist issues one of two possible reports. Furthermore, if $\delta < (\theta_{max} - \theta_{min})/12$, then a 3-partition equilibrium also exists. Repeated application of equation (4.10) with $n = 4, 5, \ldots$ gives the conditions for the existence of equilibria with larger numbers of alternative reports.

When several different partition equilibria exist for a given set of parameter values, it is impossible to say definitively which one will emerge. All of the equilibria are self-sustaining, in the sense that if the policymaker expects the lobbyist to issue one of k reports, then the lobbyist can do no better than to behave as expected. And there is little to pin down the policymaker's beliefs. Thus, we are left with an inevitable ambiguity in the model's prediction.

In some circumstances, however, the policymaker and the lobbyist might be able to coordinate on a particular equilibrium. This is most likely to be true if the two sides agree on their rankings of the alternative equilibria. We consider the rankings from an ex ante perspective; that is, before the play of the game. For the policymaker, an ex ante perspective means that she evaluates her expected welfare using her prior beliefs about the distribution of $\tilde{\theta}$. As for the interest group, we have assumed of course that it knows or learns the true value of θ. But we still may be able to evaluate the group's ex ante welfare if we can imagine a time before the group gains that knowledge. At such a time, the SIG, like the policymaker, may regard all values of θ between θ_{min} and θ_{max} as equally likely.

To see if the policymaker and the SIG concur in their ex ante rankings, we first calculate the expected welfare of the policymaker. Recall that the policymaker has the objective function $G = -(p - \theta)^2$. She expects to learn which of the n ranges contains the actual value of θ, and to set the policy $p = (\theta_{j-1} + \theta_j)/2$ when she learns that θ is in R_j. Taking all possible realizations of $\tilde{\theta}$ into account, her expected welfare in an n-partition equilibrium is[10]

$$EG^n = -\frac{1}{12(\theta_{\max} - \theta_{\min})} \sum_{j=1}^{n} (\theta_j - \theta_{j-1})^3. \tag{4.12}$$

Now we calculate the expected welfare of the interest group. Again, the expectation is taken with respect to the group's prior beliefs about the likelihood of the different possible values of θ. We assume that the group has uniform prior beliefs. Its ex ante expected welfare in an n-partition equilibrium is calculated using $U = -(p - \theta - \delta)^2$ and the policies it anticipates being implemented after each possible realization of $\tilde{\theta}$, and is given by

$$EU^n = -\frac{1}{12(\theta_{\max} - \theta_{\min})} \sum_{j=1}^{n} (\theta_j - \theta_{j-1})^3 - \delta^2. \tag{4.13}$$

Comparing (4.12) and (4.13), we see that the policymaker and the SIG do agree on their ranking of the possible equilibria. In fact, the ex ante welfare of the policymaker and the interest group always differ by the constant amount δ^2.

We can use (4.12) and (4.13) to identify the ex ante favorite equilibrium of both sides. Using (4.10), we calculate

$$-\frac{\sum_{j=1}^{n} (\theta_j - \theta_{j-1})^3}{\theta_{\max} - \theta_{\min}} = -\frac{(\theta_{\max} - \theta_{\min})^2}{n^2} - 4\delta^2(n^2 - 1). \tag{4.14}$$

Since the right-hand side of (4.14) is an increasing function of n for all values of n that satisfy (4.11), it follows that the ex ante welfare of the

---

10. We calculate expected utility from

$$EG^n = -\frac{1}{\theta_{\max} - \theta_{\min}} \sum_{j=1}^{n} \int_{\theta_{j-1}}^{\theta_j} \left(\frac{\theta_j + \theta_{j-1}}{2} - \theta \right)^2 d\theta.$$

Here $1/(\theta_{\max} - \theta_{\min})$ is the probability density of $\tilde{\theta}$ and $-[(\theta_j + \theta_{j-1})/2 - \theta]^2$ is the policymaker's utility for a given realization of $\tilde{\theta}$ in the range R_j. The formula sums the utilities for all values of $\tilde{\theta}$ in each range, sums over all ranges, and adjusts for the likelihood of each possible value of $\tilde{\theta}$.

policymaker and the interest group both increase with n.[11] Thus, both sides would agree, ex ante, that the equilibrium using the greatest number of different reports is the best among all equilibrium outcomes.[12]

4.2 Two Lobbies

So far we have considered a setting in which a single interest group lobbies the policymaker. But often policymakers are lobbied by more than one party. Several groups may have information about the policy environment, and each may try to persuade the policymaker to take decisions that it considers best. In such circumstances, the policymaker must weigh the credibility of the various groups and decide what advice to heed and what to dismiss.

But the problem of information transmission with multiple lobbies is more subtle than that. The lobbying game between an interest group and a policymaker is altered by the presence of other lobbies. A policymaker may be able to play off one information source against another by asking an informed group to confirm or contradict the reports she has already heard. The lobbyists must consider more than just their own direct relationship with the policymaker. Each must realize that the reports of others will affect how their own messages are interpreted, and that their own reports may alter the incentives that other groups have when it comes time for them to advise the policymaker.[13]

In this section we study a lobbying game with two informed interest groups. Our discussion draws heavily on Krishna and Morgan

---

11. Consider the difference between the right-hand side of (4.14) evaluated at $n = m$ and evaluated at $n = m - 1$. It equals

$$(2m - 1)\left[\frac{(\theta_{\max} - \theta_{\min})^2}{m^2(m-1)^2} - 4\delta^2\right].$$

With (4.11) being satisfied for $n = m$, this expression must be positive.

12. It may seem obvious, at first glance, that more reports are better, because information sharing improves the quality of policy decisions. But the result is not trivial, because when adding more reports, the lobbyist does not simply subdivide some of the ranges he would have used in an equilibrium with fewer reports. Rather, the ranges in the two different equilibria typically overlap.

13. Interest groups may be able to *prove* that they are telling the truth, or the policymaker may be able to detect utterly untruthful messages, as in Milgrom and Roberts (1986). Moreover, the policymaker may be able to use one interest group to confirm or disprove messages from another group, as in Lipman and Seppi (1995). We abstract from these interesting variants of the problem.

(2001). We follow them in distinguishing two different situations. In one, which they call the case of "like bias," the preferences of the two groups are biased in the same direction relative to those of the policymaker. That is, for each state of the world, either both groups prefer a policy p that is larger than what the policymaker would choose if she knew the true state, or both groups prefer a policy that is smaller than the policymaker's ideal choice. The groups may differ in the extent of their bias, with one group perhaps being more extreme than the other. The issue here is whether the two lobbyists jointly can communicate more information to the policymaker than either could convey on his own.

The second case is one of "opposite bias." In this setting, the groups' ideal points for a given state of the world lie on opposite sides of the policymaker's ideal. One group prefers a higher policy level than the politician, while the other prefers a smaller level. This pits the lobby groups against one another, to the potential advantage of the policymaker. Again we investigate what the policymaker can learn and ask whether the lobbyists can guard themselves against contradictory reports by their political adversaries.

4.2.1 Like Bias

We begin with the case of like bias. As before, the policymaker must take a decision p with consequences that depend on the state of the world, θ. The policymaker's objective is to maximize $G(p, \theta) = -(p - \theta)^2$. She has two potential sources of information about θ. These sources are two lobbyists, each of whom is fully informed about the policy environment. The lobbyist for SIG 1 seeks to maximize $U_1(p, \theta) = -(p - \theta - \delta_1)^2$, while that for SIG 2 seeks to maximize $U_2(p, \theta) = -(p - \theta - \delta_2)^2$. The case of like bias arises when the value of p that maximizes $G(p, \theta)$ is smaller (or larger) than the value that maximizes $U_1(p, \theta)$ and the one that maximizes $U_2(p, \theta)$, for every value of θ. When, as here, the welfare functions are quadratic, this case arises when δ_1 and δ_2 have the same sign. For concreteness, we suppose $0 < \delta_1 \leq \delta_2$, so that SIG 1 is (if anything) the more moderate interest group while SIG 2 is more extreme.

The outcome of the lobbying game may depend on the order in which the lobbyists meet with the policymaker and on what each knows about the advice given by the other. We can imagine at least three different scenarios. First, the meetings between the lobbyists and the policymaker might be a *secret*, so that each informant is ignorant of the fact that the policymaker has an alternative information source. Second, the meetings between lobbyist and policymaker might be *private*, in which case a lobbyist will know that another has offered advice (or will offer advice) but not the content of the discussion. Finally, a lobbyist's recommendation to the policymaker may become *public*, in which case subsequent advisers can condition their reports on the information that the policymaker already has. We will concentrate our discussion on public messages, but first say a few words about the other two scenarios.[14]

Secret Messages

When the lobbyists meet secretly with the policymaker, there can be no strategic interaction between them.[15] Neither lobbyist realizes that another meeting might take place, and so neither anticipates that the policymaker has another informant. We cannot really speak of an equilibrium in this situation, because a lobbyist's perception of how the policymaker will respond to his message will not be consistent with how the policymaker actually responds. Each lobbyist will behave as if he were the sole provider of information, and so act according to the prescriptions of one of the equilibria we studied before. The policymaker, however, will take an action based on the combined advice of the two lobbyists.

We bring this case up only to point out how the policymaker might try to combine the information contained in two distinct reports. Suppose the first lobbyist sends either a message m_1, which the policymaker interprets to mean $\theta \leq \theta_1$, or a message m_2, which the policymaker interprets to mean $\theta \geq \theta_1$. The second lobbyist, not knowing of the existence of the first, sends either $\hat{m}_1$, which means $\theta \leq \hat{\theta}_1$, or $\hat{m}_2$, which means $\theta \geq \hat{\theta}_1$. Finally, suppose for concreteness that $\theta_1 < \hat{\theta}_1$. Then, if the policymaker hears the reports m_1 and $\hat{m}_1$, she infers $\theta_{\min} \leq \theta \leq \theta_1$; these are the only values of $\tilde{\theta}$ that are consistent with her prior understanding of the distribution of the

14. It is also possible to imagine situations in which, after receiving messages from a lobbyist, the policymaker issues statements that reveal some of the information contained in these messages. We will not examine such possibilities here.

15. This statement is true when the lobbyists do not even conceive of the possibility that the policymaker has another source of information. Alternatively, the lobbyists may suspect that other secret meetings might take place, in which case they will form expectations of the likelihood of such meetings and adjust their reports accordingly. The situation then is similar to that of private messages, which we discuss below.

random variable and the pair of reports she has received. Similarly, if the policymaker hears m_2 and $\hat{m}_2$, she infers $\hat{\theta}_1 \leq \theta \leq \theta_{\max}$. Finally, if she hears m_2 and $\hat{m}_1$, she infers $\theta_1 \leq \theta \leq \hat{\theta}_1$.[16] Notice that the pair of messages convey more information about the true state of the world than does either message alone. The policymaker can combine the information contained in two messages to refine her beliefs about the policy environment

But the very fact that the meaning of a message changes when combined with another implies that the lobbyists' incentives change once each becomes aware of the other's existence. Consider, for example, a setting in which the policymaker initially believes that θ lies between 0 and 24, and that all values are equally likely. Suppose that $\delta_1 = 1$ and $\delta_2 = 2$. If only the lobbyist for SIG 1 lobbies the policymaker, there is a 2-partition equilibrium with $\theta_1 = 10$. In this case, when the state is $\theta = 10$, the lobby is indifferent between the policy $p = 5$ that would result from a report of m_1 and the policy $p = 17$ that would result from one of m_2. Each of these policies differs by 6 from the group's preferred policy of 11. Similarly, there is a unique 2-partition equilibrium when the representative of SIG 2 alone lobbies the policymaker. In this equilibrium, the lobbyist reports $\hat{m}_1$ if $\theta \leq 8$ and $\hat{m}_2$ if $\theta \geq 8$.

This pair of partitions does not, however, constitute an equilibrium when each lobby is aware that the other will also be providing information to the policymaker. If the lobbyist for SIG 1 suspects that a counterpart will report $\hat{m}_1$ when $\theta \leq 8$ and $\hat{m}_2$ when $\theta \geq 8$, then his own report of m_1 when θ slightly exceeds 10 would lead the policymaker to believe that θ lies between 8 and 10. In the event, the policymaker would set the policy $p = 9$. SIG 1 prefers this outcome to the policy $p = 17$ that would result from a truthful report of m_2. The messages m_1 and m_2 no longer are credible.

Private Messages
If the lobbyists realize that the policymaker has an alternative information source but have no way of observing the other report, then many different outcomes are possible in the lobbying game. Among

---

16. The policymaker might also hear m_1 and $\hat{m}_2$. However, this pair of messages cannot arise if both lobbyists report truthfully. Since the pair of messages occurs with zero probability "along an equilibrium path" (where the lobbyists have an incentive to report truthfully), Bayes' rule places no restriction on the policymaker's updated beliefs.

these equilibria is one in which the policymaker gains full information. To see that this is so, suppose the policymaker believes that each group will report the state of the world precisely and truthfully. She interprets a report of m from the lobbyist for SIG 1 to signify that $\theta = m$. Similarly, she interprets a report $\hat{m}$ from the lobbyist for SIG 2 to mean that $\theta = \hat{m}$. Then among her optimal strategies is one in which she sets $p = \min\{m, \hat{m}\}$. This is not the only strategy that maximizes the policymaker's expected welfare, but as long as each side reports truthfully (as it must in an equilibrium), the strategy provides the policymaker with her ideal policy in each state of the world.[17]

Now consider the incentives facing the lobbyists when they anticipate that the policymaker will follow the indicated strategy. If SIG 1 believes that its counterpart will report truthfully, this group may as well report truthfully too. For example, if the true state is $\theta = 5$, and SIG 1 expects $\hat{m} = 5$, then it expects $p = 5$ for any report it might make of a state greater than or equal to $\theta = 5$. If SIG 1 were instead to report some $m < 5$, the policymaker would take its false report at face value and the policy would be even further from the group's ideal. A truthful report by SIG 1 is a best response in this situation. The same is true for SIG 2. By using each lobbyist's report to discipline the other's, the policymaker gains full information and achieves her desired outcome in every state.

However, the equilibrium with full revelation seems fragile in these circumstances. The lobbyist for SIG 1 might believe that there is a small probability that his counterpart will announce a state larger than 5 when the true state is $\theta = 5$. This belief might reflect the possibility that the other lobbyist will make an error, or the lobbyist for SIG 1 might simply be unsure of his counterpart's intentions. If the lobbyist for SIG 2 does happen to report something larger than 5, then the lobbyist for SIG 1 would wish he had done so as well. Moreover, if the lobbyist for SIG 2 does not report a state larger than 5, there is no harm to SIG 1 if its lobbyist exaggerates his own report.

---

17. As we noted in footnote 16, Bayes' rule does not restrict what the policymaker may believe after hearing messages that would not be sent in an equilibrium play of the game. The optimal strategy we have described arises when the policymaker believes, upon hearing two conflicting reports, that the group reporting the smaller value of θ has reported honestly. With these beliefs, it is optimal for her to set $p - \min\{m, \hat{m}\}$.

Given the anticipated behavior of the policymaker, it is a weakly dominant strategy for each lobbyist to report his own group's ideal point in every state. If both lobbies recognize this, neither will report the true state.

Moreover, if the SIGs anticipate an equilibrium with full revelation of the state of the world, they may try to air their reports publicly. Whereas the policymaker achieves her first-best outcome in an equilibrium with private messages and full revelation, the interest groups with like biases may not be so happy with the situation. Each group would like the other to exaggerate the state slightly, and then it would gladly follow suit. The lobbyist for group 1 might attempt to publicize a report of, say, $m = 5.1$ when the true state is $\theta = 5$, hoping that the other lobbyist would back up his false claim.

It might be interesting to consider a game in which each lobbyist has a *choice* of whether or not to make his report public. In such a game, the policymaker would be able to draw inferences about the state of the world not only from the content of the messages, but also from the manner in which they were communicated. Moreover, the policymaker herself might have an incentive to make public what advice she has been given in some situations. But such a game is rather complicated. Instead, we turn our attention to situations in which the lobbyists are free to offer their advice publicly and have no opportunity to do otherwise.

Public Messages
When the lobbies report their information sequentially and the second lobbyist can learn what the first has said, full revelation cannot occur in any equilibrium. To see this, suppose to the contrary that there is an equilibrium in which the policymaker learns the precise state of the world from the combined reports of the two lobbyists. Then the policymaker's best response would be to set $p = \theta$ when she learns that the state is θ. But the interest groups both prefer policies greater than θ in state θ. Therefore, the first-reporting lobbyist could misrepresent the state in such a way that, if his counterpart follows suit, the policymaker will believe the state to be some $\theta' > \theta$. It would then be in the interest of the second lobbyist to corroborate the first lobbyist's (false) report.

Krishna and Morgan (2001) prove that, as in the lobbying game with a single lobby, every equilibrium with two lobbies can be rep-

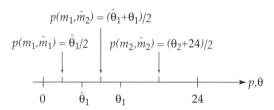

Figure 4.2
Partitions and Policies with Two Reports

resented as a partition equilibrium.[18] In a partition equilibrium, as
before, the policymaker learns that θ lies in one of a finite number of
nonoverlapping ranges. With two lobbies, the policymaker's information comes from the combined evidence in the two reports. For
example, a three-partition equilibrium arises when each lobbyist
divides the set of possible values of θ into two (nonidentical) subsets.

To show how partition equilibria can be constructed in a lobbying
game with two SIGs, we analyze further the numerical example
described above. In the example, the policymaker initially believes
that θ lies between 0 and 24. She sees each such value as equally
likely. Both interest groups have biases toward higher levels of policy
than the policymaker; specifically, $\delta_1 = 1$ and $\delta_2 = 2$.

Suppose that the lobbyist representing SIG 1 reports first, and that
his strategy is to issue one of two messages. If he sends message m_1,
the policymaker understands it to mean that $\theta \leq \theta_1$ (for some value
of θ_1 yet to be determined). If he sends the message m_2, the policymaker infers $\theta \geq \theta_1$. We hypothesize that θ_1 is reasonably large, so
that the second lobbyist will wish to distinguish further between
states that are "very low" (those that lie between θ_{min} and some $\hat{\theta}_1$)
and those that are only "reasonably low" (lie between $\hat{\theta}_1$ and θ_1). The
second lobbyist can make this distinction by choosing among two
messages. The policymaker interprets the message $\hat{m}_1$ to mean $\theta \leq \hat{\theta}_1$
and the message $\hat{m}_2$ to mean $\theta \geq \hat{\theta}_1$. The resulting partition is
depicted in figure 4.2.

First we consider the optimal response by the policymaker to the
reports she may hear. If she hears m_1 and $\hat{m}_1$, she infers that θ lies

---

18. Actually, they show that all *monotonic* equilibria are partition equilibria. A monotonic equilibrium is one in which the policy outcome in a higher state is always at least
as large as the outcome in a lower state. This property is guaranteed for the lobbying
game with one informed party, but it is not guaranteed when there is more than one
informed party. Krishna and Morgan restrict their attention to monotonic equilibria, as
we will do here.

between 0 and $\hat{\theta}_1$. By Bayes' rule, all values in this range remain equally likely. Therefore, she sets p equal to the expected value of $\tilde{\theta}$ in this range, that is, $p(m_1, \hat{m}_1) = \hat{\theta}_1/2$. This policy is shown in figure 4.2. By similar reasoning, the pair of messages m_1 and $\hat{m}_2$ induces $p(m_1, \hat{m}_2) = (\hat{\theta}_1 + \theta_1)/2$, and the pair of messages m_2 and $\hat{m}_2$ induces $p(m_2, \hat{m}_2) = (\theta_1 + 24)/2$. These policies, too, are shown in the figure.

Next we consider the incentives facing the lobbyist for SIG 2. By the time he must select a message, he will have heard his counterpart report either m_1 or m_2. If the first lobbyist has reported m_2, this signifies to the policymaker that $\theta \geq \theta_1 > \hat{\theta}_1$. Then, if the lobbyist for SIG 2 delivers the message $\hat{m}_2$, this provides no new information to the policymaker. If the lobbyist instead delivers the message $\hat{m}_1$, the policymaker will know that at least one of the reports must be false. But false reports are not part of any equilibrium. So it must be that the lobbyist for SIG 2 does not wish to send the message $\hat{m}_1$ after hearing his counterpart report m_2.[19]

In contrast, when the report by the lobbyist for SIG 1 has been m_1, the subsequent report by the second lobbyist does provide additional information to the policymaker. If the second lobbyist delivers the message $\hat{m}_1$, the policymaker infers that $\theta \leq \hat{\theta}_1$, and sets the policy $p(m_1, \hat{m}_1) = \hat{\theta}_1/2$. If he instead reports $\hat{m}_2$, the policymaker infers that $\hat{\theta}_1 \leq \theta \leq \theta_1$, and sets the policy $p(m_1, \hat{m}_2) = (\hat{\theta}_1 + \theta_1)/2$. The lobbyist for SIG 2 must have no incentive to report falsely for any value of θ, and in particular for those values slightly below and slightly above $\hat{\theta}_1$. As before, this requires the lobbyist to be indifferent between reporting $\hat{m}_1$ and $\hat{m}_2$ when the state actually is $\hat{\theta}_1$. Such indifference arises when $(\hat{\theta}_1 + \delta_2) - p(m_1, \hat{m}_1) = p(m_1, \hat{m}_2) - (\hat{\theta}_1 + \delta_2)$, or, with $\delta_2 = 2$,

$$(\hat{\theta}_1 + 2) - \frac{\hat{\theta}_1}{2} = \frac{\hat{\theta}_1 + \theta_1}{2} - (\hat{\theta}_1 + 2).$$

Rearranging terms, this gives

$$\hat{\theta}_1 = \frac{\theta_1}{2} - 4. \tag{4.15}$$

19. The incentives facing the second lobbyist when his counterpart has already reported m_2 depend on what inference the policymaker would draw upon hearing contradictory reports. Bayes' rule does not apply and therefore does not restrict the policymaker's beliefs in such an event. Without going into the details, we note that there are legitimate beliefs for the policymaker that make it undesirable for the lobbyist for SIG 2 to report $\hat{m}_1$ when $\theta \geq \theta_1$ and the other lobby has reported m_2. These beliefs support the equilibrium with truthful reporting by both lobbyists.

Finally, we consider the incentives facing the lobbyist for SIG 1. He must anticipate not only how his message will be interpreted by the policymaker, but also how it will affect the report of the other lobby. The lobbyist for SIG 1 must not have an incentive to report falsely in any state. This requires that, when the state is θ_1, his group is indifferent between the outcome that would ensue from a report of m_1 and the one that would result from a report of m_2. From what we have seen, a report of m_1 in state θ_1 leads the lobbyist for SIG 2 to report $\hat{m}_2$. A report of m_2 in state θ_1 also leads to a report of $\hat{m}_2$. Thus, in equilibrium, the lobbyist for SIG 1 anticipates a report of $\hat{m}_2$ by his counterpart, no matter which message he himself delivers. When the lobbyist for SIG 1 looks beyond the second lobbying report to the policy-setting stage, he anticipates a choice of $p = (\theta_1 + \hat{\theta}_1)/2$ in response to a report of m_1 and $p = (\theta_1 + 24)/2$ in response to a report of m_2. SIG 1 is indifferent between these outcomes in state θ_1 if and only if $(\theta_1 + \delta_1) - (\theta_1 + \hat{\theta}_1)/2 = (\theta_1 + 24)/2 - (\theta_1 + \delta_1)$, or (with $\delta_1 = 1$, and after some rearranging of terms),

$$\theta_1 = 10 + \frac{\hat{\theta}_1}{2}. \tag{4.16}$$

Equations (4.15) and (4.16) are two linear equations that relate θ_1 and $\hat{\theta}_1$. If both of these equations are satisfied, the lobbyists' messages will be credible at every stage. The equations have a unique solution with $\theta_1 = 32/3$ and $\hat{\theta}_1 = 4/3$, which is shown in panel a of figure 4.3. Evidently there is a 3-partition equilibrium in which the lobbyist for SIG 1 first reports whether θ is above or below 32/3 and then the lobbyist for SIG 2 reports whether θ is above or below 4/3. The policymaker sets the policy at either $p = 2/3$, $p = 18/3$, or $p = 52/3$, depending on what combination of reports she hears.

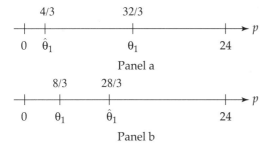

Figure 4.3
Equilibrium Partitions When SIG 1 Reports First

However, this is not the only 3-partition equilibrium that can arise when SIG 1 reports first. In constructing the equilibrium, we have assumed that $\theta_1 > \hat{\theta}_1$, so that the first lobbyist distinguishes "very low" values of θ from values that are "not so low," and the second further distinguishes "very large" values of θ from those that are only "moderately large." It is also possible to construct an equilibrium with $\hat{\theta}_1 > \theta_1$. Then the roles of the two lobbyists are reversed. The procedure for constructing the equilibrium is much the same. First, we find a state $\hat{\theta}_1$ in which the lobbyist for SIG 2 is indifferent between reporting $\hat{m}_1$ and $\hat{m}_2$, given that his counterpart has already reported m_2 (i.e., that $\theta > \theta_1$). Then we find a state θ_1 in which the lobbyist for SIG 1 is indifferent between reporting m_1 and m_2, in the light of the equilibrium responses he anticipates. The equations that are analogous to (4.15) and (4.16) are $\hat{\theta}_1 = \theta_1/2 + 8$ and $\theta_1 = \hat{\theta}_1/2 - 2$. They imply $\theta_1 = 8/3$ and $\hat{\theta}_1 = 28/3$. These partitions are depicted in panel b of figure 4.3.

So far we have assumed that the lobbyist for SIG 1 delivers his message first. We can also consider the game that arises when the order of reporting is reversed. Also in this game, there are two possible 3-partition equilibria, one with $\theta_1 > \hat{\theta}_1$ and the other with $\hat{\theta}_1 > \theta_1$. The procedure for constructing them is the same as before. It turns out that the equilibrium values for θ_1 and $\hat{\theta}_1$ are the same as when SIG 1 reports first; namely, $\theta_1 = 32/3$ and $\hat{\theta}_1 = 4/3$, or $\theta_1 = 8/3$ and $\hat{\theta}_1 = 28/3$. The possible policy outcomes also are the same.

Now let us turn our attention from the specific example with $\delta_1 = 1$, $\delta_2 = 2$, and $\theta_{\max} - \theta_{\min} = 24$ to the more general case of like bias. Krishna and Morgan (2001) have shown that, generally, it does not matter which lobby group reports first. The sets of possible equilibria are the same with either sequence of lobbying. Moreover, for any given set of parameter values, there is a maximum number of subsets in an equilibrium partition. This number rises (or remains the same) as either δ_1 or δ_2 approaches zero. In other words, the more similar are the interests of the interest groups and the policymaker, the more detailed can be the information they convey.

Krishna and Morgan also compare the equilibria that can arise when two groups lobby the policymaker to those that are possible when there is only a single lobbyist. They ask whether the addition of a second lobby improves the prospect for transfer of knowledge. Their answer is that it does not. In particular, they prove that the maximum number of subsets in an equilibrium partition with two lobbies of like bias cannot exceed the maximum number of subsets in an equilibrium partition when only the more moderate of the two lobbies the policymaker. Moreover, the ex ante welfare of the policy-maker and of each of the two SIGs is higher in an n-partition equilibrium with reports by only the more moderate of the two lobbies than in any n-partition equilibrium in which both lobbies offer their advice. Therefore, all parties would agree ahead of time (i.e., before θ is known to the SIGs) to have only the more moderate interest group advise the policymaker rather than to have both groups file reports. The more moderate group has greater credibility than the other, and thus is better able to communicate with the policymaker.

4.2.2 Opposite Bias

When interest groups share the same direction of policy bias relative to a policymaker, it is difficult for the policymaker to use one group to discipline the statements of others. If one lobbyist misrepresents the policy environment slightly, the others are happy to corroborate his report. A policymaker then must rely on keeping her conversations private in order to elicit truthful confirmation or contradiction of the reports she hears. But such privacy may be difficult to maintain, because the groups have good reasons to publicize their claims.

A policymaker can, however, use competing information sources to her advantage when lobbies have conflicting policy aims. In such a setting, if one lobbyist attempts to exaggerate his claims, another may have an incentive to bring the falsehood to light. Still, as Krishna and Morgan (2001) have shown, a policymaker can never become fully informed, even if the lobbyists do represent opposing interests.

To see why, we examine a situation in which $\delta_1 < 0$, $\delta_2 > 0$ and the lobbyist for SIG 1 reports first. We define $\theta_2^* \equiv \theta_{max} - \delta_2$; that is, θ_2^* is the state of the world in which the ideal policy for SIG 2 is equal to θ_{max}. Our argument shall be that no equilibrium of the lobbying game can reveal the precise state of the world for values of $\theta > \theta_2^*$.

Suppose, to the contrary, that the policymaker does learn the true state for such values of θ. Consider two states, θ' and θ'', such that $\theta' > \theta'' > \theta_2^*$. When the lobbying reveals the state to be θ', the policymaker sets the policy $p = \theta'$. When it reveals the state to be θ'', she sets $p = \theta''$. We take θ' and θ'' to be sufficiently close together, so that SIG 1 prefers the policy $p = \theta''$ in state θ' to the policy $p = \theta'$. This requires $\theta' - \theta'' < -\delta_1$.

Let m' denote the message that the lobbyist for SIG 1 delivers in state θ' and m'' denote the message he delivers in state θ''. Also, let $\hat{m}(m|\theta)$ denote the optimal response by the lobbyist for SIG 2 to a message m sent by his counterpart, when the true state is θ. Then, in the hypothesized equilibrium, the lobbyist for SIG 2 reports $\hat{m}' = \hat{m}(m'|\theta')$ in state θ' and $\hat{m}'' = \hat{m}(m''|\theta'')$ in state θ'', and the policymaker responds with $p(m', \hat{m}') = \theta'$ and $p(m'', \hat{m}'') = \theta''$ in these states.

We now proceed to establish that these cannot be optimal strategies for both lobbyists. To begin, suppose that the lobbyist for SIG 1 were to report m'' in state θ', instead of m'. Then the response by the second lobbyist would be $\hat{m}(m''|\theta')$. It must be that $p[m'', \hat{m}(m''|\theta')] \geq \theta''$, because the lobbyist for SIG 2 could have responded with $\hat{m}''$, in which case the policymaker would have delivered the policy θ''. So the optimal response must leave SIG 2 at least as well off as this. Furthermore, it cannot be that $p[m'', \hat{m}(m''|\theta')] = \theta''$, for if it were, SIG 1 would benefit from the proposed deviation. It follows that $p[m'', \hat{m}(m''|\theta')] > \theta''$. However, this implies that it is not optimal for the lobbyist for SIG 2 to report $\hat{m}''$ in state θ''. He could instead report $\hat{m}(m''|\theta')$ and thereby induce a policy that his group prefers to the outcome $p = \theta''$, which results when he follows the allegedly optimal strategy. Thus, the assumption of full revelation for states $\theta > \theta_2^*$ leads to a contradiction.

Although the policymaker cannot gain a complete understanding of the policy environment from two opposing lobbies, she can learn more from the two together than from either one alone. To see this, we pursue another numerical example, this time with $\delta_1 = -3$ and $\delta_2 = 3$. We again take θ to lie between 0 and 24. Then, were only SIG 1 to lobby the policymaker, the outcome would either be a babbling equilibrium or a 2-partition equilibrium. In the latter equilibrium, the lobbyist for the group sends one message if $\theta \leq 18$ and another if $\theta \geq 18$. And if only SIG 2 were to lobby, again the outcome would either be a babbling equilibrium or a 2-partition equilibrium. The lobbyist's messages would distinguish between states with $\theta \leq 6$ and those with $\theta \geq 6$. The reader may confirm that no 3-partition equilibrium is possible in either of these cases. We now proceed to show that a 3-partition equilibrium can arise when both groups lobby the policymaker.

Suppose the lobbyist for SIG 1 reports first, and that he delivers either message m_1 that indicates $\theta \leq \theta_1$ or m_2 that indicates $\theta \geq \theta_1$. The lobbyist renders his advice with the understanding that an

opposing group will report subsequently. When it is time for the
lobbyist for SIG 2 to meet with the policymaker, he delivers the
message $\hat{m}_1$ that indicates $\theta \leq \hat{\theta}_1$ or the message $\hat{m}_2$ that means
$\theta \geq \hat{\theta}_1$. Our job is to find values of θ_1 and $\hat{\theta}_1$ such that both reports
are credible when each lobbyist correctly forecasts the ensuing events.

Once the lobbyist for SIG 1 has delivered his message m_1, the report by the representative of SIG 2 gives additional information to
the policymaker. Suppose, for example, that $\theta_1 \geq \hat{\theta}_1$. Then a message
$\hat{m}_1$ suggests to the policymaker that θ lies between 0 and $\hat{\theta}_1$, while
the message $\hat{m}_2$ suggests that θ lies between $\hat{\theta}_1$ and θ_1. With the
former message, the policymaker sets the policy $p = \hat{\theta}_1/2$; with the
latter message, she sets $p = (\hat{\theta}_1 + \theta_1)/2$. SIG 2 must be indifferent
between these two outcomes when $\theta = \hat{\theta}_1$, which requires $(\hat{\theta}_1 + 3) - \hat{\theta}_1/2 = (\theta_1 + \hat{\theta}_1)/2 - (\hat{\theta}_1 + 3)$, or

$$\hat{\theta}_1 = \frac{\theta_1}{2} - 6. \tag{4.17}$$

Also, the lobbyist for SIG 1 must be indifferent between reporting
m_1 and reporting m_2 when the state is θ_1. Since this lobbyist reports
first, he must forecast the response by his counterpart. A report of
m_1, coupled with the best response by SIG 2, induces a policy of
$p = (\hat{\theta}_1 + \theta_1)/2$. A report of m_2 and the best response of SIG 2 yields a
policy of $p = (\theta_1 + 24)/2$. SIG 1 is indifferent between these two out-
comes in state θ_1 if and only if $(\theta_1 - 3) - (\theta_1 + \hat{\theta}_1)/2 = (\theta_1 + 24)/2 - (\theta_1 - 3)$, or

$$\theta_1 = \frac{\hat{\theta}_1}{2} + 18. \tag{4.18}$$

Equations (4.17) and (4.18) are the only two requirements for a
3-partition equilibrium. They are both satisfied when $\theta_1 = 20$ and
$\hat{\theta}_1 = 4$. Thus, we have identified a 3-partition equilibrium in which
the lobbyist for the group that prefers a relatively low level of the
policy variable first reports whether θ is greater or less than 20, and
the lobbyist for the group that prefers a relatively high level of the
policy subsequently reports whether θ is greater than or less than 4.
If the policymaker hears the pair of messages m_1 and $\hat{m}_1$, she sets
$p = 2$; if she hears m_1 and $\hat{m}_2$, she sets $p = 12$; and if she hears m_2 and
$\hat{m}_2$, she sets $p = 22$. These responses validate the lobbyists' reporting
strategies.

When we compare the expected welfare of the policymaker in the
3-partition equilibrium to what she can achieve when she has only a

single source of information, we find that having advisers on opposite sides of the issue works to the policymaker's benefit. What is more surprising, perhaps, is that the groups themselves gain from this, at least in an ex ante sense. Viewed from a time before the groups learn the value of θ, each has higher expected welfare in the 3-partition equilibrium that exists when both lobby than in the best equilibrium that can arise when only one group engages in lobbying. The explanation for this is simple. When a group provides information without any foil, the policymaker will be wary of its report. This wariness causes the policy outcome to differ greatly from what is warranted in some states of the world. But when a group's report must be confirmed by the report of another group that has an opposing bias, the report enjoys greater credibility. Both groups benefit from the ability to communicate information about the policy environment.

We have constructed a 3-partition equilibrium for our numerical example. But this is not the best that can be achieved. In fact, our example admits equilibria in which the policymaker becomes fully informed about the policy environment for a range of values of θ. Only for extreme values of the state variable is the policymaker forced to rely on coarse information.

Krishna and Morgan (2001) show that the properties of our numerical example are rather general. For the case of opposite bias, they establish the existence of an equilibrium with "partial revelation" whenever both lobby groups are "nonextreme." By partial revelation, we mean that lobbying enables the policymaker to infer the state of the world for a continuous range of values of θ. A group is nonextreme if it does not wish to have the policymaker believe that the state is $\theta_{\min}$ (or $\theta_{\max}$) in all states of the world. When a partial-revelation equilibrium does exist, it yields higher ex ante welfare to the policymaker and to both SIGs than does any equilibrium with lobbying by only a single group. When a partial-revelation equilibrium does not exist, then the groups' extreme preferences deprive their lobbyists of any credibility. The only equilibrium in such circumstances is a babbling equilibrium.

4.2.3   Multidimensional Information

Our discussion in this chapter has been confined to unidimensional policy issues and unidimensional uncertainty about the policy environment. Although much of the literature focuses on this case, that focus may be limiting. Indeed, a recent paper by Battaglini (2000) has shown that increasing the dimensionality of the policy problem may improve the prospects for information transmission. That is, lobby groups may be more effective in communicating information when there are many dimensions to policy than when the policy choice concerns the height of a single policy instrument.

We consider now a setting with two interest groups, two dimensions of policy, and two dimensions of policy uncertainty. The two policy dimensions might reflect different aspects of a single instrument (e.g., the tax rate on long-term capital gains and the minimum holding period for a gain to be considered "long term"), or two entirely different instruments (e.g., the tax rate on gasoline sales and the maximum allowable pollution emission). We represent the policy by a two-dimensional vector $\mathbf{p} = (p_1, p_2)$ and the state of the world by a two-dimensional vector $\boldsymbol{\theta} = (\theta_1, \theta_2)$.[20] The welfare function of the policymaker is $G(\mathbf{p}, \boldsymbol{\theta}) = -\sum_{j=1}^{2}(p_j - \theta_j)^2$, while that of SIG i is $U_i(\mathbf{p}, \boldsymbol{\theta}) = -\sum_{j=1}^{2}(p_j - \theta_j - \delta_{ij})^2$, for $i = 1, 2$. Thus, $\mathbf{p} = \boldsymbol{\theta}$ is the policymaker's ideal policy vector in state of the world $\boldsymbol{\theta}$, whereas $\mathbf{p} = \boldsymbol{\theta} + \boldsymbol{\delta}_i$ is the favorite of SIG i in that state. The vector $\boldsymbol{\delta}_i = (\delta_{i1}, \delta_{i2})$ denotes the bias in the preferences of SIG i relative to those of the policymaker. A group may prefer larger (or smaller) values of p_1 and p_2 than the policymaker in every state of the world, or it may prefer a larger value on one dimension and a smaller value on the other.

We assume that both groups know the values of both bits of information; that is, each knows the realization of the (two-dimensional) random variable $\tilde{\boldsymbol{\theta}}$. Lobbyists for the two groups meet with the policymaker privately to deliver their assessment of the policy environment.[21] The policymaker uses the advice to update her beliefs about

20. We alert the reader to a temporary change of notation. Whereas until now we have used θ_1 to denote the highest value of θ for which the lobbyist for SIG 1 sends the message m_1, we now use it to denote the first element of the vector $\boldsymbol{\theta}$. We will revert to the previous usage in the next chapter.
21. Recall from Section 4.2.1 that, with like bias and private reporting, there always exists an equilibrium with full revelation. This equilibrium arises when each lobbyist reports a state of the world and the policymaker sets the policy equal to the minimum of the two reports. However, we noted at the time the fragility of this equilibrium. It relies on each lobbyist being fully confident that the other will reveal the true state, so that each is indifferent between doing so himself or not. With even the slightest possibility that a lobby may observe the state of the world with error, the equilibrium with full revelation disappears. In contrast, the equilibrium with full revelation that we shall describe for the case of multiple policy dimensions is immune to this critique, as we shall discuss further below. Battaglini (2000) has shown that full revelation typically is not possible with sequential public reporting about multiple dimensions of policy uncertainty unless a special condition relating the groups' preferences is satisfied.

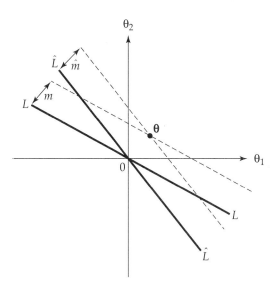

Figure 4.4
Messages with Two Policy Dimensions

$\tilde{\theta}$. Then she chooses the policy vector **p** that maximizes her expected utility.

We consider the lobbying game that arises when δ_1 is not proportional to δ_2. If δ_1 were proportional to δ_2, that would mean that the bias of SIG 1 relative to that of SIG 2 is the same in every dimension. With a lack of proportionality, each group is relatively more biased along one policy dimension.

When the groups differ in their relative biases, there exists an equilibrium with full revelation of θ. In this equilibrium, the lobbyist for SIG 1 reports the value of $m = \delta_{21}\theta_1 + \delta_{22}\theta_2$. This report informs the policymaker of the distance of θ from the line LL defined by $\delta_{21}\theta_1 + \delta_{22}\theta_2 = 0$. Meanwhile, the lobbyist for SIG 2 delivers the message $\hat{m} = \delta_{11}\theta_1 + \delta_{12}\theta_2$. This message informs the policymaker of the distance of θ from the line $\hat{L}\hat{L}$ defined by $\delta_{11}\theta_1 + \delta_{12}\theta_2 = 0$. Figure 4.4 depicts the lines LL and $\hat{L}\hat{L}$, as well as the messages m and $\hat{m}$, for a particular realization of θ. When the policymaker hears the messages m and $\hat{m}$, she can construct the two dotted lines shown in the figure. Then she can find the value of θ at the point where they intersect. Thus, the messages allow the policymaker to identify the state of the world. It remains to check only that the lobbyists have incentives to report them truthfully.

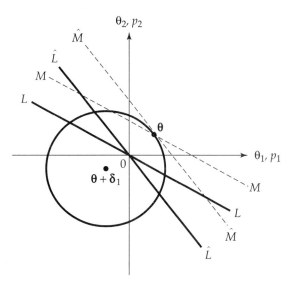

Figure 4.5
Best Response by SIG 1

Suppose the lobbyist for SIG 1 expects his counterpart to report $\hat{m} = \delta_{11}\theta_1 + \delta_{12}\theta_2$. Now consider figure 4.5, which reproduces the essential features of figure 4.4. In this figure we have added the indifference curve for SIG 1 that goes through the point θ. In general, SIG 1 is indifferent among policies that are equidistant from its ideal point of $\theta + \delta_1$; these are points on circles centered at $\theta + \delta_1$. So SIG 1 is indifferent between the policy $\mathbf{p} = \theta$ and those that lie on the circle that we have drawn, when the state of the world is θ. It prefers all such policies to those that are farther from its ideal point, that is, those that lie outside the indicated indifference curve.

If the lobbyist for SIG 2 reports truthfully, the policymaker will suspect θ to lie somewhere along the dotted line labeled $\hat{M}\hat{M}$. The report from the lobbyist for SIG 1 allows her to form beliefs about the location of θ on this line. Since the policymaker sets the policy vector equal to what she believes to be the state, a truthful report results in the policy $\mathbf{p} = \theta$. A false report can be used by the lobbyist to achieve any point along $\hat{M}\hat{M}$. But notice that SIG 1 prefers the policy $\mathbf{p} = \theta$ to any other policy on $\hat{M}\hat{M}$. It follows that the lobbyist for SIG 1 will report truthfully if he expects his counterpart to do so. The same argument applies to the lobbyist for SIG 2.

Unlike the equilibrium with full revelation that exists when the lobbyists report privately about a single item of policy-relevant information, the equilibrium here survives the introduction of small reporting mistakes by the lobbyists. Battaglini (2000) considers a game in which group i observes the correct value of θ with probability $1 - \varepsilon_i$ and observes a random, incorrect value of θ with probability ε_i. He supposes that the probabilities of error are independent for the two groups and that the groups themselves do not know if their research has been faulty or not. If the probability of a mistake is small for each group, there exists an equilibrium with (nearly) full revelation of θ when the policy environment has two dimensions of uncertainty, but not when there is only one. In the equilibrium with nearly full revelation, the policymaker learns the true value of θ except in those rare instances when one of the groups observes the state with error.

What allows for full revelation in situations with multiple policy dimensions is the ability of the policymaker to find a "direction" of policy in which her own interests align with those of each interest group. In state θ, the policymaker and SIG 1 agree that $\mathbf{p} = \theta$ is the best policy among those on $\hat{M}\hat{M}$. Thus, the policymaker can trust the lobbyist for SIG 1 to report truthfully about the distance of MM from LL. And the policymaker and SIG 2 agree that $\mathbf{p} = \theta$ is the best policy among those on MM. So, the lobbyist for SIG 2 can report credibly about the distance of $\hat{M}\hat{M}$ from $\hat{L}\hat{L}$. The prospect for finding coincident interests would be obvious, perhaps, if each SIG had unbiased preferences relative to the policymaker's along one dimension of policy, and if these dimensions of agreement were different for the two groups. Then the policymaker could rely on the lobbyist for SIG 1 to provide information about, say, θ_2, and the lobbyist for SIG 2 to provide information about θ_1. But we have seen that the same outcome can be achieved even when the groups' preferences are biased along both policy dimensions, provided that each group is comparatively more biased along a different dimension.

Battaglini's arguments can be generalized to other utility functions besides the quadratic. However, it does rely on the alignment of the different policy dimensions with the different dimensions of policy uncertainty. Suppose, for example, that the policymaker has the welfare function $G(\mathbf{p}, \theta) = -[p_1 - (\theta_1 + \theta_2)]^2 - (p_2)^2$, while the welfare

function for SIG i is $U_i(\mathbf{p}, \boldsymbol{\theta}) = -[p_1 - (\theta_1 + \theta_2) - \delta_{i1}]^2 - (p_2 - \delta_{i2})^2$.
Here, both bits of information bear on the policymaker's choice of p_1.
Since both groups are biased in their preferences along this dimension, the problem is like the unidimensional case. Each lobbyist has
an incentive to misrepresent θ_1 or θ_2 if he sees the slightest chance
that his counterpart will report one of these parameters with error.
Further research is needed to clarify the generality of Battaglini's
results and, more important, to characterize the equilibria that can
arise when there are several interest groups and several dimensions
of policy, and each group is relatively better informed about certain
aspects of the policy environment.

We have seen in this chapter how SIGs can use their knowledge of
the policy issues to influence policy choices. We have modeled lobbying as cheap talk; that is, as a game in which messages are costless
to deliver but difficult to verify. Such lobbying typically reduces the
uncertainty facing a policymaker, but cannot eliminate it entirely.
Importantly, in most cases, the sharing of information is beneficial to
both the policymaker and the interest group. Even when two groups
with disparate preferences lobby a policymaker, each group gains
relative to the outcome that would result from an uninformed policy
choice. Indeed, the gains from lobbying often are greatest when the
groups wish to pull the policymaker in opposite directions, because
then each group can serve as a credibility check on the other. The
dimensionality of the policy problem can also affect the groups'
ability to communicate information credibly. Policymakers may be
able to learn more when lobbyists convey information about several
dimensions of policy than they can when the policy advice concerns
a single policy parameter.

4.3   Appendix: A More General Lobbying Game

In this appendix we provide a more general treatment of the lobbying game of Section 4.1. We describe a setting in which the probability distribution for $\tilde{\theta}$ is an arbitrary one, and the policymaker and
interest group have objective functions that may represent a broad
class of preferences. We begin by describing the setting and then
proceed to report results that generalize our earlier findings.

4.3.1   The General Setting

We now take $G(p, \theta)$ and $U(p, \theta)$ to be general functions, not necessarily quadratic as in Section 4.1. We assume only that these functions are differentiable, strictly concave in the policy variable p, and that the cross-partial derivatives $G_{p\theta}$ and $U_{p\theta}$ are positive. The last of these assumptions means that increases in the level of the policy variable are more valuable to the policymaker and the SIG the higher is the level of θ.

The random variable $\tilde{\theta}$ now has a cumulative distribution function $F_\theta(\theta)$, with density function $f_\theta(\theta) = F'_\theta(\theta)$. We take $f_\theta(\theta)$ to be strictly positive for all values of θ between $\theta_{\min}$ and $\theta_{\max}$ and equal to zero for all values of θ outside this range. We further assume that the group's ideal policy is greater than that of the policymaker in every state of the world. Namely,

$$\arg \max_p U(p, \theta) > \arg \max_p G(p, \theta) \quad \text{for all } \theta \in [\theta_{\min}, \theta_{\max}].$$

The lobbyist learns the value of θ before the game begins. In the first stage, he communicates a "message" to the policymaker. The message is one of a finite or infinite set of possible statements, M. The lobbyist's strategy can be described by a function $\sigma(\theta)$ such that when the lobbyist observes θ, he communicates the message $m = \sigma(\theta)$ for some $m \in M$.[22]

The policymaker interprets any message according to her beliefs about the lobbyist's strategy. Let $\hat{\sigma}(\theta)$ be the strategy that the policymaker suspects the lobbyist of using. Then the policymaker interprets the message m to mean that the state is one of those for which $m = \hat{\sigma}(\theta)$. Upon hearing a message, she updates her beliefs about the distribution of $\tilde{\theta}$ by applying Bayes' rule. We define $\hat{F}_\theta(\cdot | m, \hat{\sigma})$ to be the policymaker's posterior distribution for $\tilde{\theta}$ when she hears the message m and believes the lobbyist's strategy to be $\hat{\sigma}$.[23]

The policymaker chooses p in the second stage to maximize her expected welfare, given her posterior beliefs about the policy envi-

---

22. We could allow for richer strategies. For example, the lobbyist might draw his message from a probability distribution, so that the same value of θ might give rise to one of several different messages. But we focus on pure strategies, whenever possible, to keep matters simple.

23. Bayes' rule applies for every message m that the policymaker expects to hear with positive probability. If the policymaker does not expect to hear some message m' in any state of the world, then $\hat{F}_\theta(\theta | m', \hat{\sigma})$ is not restricted.

ronment. The policy choice depends on the message she has heard and on her beliefs about the lobbyist's strategy. We denote this dependence by $p^G(m|\hat{\sigma})$. Using the posterior distribution induced by the message m given the beliefs $\hat{\sigma}$, we have

$$p^G(m|\hat{\sigma}) = \arg \max_p \int G(p,\theta) \, d\hat{F}_\theta(\theta|m,\hat{\sigma}).$$

What is an optimal strategy for the lobbyist under these conditions? We assume that the lobbyist knows how the policymaker will interpret his messages and knows the policymaker's preferences. Therefore, he can forecast the outcome $p^G(m|\hat{\sigma})$ that will result for any message. The optimal lobbying strategy, $\sigma(\theta)$, is constructed by finding, for each value of θ, the message $m \in M$ that maximizes $U[p^G(m|\hat{\sigma}), \theta]$.

In an equilibrium, the policymaker's beliefs must be consistent with the incentives faced by the lobbyist. But we have seen that the beliefs $\hat{\sigma}(\theta)$ give the lobbyist an incentive to follow the strategy $\sigma(\theta)$. Consistency thus requires that $\hat{\sigma}(\theta) = \sigma(\theta)$.[24]

4.3.2 Properties of an Equilibrium

It is easy to see that no equilibrium can be characterized by full revelation. Suppose to the contrary that the policymaker expects to learn the precise value of θ from the lobbyist's report. Then she must expect to hear a different message in each state of the world. For convenience, we let θ denote the message that the policymaker interprets as an indication that the state is θ. That is, we take $\hat{\sigma}(\theta) = \theta$. For example, the message θ might be the literal statement, "the state is θ." Upon hearing the message θ, the policymaker updates her beliefs to place a probability one on the event that the state is θ, and a probability zero on the possibility that the state is different from θ. She then implements the policy that maximizes her welfare in state θ.

We now show that it is not optimal under these circumstances for the lobbyist to use the strategy $\sigma(\theta) = \theta$. In state θ, the ideal policy for the interest group is larger than the ideal policy for the politician. If the lobbyist were to misrepresent the state to be something greater

---

24. We also need to specify beliefs "off the equilibrium path"—that is, beliefs that apply when the policymaker observes a message that is not part of the equilibrium play. We omit this part of the discussion because it has no important bearing on the main thrust of our arguments.

than θ, the policymaker would respond, given her beliefs, by setting a policy more to the group's liking. Since the beliefs $\hat{\sigma}(\theta) = \theta$ can never give rise to behavior that fulfills those beliefs, the policymaker cannot expect full revelation in any equilibrium.

It is also easy to see that a babbling equilibrium always exists. In a babbling equilibrium, the policymaker interprets all messages as providing no new information. In other words, she treats all literal statements as if they were the same message, say m^*. The policymaker's beliefs about the lobbyist's strategy can be described by $\hat{\sigma}(\theta) = m^*$ for all θ. When the policymaker forms her post-message beliefs about $\tilde{\theta}$, the posterior distribution coincides with the prior distribution.[25] Therefore, she sets the policy that maximizes her expected welfare under the distribution $F_\theta(\cdot)$. Here the policy outcome is invariant to the message. So the strategy $\sigma(\theta) = m^*$ is as good for the lobbyist as any other. In short, the beliefs $\hat{\sigma}(\theta) = m^*$ can give rise to the behavior $\sigma(\theta) = m^*$ as an optimal response. This validates the equilibrium.

Crawford and Sobel (1982) have characterized all of the possible equilibria in games such as this one. The properties they have established are generalizations of the ones that we highlighted in Section 4.1.4. They showed, first, that every equilibrium can be represented as a *partition equilibrium*. In a partition equilibrium, the lobbyist chooses one of a finite number n of messages, say $m \in \{m_1, m_2, \dots, m_n\}$. The policymaker interprets the message m_i to mean that $\theta_{i-1} \leq \theta \leq \theta_i$ for some set of numbers $\{\theta_0, \theta_1, \dots, \theta_n\}$ such that $\theta_0 = \theta_{\min}$ and $\theta_n = \theta_{\max}$. In other words, the lobbyist partitions the space of possible values of the state variable into a finite number of subsets, and advises the policymaker which subset includes the true value of θ. When the policymaker hears the message m_i, she updates her beliefs to exclude the possibility that θ lies outside the range from θ_{i-1} to θ_i. Then, by Bayes' rule, $\hat{f}_\theta(\theta|m_i) = f_\theta(\theta)/[F(\theta_i) - F(\theta_{i-1})]$ for all $\theta \in [\theta_{i-1}, \theta_i]$ and $\hat{f}_\theta(\theta|m_i) = 0$ for all $\theta \notin [\theta_{i-1}, \theta_i]$. The policymaker chooses the policy $p(m_i)$, where

$$p(m_i) = \arg \max_p \int_{\theta_{i-1}}^{\theta_i} G(p, \theta) \hat{f}_\theta(\theta|m_i) \, d\theta.$$

---

25. If the policymaker hears a message other than m^*, she cannot apply Bayes' rule to update her beliefs. In a perfect Bayesian equilibrium, the policymaker can attach any meaning at all to this sort of message. In the babbling equilibrium, her posterior distribution for $\tilde{\theta}$ is the same as her prior distribution, even if she hears a message different from m^*.

This policy maximizes the policymaker's expected welfare, conditional on her belief that $\tilde{\theta}$ must lie between θ_{i-1} and θ_i.

The lobbyist's optimal strategy must coincide with the policymaker's beliefs. This requirement pins down the boundaries of each partition. Near each boundary point, the lobbyist must have no incentive to lie when the true value of θ is just above the boundary and when it is just below it. Thus, when $\theta = \theta_i$, the lobbyist must be indifferent between the policy that results when he sends the message m_i and the policy that results when he sends the message m_{i+1}. This requires

$$U[p(m_i), \theta_i] = U[p(m_{i+1}), \theta_i]. \tag{4.19}$$

For any welfare functions $G(p, \theta)$ and $U(p, \theta)$ and any distribution $F_\theta(\theta)$, there exists a maximum number of messages that can be used in the lobbying equilibrium. This maximum number, say $n_{\max}$, depends on the degree of alignment in the interests of the SIG and the policymaker. The more similar are the welfare functions of the interest group and the policymaker, the larger is $n_{\max}$.

Crawford and Sobel prove that, if an equilibrium with n different messages exists, then an equilibrium with $n - 1$ messages also exists. Moreover, under some conditions, they can establish the uniqueness of the equilibrium with a given number of messages.[26] If these conditions hold, the lobbying game has exactly $n_{\max}$ different equilibria. These $n_{\max}$ equilibria can be ranked in terms of ex ante welfare. In particular, both the SIG and the interest group achieve higher ex ante welfare (evaluated in terms of the prior distribution for $\tilde{\theta}$, namely F_θ) in the equilibrium with n different messages than in the one with k different messages, for all $k < n$. The coincidence of ex ante preferences may be useful in selecting among equilibria, if the two sides have an opportunity to discuss the interpretation of messages before the SIG learns the state of the world.

---

26. A sufficient condition for the uniqueness of an equilibrium with a given number of messages is as follows. Consider the sets of values of θ, $\{\theta_0, \theta_1, \ldots, \}$, that satisfy $U[p(m_i), \theta_i] = U[p(m_{i+1}), \theta_i]$ for $i \geq 1$. Let $\{\hat{\theta}_0, \hat{\theta}_1, \ldots, \}$ and $\{\theta_0^*, \theta_1^*, \ldots, \}$ be two such sets with $\hat{\theta}_0 = \theta_0^*$ and $\hat{\theta}_1 > \theta_1^*$. Then uniqueness is assured if $\hat{\theta}_i > \theta_i^*$ for all $i \geq 2$. Crawford and Sobel provide, in their Theorem 2, conditions on the utility function $U(\cdot)$ and the distribution of states $F_\theta(\cdot)$ that guarantee that the above sufficient condition will be satisfied.

5   Costly Lobbying

In the last chapter we abstracted from the costs that interest groups must incur to collect and disseminate information. In reality, lobbying often entails significant costs. Interest groups hire lawyers and policy experts, engage in advertising and mailings, and sometimes pay fairly large sums to entertain policymakers in an effort to gain their sympathies. Many of these costs can be avoided by a group that elects not to participate in the lobbying game. In this chapter we examine the incentives that interest groups have to invest in lobbying and the effect that these costs have on their ability to educate policymakers.

It is useful to divide lobbying costs into three categories. Some costs are relatively fixed and outside the control of the interest group. Other costs may be varied at a group's discretion. Still other costs are imposed by the policymakers themselves. We examine each of these categories of expenses in successive sections of this chapter.

Lobbying costs that are outside a group's control are the subject of Section 5.1. We refer to these as *exogenous costs*. They may include, for example, the salaries of the technical experts who are needed to prepare policy briefs and of the lawyers who are needed to present the briefs to the policymakers. An important characteristic of exogenous costs is that they do not vary with the content of a group's message. For example, it may be that a SIG must pay roughly the same amount to hire a lawyer to argue that the policy environment warrants a moderate policy level as it would to hire a lawyer who claims that the situation is more extreme. When lobbying costs are independent of content, the policymaker cannot infer much about the policy environment from the size of these expenses. But she may be able to glean some useful information from the fact that the group was willing to bear these costs. If a group benefits differently from a given policy action in different states of the world, the fact that the group is willing to incur the cost of lobbying gives some indication about what the true state might be.[1]

Once we recognize that the mere act of lobbying can convey information, we understand why a group might be willing to incur expenses beyond those that are strictly necessary. A group might choose to run a costly advertising campaign rather than a more modest one, or to hire a stable of high-priced lawyers rather than a few articulate spokespersons. By opting for greater expense when less would suffice, the group might be able to signal the strength of its convictions or to indicate something about the nature of the policy environment. In Section 5.2 we examine *endogenous lobbying costs*— those expenses that groups bear beyond the minimum necessary to convey their messages.

A final category of costs includes those that are imposed by policy-makers. Some policymakers may insist that an interest group contribute to their campaigns before they are willing to schedule a meeting to discuss the group's concerns. More often a contribution is not a strict prerequisite for a conference, but groups see their contributions as a means to increase the likelihood of being granted a meeting. Groups often secure such access long before they know what issues will appear on the policy agenda. Accordingly, it makes sense to think of the access costs as being incurred before a group learns the state of the world. A first question to ask is, Why does the policy-maker impose these costs? After all, the information she stands to obtain from the lobbyist will be valuable to her in deciding her policy actions. One possible answer is that politicians need resources to finance their campaigns. They may be willing to sacrifice some useful information in order to raise the needed funds. Another possibility is that policymakers use the price of admission as a screen to distinguish groups that are more likely to provide valuable information from those whose reports will be less valuable. We will consider both of these explanations for *access costs* in Section 5.3.

---

1. The costs that we consider here can be avoided if an interest group decides to refrain from lobbying. They are to be distinguished from other fixed costs that a SIG must bear in order to become and remain an organized entity. Organizational costs are important for determining which interests will be active in the lobbying game, but they do not affect a group's decision of whether to lobby on a particular issue, nor do they figure in the policymaker's interpretation of a group's claims. The analysis of Chapter 4 applies to situations in which an organization bears (only) unavoidable fixed costs.

5.1   Exogenous Lobbying Costs

We begin with lobbying costs that are exogenously fixed and that are invariant to the content of a group's message. As we suggested earlier, these costs may include payments to experts and lawyers who are needed to prepare the policy briefs and to argue the group's case. We examine first the case of a single interest group that has information about a dichotomous variable. Then we proceed to situations with a continuous policy variable, and finally to situations with multiple lobbies.

5.1.1   Single Lobby, Dichotomous Information

Our discussion in this section builds on Potters and van Winden (1992). There is a single interest group, whose preferences are represented by the function $U = -(p - \theta - \delta)^2 - l$, where p is a policy variable and θ describes the state of the world. The new variable is l, which represents the cost of lobbying. In this section we take l to equal zero when the SIG chooses not to lobby and $l = l_f > 0$ when it elects to present its case. The SIG knows the state of the world, which may be either θ_H or θ_L, with $\theta_H > \theta_L$. The group's ideal policy in state θ is $\theta + \delta$, for some value of $\delta > 0$.

The policymaker has an objective function $G = -(p - \theta)^2$. Thus, the policymaker has a target policy of θ when the state is θ, but she does not know the prevailing state. She begins with the prior belief that each of the two states is equally likely. Then she updates her beliefs based on what she observes and hears. After learning what she can, she chooses p to maximize her expected utility.

As in Chapter 4, we have introduced some degree of congruence in the interests of the SIG and the policymaker, but also some conflict. Both the group and the policymaker prefer a larger value for p when the state is θ_H than when it is θ_L. This shared preference for a policy that is appropriate to the state introduces the possibility of mutually beneficial communication. However, in any given state of the world, the SIG prefers a higher value of p than the policymaker does. Thus, the policymaker must be wary of strategic manipulation. As before, the parameter δ measures the bias in the group's preferences relative to those of the policymaker—that is, the extent of the conflict in their relationship.

The lobbying game proceeds as follows. First, the interest group learns the true value of θ; then it decides whether to bear the cost l_f

of preparing a case and presenting it to the policymaker. If the SIG chooses to lobby, the policymaker updates her beliefs about θ based on the observation that a report has been made and on the content of that report. If the SIG opts not to prepare a case, the policymaker still might update her beliefs in recognition of the fact that the group opted not to appear. After updating her beliefs, the policymaker chooses the policy level to maximize her expected utility.

When $l_f = 0$, the situation is very much akin to that described in Section 4.1.2. The interest group may lobby the policymaker in all states, but only reports that are persuasive will be taken at face value. This means that the interest group must have an incentive to report truthfully in each state of the world, if any communication is to occur. When the state is θ_H, there is no risk of false reporting, since the group would never wish to report a value for θ smaller than the actual one. But when the state is θ_L, the group may be tempted to misrepresent its case. If the SIG reports "high" in state θ_L and the policymaker accepts the report as true, the resulting policy of $p = \theta_H$ may be more to the group's liking than the smaller value of $p = \theta_L$ that would result from an honest report. Recall that truthful reporting in state θ_L requires $\delta \leq (\theta_H - \theta_L)/2$; that is, the bias in the group's preferences relative to those of the policymaker must be small relative to the difference in policies indicated by the alternative states (see (4.1)). Otherwise the group's report will not be credible, and the policymaker will set $p = (\theta_H + \theta_L)/2$ no matter what report she hears.

Paradoxically, the SIG might fare better when lobbying is costly than when it is not. A positive lobbying cost can benefit the group, because it affords the group an added means to gain credibility. Consider a situation with $l_f > 0$. If the group chooses to bear this expense, its incentives for truthful reporting will be the same as those described above. Namely, the lobbyist will inevitably report truthfully when the state is θ_H, but he might be tempted to claim θ_H even when the state is θ_L. In some cases, however, the potential benefit from false reporting would not be enough to justify the lobbying cost. In such circumstances the SIG would choose to keep its lobbyist at home when the state is θ_L. But then the mere fact of the group's appearance would indicate to the policymaker that the true state must be θ_H. The content of the policy brief is no longer important, since the information has been conveyed by the group's willingness to prepare it.

We attempt now to construct an equilibrium in which the policy-maker infers the value of θ from the lobbying behavior of the interest group. In such an equilibrium the policymaker takes a group's willingness to lobby to imply that $\theta = \theta_H$ and a failure to lobby to mean that $\theta = \theta_L$. To support such beliefs, the group must be willing to bear the expense of lobbying when the state is θ_H. In this state the group faces a choice between paying the cost of l_f and achieving a policy of $p = \theta_H$, or saving itself the expense and accepting $p = \theta_L$. The SIG is willing to pay the lobbying cost in state θ_H if and only if $-\delta^2 - l_f \geq -(\theta_L - \theta_H - \delta)^2$, or

$$l_f \leq (\theta_H - \theta_L)(2\delta + \theta_H - \theta_L) \equiv k_1. \tag{5.1}$$

The group must also prefer to refrain from lobbying when the state is θ_L. By failing to lobby, it accepts a policy of θ_L, but saves l_f. If it were to opt instead to deliver a (false) report, it could induce a policy of $p = \theta_H$ at a cost of l_f. The SIG prefers to refrain from lobbying in state θ_L if and only if $-\delta^2 \geq -(\theta_H - \theta_L - \delta)^2 - l_f$, or

$$l_f \geq (\theta_H - \theta_L)[2\delta - (\theta_H - \theta_L)] \equiv k_2. \tag{5.2}$$

Since $k_1 > k_2$, there is a range of lobbying costs for which both (5.1) and (5.2) are satisfied. For these values of l_f, there exists an equilibrium in which the SIG engages in lobbying if and only if the state warrants a high level of the policy, and the mere act of lobbying signals the state of the world. Notice that $k_2 > 0$ if and only if $\delta > (\theta_H - \theta_L)/2$. This makes sense, for it says that a positive lobbying cost is required for credibility if and only if the SIG has an incentive to report falsely when $\theta = \theta_L$.

It is interesting to compare how the policymaker and the interest group each fare in an equilibrium with costly lobbying to how they would fare in the same environment were lobbying to be costless. We know that, if $\delta > (\theta_H - \theta_L)/2$, communication would be impossible in the absence of lobbying costs. Then the policymaker would set $p = (\theta_H + \theta_L)/2$, which is not her ideal policy in either state of the world. But when l_f falls between k_1 and k_2, the costly lobbying (or its absence) allows the policymaker to infer the true value of θ. Then she achieves her ideal policy in both states of the world. Clearly, the policymaker prefers the outcome with costly lobbying and full revelation to the outcome with costless lobbying that proves to be uninformative.

As for the interest group, we calculate its expected welfare at a time before it learns the realization of $\tilde{\theta}$. When lobbying is costly, the group achieves a welfare level of $-\delta^2 - l_f$ in state θ_H and a welfare level of $-\delta^2$ in state θ_L. Its expected welfare is $-\delta^2 - l_f/2$, considering that the two states are equally likely. It is easy to verify that the SIG prefers a situation in which lobbying is costly to one in which it is costless but futile if and only if $l_f < (\theta_H - \theta_L)^2/2$. It follows that both the policymaker and the interest group may benefit from having lobbying not be free.[2]

However, the opportunity to engage in costly lobbying is not always a blessing to the interest group. When $l_f > (\theta_H - \theta_L)^2/2$, the group fares worse in an equilibrium with effective lobbying than it would if lobbying were not a possibility at all. This may seem surprising, inasmuch as the SIG always has the choice not to pay the lobbying cost. But the group can suffer from an inability to tie its own hands. If the policymaker expects the SIG to lobby whenever the state is θ_H, she will interpret a failure to appear as an indication that the state is θ_L. Then, if $l_f < k_1$, the group will indeed prefer to pay the cost when the state is θ_H. But when $l_f > (\theta_H - \theta_L)^2/2$, its expected welfare with full revelation and an expected lobbying bill of $l_f/2$ still is lower than what it would be if the policy were always $p = (\theta_H + \theta_L)/2$ and the expected lobbying expense were zero. The group would lose from having the opportunity to lobby, unless it could somehow commit itself ahead of time (before learning the realization of $\tilde{\theta}$) never to come pleading for a high level of the policy.[3]

When (5.2) is violated, it is impossible for the policymaker to infer the state of the world from the lobbyist's actions and words. Still, as Potters and van Winden (1992) have shown, there may be an equilibrium in which the group's lobbying behavior conveys some limited information to the policymaker. Specifically, they construct an equilibrium in which the interest group pursues a mixed strategy. If the state is θ_H, the SIG lobbies the policymaker with probability one. But

---

2. See Banerjee and Somanathan (2001) for another example of a communication game in which both players may prefer a situation in which communication costs are positive to one in which they are zero.

3. We should note that when $\delta > (\theta_H - \theta_L)/2$, there also exists an equilibrium without any lobbying. If the policymaker expects no lobbying to occur, and if she assumes that any lobbying that does take place reflects a mistake that is equally likely to happen in either state, she will set $p = (\theta_H + \theta_L)/2$ no matter whether she is lobbied or not. Then the SIG will have no reason to bear the cost of lobbying, since it can have no effect on the policy outcome.

if the state is θ_L, it randomizes its choice, so that it sometimes lobbies and sometimes refrains. Since lobbying might occur in either state, the policymaker cannot infer from lobbying that the state must be θ_H. But she can update her beliefs based on what she sees. She will certainly put more weight on the possibility that $\theta = \theta_H$ when she observes lobbying than when she does not.

We proceed now to construct such a mixed-strategy equilibrium and to derive the limits on l_f for which it exists. Let the policymaker anticipate that lobbying will surely take place when the state is θ_H and that it will occur with a probability $\zeta < 1$ when the state is θ_L. The policymaker applies Bayes' rule to update her beliefs. If the lobbyist appears to argue his case for a high level of policy, she concludes that with probability $1/(1 + \zeta)$ the true state is θ_H and with probability $\zeta/(1 + \zeta)$ the true state is θ_L.[4] She responds to a lobbying campaign by setting a policy equal to her updated expectation of θ, which implies that $p_{lobby} = (\theta_H + \zeta\theta_L)/(1 + \zeta)$. If no lobbyist appears, the policymaker infers the state can only be θ_L. In the event, she sets $p_{no\ lobby} = \theta_L$.

We have hypothesized that the group sometimes lobbies and sometimes does not, when the true state is θ_L. For the group to behave in this manner, it must attain the same level of welfare in state θ_L regardless of its behavior; otherwise the group would simply take its preferred action. It follows that the probability of lobbying in state θ_L must be such that the induced policy response leaves the interest group indifferent between lobbying and not. The group is indifferent in state θ_L if and only if $-(p_{lobby} - \theta_L - \delta)^2 - l_f = -\delta^2$, or

$$\zeta = (\theta_H - \theta_L)\left(\frac{\delta \pm \sqrt{\delta^2 - l_f}}{l_f}\right) - 1. \qquad (5.3)$$

This equation gives two possible values of ζ that might apply in a mixed-strategy equilibrium.

Of course, the probability of lobbying must fall between zero and one. This requirement limits the combinations of lobbying costs and

---

4. Bayes' theorem states that

$$\Pr\{\theta = \theta_H \mid I = 1\} = \frac{\Pr\{I = 1 \mid \theta = \theta_H\} \Pr\{\theta = \theta_H\}}{\Pr\{I = 1 \mid \theta = \theta_H\} \Pr\{\theta = \theta_H\} + \Pr\{I = 1 \mid \theta = \theta_L\} \Pr\{\theta = \theta_L\}},$$

where I is an indicator variable, with $I = 1$ when the SIG lobbies and $I = 0$ otherwise. Since $\Pr\{\theta = \theta_H\} = \Pr\{\theta = \theta_L\} = 1/2$, we have $\Pr\{\theta = \theta_H \mid I = 1\} = 1/(1 + \zeta)$ when $\Pr\{I = 1 \mid \theta = \theta_H\} = 1$ and $\Pr\{I = 1 \mid \theta = \theta_L\} = \zeta$.

preferences that admit an equilibrium with randomization by the
interest group. In particular, the fixed costs l_f cannot be too large
(e.g., if $l_f > \delta^2$, ζ is not a real number), nor can they be too small (if l_f
is close to zero, $\zeta > 1$). Nonetheless, it is easy to find parameter values
for which a mixed-strategy equilibrium exists. Suppose, for example,
that $\theta_L = 0$, $\theta_H = 1$, $\delta = 0.9$, and $l_f = 0.72$. Then, according to (5.3),
there exists an equilibrium with $\zeta = 2/3$. In this equilibrium, the
group lobbies with probability 2/3 when the state is θ_L and always
does so when the state is θ_H. When the policymaker observes that
lobbying has occurred, she updates her belief by placing a probability of 0.6 on the event that the state is θ_H. Therefore, $p_{lobby} = 0.6$.
When no lobbying occurs, she believes $\theta = \theta_L$ with probability one.
Thus, $p_{no\ lobby} = 0$. The SIG is indifferent between lobbying in state
θ_L and not, as is required for an equilibrium with randomization in
this state.[5] When the state is θ_H, it prefers to lobby. Notice that
$l_f < k_2 = 0.8$ in this example, so that whereas an equilibrium with
partial learning exists, there is no equilibrium in which the policymaker learns the state of the world for sure.

5.1.2 Single Lobby, Continuous Information

Now we take the random variable $\tilde{\theta}$ to be continuous. Whereas the
interest group knows the precise value of θ, the policymaker initially
perceives that all values of θ between θ_{min} and θ_{max} are possible and
equally likely. This situation is identical to the one we studied in
Section 4.1.4, except that now we include a cost of lobbying.

Recall from Chapter 4 the outcome when lobbying is costless. A
moderately biased interest group can convey some useful information to the policymaker, but the group can never communicate the
exact value of θ. Any attempts by the lobbyist to make fine distinctions between similar states of the world are spoiled by the temptation to exaggerate. So the lobbyist must resort to coarse statements
that identify ranges of possibilities. We referred to such outcomes as
"partition equilibria," because the interest group uses its messages to
partition the parameter space into a set of regions.

Now, when an interest group must pay to prepare a report, the
mere act of lobbying sends a signal to the policymaker. For some

---

5. In state θ_L the SIG has an ideal policy of 0.9. By lobbying, it achieves a net welfare level of $-(0.6 - 0.9)^2 - 0.72 = -0.81$, which is the same as what it achieves by
refraining.

values of θ, the SIG may be willing to bear the lobbying cost, while for other values it will prefer to save its money. In this situation the policymaker is able to partition the parameter space into two regions even before the lobbyist utters a sound. If the lobbyist appears, the policymaker realizes that θ belongs to one set of possible values, whereas if he fails to appear a different set is indicated. Thus, lobbying may provide information even when the words cannot be trusted.

Consider, for example, a situation in which no partition equilibrium exists, except for the ubiquitous babbling equilibrium. As we noted in Section 4.1.4, this situation arises, for example, when $\theta_{min} = 0$, $\theta_{max} = 24$, and $\delta > 6$. Any 2-partition equilibrium would require the existence of a value of θ, say θ_1, at which the SIG is indifferent between the outcomes that would result from the alternative reports of "high" and "low." If such a value were to exist, the policymaker would set $p = 12 + \theta_1/2$ on hearing a report of "high" and $p = \theta_1/2$ on hearing a report of "low." But with $\delta > 6$, the SIG would always have an incentive to report "high," no matter what the value of θ_1. Therefore, there is no partition of the states that gives the group an incentive to report honestly for all values of θ. Credible communication is impossible with these parameter values when lobbying is costless.

This pessimistic conclusion need not apply when lobbying is costly. The prospective cost l_f may be large enough to discourage lobbying for a range of low values of θ when the group's desired outcome is reasonably low anyway. But if the realized value of $\tilde{\theta}$ were higher, the incentive to lobby would be greater. The group might be willing to bear the requisite cost for a range of high values of θ. A 2-partition equilibrium will exist if, for some value of θ_1 between $\theta_{min} = 0$ and $\theta_{max} = 24$, the SIG is indifferent between paying the cost l_f and attaining the policy outcome $p = (24 + \theta_1)/2$, and accepting the less desirable policy $p = \theta_1/2$ at zero cost. We now seek to identify a value of θ_1 that engenders such indifference.

We suppose that lobbying leads the policymaker to infer that $\theta \geq \theta_1$ and that an absence of lobbying leads her to infer that $\theta \leq \theta_1$. Then, her response to lobbying would be to set $p_{lobby} = 12 + \theta_1/2$, while her response to silence would be to set $p_{no\ lobby} = \theta_1/2$. If the group pays the cost l_f, it achieves welfare of $U = -(12 - \theta_1/2 - \delta)^2 - l_f$ in state θ_1. If it saves its resources, it achieves $U = -(-\theta_1/2 - \delta)^2$. Indifference requires these two welfare levels to be equal, or that

$$\theta_1 = 12 - 2\delta + \frac{l_f}{12}.$$

Finally, we must check that this value of θ_1 falls in the feasible range between 0 and 24. For $\delta > 6$ and $l_f = 0$, clearly it does not. But if, for example, $l_f = 24$, then a 2-partition equilibrium exists for $\delta < 7$. And if $l_f = 48$, such an equilibrium exists for $\delta < 8$. A group with a relatively large bias may nonetheless lobby effectively, because costly actions speak louder (or at least more credibly) than costless words.

The same intuition extends to settings where the lobbyist can in fact make some credible distinctions using only his words. Suppose, for example, that $\theta_{\min} = 0$ and $\theta_{\max} = 24$, and that $2 < \delta < 6$. If lobbying were costless, there would exist a 2-partition equilibrium in which the lobbyist advises the policymaker whether θ exceeds $12 - 2\delta$. But no 3-partition equilibrium is possible. When lobbying is costly, a 3-partition equilibrium may exist. In such an equilibrium the lobbyist would appear before the policymaker whenever $\theta \geq \theta_1$ and would not appear whenever $\theta \leq \theta_1$. Thus, the act of lobbying or not partitions the parameter space into two regions. Then, when the lobbyist appears, he informs the policymaker whether θ exceeds some critical value θ_2 or not. An equilibrium with these features exists, for example, when $l_f = 12$ and $\delta = 3$. In general, better information can be conveyed when lobbying is somewhat costly than when it is free.[6]

Lobbying costs that are independent of content cannot, however, fully resolve the SIG's credibility problem. By showing itself willing to bear the fixed cost of lobbying, the group can at best distinguish one set of states from another. For any further distinction between the states, the group must rely on its words. When a lobbyist confronts a wary policymaker, he will be forced as before to resort to coarse statements about the policy environment. So the outcome still must be a partition equilibrium, albeit one in which the act of lobbying serves as a particularly persuasive statement.

5.1.3 Two Lobbies

We return now to the case of dichotomous information, but imagine that there are two interest groups with different policy objectives. SIG

---

6. Of course, if lobbying is very costly, the SIG may not consider it worthwhile to educate the policymaker, even if the lobbyist's words would be credible.

1 has a welfare function $U_1(p,\theta,l_1) = -(p-\theta-\delta_1)^2 - l_1$, where $l_1 = l_f$ when SIG 1 engages in lobbying and $l_1 = 0$ when it does not. Similarly, SIG 2 has a welfare function $U_2(p,\theta,l_2) = -(p-\theta-\delta_2)^2 - l_2$ with $l_2 = l_f$ when SIG 2 undertakes lobbying and $l_2 = 0$ when it does not. We suppose that both groups know the precise value of θ.

Like Biases
Consider first the case of like biases, that is, $\delta_2 > \delta_1 > 0$. If SIG 1 has a moderate bias relative to the policymaker and lobbying is not too expensive, then this group alone could serve as a credible informant. In particular, if

$$l_f \leq (\theta_H - \theta_L)(2\delta_1 + \theta_H - \theta_L) \tag{5.4}$$

and

$$l_f \geq (\theta_H - \theta_L)(2\delta_1 - \theta_H + \theta_L), \tag{5.5}$$

then there exists an equilibrium in which SIG 1 lobbies whenever the state is θ_H but not when it is θ_L, and SIG 2 never lobbies.[7] The policymaker looks to SIG 1 for information, and sets $p = \theta_H$ if and only if she is lobbied by this group. With this anticipated behavior by the policymaker, SIG 1 will elect to lobby in state θ_H but not in state θ_L, by the same reasoning as was described in Section 5.1.1. And given that SIG 1 is providing the policymaker with the relevant information, SIG 2 is happy to save its resources.

Of course, for some values of δ_2, the roles of the interest groups could be reversed. If the bias of SIG 2 were such that

$$l_f \leq (\theta_H - \theta_L)(2\delta_2 + \theta_H - \theta_L) \tag{5.6}$$

and

$$l_f \geq (\theta_H - \theta_L)(2\delta_2 - \theta_H + \theta_L), \tag{5.7}$$

then SIG 2 could play the role of the informant while SIG 1 free rides. In this alternative equilibrium, the policymaker turns to SIG 2 for information and ignores any lobbying by the other group. SIG 1 has no incentive to bear the lobbying cost under these circumstances.

But if the bias of SIG 2 is sufficiently large, then condition (5.7) will be violated, and SIG 2 cannot serve as a reliable informant. The policymaker would recognize the group's incentive to report "high"

---

7. Note that (5.4) is analogous to (5.1) and (5.5) is analogous to (5.2).

even when the state is θ_L, and thus would be well justified in disregarding any report from this highly biased group. Anticipating this reaction by the policymaker, SIG 1 cannot rely on its counterpart to provide the relevant policy advice. This group would find it worthwhile to lobby itself in state θ_H, assuming that the policymaker would be responsive to its actions.

We have identified equilibria with lobbying (in some states) by only one interest group. Might there also be situations in which both groups are "forced" to lobby when the state is θ_H, for fear that the policymaker would not be convinced by a single report? The answer to this question is a qualified "yes." Suppose that for some reason, the policymaker requires lobbying by both groups before she becomes convinced that the state is θ_H. If one group or none appears, she concludes that the state must be θ_L. With these beliefs, the policymaker sets $p = \theta_H$ when both groups lobby and $p = \theta_L$ when one group or neither group does so. Then, if (5.4) and (5.5) are satisfied, SIG 1 will deem it worthwhile to lobby in state θ_H but not in state θ_L. Similarly, if (5.6) and (5.7) are satisfied, SIG 2 will lobby in state θ_H but not in state θ_L. Since the policymaker never observes lobbying by only one group, her suspicion that such an occurrence would signal $\theta = \theta_L$ never is contradicted. Therefore, her beliefs about this event do not violate the requirements of a Bayesian equilibrium.

One might argue that such skepticism on the part of the policymaker is unjustified. Imagine that SIG 2 were to deviate from its equilibrium strategy by refraining from lobbying. This would force the policymaker to confront a situation with lobbying by only one group. In the event, she should ask herself whether it is more likely that the state is θ_L and SIG 1 chose to pay the lobbying cost, or that the state is θ_H and SIG 2 opted not to come. The first possibility could arise only if SIG 1 made an error, because it is not worthwhile for this group to lobby in state θ_L even if the action convinces the policymaker that the state is θ_H.[8] In contrast, the second possibility can be rationalized as an intentional decision by SIG 2. If this group believes that the policymaker will anyway draw the "correct" conclusion about the policy environment, it prefers to stay home and save the lobbying cost. Since the event of no lobbying by SIG 2 in state θ_H can be rationalized as a reasoned choice, but the same is not true of lobbying by SIG 1 in state θ_L, it might be more reasonable to assume

---

8. Technically, lobbying by SIG 1 is a dominated strategy in state θ_L.

that the policymaker believes that $\theta = \theta_H$ in case she observes lobbying by only one group. But, if she would draw this inference, then SIG 2 indeed will opt to save the lobbying cost, as long as it expects SIG 1 to bear it. By imposing restrictions on the policymaker's out-of-equilibrium beliefs, we call into question the plausibility of an equilibrium in which each of two similarly biased groups engages in lobbying.[9]

Opposite Biases
Now suppose the groups have opposite biases, that is, $\delta_1 > 0 > \delta_2$. In such circumstances, SIG 1 has an incentive to overstate the value of θ, whereas SIG 2 is tempted to understate it. We argue first that, despite the conflict of interests, there might exist an equilibrium in which only one of the groups engages in costly lobbying, while the other free rides.

Suppose that conditions (5.4) and (5.5) are satisfied. Then, if the policymaker expects the lobbying behavior of SIG 1 to reveal the state of the world, this group indeed prefers to lobby when the state is θ_H and to refrain when the state is θ_L. The policymaker can ignore the lobbying of SIG 2 and rely on SIG 1 for information. In the event, SIG 2 has no reason to lobby in state θ_L, because the outcome anyway is the one the group prefers. And it has no reason to lobby in state θ_H, because the policymaker would pay no heed to any (false) claim that $\theta = \theta_L$.

However, this asymmetric equilibrium is not the only possible outcome under these conditions. A more symmetric equilibrium exists in which each group lobbies the policymaker in one state of the world. In state θ_H, SIG 1 has a keen interest in having the policymaker understand that a high level of policy is indicated, because underestimation of θ by the policymaker would be especially costly to the group in this state. Similarly, in state θ_L, SIG 2 wants the policymaker to be well advised that a low level of policy is needed, because this group suffers most from a high policy level in this state. The policymaker might expect that SIG 1 will come to plead its case in state θ_H and that SIG 2 will appear in state θ_L. If both groups lobby or neither does so, the policymaker might see no basis for updating her beliefs. We might suppose that, in such circumstances, she would set

---

9. Technically, the outcome with lobbying by both interest groups meets the requirements of a perfect Bayesian equilibrium, but it does not survive when a refinement is made to the equilibrium concept.

the policy based on her prior understanding that each state is equally likely. With these beliefs, the policymaker's optimal strategy is to set $p = \theta_H$ when only SIG 1 lobbies, $p = \theta_L$ when only SIG 2 lobbies, and $p = (\theta_H + \theta_L)/2$ when both groups lobby or neither does.

We must check whether the groups' chosen actions are consistent with the policymaker's beliefs. The policymaker expects SIG 1 to lobby in state θ_H, but not in state θ_L. If the group were in fact to lobby in state θ_L, it could induce a policy of $p = (\theta_H + \theta_L)/2$ in place of $p = \theta_L$, at a cost of l_f. If it were to refrain in state θ_H, it would accept a policy of $p = (\theta_H + \theta_L)/2$ in place of $p = \theta_H$, while saving l_f. The organization prefers to lobby in state θ_H and refrain in θ_L when l_f falls in an intermediate range, namely, when

$$(\theta_H - \theta_L)\left(\delta_1 - \frac{\theta_H - \theta_L}{4}\right) < l_f < (\theta_H - \theta_L)\left(\delta_1 + \frac{\theta_H - \theta_L}{4}\right).$$

The policymaker expects SIG 2 to lobby in state θ_L but not in θ_H. By analogy to the arguments for SIG 1, the organization will behave in this manner if and only if

$$(\theta_H - \theta_L)\left(-\delta_2 - \frac{\theta_H - \theta_L}{4}\right) < l_f < (\theta_H - \theta_L)\left(-\delta_2 + \frac{\theta_H - \theta_L}{4}\right).$$

When these inequalities are satisfied, there exists an equilibrium in which each group advocates its cause in the state in which it feels most strongly. The conditions are satisfied, for example, when $\theta_H = 24$, $\theta_L = 0$, $\delta_1 = 5$, $\delta_2 = -4$, and $l_f = 100$.

Unknown Biases
Lohmann (1993) has suggested a different sort of equilibrium that can arise when the policymaker is unsure of the degrees to which the interest groups are biased. We can illustrate her points in a variant of our simple model.

Lohmann observes that extremist groups may be willing to undertake costly political actions regardless of the underlying policy conditions, whereas moderately biased groups may restrict their activity to times when circumstances most warrant it. If the policymaker does not know which groups are moderate and which are extreme, then the prevalence of political activity may serve as a signal of what the state is likely to be. When lobbying is confined to a few groups, the policymaker may suspect that only the extremists are active, and thus take an action that is appropriate in a moderate state of the world. When lobbying is more widespread, she may conclude that even the moderates are active, and then she will realize that conditions call for a more extreme policy response.

To illustrate this idea, we consider again a setting with two like-biased interest groups, where SIG 2 has a greater bias relative to the policymaker than SIG 1. Suppose that the policymaker is aware that there are two groups with positive preference parameters δ_1 and δ_2, but she does not know which group is the moderate one and which is extreme. To begin, let us assume as before that both groups know the policy state, which is either θ_H or θ_L. Then, if conditions (5.4) and (5.5) are satisfied but (5.7) is violated, there can be no equilibrium in which a single lobbying report leads the policymaker to conclude that the state is θ_H. If the policymaker were to draw such a conclusion from one report, the more biased SIG 2 would have an incentive to misreport the state whenever $\theta = \theta_L$. An equilibrium does, however, exist in which both groups lobby when the state is θ_H and neither does so when the state is θ_L. The policymaker relies on confirmation from both groups to assure herself that the reliable informant is among those who are paying to send a signal. Note that it does not pay for the more biased SIG to lobby in state θ_L, because the group recognizes that its counterpart has no incentive to lobby and that its own report by itself will not be convincing.

An even more striking outcome is possible when the interest groups are unsure about the state of the world. Then the more biased group may opt to lobby the policymaker no matter what it believes about the policy environment. That is, SIG 2 may behave as a pure advocate, always alleging that the state is θ_H. The less biased SIG 1, in contrast, will engage in lobbying if and only if it believes that the state is more likely to be θ_H than θ_L. Then the policymaker can use the level of political activity as an imperfect signal of the policy state. In the equilibrium we shall describe, the policymaker chooses a relatively high level of policy when both SIGs come to argue for such, and a lower level of policy when only one group appears to plead its case.

To capture the groups' uncertainty about the policy environment, we assume that each one observes an imperfect indicator or "signal" of the true state. If SIG 1 observes the signal σ_H, then, with probability $\zeta > 1/2$, the true state is θ_H. But with probability $1 - \zeta$, the facts

observed by SIG 1 are misleading, and the true state instead is θ_L.
Similarly, if SIG 1 observes the signal σ_L, then, with probability ζ, the
true state is θ_L. With probability $1 - \zeta$, the state is θ_H. Meanwhile, SIG
2 observes an independent signal about the state of the world. Its
signal corresponds to the true state with probability ζ, but suggests a
misleading conclusion about the environment with probability $1 - \zeta$.
Both groups know the accuracy of their observations, and they know
that the other group also may be misled about the policy conditions.

Consider first what the policymaker thinks when two lobby groups
appear to argue for a high level of the policy. She knows that one or
the other of the groups has a large bias and presumes that this group
would engage in lobbying no matter what it had observed. She also
knows that the other group is more moderate, and suspects that its
willingness to bear the lobbying cost means that it has observed the
signal σ_H. The policymaker updates her beliefs about the distribution
of $\tilde{\theta}$ using Bayes' rule. This leads her to conclude that with probability ζ the state is θ_H and with probability $1 - \zeta$ it is θ_L. Using these
updated beliefs, the policymaker sets the policy level to maximize
her expected welfare, which implies that $p(2) = \zeta\theta_H + (1 - \zeta)\theta_L$. Here,
$p(j)$ denotes the policy that is implemented when j groups appear
before the policymaker to argue for a high level of policy.

Now consider the policymaker's reasoning when only one lobbyist
appears. In equilibrium, this event suggests to the policymaker that
the more moderate group chose not to bear the lobbying cost. Since
the more moderate group refrains from lobbying if and only if it
observes σ_L, the policymaker concludes that with probability ζ the
true state is θ_L and with probability $1 - \zeta$ it is θ_H. Accordingly, she
sets $p(1) = (1 - \zeta)\theta_H + \zeta\theta_L$ when only one group lobbies.

What happens if neither group chooses to lobby? A complete
absence of lobbying is inconsistent with the hypothesized strategy of
SIG 2. Accordingly, Bayes' rule does not restrict what the policymaker would make of such an event. We assume that the policymaker interprets an absence of lobbying as an indication that the
more moderate lobby observed σ_L and that the extreme lobby erred
in failing to report. Moreover, the policymaker does not see the mistake by the more extreme group as revealing anything about what
signal the group might have observed. With this interpretation of the
events that would lead neither group to lobby, the policymaker concludes that with probability ζ the true state is θ_L and with probability

$1 - \zeta$ it is θ_H. These are the same beliefs as when one group lobbies, so $p(0) = p(1) = (1 - \zeta)\theta_H + \zeta\theta_L$.[10]

Now let us investigate the incentives facing the interest groups, who anticipate the policymaker's responses to the various lobbying outcomes. We begin with the more moderate group, which is SIG 1 in our example. This group expects its counterpart to lobby no matter what signal it observes. Accordingly, it expects its own lobbying behavior to make the difference between two active lobbying campaigns and one. If SIG 1 chooses to lobby, the resulting policy will be $p(2)$. If it refrains, the policy will be $p(1)$. When the group observes σ_H, it believes that with probability ζ the true state is θ_H and with probability $1 - \zeta$ it is θ_L. By lobbying, the group achieves an expected welfare level of $-\zeta[p(2) - \theta_H - \delta_1]^2 - (1 - \zeta)[p(2) - \theta_L - \delta_1]^2 - l_f$. By refraining, it achieves $-\zeta[p(1) - \theta_H - \delta_1]^2 - (1 - \zeta)[p(1) - \theta_L - \delta_1]^2$. We have supposed that the group prefers to lobby when it observes σ_H, which requires that

$$l_f \leq (\theta_H - \theta_L)(2\zeta - 1)[2\delta_1 + (\theta_H - \theta_L)(2\zeta - 1)].$$

Similarly, when the group observes σ_L, it believes that with probability ζ the true state is θ_L and with probability $1 - \zeta$ it is θ_H. Lobbying yields the group expected welfare of $-\zeta[p(2) - \theta_L - \delta_2]^2 - (1 - \zeta)[p(2) - \theta_H - \delta_2]^2 - l_f$, whereas refraining yields welfare of $-\zeta[p(1) - \theta_L - \delta_2]^2 - (1 - \zeta)[p(1) - \theta_H - \delta_2]^2$. The group prefers to conserve its resources if and only if

$$l_f \geq (\theta_H - \theta_L)(2\zeta - 1)[2\delta_1 - (\theta_H - \theta_L)(2\zeta - 1)].$$

Now we turn our attention to the more extreme SIG 2. The lobbying behavior of this group will make a difference in two situations. First, if the true state is θ_H and SIG 1 has observed the (accurate) signal σ_H, then by lobbying the group induces a policy of $p(2)$ in place of $p(1)$. Second, if the true state is θ_L but SIG 2 has observed the (misleading) signal σ_H, then by lobbying the group again induces the policymaker to set $p = p(2)$ instead of $p = p(1)$. Since the bias of SIG 2 is large, it may prefer the higher policy $p(2)$ even when the true

---

10. Alternatively, we might assume that the policymaker interprets a failure to lobby by the more extreme group as indicating that the group more likely observed σ_L, the pattern that makes a high policy level less imperative. With this interpretation, the policymaker sees a failure to lobby by either group as a stronger indication that $\theta = \theta_L$, in which case $p(0) < p(1)$. Such an assumption would expand the range of parameters for which the hypothesized strategies constitute equilibrium behavior.

state is θ_L. Moreover, the group may be willing to bear the lobbying expense on the chance that its counterpart has (rightly or wrongly) observed the signal σ_H, so that its own lobbying behavior will make the difference to the outcome. By lobbying when it observes σ_L, SIG 2 achieves expected welfare of[11]

$$-\zeta^2[p(1) - \theta_L - \delta_2]^2 - \zeta(1 - \zeta)[p(2) - \theta_L - \delta_2]^2$$

$$-(1 - \zeta)\zeta[p(2) - \theta_H - \delta_2]^2 - (1 - \zeta)^2[p(1) - \theta_H - \delta_2]^2 - l_f.$$

By refraining, the SIG ensures that the policy will be $p(1)$, in which case its expected welfare is $-\zeta[p(1) - \theta_L - \delta_2]^2 - (1 - \zeta)[p(1) - \theta_H - \delta_2]^2$. Lobbying yields higher expected welfare for SIG 2 than not lobbying if and only if

$$l_f \leq 4\delta_2(\theta_H - \theta_L)\zeta(1 - \zeta)(2\zeta - 1). \tag{5.8}$$

When condition (5.8) is satisfied, SIG 2 prefers to lobby even when it finds evidence that the state is more likely to be θ_L. It has an even greater incentive to lobby when it sees indications that the state is θ_H. Thus, the more biased group lobbies indiscriminately. This group pays the cost of advocacy with the hope that its counterpart will observe σ_H, in which case its own message will confirm the other's report. Of course, the policymaker anticipates the more biased group's behavior and discounts its actions appropriately.

We have identified conditions for an equilibrium with pure advocacy by one interest group and informative lobbying by another. First, the policymaker must be unsure which one is the extreme group. Otherwise she would simply ignore its lobbying, and then there would be no point for the group to incur the cost. Second, the advocate must have a sufficiently large bias, so that condition (5.8) is satisfied. When SIG 2 has a large bias, it is willing to pay l_f on the off chance that its actions will make the difference to the policy outcome. This difference comes when the state is θ_H, but also when it is θ_L and yet the more moderate lobby has observed the misleading signal, σ_H. In this latter situation, the group can advocate a high level of policy (which it always prefers) and the other lobby will support its argu-

---

11. The first term in this expression is the probability that both the true state is θ_L and SIG 1 has observed σ_L, multiplied by the utility in state θ_L from a policy of $p(1)$. The second term is the probability that the true state is θ_L but SIG 1 has observed the misleading signal, σ_H, multiplied by the utility for SIG 2 in state θ_L from a policy of $p(2)$. The remaining terms have similar interpretations.

ments. Third, condition (5.8) requires that ζ not be too close to 1. The more accurate the information available to the interest groups, the less likely it is that the moderate group will observe an incorrect signal. The extreme group needs the existence of such inaccurate signals to give reason to its lobbying campaign.

5.2   Endogenous Lobbying Costs

We have seen that lobbying can serve to signal an interest group's unverifiable information. If the lobbying costs fall in a certain range, then the policymaker can learn something about the policy environment by observing whether a group is willing to pay them. However, the value of this signal is limited. If the costs are too high, the groups will rarely if ever be willing to bear them. If the costs are too low, then the willingness to pay reveals little or nothing. And, at best, a fixed lobbying cost can be used by a group to distinguish one set of policy states from another.

But lobbying costs need not be fixed. Interest groups have discretion over the size and scope of their lobbying efforts. Indeed, we often see SIGs waging lavish campaigns when it would seem that the information could be communicated more frugally. Why would an interest group pay more than is necessary to educate a policymaker? One answer might be that the group is trying to lend credibility to its words in situations where the facts are favorable to its cause. In this section we allow an interest group to choose what it wishes to spend on its lobbying campaign. We ask whether the group might spend more than is necessary, and whether the ability to overpay facilitates communication.

5.2.1   Dichotomous Information

Our model is the same as that in Section 5.1.1 in all respects but one. An interest group knows the precise value of a policy-relevant variable θ, which may be either θ_L or θ_H. The policymaker believes initially that the alternative values of θ are equally likely. The SIG has an objective to maximize $U(p, \theta, l) = -(p - \theta - \delta)^2 - l$, while the policymaker seeks to maximize $G = -(p - \theta)^2$. All of this is the same as before. But now we allow the interest group to choose the scale of its lobbying campaign; it can make the lobbying cost l large by sending a large team of lawyers and experts to the policymaker or by running a lavish advertising campaign. Or it can keep costs down by hiring a single lobbyist to argue its case.

We will show that the freedom to choose the scale of lobbying can make the difference in a group's effort to communicate dichotomous information. In particular, when lobbying costs are fixed, there exists an equilibrium with full revelation only for certain values of l_f. But when they are variable, an equilibrium with full revelation always exists. In this equilibrium, the interest group spends nothing on lobbying if the policy environment indicates a low level of the policy. If conditions indicate a high level of the policy, the group spends enough to convince the policymaker that the reality could not be otherwise.

To make this point, we need to construct an equilibrium in which the policymaker discerns the state of the world by observing the group's actions. To this end, let l_L be the amount that the SIG spends on lobbying in state θ_L and let l_H be the amount it spends in θ_H. We know that if the policymaker concludes that the state is θ_H, she will set a policy of $p = \theta_H$. And if she concludes the state is θ_L, she will set a policy of $p = \theta_L$. Our task is to find a lobbying strategy for the interest group that validates this behavior by the policymaker.

We argue first that, in an equilibrium with full revelation, $l_L = 0$. With full revelation, the policymaker infers the state of the world from the lobbying behavior of the SIG. In state θ_L, the policy outcome is $p = \theta_L$, which is worse for the interest group than the alternative of $p = \theta_H$.[12] There is no reason for the SIG to bear a cost to achieve its less desired outcome when by spending nothing on lobbying, it would suffer the same fate.

This leaves us to determine only l_H. On the one hand, the spending on lobbying in state θ_H must be large enough to be convincing. That is, it must be sufficiently large that the SIG would not wish to make the outlay in state θ_L and thereby deceive the policymaker. On the other, l_H must not be so large that the SIG would be unwilling to pay it in state θ_H. The SIG will not wish to pay the lobbying cost in state θ_L to signal falsely that the state is θ_H if and only if $-\delta^2 \geq -(\theta_H - \theta_L - \delta)^2 - l_H$, or

---

12. We are assuming here that $\delta > (\theta_H - \theta_L)/2$, or that purely verbal arguments would not be credible in state θ_L. Otherwise there is an equilibrium with full revelation with $l_L = l_H = 0$. The SIG could spend nothing on its lobbying campaign and simply report the state of the world to the policymaker.

$l_H \geq (\theta_H - \theta_L)[2\delta - (\theta_H - \theta_L)] \equiv k_2.$

This is the same condition as (5.2), except that now the SIG can choose l_H to ensure that it is met. The SIG is willing to pay the lobbying cost in state θ_H if and only if $-\delta^2 - l_H \geq -(\theta_L - \theta_H - \delta)^2$, or

$l_H \leq (\theta_H - \theta_L)[2\delta + (\theta_H - \theta_L)] \equiv k_1.$

Again, the condition is the same as (5.1). It follows that a credible lobbying campaign requires a lobbying cost between k_1 and k_2, just as before. But since $k_1 > k_2$ and the scale of lobbying is variable, it is always possible to find a value of l_H that falls in the required range.

We have established the existence of "separating equilibria." In these equilibria, the policymaker infers that the state must be θ_H when the interest group spends l_H or more on lobbying. If the group spends less than l_H, she concludes that the state must be θ_L. The lobbyist's cost l_H can be any number between k_1 and k_2. When the policymaker holds these beliefs, it is optimal for the SIG to spend l_H on lobbying if the state is θ_H and to spend nothing if the state is θ_L. The group's optimal behavior is consistent with the policymaker's beliefs.[13]

To reiterate, when an interest group can vary the scale of its lobbying effort, it can always find a way to communicate its policy-relevant information to the policymaker. This ability to communicate need not be a blessing, however. As we noted earlier, the SIG's welfare may be lower from an ex ante perspective when the policy-maker expects the group to lobby in certain policy environments than it would be if the opportunity for lobbying were nonexistent. Suppose, for example, that the policymaker expects the group to pay k_2 when the state is θ_H, which is the smallest amount that ensures credibility. If the policymaker has these expectations, the group will do so to avoid an outcome with $p = \theta_L$. In the equilibrium with signaling, expected welfare for the group (before it learns the true value

---

13. Among the separating equilibria, many would consider the one with $l_H = k_2$ to be the most compelling. When $l_H = k_2$, the cost of lobbying is the smallest it can be while remaining potentially credible. If the policymaker were to remain skeptical when she observed a campaign of size k_2, the SIG might choose to pay k_2 and offer a compelling verbal argument. The argument would be that, were the true state to be θ_L, the group would not have been willing to pay even k_2. So the group's willingness to pay k_2 ought to confer credibility on its claim that the state is θ_H. Formally, the equilibrium with $l_H = k_2$ is the only one that satisfies the "intuitive criterion" proposed by Cho and Kreps (1987) as a refinement of the equilibrium concept for signaling games.

of θ) is $EU = -\delta^2 - k_2/2$. In comparison, if there were no possibility of lobbying, then the policymaker would always set $p = (\theta_L + \theta_H)/2$, and the expected welfare of the group would be $-\delta^2 - (\theta_H - \theta_L)^2/4$. Thus, the SIG might actually be better off if there were no possibility of lobbying, as is the case when $\delta > 3(\theta_H - \theta_L)/4$.

5.2.2 Many States of Nature

The same logic applies when the policy environment has more than two possible states. The interest group might refrain from lobbying when conditions indicate the lowest possible level of policy, and it might undertake lobbying of some sort whenever conditions indicate a higher level of policy. Moreover, the policymaker might expect the scale of the lobbying effort to vary with the underlying conditions, so that the SIG devotes more resources to lobbying the greater is the value of θ. Then the policymaker would respond to more costly lobbying campaigns with ever greater levels of policy. We illustrate this logic first for the case of three states of nature and then for the case of a continuous random variable $\tilde{\theta}$.

First, let there be three possible values of θ, θ_H, θ_M, and θ_L, with $\theta_H > \theta_M > \theta_L$. Suppose the policymaker expects the group's lobbying behavior to be revealing about the policy environment. In particular, she expects the group to spend nothing on lobbying when the state is θ_L, to spend at least $l_M > 0$ when the state is θ_M, and to spend at least $l_H > l_M$ when the state is θ_H. Then she responds by setting $p = \theta_L$ when the SIG fails to lobby, $p = \theta_M$ when the lobbying expense is at least l_M but less than l_H, and $p = \theta_H$ when the lobbying expense is l_H or more.

To justify beliefs of this sort, we need to find values of l_M and l_H that give the SIG the appropriate incentives. We seek the smallest such values that do the trick. Note first that the incentives facing the SIG in state θ_L are similar to those in a two-state environment. The group can pay nothing for lobbying and accept a policy of $p = \theta_L$, or it can conduct a moderate lobbying campaign and induce an outcome of $p = \theta_M$. The smallest lobbying cost l_M that leaves the group with no incentive to lobby in state θ_L is

$$l_M = (\theta_M - \theta_L)[2\delta - (\theta_M - \theta_L)].$$

The group also has the option to conduct a vigorous lobbying campaign in state θ_L so as to fool the policymaker into setting $p = \theta_H$.

However, this option will never be attractive to the SIG in circumstances in which it has no incentive to engage in large-scale lobbying even when the true state is θ_M.

We consider next the group's incentives in state θ_M. With $l_M = (\theta_M - \theta_L)[2\delta - (\theta_M - \theta_L)]$, the group always prefers to lobby in state θ_M than to accept a low level of policy. The group might, however, be tempted to intensify its lobbying effort and thereby induce a higher level of policy. For the group not to engage in such misleading behavior, we need the *extra* cost of the larger lobbying campaign to offset the benefit from having a high level of policy in state θ_M instead of an intermediate level of policy. Thus, $l_H - l_M = (\theta_H - \theta_M)[2\delta - (\theta_H - \theta_M)]$, which (with the equation for l_M) implies

$$l_H = 2\delta(\theta_H - \theta_L) - (\theta_H - \theta_M)^2 - (\theta_M - \theta_L)^2.$$

The final thing we need to verify is that the SIG is willing to bear the high cost of lobbying when the state actually is θ_H. But we know by construction that the group is indifferent between conducting a modest campaign and an elaborate one when the true state is θ_M. The group places an even greater value on a high level of policy when the state is θ_H than when it is θ_M. It follows that the group must be willing to spend l_H when the state is θ_H to avoid an outcome with $p = \theta_M$.

We have thus identified a pair of lobbying costs, l_M and l_H, with the property that, if the policymaker expects the group to undertake lobbying of these differing intensities in the different states, the SIG will find it optimal to do as expected. In other words, we have described a separating equilibrium in which the policymaker discerns the policy state from the interest group's lobbying behavior.

We have assumed in this section that all lobbying expenses are voluntary. That is, the SIG might choose to bear costs in order to buy credibly, but none of these costs are strictly necessary for it to prepare and transmit its report. As long as we maintain this assumption, we can readily extend the arguments to any number of states of the policy environment. Even if θ is a continuous variable, there exists a lobbying equilibrium in which the group's lobbying behavior signals the state of the world. Our next task is to construct this equilibrium with full revelation of a continuous variable. After that, we will show that problems reappear when lobbying requires some minimum expense.

Let $\tilde{\theta}$ represent a continuous random variable that lies between $\theta_{\min}$ and $\theta_{\max}$. The policymaker believes initially that all values in the range are equally likely.[14] But she updates her beliefs based on the size of the interest group's lobbying effort. In particular, she anticipates that the SIG will spend an amount $l(\theta)$ in state of the world θ, where each state gives rise to a different level of expenditure. Because she associates each level of spending with a different state, she believes that her observation of the SIG's behavior allows her to identify the state of the world. Her response is to set $p = \theta$ for the value of θ she believes to prevail.

As before, we must ensure that the policymaker's beliefs are in line with the interest group's incentives. Two properties of the function $l(\theta)$ are needed to ensure this. First, we need $l(\theta_{\min}) = 0$, because the SIG has no reason to spend on lobbying when the result will anyway be the lowest conceivable level of policy. Second, we need the marginal cost of signaling a slightly higher value of θ to match the marginal benefit to the SIG in any state from having the policymaker believe that θ is a bit higher. The marginal benefit to the SIG from gaining a slightly higher policy than $p = \theta$ in state θ is 2δ. The marginal cost of signaling a higher value of θ is $l'(\theta)$. Equating the two gives $l'(\theta) = 2\delta$. Finally, combining the two requirements, we have a candidate for the lobbying function, namely

$$l(\theta) = 2\delta(\theta - \theta_{\min}). \tag{5.9}$$

We need to check that when the policymaker expects the SIG to spend according to $l(\theta) = 2\delta(\theta - \theta_{\min})$, the SIG actually has an incentive to behave in this manner. In state θ, the group could fool the policymaker into believing that the state is instead x by spending $l(x)$ on its lobbying campaign, where $l(x) = 2\delta(x - \theta_{\min})$. If it did so, the policymaker would set the policy $p = x$, and the SIG would achieve a welfare level of $U(x) = -(x - \theta - \delta)^2 - 2\delta(x - \theta_{\min})$. But note that $U(x)$ reaches a maximum at $x = \theta$ for all values of θ, which implies that the interest group has no incentive to mislead the policymaker. Thus, we have identified a lobbying function that generates full revelation when lobbying entails no fixed cost.[15]

---

14. Nothing in the remainder of this section hinges on this assumption.

15. Ball (1995) solves a related problem with more general utility functions, but with the added restriction that the function $l(\theta)$ must be linear. We have restricted the utility function to be quadratic, but we placed no restrictions on the shape of $l(\theta)$. With quadratic utility, the equilibrium lobbying function is linear, but it would not be so with other forms of the utility function.

Now let us suppose that the interest group must spend at least l_f to prepare a policy brief and present it to the policymaker. It can spend more than this amount if it wishes, but it can avoid the expense only by choosing not to lobby at all. We first observe that a minimum lobbying expense of l_f precludes the existence of an equilibrium in which the policymaker becomes fully informed. If the policymaker were to learn the policy state for all values of θ, she would implement $p = \hat{\theta}$ in state $\hat{\theta}$ and $p = \theta_{min}$ in state θ_{min}. But if $\hat{\theta}$ is very close to θ_{min}, the benefit to the SIG from having a policy of $\hat{\theta}$ instead of θ_{min} is very small. The interest group would not be willing to pay the minimum cost of l_f in order to persuade the policymaker that the state is $\hat{\theta}$, when a policy of θ_{min} could be had at zero cost.

We construct an equilibrium in which the SIG refrains from lobbying for a range of values of θ between θ_{min} and some θ_1, and its lobbying behavior reveals the state of the world for all values of $\theta \geq \theta_1$. In such an equilibrium, the policymaker sets the policy $p = (\theta_{min} + \theta_1)/2$ whenever no lobbying takes place, and she sets $p = \theta$ when she infers that the state must be θ from the fact that the SIG has borne a lobbying expense of $l(\theta)$. To construct this equilibrium, we need to find a value of θ_1 and a function $l(\theta)$ with the properties that (i) $l(\theta) \geq l_f$ for all $\theta \geq \theta_1$; (ii) the SIG has no incentive to lobby for any $\theta < \theta_1$; and (iii) the SIG wishes to spend exactly $l(\theta)$ on lobbying for all $\theta \geq \theta_1$.

For (ii) to be true, the SIG must be indifferent between lobbying and not lobbying in state θ_1. Let us suppose that the group could convey the information that $\theta = \theta_1$ by conducting the minimally feasible lobbying campaign, which costs l_f. Then the SIG will be indifferent between paying this expense and not in state θ_1 if and only if $-[(\theta_{min} + \theta_1)/2 - \theta_1 - \delta]^2 = -\delta^2 - l_f$, or

$$\theta_1 = \theta_{min} + 2\left(\sqrt{\delta^2 + l_f} - \delta\right). \tag{5.10}$$

For (iii) to be true, the spending schedule must have a marginal benefit of signaling a higher state equal to the marginal cost. This in turn requires $l'(\theta) = 2\delta$, as we have seen before. A lobbying function that has all the required properties is depicted in figure 5.1. Its equation is

$$l(\theta) = \begin{cases} 0 & \text{for} \quad \theta_{min} \leq \theta < \theta_1 \\ l_f + 2\delta(\theta - \theta_1) & \text{for} \quad \theta_1 \leq \theta \leq \theta_{max} \end{cases}.$$

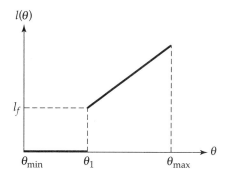

Figure 5.1
Equilibrium Lobbying Function with a Minimum Cost of Lobbying

To summarize, when lobbying requires a minimum outlay, the policymaker cannot discern the appropriate policy in all states of the world. In particular, there is a range of states that indicate a low level of policy for which the interest group refrains from lobbying. Then the policymaker must set a policy that is suitable for an average state in this (low) range. For states that indicate a higher level of policy, the interest group is able to communicate a precise report about θ. It does so by varying its lobbying expenses positively with θ in such a way that the size of its campaign signals the prevailing state.

5.2.3   Multiple Interest Groups

If there is no minimum cost to lobbying, then the presence of additional interest groups that know the state of the world does not change the story much. In particular, there always exist equilibria in which the policymaker becomes fully informed. The policymaker might rely on a particular group to signal the state of the world while the others enjoy a free ride. Or she may insist that several groups incur lobbying expenses before she is ready to update her views about θ. Although the policymaker has no reason to insist on confirmation from several groups when each group is fully informed, the SIGs would be willing to bear the expense if that is what it would take to convince her.

Lohmann (1995) has studied the more interesting situation that arises when several groups have some knowledge about the policy environment but none is perfectly informed. In our setting, we can imagine a situation with two like-biased SIGs, each of which observes an independent, and possibly misleading, indicator of the state of the world. For example, when the state is θ_H, either SIG may observe with some reasonably high probability an indication that the value of θ is high. But with a smaller probability, a particular group may instead observe a signal that the state is θ_L. Similarly, a group may observe indications that the state is θ_L when actually it is so, or it may be misled into thinking that it is more likely that the state is θ_H.

If the groups' biases cause them to prefer higher levels of policy than the policymaker prefers in both states of the world, they may prefer that the policymaker believe the state is θ_H no matter what evidence they have observed. But they will be especially keen to have her believe the state is θ_H when they have observed indications that this actually is so. For this reason, it is possible to construct an equilibrium in which SIG 1 spends l_1 on lobbying when it observes a signal that the state is θ_H and spends nothing on lobbying when it observes a signal that the state is θ_L, and SIG 2 similarly spends l_2 on lobbying when it observes indications that the state is θ_H and nothing when it observes otherwise. In the equilibrium, the policymaker takes the acts of lobbying to reveal the evidence that each SIG has observed, and sets a policy accordingly. The endogenous lobbying costs l_1 and l_2 that apply in equilibrium are such that each group has an incentive to behave as expected. Since the calculation of these costs is a bit tedious, we will suppress the details and discuss only the qualitative features of the equilibrium.

First, consider the policymaker. She will observe lobbying by either two SIGs, or one, or none. If both groups lobby, this is an indication (in equilibrium) that each has observed the signal that the state is more likely to be θ_H. This can happen in state θ_L only if both signals happen to be inaccurate, that is, with probability $(1 - \zeta)^2$, where ζ again denotes the probability that a given observation by a SIG is not misleading. The policymaker updates her beliefs after being lobbied by both SIGs and sets the policy equal to her new expected value of $\tilde{\theta}$, which implies $p(2) = [1 - (1 - \zeta)^2]\theta_H + [(1 - \zeta)^2]\theta_L$. Here we use $p(2)$ to denote the policy that results when two groups lobby (an analogous notation for the other cases).

Similarly, if neither group engages in lobbying, the policymaker infers that both must have observed a signal that the state is θ_L. This suggests to her that the state is θ_L with probability $1 - (1 - \zeta)^2$ and is θ_H with probability $(1 - \zeta)^2$, where the latter is the probability that both signals of θ_L were misleading. A policymaker who sees no lobbying sets $p(0) = [1 - (1 - \zeta)^2]\theta_L + [(1 - \zeta)^2]\theta_H$.

Finally, if one group lobbies and the other does not, then in equilibrium the two SIGs must have observed different signals. Each signal has the same precision, and each state has the same ex ante probability. It follows from Bayes' rule that the policymaker's beliefs do not change in the face of such conflicting evidence. Accordingly, she sets $p(1) = (\theta_H + \theta_L)/2$ when she sees lobbying by exactly one interest group.

To complete the construction of the equilibrium, we would need to find the values of l_1 and l_2 that give the SIGs an incentive to lobby when they think it more likely that the state is θ_H, but not when they think it more likely that the state is θ_L. Suppose, for example, that SIG 1 has observed an indication that the state is θ_L. Based on this observation, the group can update its beliefs about the likelihood that its counterpart has observed the same signal as it has, or that it has observed a conflicting indication that the state is θ_H. Then it can calculate the probability that its own lobbying campaign would make the difference between policy outcomes of $p(1)$ versus $p(0)$ or the difference between outcomes of $p(2)$ versus $p(1)$. Furthermore, it can calculate the probability of each of these events happening when the true state is θ_H and when the true state is θ_L. (Note that the interest group is aware that its own observations may have been misleading.) Putting all of this together, the group can calculate the increase in its expected welfare that comes from lobbying after it has observed an indication that the state is θ_L, compared to its expected welfare from not lobbying in that situation. An equilibrium value of l_1 must be large enough to dissuade the group from lobbying when it has observed an indication that the state is θ_L but not so large as to discourage lobbying when the group has observed an indication that the state is θ_H. A similar calculation applies for l_2.

The equilibrium described here has two noteworthy features. First, the greater the bias in a group's preferences relative to the policymaker's preferences, the more it must spend to convince her that its evidence indicates a high level of policy. Thus, if both groups lobby, the more lavish campaign will be conducted by the group with the more extreme preference bias. Second, the greater the number of groups that are active in lobbying, the higher the policy level that results in equilibrium. Lohmann has shown, in a related model, that these findings extend to situations with any number of SIGs.

5.3   Access Costs

Not all lobbying expenses are real costs of collecting and disseminating information. Sometimes the policymakers impose costs on interest groups by insisting that they contribute to their reelection campaigns before agreeing to meet with them. Indeed, when interest groups contribute to political campaigns, they often claim that what they are buying is access. Access allows a group a chance to plead its case. If the politicians require such payments, many groups will be ready to comply.

In this section we study situations in which an interest group must contribute to a politician's campaign if it wishes to lobby for a preferred policy. Why might a politician require such a payment, when the information the group has to report is potentially valuable to her? We entertain three possible answers to this question. First, the policymaker might consider her time to be a scarce resource. Then she may use an access fee to ensure that the value of the information exceeds the opportunity cost of her time. Second, the policymaker may value campaign contributions in their own right, as we shall emphasize in Chapter 7 and beyond. She may be willing to trade off a loss of information from those who are unwilling to pay the fee for the benefit of raising valuable funds. Finally, the politician may use access fees to help distinguish moderate interest groups from ones that are more extreme, in situations where she is unsure about the extent of a group's policy bias.

An issue that immediately arises when we think about access fees is the timing of when they must be paid. Must a SIG secure its visitation privileges before it knows exactly what its lobbyist will advise the policymaker, or can it wait to buy access until after it becomes better informed? In reality, both of these sequences are relevant. The descriptive literature tells of cases in which contributions are paid well before the groups know what issues will be on the table and even before they know whether a politician will succeed in her election bid.[16] In these cases, the purchase of access can be seen as happening when the group has little or no informational advantage vis-à-vis the policymaker. In other cases, however, groups approach policymakers with requests for an audience in order to lobby on specific issues. These may be issues that appear on the legislative

---

16. See, for example, Bauer, de Sola Pool, and Dexter (1963) or Sabato (1981).

agenda, and the groups may already be knowledgeable about them. Under these circumstances, a willingness to lobby conveys information to the policymaker about the state of the world. Since such situations are similar to what we have already studied in Section 5.2,[17] we shall focus our attention here on access fees that must be paid when the groups are still imperfectly informed.

In this section we investigate the interaction between a policymaker and a single interest group. The policymaker wishes to enact a policy that is appropriate to the policy environment. But she also values campaign contributions and recognizes the opportunity cost of her time. We write her welfare function as the sum of three components, each representing one of these concerns. In particular, we take $G = -\lambda(p - \theta)^2 + (1 - \lambda)c - \hat{\tau}$, where c denotes the contributions amassed by the policymaker, and $\hat{\tau}$ equals some $\tau > 0$ if the policymaker devotes time to listening to the lobbyist and zero if she does not. As before, the policymaker does not initially know the value of θ but regards it as the realization of a uniformly distributed random variable that may take on values between θ_{min} and θ_{max}.

For simplicity, we ignore any asymmetries of information that may exist at the time that access must be secured. Instead, we assume that the SIG, like the policymaker, initially regards the values between θ_{min} and θ_{max} as being equally likely. The SIG's objective is to maximize $-E(\tilde{p} - \tilde{\theta} - \delta)^2 - c$, where the expectation is taken over the possible values that $\tilde{\theta}$ might take and the policies that would ensue. If the SIG buys itself a place on the policymaker's schedule, it will have an opportunity to lobby before the policy decision is made. By then the SIG will know the true value of θ and can make any report about it that would be credible to the policymaker.

5.3.1 Group with a Known Bias

Suppose, to begin, that the policymaker knows the extent of the interest group's bias. If the policymaker can dictate the terms of access, she can require a contribution equal to the largest amount that the SIG would be willing to pay. We ask now, How much would

17. Indeed, the previously cited paper by Lohmann (1995) on signaling by multiple interest groups refers to the costs borne by the groups as "campaign contributions" and the quid pro quo as "access." When the costs are borne ex post in order to lend credibility to a report, it does not matter for the argument whether these funds go to public displays (e.g., advertising) or whether they go into the politician's campaign coffers.

the group pay for an opportunity to lobby, and will that amount be enough, together with the expected value of the information, to cover the opportunity cost of the policymaker's time?

In Chapter 4 we saw that if lobbying takes place, the SIG at best will be able to advise the policymaker of a range of values that includes θ. The lobbying game may have several different equilibria, each with a different number of messages that the lobbyist might use. We also learned that the maximum number of messages decreases with the extent of the group's bias relative to the policymaker. Moreover, the ex ante welfare of each side grows with the number of messages among which the lobbyist chooses.

More specifically, we derived conditions on δ, θ_{min}, and θ_{max} that allow for the existence of an n-partition equilibrium (see (4.11)) and characterized an equilibrium by the values of θ at which the lobbyist is indifferent between sending one message and the next. Then we used the conditions that determine $\theta_1, \theta_2, \ldots, \theta_{n-1}$ to express the expected welfare of each side as a function of n alone (see (4.12), (4.13), and (4.14)). Of course, these calculations did not include any adjustments for campaign contributions or for the opportunity cost of the policymaker's time.

Using the results from the earlier calculations, we can compute the maximum amount that the SIG would be willing to pay for access to the policymaker. This figure is just the difference between the expected welfare it can achieve in a lobbying equilibrium and the welfare it would achieve in an equilibrium with no lobbying. Let us suppose that the group anticipates that if it buys access, the outcome will be the lobbying equilibrium with the maximum feasible number of messages, n_{max}. Then the largest amount the SIG would pay for access is given by[18]

$$c_{max} = \frac{n_{max}^2 - 1}{12} \left[\frac{(\theta_{max} - \theta_{min})^2}{n_{max}^2} - 4\delta^2 \right].$$

Notice that c_{max} is larger, the smaller is δ. That is, a group that has a modest bias in its preferences relative to the policymaker is willing to pay more for access than a group that has a larger bias. This is true for two reasons. First, given the number of partitions in the equilibrium, the communication between a group and the policymaker

---

18. Using (4.13) and (4.14), we evaluate $c_{max} = EU^{n_{max}} - EU^1$ to obtain the expression in the text.

imparts better information the smaller is δ. In a 2-partition equilibrium, for example, the dividing point that separates the two regions is closer to the midpoint of the range between θ_{min} and θ_{max}, the more aligned are the interests of the SIG and the policymaker. Second, the maximum number of partitions also grows as δ shrinks. For these two reasons, it is possible for a SIG to communicate better information to a "friendly" politician than to one whose policy objectives are very different from its own. Since a group cannot fool the policymaker in a lobbying equilibrium, its expected welfare grows with the amount and quality of information that it can convey.

Next consider the policymaker. If she were to grant access to the lobbyist in exchange for a contribution of c_{max}, she would gain new understanding of the policy environment. This would allow her to make a better informed policy choice. Using expressions (4.12) and (4.14) from Chapter 4, we can calculate the contribution of the lobbying report to the policymaker's expected welfare. We find the expected gain in W to be equal to λc_{max}. The direct value of the campaign gift is, of course, $(1 - \lambda)c_{max}$. Thus, the direct and indirect benefit to the policymaker from granting access to the SIG sum to c_{max}. If $c_{max} > \tau$, the benefit exceeds the scarcity value of the policymaker's time, and so she will grant access for a fee of c_{max}. If $c_{max} < \tau$, she will make herself unavailable to the SIG by charging a fee in excess of c_{max}.

Our discussion suggests an inverse relationship between contributions and bias. A group with preferences that are rather different from those of the policymaker has relatively little to gain from lobbying, and so is willing to pay less for the opportunity. And a group with quite a large bias in its preferences would be willing to pay so little for access, and would provide the policymaker with so little by way of useful information, that the value of the meeting would not be worth the policymaker's time. This pattern of contributions is depicted by the boldface curves in figure 5.2. Up to $\delta = \delta_1$, contributions decline as the relative bias increases. For even greater degrees of bias than δ_1, the SIG does not buy access, and contributions are nil. This pattern is in keeping with the empirical evidence, inasmuch as groups seem to contribute most to politicians they perceive as sympathetic to their cause.[19]

---

19. See, for example, McCarty and Poole (1998), who provide evidence that contributions by political action committees are inversely related to the disparity between the group's preferences and those of the recipients. Further evidence is presented by Welch (1980) and Poole and Romer (1985).

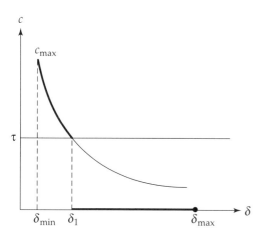

Figure 5.2
Contributions as a Function of δ

Our conclusion does not require the assumption that all bargaining power resides with the politician. We have so far assumed that the policymaker sets the requirements for a meeting, and that the group must either accept or reject her terms. Alternatively, the two sides might negotiate over the price of access. For example, the SIG might reject the politician's demand for a contribution of c_{max} and respond with a counterproposal. One possible outcome of bargaining is that the two sides will share equally in the gains from informative lobbying. In the event, the gain to the politician from having the SIG's report and a contribution of size c (net of the opportunity cost of meeting with the group) would match the gain to the SIG from making the report at a cost of c. An equal division of the surplus implies a contribution of size[20]

$$c_b = \frac{1}{2-\lambda}[\tau + (1-\lambda)c_{max}].$$

Notice that c_b decreases with δ, because c_{max} does. Therefore, in this case too, the size of the contribution is inversely related to the disparity in preferences between the donor and the recipient.[21]

---

20. The surplus for the policymaker from the information and the contribution equals $\lambda c_{max} + (1-\lambda)c - \tau$. The surplus for the interest group equals $c_{max} - c$. By equating the two, we obtain the expression in the text.

21. More generally, if the two sides reach a Nash bargaining solution in which the policymaker captures a fraction η of the surplus, then the contribution will vary inversely with δ provided that $\eta > \lambda(1-\eta)$.

5.3.2 Group with an Unknown Bias

Now suppose that the policymaker is unsure about the interest group's preferences. The policymaker knows that the group has an objective function of the form $U = -(p - \theta - \delta)^2 - c$, but she does not know the extent of its policy bias. She suspects that δ falls in a range between $\delta_{\min}$ and $\delta_{\max}$, and regards all values in this range as equally likely.

To keep our discussion simple, we shall impose some limits on the values of $\delta_{\min}$ and $\delta_{\max}$. First, we assume that $\delta_{\min} > (\theta_{\max} - \theta_{\min})/12$, so that even if the group's bias is as small as is imaginable to the policymaker, the largest number of messages that the lobbyist can choose in a lobbying equilibrium is two. Second, we assume that $\delta_{\max} < (\theta_{\max} - \theta_{\min})/4$, so that even if the bias is as large as is imaginable, a 2-partition equilibrium always exists. With these restrictions, the policymaker is justified in expecting the lobbyist to report either "θ is low" or "θ is high." Her problem is to interpret the meaning of these reports in view of her uncertainty about the interest group's preferences.

For now we let the policymaker dictate the terms of access. To find the optimal fee for the policymaker, we need first to compute the likelihood that the SIG would pay a given price, c. Then we need to gauge the information that the policymaker would receive in circumstances in which a meeting would take place. Once we have done all of that, we can examine how a change in the fee affects the quality of the policy decision and the policymaker's expected revenues, and find the contribution level that maximizes her expected welfare.

We will see that lobbying is most attractive to the interest group when its bias is either small or large. In other words, if there are values of δ for which the SIG would refrain from lobbying, these are values that fall in the interior of the range between $\delta_{\min}$ and $\delta_{\max}$. This is very different from what was true for a group with a known bias, where the value of lobbying declined monotonically with δ.

Let us hypothesize that the SIG buys a chance to lobby if and only if δ falls between $\delta_{\min}$ and δ_1, or between δ_2 and $\delta_{\max}$, for some values of δ_1 and δ_2 that depend on the cost of access, c. With this conjecture about the SIG's behavior, we can investigate what the policymaker's optimal response would be to the alternative reports she might hear.

Consider first the possibility that the SIG has opted to pay c and that its lobbyist reports that "θ is low." For each possible value of δ

for which the SIG would lobby, there is a cut-off point $\theta_1(\delta)$ with the property that the SIG would report "low" if and only if $\theta \le \theta_1(\delta)$. The cut-off point is the state that leaves the SIG indifferent between reporting "low" and "high" when its bias is δ and it correctly anticipates the policymaker's response to either report. Such indifference occurs when the policy p_l that the group expects to see implemented after a report of "low" is the same distance from the group's ideal point of $\theta + \delta$ as the policy p_h that it expects to see implemented after a report of "high"; that is, $\theta_1(\delta) + \delta - p_l = p_h - \theta_1(\delta) - \delta$. Thus,

$\theta_1(\delta) = \frac{1}{2}(p_l + p_h) - \delta.$

With this understanding of the group's reporting strategy, the policymaker can calculate an average value of θ conditional on hearing a report that "θ is low." This calculation takes into account not only the different possible values of θ for a given $\theta_1(\delta)$, but also the different possible values of δ that would result in lobbying. It yields $E[\tilde{\theta}|"low"] = (3\theta_{\min} + \theta_{\max})/4 - \bar{\delta}$, where $\bar{\delta}$ is the average value of δ among those values that the policymaker believes will result in lobbying.[22] The policymaker sets the policy equal to her updated mean value for $\tilde{\theta}$, which implies that

$$p_l = \frac{3\theta_{\min} + \theta_{\max}}{4} - \bar{\delta}. \tag{5.11}$$

By a similar calculation, we find that $E[\tilde{\theta}|"high"] = (\theta_{\min} + 3\theta_{\max})/4 - \bar{\delta}$, and thus

$$p_h = \frac{\theta_{\min} + 3\theta_{\max}}{4} - \bar{\delta}. \tag{5.12}$$

Now let us consider the interest group's decision about whether to buy access when its bias is δ and when it anticipates the policymaker's responses as described above. First we calculate what the SIG stands to gain from lobbying, considering the report it would give in each possible state and the policy outcome that would result. This gain, which we denote by $B(\delta, \bar{\delta})$, is the expected difference between the group's utility from a policy of p_l (should it report "low") or p_h (should it report "high") and the utility it would derive from a

22. Specifically,

$$\bar{\delta} = \frac{1}{2}\left[\frac{(\delta_1)^2 - (\delta_{\min})^2}{\delta_1 - \delta_{\min} + \delta_{\max} - \delta_2}\right] + \frac{1}{2}\left[\frac{(\delta_{\max})^2 - (\delta_2)^2}{\delta_1 - \delta_{\min} + \delta_{\max} - \delta_2}\right].$$

$B(\delta,\bar{\delta}),c$

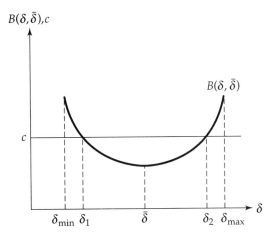

Figure 5.3
The SIG's Incentive to Lobby

policy of $p = (\theta_{\min} + \theta_{\max})/2$. The latter policy is the one that would be implemented in all states of the world if the group were to refrain from lobbying. The calculation of the expected gain is tedious, but not difficult, and yields

$$B(\delta,\bar{\delta}) = \tfrac{1}{2}(\delta - \bar{\delta})^2 - \bar{\delta}^2 + \tfrac{1}{16}(\theta_{\max} - \theta_{\min})^2.$$

The function $B(\delta,\bar{\delta})$ is shown figure 5.3. Notice that it reaches a minimum at $\delta = \bar{\delta}$. That is, the incentive to lobby is least for a group whose bias is equal to the average of the values for which lobbying would take place and greatest when the group's bias is far from this average. It follows that, if the SIG is just indifferent between paying the access fee and not when its bias is δ_1, then it will be unwilling to pay the fee when its bias slightly exceeds δ_1. Similarly, if the SIG is just indifferent between bearing the access fee and not when its bias is δ_2, it will not be willing to pay the fee when its bias is slightly less than δ_2. This validates our hypothesis that the SIG will lobby only if its bias is either small or large.

For a given access fee, the lobbying equilibrium is characterized by three equations. The first two define δ_1 and δ_2, the degrees of bias that leave the SIG indifferent between purchasing access at price c and not. They are $B(\delta_1,\bar{\delta}) = c$ and $B(\delta_2,\bar{\delta}) = c$. The third equation ensures that the policymaker's view of the group's expected bias is consistent with the group's optimal behavior. Specifically, from the definition of $\bar{\delta}$ we obtain

$$\bar{\delta} = \frac{1}{2}\left[\frac{(\delta_1)^2 - (\delta_{min})^2}{\delta_1 - \delta_{min} + \delta_{max} - \delta_2}\right] + \frac{1}{2}\left[\frac{(\delta_{max})^2 - (\delta_2)^2}{\delta_1 - \delta_{min} + \delta_{max} - \delta_2}\right].$$

These three equations determine δ_1, δ_2, and $\bar{\delta}$, which in turn determine p_h and p_l. Note that $B(\delta_1, \bar{\delta}) = B(\delta_2, \bar{\delta})$ implies that δ_1 and δ_2 are symmetrically placed around $\bar{\delta}$, which in turn implies that

$$\bar{\delta} = \tfrac{1}{2}(\delta_{min} + \delta_{max}).$$

Now we turn to the policymaker's choice of the access fee. Starting from a given value of c, a small increase in the fee has three effects. First, it narrows the range of values of δ for which the SIG would elect to purchase access (see figure 5.3). This means a smaller probability that the policymaker will need to spend time with the lobby, and hence a reduced expected cost of the policymaker's time. Second, it changes the quality of the policymaker's decision. An increase in c does not change $\bar{\delta}$, and hence it does not change the policymaker's response to a report of "low" or "high." An increase in the fee does, however, change the likelihood that any lobbying will take place. Since the expected quality of the policymaker's decision improves when she has a greater likelihood of becoming better informed, an increase in the fee imposes a cost on her for this reason.[23] Finally, an increase in c affects the expected revenues for the politician. The expected contribution is equal to the probability that access will be purchased times the size of the typical gift, and thus it can rise or fall with an increase in c.

The optimal fee balances these various effects. If the policymaker places a great weight on making the correct policy decision (i.e., if λ is large) and if the opportunity cost of her time is relatively small, then she may set a fee of $c = B(\bar{\delta}, \bar{\delta})$, which is the largest value of c for which the probability of lobbying is one. Alternatively, if the opportunity cost of her time is large and the policy issue is not so important to her, she may set a high fee that precludes lobbying even if $\delta = \delta_{min}$ or $\delta = \delta_{max}$. For intermediate cases, the optimal fee will induce lobbying by the group if its interests are closely aligned with those of the policymaker, or if its bias is rather extreme. On the margin, the welfare that the policymaker could gain by setting a lower fee, thereby increasing the probability of attaining useful information, is offset by

23. The reader may verify that the policymaker's expected welfare $E[-(\tilde{p} - \tilde{\theta})^2]$ rises with δ_1 and declines with δ_2, as long as $\delta_{max} < \tfrac{1}{4}(\theta_{max} - \theta_{min})$. Since an increase in c decreases δ_1 and increases δ_2, it must lower $E[-(\tilde{p} - \tilde{\theta})^2]$.

the potential loss of expected revenue and by the expected loss of her valuable time.

5.3.3 Access Fees as Signals of SIG Preferences

In the last section we allowed the policymaker to dictate the terms of access. She might prefer, however, to allow the SIG to choose the size of its contribution. By suggesting to the SIG that it make a voluntary contribution of any size, the policymaker affords the group an opportunity to signal the extent of its policy bias. Then she can use what she learns about the group's willingness to pay in assessing the meaning and credibility of its messages.

We have seen that voluntary spending can be used by an interest group with a known bias to signal the state of the policy environment. Might voluntary contributions by a group with an unknown bias similarly allow it to signal the nature of its preferences? Austen-Smith (1995) has posed this question in a model that is related to our own. He has shown that in fact, full revelation of the group's bias cannot occur in any equilibrium. We proceed now to illustrate his finding and to explain why it is so.

In the same setting as in the last section, let us imagine that the interest group is left to decide how much to pay for access to the policymaker. The policymaker takes the size of the contribution to indicate the extent of the SIG's policy bias. To show that there can exist no equilibrium with full revelation of δ, we suppose the opposite to be true. We attempt to construct an equilibrium in which the group contributes $c(\delta)$ when its bias is δ, where $c(\cdot)$ is a function that takes on a different value for every δ in the range from δ_{min} to δ_{max}. When each contribution level can be associated with a distinct bias (which requires that $c(\cdot)$ be either monotonically increasing or monotonically decreasing), the policymaker can infer the group's exact bias from the size of its contribution. We will show that the monotonicity assumption leads to a contradiction.

Consider first the policymaker's response to the alternative reports she might hear. If the SIG reports "low," she will believe that θ falls between θ_{min} and $\theta_1(\delta) = (\theta_{max} + \theta_{min})/2 - 2\delta$.[24] She will also believe

---

24. We compute $\theta_1(\delta)$ from

$$\theta_1(\delta) + \delta - p_l(\delta) = p_h(\delta) - \theta_1(\delta) - \delta$$

where $p_l(\delta) = [\theta_{min} + \theta_1(\delta)]/2$ and $p_h(\delta) = [\theta_{max} + \theta_1(\delta)]/2$.

that she knows δ, which she has deduced from the size of the group's contribution. Thus, she will set the policy equal to her updated beliefs of $E[\tilde{\theta}|\text{"low"}] = [\theta_{\min} + \theta_1(\delta)]/2$. This implies

$$p_l(\delta) = \frac{3\theta_{\min} + \theta_{\max}}{4} - \delta.$$

If the SIG instead reports "high," the policymaker will set the policy equal to $E[\tilde{\theta}|\text{"high"}] = [\theta_1(\delta) + \theta_{\max}]/2$. This implies

$$p_h(\delta) = \frac{\theta_{\min} + 3\theta_{\max}}{4} - \delta.$$

Now we turn to the incentives facing the interest group, which anticipates the policymaker's response. The group must decide how much to contribute, knowing that the policymaker will take its generosity as an indication of the extent of its bias. Let $c(x^*)$ denote the size of its optimal contribution, which induces the policymaker to believe that its bias is x^*. For an equilibrium with full revelation, the group must have an incentive to set $x^* = \delta$ for all values of δ; that is, it must not see a potential benefit from misleading the policymaker by contributing an amount different from what would be expected given its true bias.

If the SIG signals a bias of x, it expects the policymaker to set $p = p_l(x)$ in response to its own subsequent report that "θ is low" and to set $p = p_h(x)$ in response to a report that "θ is high." Of course, it will be able to choose the content of its report optimally once it learns the state of the world. Having signaled a bias of x when its true bias is δ, the optimal strategy for the SIG is to report "low" when $\theta \le \theta_1(x;\delta) = (\theta_{\min} + \theta_{\max})/2 - \delta - x$, and to report "high" otherwise.[25] Anticipating the policymaker's response to its optimal reports, the group can calculate the expected welfare that it achieves by a contribution of $c(x)$ when its bias is δ. We find that

$$U(x;\delta) = -\tfrac{1}{48}(\theta_{\max} - \theta_{\min})^2 - \tfrac{1}{2}(\delta + x)^2 - c(x), \qquad (5.13)$$

where $U(x;\delta)$ denotes this expected welfare level.

---

25. The optimal reporting strategy for the SIG when its bias actually is δ but the policymaker believes it to be x is found by solving

$$\theta_1(x;\delta) + \delta - p_l(x) = p_h(x) - \theta_1(x;\delta) - \delta,$$

where $p_l(x) = (3\theta_{\min} + \theta_{\max})/4 - x$ and $p_h(x) = (\theta_{\min} + 3\theta_{\max})/4 - x$.

$U(x;\delta)$

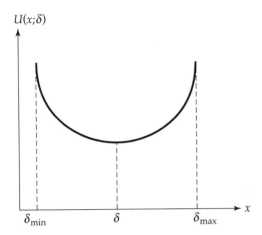

Figure 5.4
Expected Utility for a SIG with Bias δ

The optimal contribution for a SIG with a bias δ is $c(x^*)$, where x^* is the value of x that maximizes $U(x;\delta)$. To find x^*, we compute the first-order condition, which implies $c'(x^*) = -(\delta + x^*)$. If the SIG is to signal truthfully for all values of δ, it must be true that $x^*(\delta) = \delta$ for all δ. This can be satisfied only if $c'(x) = -2x$, and thus $c(x) = A - x^2$, for some constant value of A. Thus, $c(x) = A - x^2$ is our candidate contribution function. Notice that this function is monotonic for $x > 0$, so in principle it would allow the policymaker to identify δ as long as $\delta_{min} > 0$.

There is a problem, however. If $c(x) = A - x^2$, the second-order condition for maximizing $U(x;\delta)$ is not satisfied at $x = \delta$, because $\partial^2 U / \partial x^2 = 1$ is positive. In other words, the group's expected welfare of $U(x;\delta)$ reaches a minimum, not a maximum, at $x = \delta$, as can be seen in figure 5.4. Thus, the incentive facing a SIG with a bias δ is not to contribute $c(\delta)$, but rather to contribute either $c(\delta_{min})$ or $c(\delta_{max})$. It follows that the hypothesis of full revelation of the group's bias cannot be sustained.

Our finding can be understood as follows. As we saw in Section 5.3.2, when the policymaker does not know the group's bias, the group gains the most from lobbying when its bias actually is either small or large. Hence, it has the greatest willingness to pay for access when its bias is small or large. But a signaling equilibrium with full revelation requires a monotonic relationship between the unobserved characteristic and the willingness to pay. Either the group must be willing to pay more when its bias is small than when it is larger, in which case a large contribution would signal a small bias, or the group must be willing to pay more when its bias is large than when it is smaller, in which case a large contribution would signal a large bias. Since the benefit from lobbying falls with δ for $\delta < \bar{\delta}$, and rises with δ for $\delta > \bar{\delta}$, the policymaker cannot rely on the contribution to distinguish between cases in which δ is quite small and those in which it is quite large.

Austen-Smith (1995) has established a similar result in a related model for a wider class of utility functions than the quadratic. He shows that if the contribution reveals anything at all to the policymaker about the group's bias, there must be ranges of values of δ with the property that all values of δ in the range give rise to the same level of contribution. Moreover, it is possible that the same contribution will be made for all δ between some δ_1 and δ_2 as well as for all δ between some δ_3 and δ_4 (with $\delta_1 < \delta_2 < \delta_3 < \delta_4$), and yet for δ between δ_2 and δ_3 the contribution will be something different. Voluntary contributions can only partially resolve a policymaker's uncertainty about an interest group's preferences and thus its reliability.

In this chapter, we have studied lobbying in settings where collecting and presenting information are costly. We began with the assumption that lobbying costs are fixed and independent of the content of a group's message. We showed that a group's willingness to bear these costs conveys information to the policymaker, independent of anything the group might say to her in a meeting. In settings in which the group's claims about the policy environment would not be credible, its lobbying may nonetheless have real effects. And when a group can communicate some information with its words alone, the demonstration of a willingness to pay can further enhance its credibility.

Interest groups often spend more on lobbying than would seem necessary to deliver their messages. This behavior can be understood in the light of the discussion in this chapter. By showing their willingness to bear a large cost of lobbying, groups may signal the urgency of their message. The policymaker may be able to infer quite a lot from the scale of a lobbying effort, and make a better policy decision as a result. However, when lobbying uses real resources, an interest group may suffer from being expected to reveal its information in this manner.

Sometimes the costs of lobbying are imposed by policymakers themselves. Interest groups often claim that their political contributions serve to buy access. We asked, Why would a policymaker place a price on access, and what effect do such fees have on the quality of her policy decision? Policymakers might levy fees in order to ration their time, or because they covet contributions for their usefulness in waging a campaign. When an interest group voluntarily contributes to a policymaker before it becomes informed about the policy issues and environment, the amount of its gift might also signal something about the nature of its preferences.

6   Educating Voters

In the last two chapters we examined how interest groups can use their knowledge of the policy environment to lobby policymakers and influence their decisions. Policymakers are not the only targets of the lobbying waged by special interests. Groups also aim their educational campaigns directly at the public. The voting public, even more so than politicians, often lacks the in-depth knowledge of policy issues that is needed to evaluate the various policy options. An individual voter has little incentive to collect such information, because her vote is so unlikely to make the difference in the election. To the extent that interest groups can make information available to voters at little or no cost to them, the voters should be keen to have it.

The interest groups, for their part, should be eager to provide the public with policy-relevant information. In so doing, a group can try to portray the issues in a light that is favorable to its own cause. Many interest groups seek to shape public opinion by advertising in the media, by undertaking mass mailings, and sometimes by waging highly visible demonstrations and protests. Some groups also target communication to more narrow audiences. Organizations can deliver information to specific groups—such as their own rank-and-file members and others who might be sympathetic to their cause—by advertising in trade publications and special interest magazines, by conducting directed mailings, and by engaging in discussions at membership meetings and social gatherings.

Many authors who have written on campaign spending have pointed to the "rational ignorance" of voters as a reason why such spending might be effective.[1] A typical approach has been to assume

---

1. See, for example, Denzau and Munger (1986), Baron (1994), and Grossman and Helpman (1996b).

that poorly informed voters respond to campaign advertising—coming from the political contestants themselves or from interested parties—by voting in greater numbers for the party or position that has sponsored the ad. Indeed, we shall take a similar approach in Chapter 10, when we discuss the parties' use of the receipts from campaign contributions. But here our focus is distinctly different. We consider not the effects of the groups' contributions per se, but rather the informational content of their messages. Voters may not be able to verify the various claims made in a group's advertisement or other communication, but they may nonetheless listen to the arguments and try to assess their credibility.

As with their efforts to advise policymakers, SIGs can educate voters with messages that are directly informative or indirectly so. A directly informative message might describe, for example, the voting records of the candidates or the alleged facts about a policy issue. An indirect message is one that contains no specific content but still conveys information because it demonstrates the group's willingness to bear an avoidable expense. In this chapter we focus on costless communication, following the approach we took in Chapter 4. Costly signaling could also be studied in a manner similar to Chapter 5, but we leave this extension to the interested reader.

We begin by examining situations in which an organized group supplies information to a broad audience of voters. We endow the group with information that bears on the welfare effects of a policy instrument. In particular, the organization can gauge what level of the policy would be best for its members and how these members would fare under alternative policy options. The organization's information might also be relevant to voters who are not members of the group, but typically it will be less informative for these others.

Consider first how the members of an interest group will interpret messages from their organization. If the political objectives of an organization and all of its members were exactly the same, then the members would be able to take the organization's claims at face value. However, typically this will not be the case. When the leaders of a SIG pursue the group's collective interest, they will wish to have all members of the group vote for the party whose platform better serves the membership. But individual members will cast their votes so as to further their personal political goals. When the members of a group hold differing views on some issues, they will not all be inclined to vote the same. In the event, the leaders will be tempted to misrepresent their information so as to fool some members into voting for a party that would not be their choice if they were fully informed. Of course, astute members will recognize the leaders' incentives and will not be fooled. But the possibility of misrepresentation colors what information the organization can communicate.

The divergence in political interests between an organization and the public at large will, if anything, be greater than that which separates the leadership from its members. Still, the credibility issues that arise are similar for the two audiences. A voter who is not a member of the group must also ask herself whether the group's claims about the policy environment can be trusted. If so, she should use the information to update her beliefs about the issues. The extent of updating will depend, of course, on how relevant the organization's information is to her own concerns.

The incentive that an organization has to misrepresent the policy environment makes the timing of its communication important for determining what information it can convey. If an educational campaign takes place before the parties have announced their positions on the issues of concern to the SIG, the organization must anticipate the response of the politicians to its messages. In contrast, if the campaign comes closer to the time of the election, the organization may be able to observe the parties' positions and use its public messages to steer the voting. In Section 6.2 we study the effects of information provided to voters before the parties have announced their positions on an issue of concern to the group, whereas in Section 6.3 we examine public pronouncements that take place after the parties' positions are known.

Section 6.4 focuses on campaign endorsements. Endorsements are a particularly simple type of message that some SIGs issue after the candidates have taken their positions. In an endorsement, a group designates one candidate or another as its preferred choice in the election. The common use of endorsements may be explained by the ease with which these messages can be communicated and by the relatively low cost they impose on the recipients. But, as we shall see, an endorsement sometimes can provide as much information as a more detailed message, considering the credibility problem that exists once the parties' positions are known.

The last part of this chapter deals with information that interest groups target to more narrow audiences. In particular, we discuss the efforts that an organization might make to educate its members about the policy environment and about the relative merits of the different candidates for office.

6.1 The Election

To begin, we need a model of an election with imperfectly informed voters. We develop a model similar to the one we used in Chapter 3. There are two political parties that are vying for control of a legislature. Each party holds some immutable positions on a set of issues of immediate concern. But there is another matter on the political agenda about which the parties' views are more pliable. We assume that the parties choose their positions on this issue in order to maximize their chances of capturing a majority. The party that wins a majority of the votes will implement its platform after the election.

The voters begin with an imperfect understanding of the pliable policy issue. In particular, each voter does not know what policy level would best serve her own personal interests. A SIG represents a group of voters whose welfare will be affected similarly by the pliable policy. The central organization has information that bears on the welfare effects of the various options. The organization endeavors to educate the public in a way that promotes the collective welfare of its members.

6.1.1 The Voters

There are two types of voters, those who are members of the interest group and those who are not. We refer to the latter as the "general public" or the "public at large." The interest group represents individuals who will be affected similarly by the pliable policy, whereas the general public comprises individuals with a variety of interests in the matter. Voters hold diverse views about the remaining policy issues, whether they are members of the SIG or not.

Let π_S denote the ideal pliable policy for a member of the interest group.[2] A typical group member i derives utility $u_{iS} = -(p^k - \pi_S)^2 + v_{iS}^k$ from the policies of party k, $k = A, B$, where p^k is the pliable policy that is implemented by party k after the election and v_{iS}^k is the member's evaluation of the fixed positions of that party.

---

2. We use an "S" subscript throughout this chapter to denote a variable relating to a member of the SIG.

Notice that the members have heterogeneous preferences regarding policies other than p^k (as reflected by the subscript i on v_{iS}^k), but all wish to have the pliable policy as close to their common ideal level as possible. A voter i who is not a member of the SIG has an ideal pliable policy of π_{iP} (here, "P" stands for public at large). This voter has a utility function $u_{iP} = -(p^k - \pi_{iP})^2 + v_{iP}^k$ from the policies of party k.

Every SIG member has a limited understanding of the pliable policy issue. Specifically, the members do not know what level of the policy instrument would best serve their interests. This lack of information translates into uncertainty about π_S. The members have some prior beliefs about what pliable policies would be likely to serve them well. We suppose that members of the group initially view their ideal pliable policy as the realization of a random variable, $\tilde{\pi}_S$, the distribution of which indicates the perceived likelihood of different values.

The group members may update their beliefs about the policy environment based on information they receive from their leaders.[3] On election day, each SIG member casts her vote so as to maximize Eu_{iS}, where the expectation is taken over her election-day beliefs about the distribution of $\tilde{\pi}_S$ as well as her beliefs about how her own vote will affect the outcome of the election.

Voters who are not members of the interest group also are imperfectly informed about the policy environment. A voter i in the public at large believes that her ideal policy level might be any one in a range of possible values, as represented by the random variable $\tilde{\pi}_{iP}$. Each such voter seeks to maximize Eu_{iP}.

Now consider an individual's behavior in the voting booth. Voters are assumed to know the candidates' stated positions on the issues. In what follows, every vote for a party increases the probability that the designated party will win a majority of the votes. Therefore, it is a dominant strategy for an individual voter to cast her ballot for a

---

3. They may also update their beliefs based on the positions that are taken by the parties. In fact, Bayes' rule requires such updating in some equilibria. However, in those circumstances where the equilibrium positions reveal something about the voters' interests, the parties have the same pliable positions, so the updating does not affect their preferences among the parties. We assume that voters do not use the parties' announced positions to update their beliefs out of equilibrium. That is, were a party to deviate from its equilibrium position to another, the voters would judge the parties based on updated beliefs that reflect only the group's report.

party if and only if she expects to fare better under its proposed policies.

It is convenient to define $v_{iS} = v_{iS}^B - v_{iS}^A$, as we did in Chapter 3. Thus, v_{iS} measures the extent to which voter i in the SIG prefers the positions of party B to those of party A on issues other than the one on which the group shares a common view. Of course, v_{iS} might be negative, if individual i in fact regards the fixed positions of party A as the more desirable. SIG member i will vote for party A if and only if $E[-(p^A - \tilde{\pi}_S)^2] > E[-(p^B - \tilde{\pi}_S)^2] + v_{iS}$, which, after canceling and rearranging terms, implies[4]

$$v_{iS} < 2(\bar{p} - \bar{\pi}_S)(p^B - p^A). \tag{6.1}$$

Here, $\bar{p} = (p^A + p^B)/2$ is the average of the parties' pliable policy positions and $\bar{\pi}_S = E\tilde{\pi}_S$ is the mean value of the (posterior) distribution of $\tilde{\pi}_S$, as seen by the SIG member on election day.[5] An individual group member calculates a mean value of $\tilde{\pi}_S$ after gleaning what she can about the policy environment from the information provided by the organization.

We take the distribution of v_{iS} among SIG members to be uniform in the interval extending from $(-1 + 2b)/2f$ to $(1 + 2b)/2f$. This specification makes the density of the distribution constant and equal to f. The mean of the distribution, b/f, tells us which platform of fixed policy positions is more popular among group members, and by how much. If $b = 0$, exactly half of the group members prefer the fixed positions of either party. If $b < 0$, more than half of the members prefer the fixed positions of party A, while if $b > 0$, more than half of the members prefer the fixed positions of party B.

We can now calculate the fraction of votes by SIG members that go to each party when their pliable platforms are p^A and p^B and when the members have an expected ideal policy (based on their updated information) of $\bar{\pi}$. Using the voting rule in (6.1) and the fact that v_{iS} has a uniform distribution, we find that

---

4. The voter should condition her calculation of the expectations on the event that her vote is decisive in the election, as described by Feddersen and Pesendorfer (1996). However, the conditional expectation is the same as the unconditional expectation here, because the event of being pivotal provides no new information about the distribution of $\tilde{\pi}_S$. For given p^A and p^B, whether voter i is pivotal depends only on how popular the parties' fixed positions prove to be among voters other than herself.
5. Note that it does not matter how the indifferent voters cast their ballots, because there is a negligible fraction of such individuals in the voting population.

$$s_S = \tfrac{1}{2} - b + 2f(\bar{p} - \bar{\pi}_S)(p^B - p^A), \tag{6.2}$$

where s_S denotes the fraction of SIG members who vote for party A.

We assume that the distribution of views about the fixed policy issues is the same in the general public as it is among SIG members. Moreover, we take the distribution of v_{iP} to be independent of a voter's perceived ideal policy, π_{iP}. A voter who believes that her ideal policy has a distribution with mean $\bar{\pi}_{iP} = E\tilde{\pi}_{iP}$ will vote for party A if and only if $v_{iP} < 2(\bar{p} - \bar{\pi}_{iP})(p^B - p^A)$. The fraction of votes that will go to party A among voters with this belief is $s_{iP} = 1/2 - b + 2f(\bar{p} - \bar{\pi}_{iP})(p^B - p^A)$. Summing across all the different values of $\bar{\pi}_{iP}$, and weighing each s_{iP} by the number of voters with the particular prior $\bar{\pi}_{iP}$, gives

$$s_P = \tfrac{1}{2} - b + 2f(\bar{p} - \bar{\pi}_P)(p^B - p^A), \tag{6.3}$$

where s_P denotes the fraction of votes for party A among all voters who are not members of the SIG, and $\bar{\pi}_P$ is the population mean of $\bar{\pi}_{iP}$.

Finally, let ω be the fraction of voters who belong to the interest group and $1 - \omega$ be the fraction of voters who do not. We can weight (6.2) and (6.3) by the respective fractions in the voting population and sum the resulting equations to derive

$$s = \tfrac{1}{2} - b + 2f(\bar{p} - \bar{\pi})(p^B - p^A). \tag{6.4}$$

Here s denotes the aggregate share of votes that goes to party A and $\bar{\pi} = \omega\bar{\pi}_S + (1 - \omega)\bar{\pi}_P$ is the mean expected ideal pliable policy in the entire electorate. Note that this mean expectation is formed based on the voters' updated beliefs after the SIG wages its publicity campaign.

6.1.2   The Parties

The political parties choose their respective positions on the pliable issue in order to maximize their chances of winning the election.[6] Unlike in Chapters 4 and 5, we assume that the politicians are fully informed about this issue. In particular, they understand how the

---

6. We could alternatively assume that a party seeks to maximize its expected number of votes. This objective might be more appropriate, for example, if the parties are most interested in awarding patronage, and the ability of each to do so depends on the number of its seats in the legislature. The choice of objective is not important here, as both give rise to the same equilibrium positions and distribution of policies.

various levels of the policy instrument p would affect the different constituencies. The political parties must announce their pliable positions before they know which of the platforms of fixed positions will prove to be more popular to voters. Recall that b measures the aggregate preference for the fixed positions of party B. The parties regard b as the realization of a random variable, $\tilde{b}$. Their beliefs about b are summarized by a distribution function for $\tilde{b}$.

The election winner is the party that captures a majority of the votes. The probability that $s > \frac{1}{2}$ can be calculated from equation (6.4), and is equal to the probability that

$$b < 2f(\bar{p} - \bar{\pi})(p^B - p^A). \tag{6.5}$$

Party A maximizes this probability by choosing p^A to maximize the expression on the right-hand side of (6.5). Party B maximizes its own chances by choosing p^B to minimize the same expression. If the parties adopt their positions before the SIG wages its publicity campaign, they must anticipate how their choices will affect the content of the group's report, which in turn will determine $\bar{\pi}$. Otherwise, the parties take $\bar{\pi}$ as given. A Nash equilibrium obtains when each party's pliable position is a best response to the optimal choice of the other.

6.1.3 The Interest Group

The central organization of the interest group has information about the policy environment. To highlight the similarities with Chapters 4 and 5, we adopt the same notation to describe their information. In particular, the SIG knows the value of a policy-relevant variable, θ. The politicians also know the value of θ, but the voters do not. They regard θ as being the realization of a random variable, with all values between $\theta_{\min}$ and $\theta_{\max}$ being possible and equally likely.

The information in the hands of the organization bears on the welfare effects of the pliable policy instrument. We assume that the group's information has particular relevance to its members. This is plausible, because the SIG is most likely to conduct research that provides information about how its members would fare under the alternative policy options. The organization's research results may or may not be relevant to the public at large. We allow for a range of possibilities in this regard.

More specifically, we suppose that the organization's research identifies the ideal pliable policy for SIG members. With this assumption, it is convenient to describe the information in terms of what it says about the members' ideal; that is, we take $\pi_S = \theta$. As for the others, a typical voter i has an ideal policy π_{iP}. We denote the sample mean of π_{iP} in the public at large by π_P, and assume that $\pi_P = \rho\theta + \delta$. Here, ρ measures the extent to which the results of the organization's research are informative about the interests of non-members. If $\rho = 1$, the interests of the typical group member and the average nonmember move in tandem, so that their ideal policies differ by δ in all states of the world. Another possibility is that $\rho = 0$, in which case the organization's research reveals nothing about the interests of the general public. There will also be policy issues for which ρ is negative. A negative value of ρ implies a conflict of interest between SIG members and the general public; when the state of the world is such that a high value of p would benefit group members, such a policy would be harmful to the average individual who is not a member of the group. To simplify the exposition, we limit our attention to values of ρ that lie between -1 and 1.

The job of the organization is to communicate something of its knowledge to the voters. The SIG might report, for example, that "$\theta = 3$" or that "θ falls in a range between 1 and 5." The public must assess the credibility of the group's report. If the report is credible, each voter will consider what it means for her own likely interests, and will update her beliefs about π_S or π_{iP} accordingly. If the report is not credible, it will be appropriately discounted.

In assessing credibility, the voters who hear the report must take into account the organization's objectives in sending it. There are at least two possibilities to consider. First, the group might endow its leaders with a *narrow mandate* to focus only on the pliable policy issue. That is, the rank and file might instruct its leaders to pursue a policy outcome p that best serves the group's interest in this single policy dimension. Alternatively, the group might grant its leaders a *broad mandate* to pursue the members' aggregate expected welfare. Whatever the mandate, we assume the leaders execute it faithfully. In other words, we overlook any problems that the group may encounter in motivating the leaders to carry out its orders.

If the mandate is narrow, the group leaders will not be concerned about outcomes other than p. Rather, their objective will be to issue public statements so as to maximize $E[-(\tilde{p} - \pi_S)^2]$, where the expectation here refers to their uncertainty about which party will prove to be more popular and hence which will win the election.[7] If instead the mandate is broad, the leaders will seek to maximize $E[-(\tilde{p} - \pi_S)^2 + \tilde{v}_S]$, where $\tilde{v}_S$ is the average utility among members associated with the package of fixed policies.[8] Note that b/f measures the average bias among voters in favor of the fixed positions of party B. The SIG leaders do not know b at the time they send their message. Rather, like the politicians, they view the relative popularity index b as the realization of a random variable, $\tilde{b}$.

We will find that the nature of the mandate does not affect the policy outcome when the organization issues its messages before the parties announce their positions. But when the messages are sent after the positions are known, the distinction does matter. Then, if the mandate is narrow, the SIG leadership knows straightaway which party it wishes to cast in a favorable light. If the mandate is broad, the leaders' decision problem is more subtle. They must consider what the preferences of the membership on the fixed policy issues are likely to be in situations where their report will make the difference in the election. We concentrate on the simpler case of a narrow mandate in the main text, leaving the broad mandate for an appendix. When we compare the two outcomes in the appendix, we find that the SIG members typically fare better when the leaders' mandate is narrow than when it is broad. This may justify our focus on the narrow mandate, inasmuch as the members will wish to issue such instructions if they are in a position to do so.

6.2   Early Communication

In this section, we allow the SIG leaders to educate the voters early in the election cycle. Their effort to do so may involve an advertising campaign, or a mass mailing, or some combination of these and other means. For simplicity, we assume that all voters hear the group's message. Importantly, the communication considered here occurs before the parties take their positions on the pliable issue. Thus, the parties are able to react to any changes in the political climate that result from the group's publicity campaign.

---

7. The random variable $\tilde{p}$ takes the value p^A with probability ζ^A and the value p^B with probability $1 - \zeta^A$, where ζ^A is the probability that party A will win the election.
8. The SIG leaders see $\tilde{v}_S$ as a random variable for two reasons. First, they do not know for sure which party will win the election. Second, they do not know what the members' evaluation of the fixed positions will turn out to be.

The SIG issues a statement about θ. To understand what statements would be credible and which will be sent, we need to analyze how the election game would play out after the various possible reports. We therefore start our analysis with the final stages of the game, and work our way backward.

6.2.1   Party Competition and Voting

The last stage of the game is when the voting occurs. We know that if SIG members have an expectation of their ideal policy at this stage of $\bar{\pi}_S$ and the positions are p^A and p^B, their votes will divide according to (6.2). Similarly, if the average expected ideal policy among the public at large is $\bar{\pi}_P$, (6.3) gives the split of these votes. Thus, (6.4) gives the fraction of votes that party A will win, if the positions are p^A and p^B and $\bar{\pi} = \omega\bar{\pi}_S + (1-\omega)\bar{\pi}_P$ is the average expected ideal pliable policy in the population as a whole.

At the preceding stage, the parties set their pliable positions to maximize their chances of winning a majority of the votes. At this stage, they take voters' beliefs about π_S and π_{iP} as given.[9] Party A seeks to maximize the probability that $s > 1/2$, which means it wishes to maximize the right-hand side of (6.5). The first-order condition for this maximization yields $p^A = \bar{\pi}$. Similarly, party B seeks to minimize the right-hand side of (6.5), which yields $p^B = \bar{\pi}$. Evidently, the parties' pliable positions converge at the mean expected ideal policy in the population of voters. This, then, is the pliable policy outcome no matter which party wins the election.

6.2.2   Credible Messages

Now we come to the behavior of the SIG. The leaders anticipate the subsequent competition between the parties. They foresee an outcome in the position-taking stage in which the parties will adopt a common platform equal to $\bar{\pi}$. Their goal is to use their educational campaign to induce a favorable value of $\bar{\pi}$. Since the voters will be

---

9. In forming their best responses, the parties consider π_S and π_{iP} to be fixed. By assumption, this is true of voters' beliefs out of equilibrium. In the equilibrium, the voters may be able to update their beliefs about π_S and π_{iP} based on the positions they observe the parties having taken. However, in the equilibrium we describe, the positions reveal only that the average ideal policy is $\bar{\pi}$, which is what the voters believed anyway before observing the positions. Thus, the parties are justified in taking $\bar{\pi}$ as fixed.

aware of this aim, they will accept the group's report about θ only if the leaders have an incentive to tell the truth. As in Chapters 4 and 5, the leaders are constrained by the requirement that their messages be credible.

Before we address the issue of credibility, we note that the outcome will be the same no matter what the leaders' mandate is. If the mandate is narrow, the objective of the leaders is to induce beliefs about θ such that $\bar{\pi}$ is as close to π_S as possible. This will give the best possible pliable outcome for the group, and that is all the leaders with a narrow mandate care about. If the mandate is broad, the leaders' objective is to maximize total expected welfare. But since the leaders anticipate convergence in the pliable positions of the two parties, they expect party A to win the election if and only if its fixed policies prove to be the more popular. The group's educational campaign will not affect the popularity of the fixed positions, so it will not affect the probability that one set of fixed positions will be implemented instead of the other. The leaders with a broad mandate can do no more for the members than to behave as if their mandate was narrow.

We ask first whether the SIG leaders can report fully and faithfully on the information they have (i.e., whether they can reveal the precise value of θ). Clearly, any such report would not be credible, for reasons that should be familiar by now. If the voters were to anticipate a complete report about θ, they would update their beliefs accordingly. Upon hearing a report that "θ is precisely equal to $\hat{\theta}$," for some value $\hat{\theta}$, a SIG member would infer that $\pi_S = \hat{\theta}$, while others would infer that $\pi_P = \rho\hat{\theta} + \delta$. Then the result of the political process would be $p = \bar{\pi} = \omega\hat{\theta} + (1 - \omega)(\rho\hat{\theta} + \delta)$. If $\omega\hat{\theta} + (1 - \omega)(\rho\hat{\theta} + \delta) < \theta$, the leaders would have an incentive to overstate the true value of θ in order to induce a larger p than the one that would result from accurate reporting. Similarly, if $\omega\theta + (1 - \omega)(\rho\theta + \delta) > \theta$, the leaders would have an incentive to understate θ. Only if $\omega\theta + (1 - \omega)(\rho\theta + \delta) = \theta$ could the leaders be expected to report truthfully; but such truthful reporting could only happen for one particular value of θ, and not for all values between θ_{min} and θ_{max}.

In fact, the strategic setting is much like the one in Chapter 4. Here, as there, the SIG wishes to educate, but has an incentive to exaggerate. In an equilibrium, the voters must interpret the messages they hear in a way that is consistent with the organization's incentives in sending them. To characterize an equilibrium, we must draw once again on the insights of Crawford and Sobel (1982). Their results imply that the outcome of the communication game must take the form of a partition equilibrium.

Let us try to construct an equilibrium in which the SIG issues one of two distinct messages. One possible message would indicate that the common interests of the members are best served by a "low" value of the policy variable p, while the other would indicate the greater desirability for members of a "high" value of p. The voters would interpret the former message to mean that θ falls between θ_{min} and θ_1 for some value of θ_1, and the latter to mean that θ falls between θ_1 and θ_{max}. For these alternative messages to be credible, we need the leaders to have an incentive to report "low" whenever $\theta \leq \theta_1$, and to report "high" whenever $\theta \geq \theta_1$.

Voters use Bayes' rule to update their beliefs. If they take a report of "low" at face value, they rule out values of θ greater than θ_1. This leaves them believing that θ must lie between θ_{min} and θ_1, with all values in this range seeming equally likely. Thus, a report of "low" induces an expected ideal policy for SIG members of $\bar{\pi}_S = (\theta_{min} + \theta_1)/2$. The public at large is led by this report to believe that $\bar{\pi}_P = \delta + (\theta_{min} + \theta_1)\rho/2$. In the event, political competition would drive the political parties to announce identical pliable platforms of $p^A = p^B = p_{low}$, where

$$p_{low} = [\omega + \rho(1 - \omega)]\left(\frac{\theta_{min} + \theta_1}{2}\right) + (1 - \omega)\delta.$$

In contrast, a report of "high" would lead voters to exclude values of θ less than θ_1. They would conclude that θ lies between θ_1 and θ_{max}, with an expected value of $(\theta_1 + \theta_{max})/2$. Then the parties' platforms would converge to

$$p_{high} = [\omega + \rho(1 - \omega)]\left(\frac{\theta_1 + \theta_{max}}{2}\right) + (1 - \omega)\delta.$$

For the organization's incentives to be consistent with the voters' interpretations, the leaders must be indifferent between sending a report of "low" and a report of "high" when $\theta = \theta_1$. Such indifference requires

$$-(p_{low} - \theta_1)^2 = -(p_{high} - \theta_1)^2$$

or

$$\theta_1 = \left[\frac{\omega + (1-\omega)\rho}{2 - \omega - (1-\omega)\rho}\right]\left(\frac{\theta_{\min} + \theta_{\max}}{2}\right) + \left[\frac{2(1-\omega)}{2 - \omega - (1-\omega)\rho}\right]\delta. \quad (6.6)$$

Also, the leaders must prefer to report "high" when θ is greater than θ_1 and to report "low" when θ is less than θ_1 (and not the other way around). This requires $p_{high} > p_{low}$, which in turn requires $\omega + (1-\omega)\rho > 0$.

If $\omega + (1-\omega)\rho > 0$ and the solution for θ_1 in (6.6) falls between $\theta_{\min}$ and $\theta_{\max}$, then we have identified a legitimate, 2-partition equilibrium. In this equilibrium, voters are educated by a report that informs them whether the value of θ is low or high. For θ_1 to fall between $\theta_{\min}$ and $\theta_{\max}$, δ cannot be too large in absolute value. That is, the interests of the SIG members and the public at large cannot differ by too much. With a great divergence of interests, the equilibrium policy that would result from political competition with (partially) informed voters is far from the group's ideal policy. Under these circumstances, the organization has too great an incentive to misrepresent the policy environment; none of its reports are credible.

The case that is most similar to what we discussed before arises when $\rho = 1$, that is, when the preference bias of SIG members relative to the average nonmember is a constant. For $\rho = 1$, (6.6) implies that $\theta_1 = (\theta_{\min} + \theta_{\max})/2 + 2(1-\omega)\delta$. In this case, a two-partition equilibrium exists if and only if $4(1-\omega)|\delta| < \theta_{\max} - \theta_{\min}$. Now it is easy to see that the group's bias cannot be too great if there is to exist an equilibrium with informative reports.

If the solution for θ_1 in (6.6) does not fall between $\theta_{\min}$ and $\theta_{\max}$, or if $\omega + \rho(1-\omega) < 0$, then even a binary report from the SIG would not be credible. In such circumstances, the only possible outcome at the communication stage is the ubiquitous babbling equilibrium. The organization issues a report that contains no new information about the policy environment, and the voters hold on to their prior beliefs. These beliefs are that $\bar{\pi}_S = (\theta_{\min} + \theta_{\max})/2$ and $\bar{\pi}_P = (\theta_{\min} + \theta_{\max})\rho/2 + \delta$. Since the political competition leads the parties to adopt positions at the average expected ideal policy, the outcome in these cases must be

$$p = [\omega + \rho(1-\omega)]\left(\frac{\theta_{\min} + \theta_{\max}}{2}\right) + (1-\omega)\delta.$$

We have so far considered only a 2-partition equilibrium and a babbling equilibrium as possible outcomes in the communication subgame. For some values of ρ, δ, and ω, there are further possibilities. Sometimes the organization can use a richer vocabulary than just "low" and "high" to describe the policy environment. For example, it might be able to credibly issue one of three different reports. In fact, we can apply the results of Crawford and Sobel (1982) to characterize the set of possible equilibria at the communication stage. When parameter values are such that there is no value of θ between $\theta_{\min}$ and $\theta_{\max}$ at which the ideal policies of the SIG members and the average nonmember are exactly the same, the number of distinct messages used in a partition equilibrium must be finite. The maximum number of messages will be larger, the more similar are the interests of the SIG and the general public—for example, the smaller is $|\delta|$ when $\rho = 1$. If there does exist some value of θ between $\theta_{\min}$ and $\theta_{\max}$ at which the ideal policies of the representative SIG member and the average member of the general public happen to be the same, then the number of credible messages in the SIG leader's vocabulary can be infinite.[10]

6.2.3   Who Gains and Who Loses?

We have described equilibria in which the interest group's educational activities alter the policy outcome. We now ask, Who benefits from these activities? Will interest group members necessarily achieve higher welfare when their leaders are able to publicize announcements about the policy environment? If so, do these gains come at the expense of other voters, or might all voters gain from having a better informed electorate? To address these questions, we focus on the 2-partition equilibrium of the communication subgame, and compare the outcome with that which would emerge if the SIG could not engage in educational activities. Recall that the existence of a 2-partition equilibrium requires $\omega + \rho(1 - \omega) > 0$ and also that θ_1 in (6.6) fall between $\theta_{\min}$ and $\theta_{\max}$.

To make the comparison, we consider a voter i who has an ideal policy $\pi_i = \rho_i\theta + \delta_i$. Note that $\rho_i = 1$ and $\delta_i = 0$ for all members of the

---

10. As a technical point, even if the number of messages is infinite, the communication from the SIG cannot be fully revealing. In fact, the organization will use many messages to distinguish states that are close to the one where the interests are the same, but relatively few messages to distinguish states where the interests diverge. The condition for the existence of a θ for which the ideal policies of the SIG members and the average member of the general public are the same is $\theta_{\min} \leq \delta/(1 - \rho) \leq \theta_{\max}$.

interest group. The average voter in the public at large has $\rho_i = \rho$ and $\delta_i = \delta$, while the average voter in the population as a whole (including group members and nonmembers) has $\rho_i = \omega + (1 - \omega)\rho$ and $\delta_i = (1 - \omega)\delta$.

If the SIG were unable to educate voters, the pliable policy outcome would be $p = [\omega + (1 - \omega)\rho](\theta_{min} + \theta_{max})/2 + (1 - \omega)\delta$. Whether it can undertake such an effort or not, the parties' pliable positions will converge in equilibrium, and the election will be won by the party whose fixed positions prove to be the more popular. So we can assess the distributional effects of the group's educational activities by comparing the component of expected welfare that reflects the pliable policies in an equilibrium in which $p = p_{low}$ for $\theta \leq \theta_1$ and $p = p_{high}$ for $\theta > \theta_1$ with the same component for an equilibrium in which $p = [\omega + (1 - \omega)\rho](\theta_{min} + \theta_{max})/2 + (1 - \omega)\delta$ for all values of θ. We find that individual i gains from the group's campaign if and only if[11]

$$\rho_i > \frac{\omega + (1 - \omega)\rho}{2}. \tag{6.7}$$

The inequality in (6.7) has several implications. First, since $\omega + (1 - \omega)\rho > 0$ in any 2-partition equilibrium, no voter whose ideal policy varies inversely with θ can benefit from the educational activities of the interest group. Indeed, only voters whose interests have a sufficiently high positive correlation with those of SIG members across states of the policy environment stand to gain from the group's efforts. Second, the average voter in the public at large will benefit from the group's early communication if and only if $\rho > \omega/(1 + \omega)$—that is, if the correlation between this voter's ideal policy and that of the interest group is relatively high compared to

---

11. An individual with an ideal point of $\pi_i = \rho_i\theta + \delta_i$ fares better in the 2-partition equilibrium than in an equilibrium with no communication if and only if $D(\rho_i, \delta_i) > 0$, where

$$D(\rho_i, \delta_i) = -\int_{\theta_{min}}^{\theta_1} (p_{low} - \rho_i\theta - \delta_i)^2 \, d\theta - \int_{\theta_1}^{\theta_{max}} (p_{high} - \rho_i\theta - \delta_i)^2 \, d\theta + \int_{\theta_{min}}^{\theta_{max}} (p - \rho_i\theta - \delta_i)^2 \, d\theta.$$

Using the values of p_{low} and p_{high} in the 2-partition equilibrium and the value of p in an equilibrium with no communcation, it is straightforward to verify that changes in δ_i do not affect $D(\rho_i, \delta_i)$. Also, increases in ρ_i increase $D(\rho_i, \delta_i)$ whenever $\theta_{min} < \theta_1 < \theta_{max}$. Thus, the individual fares relatively better with an active SIG the greater is the correlation between his ideal point and that of the group. By solving for the ρ_i that makes $D(\rho_i, \delta_i) = 0$, we find that an individual i has the same expected welfare in the two equilibria if $\rho_i = [\omega + (1 - \omega)\rho]/2$. This justifies our claims in the text.

the fraction of group members in the voting population. Third, since $\rho_i = 1$ for SIG members and the right-hand side of (6.7) is at most one-half, the organization's activities do benefit all of its members. Finally, the group's educational activities raise the expected welfare for the average voter in the overall population, including those who are members of the interest group and those who are not. Notice that δ_i does not enter into the welfare comparison; the effect of the group's educational activities about θ on a voter i depends only on how this voter's ideal pliable policy varies with that of the SIG members, and not on the absolute difference between the voter's ideal and the group's ideal.

6.3   Late Communication

In the last section we studied the efforts that a SIG might make to educate voters early in the election cycle, before the parties have committed to their positions on the pliable policy issue. If the parties realize that voters are gaining a better understanding of the issues, they will tailor their positions more to the voters' liking. In this way, a SIG might use its knowledge of the issues to benefit its members.

In this section we examine informational campaigns that take place closer to election time. In particular, we allow the SIG to make public statements about the policy environment after the parties have taken their positions. A SIG faces very different incentives after the positions have been announced than it does beforehand. At the later stage, the organization can no longer hope to influence the policy choice via competition between the parties. Instead, it must attempt to steer voters to the party whose positions would better serve its members. This does not mean, however, that the possibility of late communication has no effect on its positions. When a party expects the SIG to issue a statement late in the election cycle, it may opt to take a position favorable to the group in the hope that the organization's message will cast the party's position in a favorable light. In other words, political parties may cater to interest groups in anticipation of their late announcements.

When communication from a SIG comes late in the game, the content of its message may vary with the leaders' mandate. For example, if the leaders have a narrow mandate to induce the best possible pliable policy for the group, they will issue statements that point the voters to the party whose pliable position is closer to the group's ideal. If instead the mandate is broad, the leaders must take into account their imperfect information about the members' preferences. The leaders should be wary of issuing statements that might benefit a party whose positions on the fixed issues will prove to be unpopular among the membership. To minimize this risk, they should ask themselves what the preference bias of the members is likely to be in situations where the content of their message makes the difference in the election. In other words, the leaders should condition their statements on the event that their report will be decisive. Such conditioning requires a subtle and more difficult calculation, so we choose to leave the technical discussion of this case for an appendix. In the main text, we focus on situations where the leaders' mandate is narrow.

6.3.1 Reports and Voting

As before, we begin our analysis from the final stage of the game, and work our way backward. The final stage is when voting takes place. By the time a voter enters the voting booth, she knows the pliable positions of the parties and has some (possibly) updated expectations about her own ideal policy. The voters' views about the policy environment are summarized by the variable $\bar{\pi}$. Given $\bar{\pi}$, we can use equation (6.4) and the distribution of b to calculate the probability that each party will win the election.

At the preceding stage, the organization issues its report to the public. The report is a statement about the variable θ. The leaders know the parties' pliable positions, but not their relative popularity. Their goal is to minimize the expected distance of the pliable policy from the group's ideal. It follows that if p^A is closer to π_S than is p^B, the leaders will attempt to maximize the probability that party A will win the election. Otherwise, they will attempt to maximize the probability that party B will win the election.

To be more specific, let us look carefully at a case where $\pi_S > \bar{p}$ and $p^A > p^B$. Since the group's ideal policy is above the midpoint between the two positions, the SIG prefers the (higher) pliable position of party A. This implies that the organization will seek to use its message to further the electoral fortunes of party A. The probability of a victory for party A is maximized when the right-hand side of (6.5) is maximized, or when the value of $\bar{\pi}$ is maximized. In other words, the organization wishes to make the average voter believe that a very high level of the pliable policy will best serve her interests. When the average voter believes this, she is most inclined to vote for party A, for any given feelings she may have about the fixed policy positions. The fact that the organization wishes to maximize $\bar{\pi}$ means that it has a powerful incentive to exaggerate.

But the temptation to exaggerate hinders the effort to educate. Once the positions have been announced, the organization cannot be trusted to provide accurate information about the size of θ. If voters were to expect the organization to use as few as three distinct messages in its report, the leaders would never issue the "middle" of the three possible reports. This report would be dominated by one of the others that generates a more extreme expectation about $\bar{\pi}$.

Since the SIG cannot credibly use a vocabulary with three or more messages, we focus on the possibility that there is a 2-partition equilibrium in the communication subgame. If such an equilibrium exists, the organization reports "low" when $\theta \leq \theta_1(p^A, p^B)$ and reports "high" when $\theta \geq \theta_1(p^A, p^B)$. The cut-off point θ_1 can be a function of p^A and p^B here, because the leaders know the parties' positions when they decide what message to send. If the SIG reports "low," it leads voters to believe that $E\tilde{\theta} = (\theta_{\min} + \theta_1)/2$. Then $\bar{\pi}_S = (\theta_{\min} + \theta_1)/2$ and $\bar{\pi}_P = (\theta_{\min} + \theta_1)\rho/2 + \delta$. If the SIG reports "high," $E\tilde{\theta} = (\theta_{\max} + \theta_1)/2$. Then $\bar{\pi}_S = (\theta_1 + \theta_{\max})/2$ and $\bar{\pi}_P = (\theta_1 + \theta_{\max})\rho/2 + \delta$.

As always, the incentives facing the SIG must coincide with the voters' interpretation of its messages. The organization must not prefer to report "low" for any value of $\theta > \theta_1(p^A, p^B)$, or to report "high" for any $\theta < \theta_1(p^A, p^B)$. For this to be so, it is necessary that the leaders be indifferent between issuing the alternative reports when $\theta = \theta_1(p^A, p^B)$. But the alternative reports induce different probabilities of election for the two parties. The SIG will not be indifferent among two situations with different election odds unless its members would be equally happy with the two pliable policy outcomes that might result. This in turn requires that π_S be equidistant from the parties' proposals—that is, that $\theta = \bar{p}$. We conclude that, if a 2-partition equilibrium exists for some pair of positions p^A and p^B with $p^A \neq p^B$, then $\theta_1(p^A, p^B) = \bar{p}$.

A 2-partition equilibrium does not exist if $\omega + (1 - \omega)\rho < 0$ or if the midpoint between the positions falls outside the range between $\theta_{\min}$ and $\theta_{\max}$. A situation with $\omega + (1 - \omega)\rho < 0$ can arise when the general public knows that what is good for the group is bad for them ($\rho < 0$), and when there is a sufficient number of these voters to make the SIG wish to practice deception. Then the SIG leaders will have an incentive to report "high" when θ actually is low, and to report "low" when θ actually is high. No reports can be credible under such conditions, so the only equilibrium is the babbling equilibrium. If $\omega + (1 - \omega)\rho > 0$ but $\bar{p} < \theta_{\min}$, the SIG also has an inevitable credibility problem. Then its leaders have an incentive to report "low" for all values of θ. Or, if $\omega + (1 - \omega)\rho > 0$ but $\bar{p} > \theta_{\max}$, they have an incentive to report "high" for all values of θ. In each of these situations as well, the only possible outcome is a babbling equilibrium.

In all other cases—that is, when $\omega + (1 - \omega)\rho > 0$ and $\theta_{\max} > \bar{p} > \theta_{\min}$—there does exist a 2-partition equilibrium in the communication subgame. In this equilibrium, the SIG reports "high" when the state θ exceeds the midpoint between the parties' pliable positions and reports "low" otherwise. The former message leads voters to believe that $E\tilde{\theta} = (\theta_{\max} + \bar{p})/2$, while the latter message leads them to believe that $E\tilde{\theta} = (\theta_{\max} + \bar{p})/2$. Voters update their beliefs about their own ideal policies based on this new understanding of the policy environment.[12]

6.3.2 Political Competition

We turn now to the competition between the parties. The parties choose their positions in anticipation of the SIG's report to the public and the subsequent voting. We assume that $\omega + (1 - \omega)\rho > 0$, so that an equilibrium with meaningful communication exists for some values of p^A and p^B. We also assume that the parties anticipate a 2-partition equilibrium in the communication subgame whenever their positions are in the range such that an equilibrium of this sort exists.

---

12. This statement requires some further clarification. Voters update their beliefs based on the organization's announcement for all p^A and p^B such that $p^A \neq p^B$ and $\theta_{\min} < \bar{p} < \theta_{\max}$. However, the equilibrium that we shall describe in the next section is characterized by convergence in the parties' positions. The (identical) positions that the parties adopt in equilibrium give voters some additional information about the value of θ, whereas the report from the SIG, in the case of identical positions, does not. In equilibrium, therefore, the voters update their beliefs based on the positions and not on the report. The equilibrium updating of beliefs about θ does not affect voting in this case, because voters base their vote on the fixed positions when the pliable positions are the same. The out-of-equilibrium updating that we describe here is important for identifying the equilibrium, however, inasmuch as it allows us to calculate the implications for the election odds of any deviation that a party might contemplate.

Suppose that party A expects its rival to announce a position p^B different from the group's ideal of $\pi_S = \theta$, but between $\theta_{\min}$ and $\theta_{\max}$. If party A were to announce the same position, its chance of winning the election would be $F_b(0)$, where $F_b(\cdot)$ is the cumulative distribution function of the random popularity variable $\tilde{b}$. Alternatively, party A might take a position a bit closer to π_S than its rival. For example, if $p^B < \pi_S$, party A might contemplate a position of $\hat{p}^A = p^B + e$, for some small but positive value of e. Such positioning would leave the midpoint between the parties' positions a bit below the group's ideal (i.e., $\bar{p} = p^B + e/2 < \pi_S$), and thus would induce the SIG leaders to report "high." This report would cause voters to update their beliefs such that $E\tilde{\theta} = (\bar{p} + \theta_{\max})/2$, thereby generating an expected ideal policy in the voting population of $\bar{\pi} = [\omega + (1 - \omega)\rho](\bar{p} + \theta_{\max})/2 + (1 - \omega)\delta$.[13] Then, by (6.4), party A would win a majority of votes with probability $F_b[2f(\bar{p} - \bar{\pi})(-e)]$.

If $2f(\bar{p} - \bar{\pi})(-e) > 0$, the announcement of $\hat{p}^A$ would give the party a better chance of winning the election than an announcement of $p^A = p^B$. So, if $p^B < [\omega + (1 - \omega)\rho](p^B + \theta_{\max})/2 + (1 - \omega)\delta$, party A wishes to locate a bit closer to π_S than its rival. But if party A has an incentive to shade its rival's position in the direction of the SIG's preferences, then party B has an incentive to do this as well. Each party anticipates that the SIG's education campaign might help or harm its electoral prospects, depending on the location of its pliable position relative to that of its rival. The competition to induce a helpful report drives the parties to cater to the special interest.

In an equilibrium, neither party can have an incentive to outdo its rival. The equilibrium, therefore, has convergent positions. We now describe these positions. To this end, we define

$$\theta_l = \frac{[\omega + (1 - \omega)\rho]\theta_{\min} + 2(1 - \omega)\delta}{2 - \omega - (1 - \omega)\rho} \tag{6.8}$$

and

$$\theta_h = \frac{[\omega + (1 - \omega)\rho]\theta_{\max} + 2(1 - \omega)\delta}{2 - \omega - (1 - \omega)\rho}, \tag{6.9}$$

and assume, for the time being, that $\delta \geq (1 - \rho)\theta_{\min}$ and $\delta \leq (1 - \rho)\theta_{\max}$. The restrictions on δ ensure that $\theta_l \geq \theta_{\min}$ and $\theta_h \leq \theta_{\max}$.

---

13. To calculate this value of $\bar{\pi}$, we use $\theta_1 = \bar{p}$, $\pi_S = (\theta_1 + \theta_{\max})/2$, $\bar{\pi}_P = (\theta_1 + \theta_{\max})\rho/2 + \delta$, and $\bar{\pi} = \omega\bar{\pi}_S + (1 - \omega)\bar{\pi}_P$.

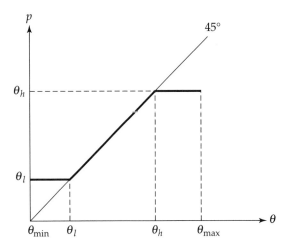

Figure 6.1
Equilibrium Policies with Late Communication

Then, if θ falls between θ_l and θ_h, the parties position themselves at the group's ideal pliable policy, or $p^A = p^B = \theta = \pi_S$. If $\theta > \theta_h$, the parties announce a common position of $p^A = p^B = \theta_h$, whereas if $\theta < \theta_l$ they announce a common position of $p^A = p^B = \theta_l$.

With these strategies for the parties, the equilibrium outcome in different states of the world is illustrated by the boldface line in figure 6.1. For intermediate values of θ, the political competition allows the interest group to achieve its favorite pliable policy in the given state. This is true, of course, no matter which party wins the election. For high values of θ, the outcome is $p = \theta_h$. For low values of θ, it is $p = \theta_l$. Since both θ_h and θ_l are constants, independent of θ, the policy outcome does not respond to the policy environment for extreme values of θ. The fraction of states in which the SIG obtains its ideal policy is larger, the greater is ω (the fraction of SIG members in the population) and the greater is ρ (the correlation in the interests of members and nonmembers).[14]

To understand why the indicated strategies are mutual best responses, consider a situation in which $\theta_l < \theta < \theta_h$ and $\pi_S > \pi_P$; in other

---

14. The fraction of states in which the SIG members achieve their ideal is

$$\frac{\theta_h - \theta_l}{\theta_{max} - \theta_{min}} = \frac{\omega + (1 - \omega)\rho}{2 - \omega - (1 - \omega)\rho}.$$

The statement in the text follows immediately.

words, the ideal pliable policy for the SIG exceeds the mean ideal policy for the public at large (the opposite case is analogous). Suppose that party A were to deviate from its position at $p^A = \pi_S = \theta$ and announce instead a position $\hat{p}^A$ that is smaller than π_S and thus closer to π_P. Then θ would exceed $\bar{p}$, and the SIG would report a "high" value of θ. The deviation and subsequent statement by the SIG would perhaps make party A more attractive to voters in the general public. But for every b, the fraction of total votes that party A could "win" by this deviation amounts to only $(1 - \omega)f[(2 - \rho)\bar{p} - \rho\theta_{max} - 2\delta](p^B - \hat{p}^A)$, in view of equation (6.3).[15] Meanwhile, the deviation would reduce the attractiveness of party A to SIG members. These members would interpret the report "high" to mean that the true value of θ exceeds $\bar{p}$, and some of them would switch their allegiance to party B. For a given value of b, the loss of support among SIG members would amount to a fraction $\omega f(\theta_{max} - \bar{p})(p^B - \hat{p}^A)$ of the total vote. Using the fact that $\bar{p} < \theta \leq \theta_h \leq \theta_{max}$, it is possible to show that the latter effect must dominate. This means that the deviation reduces the party's vote count for any given value of b, and thus it reduces its chances of winning the election. For intermediate values of θ, the best response to $p^B = \theta$ is for party A to set $p^A = \theta$.

Now consider a situation with $\theta > \theta_h$, and suppose that $p^B = \theta_h$. If party A were to deviate from $p^A = \theta_h$ to a policy closer to π_S, it would induce the SIG to issue a report of "high." This would enhance the party's attractiveness among group members but reduce its attractiveness to the general public. It is easy to confirm that, with such an extreme value of θ, the extra support among SIG members does not compensate for the loss of votes in the public at large.[16] Evidently, the parties will cater to the SIG in the hope of generating a favorable report, but only up to a point.

Similarly, if $\theta < \theta_l$, it is a best response for either party to announce a position of θ_l when it expects its rival to do so. A deviation in either

---

15. We calculate the vote change using $\bar{\pi}_P = \delta + \rho(\theta_1 + \theta_{max})/2 = \delta + \rho(\bar{p} + \theta_{max})/2$, and recognizing that the general public accounts for a fraction $1 - \omega$ of the total electorate. The use of quotation marks around "win" is meant to convey that this vote change could be negative.

16. If party A were to deviate from θ_h to $\hat{p}^A > \theta_h$, for example, its vote share for a given value of b would change by

$$f(p^B - \hat{p}^A)\{[2 - \omega - (1 - \omega)\rho]\bar{p} - [\omega + (1 - \omega)\rho]\theta_{max} - (1 - \omega)\rho\delta\}.$$

The expression in curly brackets is positive, because $\bar{p} > \theta_h$. Thus, with $p^B = \theta_h < \hat{p}^A$, the deviation by party A must cause it to lose votes.

direction is bound to cost a party some votes. It is interesting to note that, in this situation, the policy outcome may exceed both the ideal policy for group members and the ideal policy for the average voter in the general public. It might seem that either party could benefit by announcing a smaller level of the policy instrument than θ_l, if $\theta_l > \pi_S$ and $\theta_l > \pi_P$. However, the move toward π_P would actually cost the deviant party votes among the general public, because these voters would not know that π_P actually is small. In fact, their updated beliefs after the deviation and the report would be that $\bar{\pi}_P = (\theta_{\min} + \theta_1)\rho/2 + \delta$, which exceeds the true value of π_P when θ is small. The parties do not move their positions in a direction that benefits the average voter when $\theta < \theta_l$, because the voters in the general public would not recognize the move as one that served them well.

Up until now, we have assumed that $(1-\rho)\theta_{\max} > \delta > (1-\rho)\theta_{\min}$. Now let us consider what happens when $\delta < (1-\rho)\theta_{\min}$, so that $\theta_l < \theta_{\min}$. There are two cases to consider. The first such case arises when $\theta_h > \theta_{\min}$, as will be true if

$$\delta > \frac{\theta_{\min} - \frac{1}{2}(\theta_{\min} + \theta_{\max})[\omega + (1-\omega)\rho]}{1-\omega}.$$

Then the play of the game is similar to what we have just described. There is a range of values of θ extending from $\theta_{\min}$ to θ_h for which the parties' pliable positions match the SIG's ideal policy in every state, and a second range of values from θ_h to $\theta_{\max}$ for which $p^A = p^B = \theta_h$. The only difference from the situation depicted in figure 6.1 is that there is no range of values of θ for which $p^A = p^B = \theta_l$.

The second case arises when $\theta_h < \theta_{\min}$. Then the game plays out rather differently. The positions that the parties might otherwise take to induce a favorable message from the organization fall outside the range of feasible values for θ. Recall from Section 6.3.1 that if $\bar{p} < \theta_{\min}$, the messages from the SIG lack credibility. Since the leaders would announce "high" for all possible realizations of $\tilde{\theta}$, the voters simply ignore their reports. In the event, the outcome at the communication stage is a babbling equilibrium, which leaves the voters no better informed than they were at the outset of the game. With $\bar{\pi}_S = (\theta_{\min} + \theta_{\max})/2$ and $\bar{\pi}_P = (\theta_{\min} + \theta_{\max})\rho/2 + \delta$, the mean expected ideal policy in the electorate is $\bar{\pi} = (\theta_{\min} + \theta_{\max})[\omega + (1-\omega)\rho]/2 + (1-\omega)\delta$. The unique equilibrium has both parties announcing pliable positions at this level in all possible states of the world.

6.3.3   Early and Late Communication

Until now, we have assumed that the SIG has a single opportunity to convey information, which comes either before the parties have adopted their pliable positions or after they have done so. It may be possible, however, for the organization to undertake educational activities both early and late in the election cycle. The SIG might make some limited claims about the policy environment before the parties have taken their positions, and further claims after their positions have become clear.

It is straightforward to apply the modeling tools that we have developed to such a situation. To do so, we again must solve the game backward. Assuming that an n-partition would result from the initial communication, the voters will infer from the group's early announcement that θ lies in a range between, say, θ_j and θ_{j+1}. From this point forward, the game is exactly like the late-communication scenario, except that θ_j and θ_{j+1} play the role that $\theta_{\min}$ and $\theta_{\max}$ played in our earlier analysis. For realizations of $\tilde{\theta}$ between θ_j and θ_{j+1}, the parties might converge on pliable positions equal to some $\theta_{j,l}$ for low values of θ between θ_j and $\theta_{j,l}$; they might adopt the group's ideal policy for an intermediate range of values of θ; and they might converge on positions of $\theta_{j,h}$ for values of θ between $\theta_{j,h}$ and θ_{j+1}. In other words, the outcome in the subgame might be qualitatively the same as that depicted in figure 6.1, except that voters would already know from the earlier message that θ falls between θ_j and θ_{j+1}. The values of $\theta_{j,l}$ and $\theta_{j,h}$ can be calculated as functions of θ_j and θ_{j+1}, using the formulas in (6.8) and (6.9), but with θ_j taking the place of $\theta_{\min}$ and θ_{j+1} taking the place of $\theta_{\max}$.

All that is needed to complete the story are values of $\theta_1, \theta_2, \ldots, \theta_n$ that describe an n-partition equilibrium for the early-communication subgame. At $\theta = \theta_j$, the SIG must be indifferent between announcing that θ lies between θ_{j-1} and θ_j and announcing that it lies between θ_j and θ_{j+1}. At this stage, the organization anticipates that the former announcement will result in a pliable policy of $\theta_{j-1,h}$ and the latter will result in a pliable policy of $\theta_{j,l}$, in view of the events (positioning, announcement, voting) that will follow. The indifference conditions give a second set of relationships between the $\theta_{j,l}$ and $\theta_{j,h}$ variables and the θ_j's, which can be solved with the earlier ones for all the equilibrium values. We leave the details of this to the interested reader.

6.4 Endorsements

Many interest groups issue communiqués that serve only to identify their favorite candidate in an election. These messages, commonly known as *endorsements*, are a particularly simple form of public communication. They provide a summary account of the organization's preferences without going into any of the details.

One possible explanation for the prevalence of endorsements is the very fact of their simplicity. As we have noted, voters may be disinclined to invest a great deal of time and effort to educate themselves before voting. Thus, they may be unwilling to read a long message that provides details about the policy environment and the candidates' positions on the issues. But an endorsement requires hardly any input from the recipient. A voter can get the message by listening to a 30-second advertisement while driving to work, or by examining a single sheet of paper with block printing of a candidate's name. Moreover, an endorsement may well be cheaper for an interest group to send than more detailed reports.

Our analysis in the last section provides an alternative explanation for the common use of this type of message. Endorsements may convey as much information to voters as more detailed reports, once the credibility constraints on information transmission are taken into account. Moreover, an endorsement can be a very effective tool for a group to achieve its policy aims, especially if the ideal policy for the interest group is not too different from the average voter's ideal. We elaborate on these points below.

As we have seen, the leaders of a SIG who have been given a narrow mandate to pursue a single policy issue are limited in the vocabulary they can use to educate voters. Once the parties have adopted their positions, these leaders have a powerful incentive to exaggerate. If they favor one party's position over the other's, they will be tempted to portray the policy environment in a manner that shows their preferred party in the most favorable light. Astute voters will discount their claims and interpret them as indicating only the direction of the group's leanings. We saw that the resulting equilibrium can involve the use of at most two distinct messages.

In our discussion of late communication, we referred to the alternative messages as "high" and "low." These messages can be given a literal interpretation. They may take the form of a letter or an advertisement that makes the case for either a high or a low level of the pliable policy variable. With this literal interpretation, each voter is left to infer for herself which party has a position that is better suited to her interests.

But, clearly, the same outcome can be achieved with a different pair of messages. Namely, the SIG could announce "vote for party A" in states of the world in which the distance of p^A from the group's ideal pliable policy is smaller than the distance of p^B from π_S, and "vote for party B" when the opposite is true. In other words, a group can use an endorsement to effect a 2-partition equilibrium in the communication game.

The endorsement equilibrium is easy to describe. At the communication phase, the SIG endorses the party whose position is closer to the group's ideal. Then, if $\theta_{\min} \leq \bar{p} \leq \theta_{\max}$, the public infers from the endorsement whether θ is greater or less than $\bar{p}$. An endorsement of the party with the lesser proposal indicates $\theta \leq \bar{p}$; an endorsement of the other party implies $\theta \geq \bar{p}$. The voters gain no information from the endorsement when $\bar{p} < \theta_{\min}$ or $\bar{p} > \theta_{\max}$. In these situations, the SIG endorses the same party no matter what it knows about θ.

Anticipating this behavior, the parties compete for the group's endorsement. That is, they choose their pliable positions with an eye toward being named by the group as its preferred choice. The outcome of this competition is the same as described in Section 6.3.2. Namely, the parties take as their common positions the interest group's ideal policy level $\pi_S = \theta$ if θ falls between θ_l and θ_h. Otherwise they choose θ_h (for high values of θ) or θ_l (for low values of θ). Evidently, the SIG members fare quite well in the competition for the endorsement, especially when their ideal policy is not too extreme.

It is also possible to analyze the endorsement game when there is more than one organized interest group with a stake in the pliable policy decision. Such settings were considered in Grossman and Helpman (1996a), where we used a model of the election process similar to the one described here.[17] With several interest groups issuing endorsements, the parties recognize that by taking positions favorable to some, they may alienate others. Each party must decide which endorsements to seek, and which they are ready to concede. The relative sizes of the different interest groups are important for this—each party would like to have endorsements from a set of SIGs

---

17. The interested reader should also see Grossman and Helpman (1999), which has a more general model and additional discussion.

that comprises a large share of the voting population. In the equilibrium, the parties adopt a position that is favorable to an appropriately chosen "moderate" group, so that a deviation to either side would harm a party's prospects, in view of the endorsements that would thereby be gained and lost.

6.5 Educating Members

So far we have discussed educational campaigns aimed at a broad spectrum of voters. Many interest groups also target information flows more narrowly. They seek to educate voters who are already sympathetic to their cause, especially their own rank-and-file members. Most interest groups endeavor to keep their members informed about new and prospective legislation and about other political developments that are likely to have an impact on their welfare.

It might seem that the credibility problems that arise when a SIG tries to educate a suspicious public about the policy environment would not be present when the organization seeks to educate its own like-minded members. But, as we have observed before, that is not always the case. The leaders of an interest group will aim to serve the aggregate or average interests of their constituents, whereas an individual member will be concerned with her own well-being. To the extent that the preferences of different members of a group diverge on at least some policy issues, the leaders and members need not share the same electoral objectives. The central organization has reason to mislead its rank and file if by doing so it can induce individual members to vote in a manner that serves the group as a whole. For this reason, the members must be wary of the information they receive from their own organization.

First we discuss messages that are delivered to a group's members before the parties have adopted their pliable positions. These messages might be conveyed in a group newsletter or magazine, or in a more detailed policy brief. As before, we assume that the SIG knows something about the policy environment that voters do not, as summarized in a variable θ. The information bears on the members' interest in a pliable policy issue, and possibly is relevant to other voters as well. We continue to assume that $\pi_S = \theta$ and $\pi_P = \rho\theta + \delta$, but now suppose that the general public does not observe the content of the group's report about θ.

One possible outcome is that the political parties will respond to the updated beliefs of SIG members, but will take the beliefs of other voters as given. In the event, the parties will announce identical positions on the pliable issue of $p^A = p^B = \omega\bar{\pi}_S + (1 - \omega)\bar{\pi}_P$, where $\bar{\pi}_S$ is the members' updated expectation of their ideal policy (reflecting the message they receive) and $\bar{\pi}_P = (\theta_{min} + \theta_{max})\rho/2 + \delta$ is the prior expectation of the average nonmember about her own ideal policy. With this assumed behavior on the part of the parties, the organization can forecast the relationship between its own messages and the final policy outcome by taking $\bar{\pi}_P$ as given. An equilibrium in the communication game involves a reporting scheme in which leaders' incentives are consistent with the members' interpretation. This requirement should be familiar by now, as should the resulting partition equilibria. The only difference between these equilibria and those that arise when the group's reports are issued publicly is that now the general public does not update its beliefs based on the report. In this sense, these equilibria are similar to the ones that can arise with public communication when $\rho = 0$.

But with targeted policy reports, other equilibria may be possible as well. The outcome in the political competition clearly depends on what inferences the voters draw from the positions they see the parties taking. Suppose, for example, that $\theta < \theta_1$. The equilibrium just described has $p^A = p^B = \omega(\theta_{min} + \theta_1)/2 + (1 - \omega)[(\theta_{min} + \theta_{max})\rho/2 + \delta]$ for such low values of θ. If the voters who are not members of the interest group see the parties take these positions, they will be able to infer that the group's report to its members must have been "low." Thus, they will be able to update their beliefs about θ without observing the message directly. However, such updating has no effect on their voting, because their understanding of the pliable issue does not matter when the parties' positions are the same.

The important question for us to ask is, How will voters react if they observe a pair of positions that are not the same? With $\theta < \theta_1$, suppose that party A were to announce a position slightly different from the one described above. One possibility is that voters who do not observe the group's message might say to themselves, "This is not consistent with my understanding of the equilibrium, so I remain completely agnostic about the value of θ." With this interpretation of events by the uninformed voters, the deviation by party A will be harmful to its election prospects. But another possibility is that voters outside the group might instead say to themselves, "This is not what I expected to observe, but since both positions are quite low, it is likely that the SIG sent its members a message of 'low'." With this alternative interpretation of events by the uninformed voters, the deviation by party A might well prove beneficial to its electoral prospects. If so, the parties would not announce the positions described above, but some others that would depend on the precise manner in which the voters outside the group update their beliefs. There is little to pin down the response by voters in the public at large. But the assumption that these voters will maintain their prior beliefs is not especially compelling.

Now let us turn our attention to the game in which the SIG sends messages to its members after the parties have announced their positions. In this situation there is nothing to tip off the general public about the content of the group's message. It seems more justifiable, then, to assume that voters in the public at large would retain their prior beliefs. We will proceed with the assumption that $\bar{\pi}_P = (\theta_{\min} + \theta_{\max})\rho/2 + \delta$ no matter what late message the SIG sends to its members.

Consider first the communication game for a given pair of positions p^A and p^B, with $\bar{p} = (p^A + p^B)/2$. As before, the leaders report "low" if $\theta < \bar{p}$, and report "high" otherwise. For p^A and p^B such that $\theta_{\max} > \bar{p} > \theta_{\min}$, the report allows SIG members to identify which pliable position is closer to their ideal. For other levels of p^A and p^B, the report provides no information to the members. Of course, the report never provides any new information to the voters in the general public, because they do not observe its content.

Now consider once more the political competition between the parties. The parties anticipate the organization's report and compete to be portrayed by it in a favorable light. But this time they suspect that the voting behavior of the general public will not be affected by the group's (private) report. We assume that the parties take $\bar{\pi}_P$ as given. Then we can compute the best responses for the parties under the hypothesis that $\bar{\pi}_P = (\theta_{\min} + \theta_{\max})\rho/2 + \delta$.

We find, as before, that the competition gives the SIG members their ideal pliable policy for a range of values of θ. The range extends from some θ_l to some θ_h, as it did before, although the values of θ_l and θ_h are not the same as with public messages. Using the assumption that $\bar{\pi}_P$ is fixed, we can calculate the largest and smallest policy that the parties would be willing to announce in order to induce a favorable message. These are[18]

$$\theta_h = \frac{(1-\omega)\rho(\theta_{min}+\theta_{max})+\omega\theta_{max}+2(1-\omega)\delta}{2-\omega}$$

and

$$\theta_l = \frac{(1-\omega)\rho(\theta_{min}+\theta_{max})+\omega\theta_{min}+2(1-\omega)\delta}{2-\omega}.$$

For $\theta > \theta_h$, $p^A = p^B = \min\{\theta_h, \theta_{max}\}$, while for $\theta < \theta_l$, $p^A = p^B = \max\{\theta_l, \theta_{min}\}$. This completes our discussion of the political game that arises when a SIG sends late messages to its members, the contents of which are not observed by the general public.

In this chapter, we have studied how interest groups may further their political objectives by using their knowledge of the policy environment to educate the public. We have seen how the temptation to exaggerate can hinder the effort to communicate. This problem is especially severe late in the election cycle, when the candidates have already announced their positions on the issues. Then the interest group is tempted to paint a picture of the policy environment that casts its preferred party in a very favorable light. At this stage, its detailed reports about the policy issues will not be credible, and the best it can do is to identify the party whose proposal would better serve the rank-and-file members. Paradoxically, the members of the SIG fare particularly well when their organization has such a limited ability to communicate. When the language of communication is blunt, the competition between parties for a report that wins them support is especially intense.

An interest group also benefits from the ability to issue early reports. Such reporting can be used to provide voters with background information about the policy issues. When the SIG controls the flow of information, the need for credibility again limits the amount of detail that can be supplied. Still, the education of the public allows the group to achieve a policy closer to its ideal than would be the case in the absence of any publicity campaign.

---

18. The value of θ_h is derived by setting $\theta_h = \bar{p} = \bar{\pi}$, with

$$\bar{\pi} = (1-\omega)[\tfrac{1}{2}(\theta_{min}+\theta_{max})\rho+\delta]+\omega\tfrac{1}{2}(\bar{p}+\theta_{max}).$$

This is the largest value of θ at which it is a best response for a party to set its position equal to θ when its rival does likewise and $\bar{\pi}_P = (\theta_{min}+\theta_{max})\rho/2+\delta$. The value of θ_l is derived analogously.

6.6   Appendix: SIG Leaders with a Broad Mandate

In the main text, we distinguished two alternative objectives that the leaders of an interest group might have. The leaders might pursue the group's collective interests in areas where the members have similar preferences. Or they might pursue the group's aggregate welfare from all dimensions of government policy. In the case of a narrow mandate, the organization takes actions to induce a pliable policy that is as close to the group's ideal as possible. If the mandate is broad, the leaders aim instead to maximize the members' total expected utility, including the utility that they derive from policy issues on which they have no common views.

We have seen that the form of the mandate does not bear on the leaders' communication early in the election cycle. When an organization issues early reports, the leaders anticipate subsequent convergence in the parties' pliable platforms. They realize that the election outcome will hinge on the popularity of the parties' fixed positions, which their message does not affect. Therefore, the leaders focus their efforts on achieving a favorable pliable policy, no matter what their mandate happens to be.

However, the mandate becomes important when communication takes place after the parties have announced their positions. In the text, we focused on the simpler case of a narrow mandate. We found that, with such a mandate, the leaders are inclined toward extreme statements about the policy environment. In contrast, leaders who perceive a broader mandate will be more restrained in their claims. Such leaders will recognize that they do not know the relative popularity of the parties' fixed positions, and they will be reluctant to overstate their case, lest they engineer a victory for a party that proves to be unpopular with their average member.

In this appendix, we study late communication by an interest group whose leaders have a broad mandate. We find that such leaders have only a limited incentive to exaggerate about the policy environment. In some circumstances, their reticence permits greater communication than would be possible if their mandate were narrow. After discussing the equilibria that are possible in the communication subgame, we revisit the competition between the political parties. Finally, we compare the policy outcomes that result from the different mandates.

6.6.1 Communication Game When SIG Leaders Have a Broad Mandate

We consider the incentives facing an organization that has detailed knowledge of the policy environment. As before, the information in the hands of the leaders allows them to identify the ideal pliable policy for SIG members. The information also may be relevant to the general public.

The leaders seek to maximize the average expected utility of group members. We can write the maximand as

$$EU_S = \bar{v}_S^A + \int_{b_{\min}}^{\beta} -(p^A - \theta)^2 f_b(b)\, db + \int_{\beta}^{b_{\max}} \left[-(p^B - \theta)^2 + \frac{b}{f} \right] f_b(b)\, db.$$

(6.10)

Here, $\bar{v}_S^A = E\tilde{v}_S^A$ is the expected utility that the average SIG member would derive from the fixed positions of party A, $f_b(\cdot)$ is the probability density function that describes the leaders' beliefs about the likely popularity of the two parties, $b_{\min}$ and $b_{\max}$ are the minimum and maximum values of b in this distribution, and β is the cutoff value for b at which party A wins the election; that is, $b = \beta$ implies $s = 1/2$. Note that $\bar{v}_S^A$ is outside the leaders' control. Note too that the second integral includes the realization of $\tilde{b}$, which is the "extra" utility (positive or negative) that members would derive from the fixed positions of party B, were that party to win the election. The leaders recognize that their message can affect this component of utility, because the report might change the winner of the election. When deciding what message to send, the leaders must consider what values of b are most likely to prevail when their communiqué makes the difference in the election.[19]

The leaders are concerned with how their pronouncement will affect EU_S. Their message will alter voters' beliefs about θ, thereby changing $\bar{\pi}$ and β. From equation (6.4), we know that

$$\beta = 2f(\bar{p} - \bar{\pi})(p^B - p^A).$$

(6.11)

We can use (6.10) to calculate the effect of a change in β on the average expected utility of group members. We find

---

19. Some readers will recognize a parallel with the work of Feddersen and Pesendorfer (1996). These authors discuss how an imperfectly informed voter ought to condition his vote on the states of the world in which his vote is pivotal.

$$\frac{dEU_S}{d\beta} = \left[(p^B - \theta)^2 - (p^A - \theta)^2 - \frac{\beta}{f}\right] f_b(\beta).$$

After substituting for β using (6.11), this equation can be rewritten as

$$\frac{dEU_S}{d\beta} = 2(p^A - p^B)(\theta - \bar{\pi}) f_b(\beta).$$

Finally, since $d\beta/d\bar{\pi}$ is positive if and only if $(p^A - p^B)$ is positive, we see that the SIG wishes to deliver a message that raises $\bar{\pi}$ if and only if $\bar{\pi} < \theta$. Evidently, SIG leaders with a broad mandate will exaggerate their statements about θ only up to a point. Once $\bar{\pi} = \theta$, they have no desire to induce still higher expectations of π_S and π_P.

We now attempt to construct a 2-partition equilibrium for the communication subgame. As before, voters take the message "low" to mean that θ lies between $\theta_{\min}$ and θ_1 for some value of θ_1, and the message "high" to mean that θ lies between θ_1 and $\theta_{\max}$. The alternative messages induce different values of β, the greatest value of the bias parameter b for which party A wins the election. In particular, if the SIG reports "low," the cutoff point for a victory by party A is $\beta_{low} = 2f\{\bar{p} - [\omega + (1 - \omega)\rho](\theta_{\min} + \theta_1)/2 - (1 - \omega)\delta\}(p^B - p^A)$, considering that $\bar{\pi} = [\omega + (1 - \omega)\rho](\theta_{\min} + \theta_1)/2 + (1 - \omega)\delta$ when voters believe that $\theta \leq \theta_1$. If the SIG reports "high," the cutoff point instead is $\beta_{high} = 2f\{\bar{p} - [\omega + (1 - \omega)\rho](\theta_1 + \theta_{\max})/2 - (1 - \omega)\delta\}(p^B - p^A)$.

The organization must be indifferent between sending the alternative messages when $\theta = \theta_1$. This requires

$$\int_{b_{\min}}^{\beta_{low}} -(p^A - \theta_1)^2 f_b(b)\, db + \int_{\beta_{low}}^{b_{\max}} \left[-(p^B - \theta_1)^2 + \frac{b}{f}\right] f_b(b)\, db$$

$$= \int_{b_{\min}}^{\beta_{high}} -(p^A - \theta_1)^2 f_b(b)\, db + \int_{\beta_{high}}^{b_{\max}} \left[-(p^B - \theta_1)^2 + \frac{b}{f}\right] f_b(b)\, db$$

or

$$2(\theta_1 - \bar{p})(p^A - p^B) = \frac{1}{F_b(\beta_{high}) - F_b(\beta_{low})} \int_{\beta_{low}}^{\beta_{high}} \frac{b}{f} f_b(b)\, db. \qquad (6.13)$$

The left-hand side of (6.13) gives the extra utility (positive or negative) that a group member would derive from having a pliable policy of p^A instead of p^B when his actual ideal policy is θ_1. The right-hand side gives the leaders' expectation of the extra utility (positive or negative) that the average member would derive from the fixed positions of party B, conditional on b falling in the range between β_{low} and β_{high}. Thus, equation (6.13) determines a value of θ at which the group's preference for one party's pliable position matches the leaders' guess of their likely preference for the other party's fixed positions, where the assessment of the latter applies only to those values of $\tilde{b}$ at which the group's announcement will make the difference in the election.

To proceed further, we assume that the leaders have a uniform prior distribution on the relative popularity of party B. That is, we take $\tilde{b}$ to be uniformly distributed between b_{min} and b_{max}, so that $F_b(\cdot)$ is linear and f_b is a constant. In this case, the conditional expectation of b/f on the right-hand side of (6.13) equals $(\beta_{low} + \beta_{high})/2f$. This, together with the expressions for β_{low} and β_{high}, implies that

$$\theta_1 = \left[\frac{\omega + (1 - \omega)\rho}{2 - \omega - (1 - \omega)\rho}\right]\left(\frac{\theta_{min} + \theta_{max}}{2}\right) + \left[\frac{2(1 - \omega)}{2 - \omega - (1 - \omega)\rho}\right]\delta. \quad (6.14)$$

Note that the value of θ_1 in (6.14) is independent of p^A and p^B. This means that, with a broad mandate, the credibility of the leaders' late message does not depend on the positions that the parties have adopted. The leaders have the same incentive to announce that θ is low when, say, both parties have announced positions close to the group's ideal policy as when one party has taken a position a bit below θ_1 and the other has taken one much farther away. This property of the partition equilibrium is special to the case of a uniform distribution for $\tilde{b}$; with a different function $F_b(\cdot)$, the cutoff point θ_1 typically would vary with p^A and p^B.

If the value of θ_1 in (6.14) falls between θ_{min} and θ_{max}, then we have a legitimate 2-partition equilibrium of the subgame with late communication. Clearly, the existence of a 2-partition equilibrium depends on the values of ω, δ, and ρ. Notice that when a 2-partition equilibrium does exist, the point at which the organization switches from sending one message to sending the other does not come at $\theta_1 = \bar{p}$. In other words, the organization does not switch from reporting "low" to reporting "high" at a value of θ at which the group is indifferent between the pliable positions of the two parties.

To understand why this is so, consider a concrete example. Suppose that $p^B > p^A$, $\bar{p} = (\theta_{min} + \theta_{max})/2$, $\delta < 0$, $\rho = 1$, and that θ is a bit less than $\bar{p}$. In this situation, if the leaders had a narrow mandate, they would report "low" in order to steer votes to party A. But with a broad mandate, the leaders report differently. Given voters' prior beliefs, the average voter prefers the pliable position of party A before he learns anything about θ from the interest group. Thus, the election will be close only if the fixed positions of party B prove to be the more popular. These are the only conditions under which the organization's message might make the difference in the election. Since θ is close to $\bar{p}$, the SIG members will fare almost as well under p^B as under p^A. A report of "high" improves the average member's overall welfare by helping party B to win in situations where it is likely that $b > 0$.

There is another special property of the 2-partition equilibrium that arises when the leaders' prior beliefs about $\tilde{b}$ are uniformly distributed. Notice that the value of θ_1 in (6.14) is the same as that in (6.6). In other words, the leaders with a broad mandate convey the same information with their late communication as they would if their message were sent earlier. This property of the equilibrium would not hold for other distributions of $\tilde{b}$. But no matter what the leaders' beliefs about $\tilde{b}$, their late messages have greater credibility than they would if their mandate were narrow. As we have seen, leaders with a narrow mandate can use at most two distinct messages to describe the policy environment in the communication subgame. But leaders with a broad mandate may be able to go beyond a 2-partition equilibrium. Depending on parameter values and the shape of $F_b(\cdot)$, it may be possible for them to choose from three or more distinct messages in their late communication about the policy environment. The extra credibility reflects their limited incentive to exaggerate, as compared to the unlimited incentive that confronts leaders with a narrow mandate once they know the parties' positions.

6.6.2 *Political Competition When SIG Leaders Have a Broad Mandate*

We turn now to the competition between political parties that anticipate the announcements of the SIG leaders. To illustrate the nature of this competition, we focus on a special case with $\rho = 1$ and $\delta < 0$. We also assume that the parties expect the organization to choose from at most two distinct messages, no matter what the parties' positions happen to be. In this case, (6.14) implies

$$\theta_1 = \frac{\theta_{\min} + \theta_{\max}}{2} + 2(1 - \omega)\delta. \tag{6.15}$$

As in the case of early communication, the political equilibrium features convergence of the pliable positions of the two parties. For $\theta \geq \theta_1$ the parties adopt the pliable positions

$$p^A = p^B = \theta_{\max} + 2(1 - \omega)\delta - \tfrac{1}{4}(\theta_{\max} - \theta_{\min}) \qquad (6.16)$$

while for $\theta \leq \theta_1$ they adopt the pliable positions

$$p^A = p^B = \theta_{\min} + 2(1 - \omega)\delta + \tfrac{1}{4}(\theta_{\max} - \theta_{\min}). \qquad (6.17)$$

These are the same positions that result with early communication. Here they reflect the parties' expectation that the SIG will educate voters about the size of θ, but that the organization will not alter its intended message in response to the parties' position.

6.6.3   A Comparison of Two Mandates

Having described outcomes of the communication-cum-election game under alternative assumptions about the organization's mandate, we can now pose a further question. Suppose the interest group could choose the objective function of its leaders. Should the group direct its leaders to focus narrowly on the pliable policy issue or more broadly on the members' overall welfare? Of course, the instructions would have to be issued behind a veil of ignorance, that is, at a time when the members know only the prior distribution of $\tilde{\theta}$, and not the actual realization of the state of the world. The instructions would also need to be observable to the political parties and binding, or else the parties might choose their positions in expectation of different behavior by the leaders than would actually be the case.

A comparison of the two mandates teaches an interesting lesson. On the one hand, the leaders who concern themselves with the overall welfare of the members have greater credibility. Such leaders are better able to educate group members about the policy environment. This education is valuable to the members, because it allows them to elect with higher probability the party that would provide them with higher welfare. Such considerations alone would suggest that the leaders ought be granted a broad mandate. On the other hand, the competition between the political parties for favorable publicity is more intense when the leaders focus narrowly on the pliable issue. As we have seen, leaders with such a focus can only report credibly about which of the parties' pliable positions would better serve the group. Knowing that the organization will provide voters with only this information, the parties are led to adopt positions at or close to the group's ideal policy.

The analysis we have performed allows us to compare outcomes for the special case where $\rho = 1$ and the SIG leaders send one of two distinct messages. In the case of a narrow mandate, the equilibrium pliable policy matches the group's ideal for all values of θ between $\theta_l = \theta_{\min} + 2(1 - \omega)\delta$ and $\theta_h = \theta_{\max} + 2(1 - \omega)\delta$. So the only time that the broad mandate might conceivably deliver a better pliable policy to the group members is when $\theta < \theta_l$ or $\theta > \theta_h$. Since $\theta_l < \theta_1 < \theta_h$ (see (6.15)), it follows that for $\theta < \theta_l$ the pliable policy exceeds the SIG's ideal policy under either mandate, and the policy outcome is larger (and thus farther from the group's ideal) in the case of a broad mandate.[20] Similarly, when $\theta > \theta_h$, the pliable policy falls short of the SIG's ideal policy under either mandate, but the shortfall is larger when the leaders have a broad mandate.[21] Thus, no matter what the actual value of θ, the SIG members achieve a more favorable pliable policy when their leaders pursue a narrow mandate than when they pursue a broad one. Moreover, the parties' pliable positions coincide in every equilibrium. This means that the probability that either party will win the election is the same with the two different mandates. The chances for implementation of the alternative fixed platforms are also the same. It follows that the group members fare better when their leaders focus narrowly on the pliable issue than when they are more broadly concerned, at least when their communication creates a 2-partition equilibrium.

It is possible that a group might wish to grant its leaders a broad mandate if by doing so it allowed them to provide detailed information about the policy environment. We cannot rule out the possibility that members' ex ante welfare would be higher with welfare-maximizing leaders, were the latter able to achieve an equilibrium in the communication game with more than two messages. But the SIG members will often fare better when their leaders are instructed to ignore issues besides those of common interest to the membership. The constraint that this narrow mandate imposes on the leaders' communication serves the members well in the political competition.

---

20. Note from (6.17) that the equilibrium policy exceeds θ_l in this case.
21. Note from (6.16) that the equilibrium policy falls short of θ_h in this case.

III   Campaign Contributions

7   Buying Influence

We have seen how interest groups can use their knowledge of the issues and candidates as a tool for political influence. Our focus switches now from information to money. As we noted in Chapter 1 (and as should be plain to anyone who heeds the popular press), SIGs play a large and growing role in political financing. In the 1997–1998 U.S. federal election cycle, for example, political action committees disbursed more than $470 million. The PACs contributed almost one-third of the funds raised by candidates for the U.S. Congress and accounted for a goodly share of the revenues of the political parties.[1]

What do the interest groups buy with their contributions? This is a sensitive question, and one that generates considerable controversy. The groups themselves claim that their giving is intended only to secure access to the policymakers. In Chapter 5 we saw that policymakers indeed have reason to place a price on their time in order to conserve this valuable resource and to screen lobbyists whose positions are unknown to them. But most observers do not believe that access is the groups' only aim. In the remainder of the book, we consider two obvious alternatives. In this chapter and the next two, we suppose that SIGs contribute to parties and politicians in a more or less direct attempt to influence their policy decisions. Then, in Chapter 10, we allow for an electoral motive in political giving. When groups contribute for this reason, they exert their influence on policy indirectly by helping their preferred candidates to get elected.

The suggestion that SIGs are trading money for influence conjures up a sordid image. Some readers might envision corrupt politicians in smoke-filled rooms peddling favors and haggling over the price.

---

1. See http://www.fec.gov/press/pacsum98.htm (accessed November 30, 2000).

But the reality can be quite different from this. The interaction between SIG and policymaker need not involve any explicit discussion of a quid pro quo. Rather, influence can be bought and sold by a subtle exchange in which both sides recognize what is expected of them. The SIG can make known by its words and deeds that it supports politicians who are sympathetic to its cause. Then the policymaker can appear to be taking actions to promote a constituent's interests while gratefully accepting the group's support. Campaign funds are an obvious necessity in modern politics, and one should not be surprised that politicians respond to the incentives they face.

To begin our study of campaign contributions, we examine the interaction between a single interest group and a single policymaker. The policymaker may be either an individual who has authority for some policy decisions or a cohesive political party. We postpone until Chapter 8 all discussion of the competition for influence between two or more SIGs. Chapter 9 examines a SIG's strategies for buying influence in situations where a group of politicians share responsibility for setting policies and where party discipline is weak.

In the next section we investigate a group's bid for influence over a single policy decision. We consider the determinants of its willingness to pay and the policy that results when it makes a take-it-or-leave-it offer. Section 7.2 presents an application of the theory to the allocation of spending on local public goods. Then, in Section 7.3, we extend the theory to situations in which a single SIG can influence the policymaker's choice of several policy instruments. This is followed again by an example, this one concerning an industry that seeks both protection from import competition and relief from costly environmental regulations. In the final section we relax the assumption that the SIG makes take-it-or-leave-it offers and examine the outcome of bargaining between the group and the policymaker.

7.1 One-Dimensional Policy Choice

To begin, we consider a setting in which a single individual (or political party) has unilateral authority to set a policy variable, p. This is the same as in Chapters 4 and 5. The policymaker's objective is to maximize a political utility function, $G(p,c)$, where c is the campaign contribution that she receives from the sole organized interest group. The utility function is meant to capture the policymaker's personal preferences over the various possible policy outcomes, as well as her concern for her future electoral prospects. The policy p will affect the politician's chances of being reelected if voters look retrospectively at her record when deciding whether to vote for her in subsequent elections. The utility function $G(\cdot)$ is assumed to be increasing in c; this reflects an assumption that the politician can use any funds she receives from the interest group to finance campaign spending or otherwise purchase political gain.[2]

The objective function of the interest group is $U(p, c)$. This function reflects the members' concern about the policy outcome and the costliness of the contributions to them. We do not address the issue of how this utility function relates to the policy preferences of the individual members, nor do we concern ourselves with the internal distribution of the burden for paying the contribution. Rather, we simply assume that the group has managed to overcome its collective action problem, and that $U(\cdot)$ represents its internally agreed objective. The group's utility is strictly decreasing in the size of the contribution, c.

In Chapters 4 through 6, we typically assumed that the policymaker and the SIG have favorite policy levels, and that the welfare of each declines with the square of the distance of the policy from their respective ideal levels. Here we place fewer restrictions on these utility functions, although the earlier specification is surely a legitimate special case. We assume that $G(\cdot)$ is single-peaked as a function of p for any given level of c. The ideal policy for the policymaker might or might not be different at different contribution levels. Also, the policymaker's welfare might be the same for a policy that is a certain amount greater than her ideal as it is for one that is the same amount less than her ideal (as with the quadratic), or she may view overshooting and undershooting of her favorite policy level differently. As for the interest group, it too may have an ideal policy for a given size of contributions, or its welfare might be everywhere increasing or decreasing with the level of p. We assume that both utility functions are continuous in their variables and that contributions cannot be negative.

There are different ways in which the politician and the SIG might strike a deal. The policymaker might suggest a contribution level to the group and indicate a policy she is willing to enact in return. Or the policymaker might meet with a representative of the SIG and the two might negotiate over a policy and a contribution. We will consider some of these possibilities later in the chapter, but for now we suppose that it is the interest group that takes the initiative in trying to influence the policy outcome. In particular, we assume that the representative of the SIG confronts the politician with a *contribution function*. This function indicates the size of the contribution the group intends to make in response to every possible level of the policy. We denote the contribution function by $C(p)$, with the interpretation that when the policymaker chooses the policy p, the interest group contributes $c = C(p)$. The SIG designs the function so as to maximize its own objective function.

The contribution function captures well the idea that different actions by the policymaker lead to different levels of campaign support. Nonetheless, it is obviously an abstraction from reality. No interest group would take the time to construct such a detailed and complete set of offers, and even it did so, it would have difficulty communicating such a function to the policymaker. Also, we think of the offer as being implicit rather than explicit. An explicit offer of contributions for policies might offend many a well-intentioned politician, who recognizes the need for campaign financing but does not like to think herself as for sale. Even a less scrupulous politician might worry that influence peddling would cost her politically if the deals became known to voters. Instead, the contribution function might be conveyed in a general discussion about the strength of the interest group's feelings about an issue and its relative preferences among the alternative possible outcomes. From such a discussion, the policymaker might come to realize that the size of the group's contribution would vary with its degree of satisfaction with the policy outcome. Finally, we note that the contribution function is only a promise, not a contract, and a vague one at that. The politician might worry that the SIG will renege on such a promise, or the SIG might worry that the policymaker will undo the policy action once the gift has been paid. We will assume that the relationship between the two is ongoing, so that promises are carried out to preserve the possibility of subsequent cooperation.

We ask now, What contribution function $C(p)$ should the SIG offer to the politician if the group anticipates that she will take the action that maximizes her own political welfare? This type of question

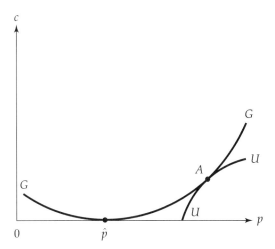

Figure 7.1
Candidate Equilibrium

arises frequently in other areas of economics and politics: it is the question of how a principal should design a payment scheme so as to give an agent the appropriate incentives to act on his behalf. Here we may think of the interest group as the principal and the politician as the agent. As in other contexts, the actions of the agent are not without cost; it is costly for the politician to pander to the SIG, because doing so means abandoning to some extent her own policy preferences as well as the interests of the general public.[3]

Figure 7.1 illustrates the solution to the SIG's problem of designing a contribution schedule to influence a single policy decision. In the figure, GG represents a typical indifference curve for the policymaker. Since the policymaker has preferences that are single-peaked as a function of p for a given value of c, and are everywhere increasing in c, the indifference curves have the shape that is shown; each reaches a minimum at some (possibly different) value of p and slopes downward to the left and upward to the right of this point. The minimum point corresponds to the politician's favorite policy, given the associated size of the contribution c.

---

3. Often, principal–agent problems are cast in a setting of asymmetric information. For example, the principal might not know the incentives facing the particular agent, or might not be able to observe the actions she takes. Here we abstract from such informational asymmetries, which greatly simplifies the problem. For models of contribution games with imperfect information, see Ball (1995) and Epstein and O'Halloran (1994).

Special meaning attaches to the particular indifference curve depicted in the figure. Notice that the curve reaches a minimum where $c = 0$. The policy marked $\hat{p}$ is the policymaker's favorite when contributions are zero. The curve thus depicts the points that give the politician the same level of welfare as what she could achieve in the absence of any dealings with the SIG. The group's offer must provide her with at least this level of welfare, for otherwise she would reject the offer and attain it on her own.

In the figure we also show a typical indifference curve for the SIG. This curve is labeled UU. If the group has a favorite policy for a given c, then the curve reaches a maximum at this policy level. If the group's welfare rises monotonically with p, then the curve is everywhere upward sloping. If its welfare falls monotonically with p, the curve is downward sloping. In any case, lower curves (with smaller contributions for a given level of p) correspond to higher levels of SIG welfare. The group's problem, then, is to induce a policy p° with a contribution c° such that p° and c° fall on the lowest curve possible.[4]

The point labeled A is a candidate solution. This point yields the greatest utility to the SIG among those that leave the policymaker at least as well off in the political equilibrium as she would be with a policy of $\hat{p}$ and no contributions from the interest group. All other points on or above GG fall on indifference curves above the one labeled UU, which means they give the SIG a lower level of welfare. What remains to be shown is that the SIG can achieve the welfare associated with point A by an appropriate (and feasible) choice of contribution schedule.

In fact, there are many schedules that would do the trick. Figure 7.2 illustrates two such schedules. The curves OCC and $OC'C'$ both coincide with the horizontal axis for some range of policies. This means that no contributions are offered unless the policy exceeds some minimum level. Both curves lie everywhere below GG, except that each touches GG at points A and B. Since the curves are everywhere non-negative, they are certainly feasible. And when confronted with either schedule, the politician can do no better than to choose p°. In fact, the politician is indifferent between $\hat{p}$ and p°, but the SIG could break the tie to its benefit by offering a tiny bit more for p° than what is indicated in the figure.

---

4. While we have drawn GG as convex and UU as concave, nothing we have assumed ensures these curvatures. However, these properties of the curves are not needed for the conclusions we draw.

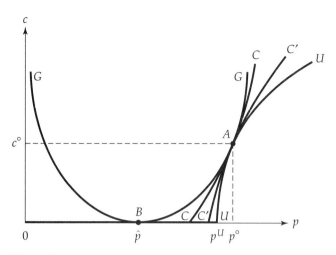

Figure 7.2
Optimal Contribution Functions

More formally, the equilibrium policy p° is the one that maximizes $U(p,c)$ subject to the constraint $G(p,c) \geq G(\hat{p},0)$. In the equilibrium, the SIG contributes c°, where $G(p^\circ,c^\circ) = G(\hat{p},0)$. Notice that this pair of policy and contribution is jointly efficient for the interest group and the policymaker. That is, no other policy choice and campaign gift can make either one better off without harming the other.[5] We will find that this property of the equilibrium generalizes to situations with many policy issues, to situations with bargaining between the politician and the SIG, and to many situations with competing interest groups.

The efficiency property of the equilibrium has particular force when the policymaker's utility function takes a special form. Suppose the policymaker derives her policy preferences from a concern for the welfare of the general public. This might reflect her desire to do well by her constituency, or it may be because she perceives a connection between voter well-being and her reelection prospects. Suppose further that she perceives a constant marginal utility of contributions, at least in the relevant range. Then we can write her objective as $G = \lambda W(p) + (1 - \lambda)c$, where $W(p)$ gives aggregate

---

5. This property of the equilibrium is reflected in the tangency between GG and UU at point A. Points on GG above the common tangent at A (besides A itself) give lower utility to the interest group. Points on UU below the tangent yield lower welfare to the politician.

welfare as a function of the policy variable. Finally, suppose the SIG, too, has a constant marginal utility of income, $U(p,c) = W_s(p) - c$. Then the fact that the equilibrium policy is jointly efficient implies that this policy maximizes $\lambda W(p) + (1 - \lambda)W_s(p)$; that is, it maximizes a weighted average of the welfare of interest group members and the general public. The weights reflect the policymaker's concern for the public's well-being relative to her taste for campaign funding.

Before we leave this section, we would like to identify a particular contribution schedule that the SIG can use to implement the equilibrium outcome. This schedule—which we refer to as a *compensating contribution function*—has some appealing properties that we will explain later.[6] A compensating contribution schedule is one that coincides with the group's indifference curve whenever the latter involves non-negative contributions, and coincides with the horizontal axis elsewhere. It is "compensating" in the sense that when the SIG makes positive offers for two different levels of the policy, the difference between the two offers compensates for the difference in the SIG's evaluation of the two policies. In other words, if $C(p)$ is a compensating function with $C(p_1) = c_1 > 0$ and $C(p_2) = c_2 > 0$ for some p_1 and p_2, then $U(p_1, c_1) = U(p_2, c_2)$. In figure 7.2 there is a compensating contribution function that coincides with the horizontal axis to the left of point p^U and coincides with UU to the right of that point. Notice that if the SIG were to propose this contribution schedule, the policymaker would respond by choosing the policy p° at point A.[7]

---

6. Bernheim and Whinston (1986a) were the first to discuss the properties of these functions, which they called "truthful." Some game theorists consider this terminology to be misleading, because it suggests the possibility of hiding the truth, when in fact the setting is one of complete information. We choose the term "compensating" to reflect the relationship between these functions and the economic concept of (Hicksian) compensating variation. The compensating varation is the amount an agent must be paid (or taxed) in a new situation to leave him exactly as well off as he was in an initial situation. When the SIG proposes a compensating contribution function, it offers the compensating variation relative to some reference level of utility (if that amount is non-negative).

7. More formally, let $\mu(p, U)$ be the contribution (possibly negative) that leaves the SIG with utility U when the policy is p. Then we define a compensating contribution schedule relative to the utility level U by

$$H(p, U) = \max[0, \mu(p, U)].$$

The equilibrium is achieved when the SIG offers the compensating schedule $H(p, U^\circ)$, where $U^\circ = U(p^\circ, c^\circ)$.

7.2   The Allocation of Public Spending

Let us turn to a simple application of the model to gain a better understanding of its implications. Suppose a politician has the authority to allocate a budget of size g to two different public services. Each of these services will benefit a distinct group of citizens. For example, the services might be health care for the elderly and day care for children, or road projects that will reduce transport costs for firms in one region or another. We label the groups with an index $i = 1$ or $i = 2$ and assume for simplicity that the benefit functions are symmetric. That is, when an amount g_i is spent on services of value to group i, the group enjoys gross benefits of $V(g_i)$. The benefit functions are increasing and concave, and give surplus for each group measured in dollars.

Now suppose that one group is politically organized but the other is not. The organized group offers campaign support with the aim of influencing the policymaker's allocation decision. The unorganized group refrains from any political activity.

The organized group has as its objective to maximize $U_1(g_1, c) = V(g_1) - c$, where c is the size of its political gift. The politician, on the other hand, sees the two groups as equally worthy, but also covets campaign funding. We suppose that her objective function takes the form $G(g_1, c) = \lambda[V(g_1) + V(g - g_1)] + (1 - \lambda)c$, where $V(g_1) + V(g - g_1)$ is the joint benefits of the two groups (gross of contributions) and λ gives the weight she attaches to aggregate welfare relative to campaign funds.

According to our earlier findings, the equilibrium allocation must be jointly efficient for the organized group and the politician. That is, it must maximize the welfare of one, given the welfare of the other. The allocation that maximizes $V(g_1) - c$ subject to $G(g_1, c) \geq \hat{G}$, where $\hat{G} = \lambda \max_{g_1}[V(g_1) + V(g - g_1)] = 2\lambda V(g/2)$, is the same as that which maximizes $V(g_1) + \lambda V(g - g_1)$.[8] This allocation, which satisfies

---

8. Note that the politician must be paid a contribution of

$$c = \frac{\hat{G}}{1 - \lambda} - \frac{\lambda}{1 - \lambda}[V(g_1) + V(g - g_1)]$$

in order to achieve a welfare level $\hat{G}$. Thus, the efficient policy maximizes

$$V(g_1) + \frac{\lambda}{1 - \lambda}[V(g_1) + V(g - g_1)] - \frac{\hat{G}}{1 - \lambda},$$

which is the same as maximizing $V(g_1) + \lambda V(g - g_1)$.

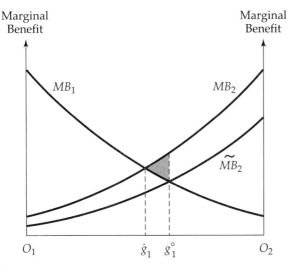

Figure 7.3
Budget Allocation

$$V'(g_1^\circ) = \lambda V'(g - g_1^\circ),\tag{7.1}$$

is depicted in figure 7.3.

In the figure, the total budget g is represented by the horizontal distance from O_1 to O_2. An allocation g_1 is measured rightward from the point labeled O_1, while $g_2 = g - g_1$ is measured leftward from the point labeled O_2. We depict the marginal benefit curves for the organized and unorganized groups respectively as MB_1 and MB_2. They intersect at $\hat{g}_1 = g/2$, where the budget is divided equally. This allocation maximizes aggregate welfare.

According to equation (7.1), the political equilibrium occurs at point g_1°, where MB_1 intersects a curve $\widetilde{MB}_2$, which is at a fraction λ of the height of MB_2. By offering contributions linked to the budget allocation, the organized group induces the politician to treat its rival's well-being with a reduced weight. The resulting division is skewed toward service 1, the more so the smaller is the politician's concern for aggregate well-being relative to her taste for campaign funds. In the limit, as λ approaches zero, the service that benefits the organized group receives all of the available public funds.

The model also predicts the size of the equilibrium contribution. The interest group must compensate the policymaker for the loss of political welfare arising from her failure to allocate the funds as she otherwise would. From the policymaker's perspective, the first-best allocation has equal shares, $g_1 = g_2 = g/2$. This allocation yields political welfare of $\hat{G} = 2\lambda V(g/2)$ when the organized group contributes nothing. The politician achieves this same level of welfare in the political equilibrium, which means that contributions satisfy $\lambda[V(g_1^\circ) + V(g - g_1^\circ)] + (1 - \lambda)c^\circ = 2\lambda V(g/2)$, or

$$c^\circ = \frac{\lambda}{1 - \lambda}\left[2V\left(\frac{g}{2}\right) - V(g_1^\circ) - V(g - g_1^\circ)\right]. \tag{7.2}$$

The size of the contribution can also be computed from the figure. The shaded area shows the loss of aggregate welfare resulting from the unequal distribution of public spending. The politician must be compensated for the political cost of this welfare loss, which means that contributions are $\lambda/(1 - \lambda)$ times this dollar amount.

It is interesting to observe that total contributions need not respond monotonically to the politician's taste for campaign funding. In our example, if $\lambda = 0$, then $c^\circ = 0$; the policymaker would require little by way of influence payment if she had little concern for public welfare. But contributions might also approach zero when λ approaches one. If it is too costly for an interest group to purchase a politician's favor, the group might refrain from doing so.

7.3 Multiple Policy Instruments

It is easy to extend the model to settings in which the policymaker sets the levels of several different policy instruments (or decides several dimensions of the same general policy). Suppose the policymaker has responsibility for setting a vector of policies $\mathbf{p} = (p_1, p_2, \ldots, p_m)$. Each p_i represents a different policy level, such as an emissions standard, a subsidy for pollution abatement equipment, and so on. The policymaker aims to maximize $G(\mathbf{p}, c)$, while the SIG aims to maximize $U(\mathbf{p}, c)$. The SIG designs a contribution schedule that relates the promised gift to the *vector* of government policies.

Although this problem may seem complex, the logic here is the same as before. The politician can unilaterally achieve political welfare of $G(\hat{\mathbf{p}}, 0)$ by setting the policies $\hat{\mathbf{p}} = \arg\max_{\mathbf{p}} G(\mathbf{p}, 0)$ and declining all gifts from the interest group. Surely she will not accept a deal that offers a lower welfare level than this. So the best the SIG can hope is to induce the policies that maximize $U(\mathbf{p}, c)$ subject to $G(\mathbf{p}, c) \geq G(\hat{\mathbf{p}}, 0)$. If attainable, these policies again would be jointly efficient for the interest group and the policymaker.

Once again, the SIG has many ways to achieve the constrained optimum. It can design any schedule that is tangent to the indifference surface passing through $G(\hat{\mathbf{p}}, 0)$ and that otherwise lies below it. We will illustrate by constructing the compensating schedule that implements an equilibrium policy outcome. Here a compensating schedule is one that takes the form

$$H(\mathbf{p}, U) = \max[0, \mu(\mathbf{p}, U)]$$

for some value of U, where $\mu(\mathbf{p}, U)$ is the contribution (possibly negative) that leaves the SIG with utility U when the policy vector is $\mathbf{p}$.

Suppose the SIG offers the particular compensating schedule $H(\mathbf{p}, U^\circ)$, where $U^\circ = U(\mathbf{p}^\circ, c^\circ)$ and $\mathbf{p}^\circ$ and c° maximize $U(\mathbf{p}, c)$ subject to $G(\mathbf{p}, c) \geq G(\hat{\mathbf{p}}, 0)$. How should the policymaker respond to this schedule? If she chooses $\mathbf{p}^\circ$, the schedule promises a gift of c°, leaving her with political welfare of $G(\mathbf{p}^\circ, c^\circ)$. If she chooses something different, say $\mathbf{p}^a$, then her welfare could be no higher. For suppose it were in fact higher, that is, $G[\mathbf{p}^a, H(\mathbf{p}^a, U^\circ)] > G(\mathbf{p}^\circ, c^\circ)$. Then it must be that $G[\mathbf{p}^a, H(\mathbf{p}^a, U^\circ)] > G(\hat{\mathbf{p}}, 0)$, because $G(\mathbf{p}^\circ, c^\circ)$ is no smaller than $G(\hat{\mathbf{p}}, 0)$. But this implies $H(\mathbf{p}^a, U^\circ) > 0$. Now, since a compensating schedule provides the SIG with the same utility at all policies that induce positive contributions, it must be that $U[\mathbf{p}^a, H(\mathbf{p}^a, U^\circ)] = U^\circ$. But here we have a contradiction, because this reasoning suggests that the SIG could have achieved higher utility than U^υ by inducing the policy vector $\mathbf{p}^a$ and offering a contribution slightly smaller than c°. Since $\mathbf{p}^\circ$ and c° are defined such that no such superior outcomes exist, it follows that the policymaker would willingly choose $\mathbf{p}^\circ$ when offered the schedule $H(\mathbf{p}, U^\circ)$.

We conclude this section by stating more formally what we mean by an equilibrium in the contribution game. This definition will be handy when we come to consider competing interest groups in Chapter 8.

Our formal definition is motivated by the following problem. The SIG does not wish to pay more for influence than is absolutely necessary. So the group pares its contribution just to the point of making the policymaker indifferent between its preferred outcome and another. But if the policymaker literally were indifferent, she might make the wrong choice. So the SIG must give the policymaker a tiny bit extra to break the tie. Of course, however much extra the SIG gives for this purpose, it can gain (slightly) by cutting that amount in half. We are left with a technical ambiguity, but one that is of no real importance.

To resolve this ambiguity, we allow the SIG to select among policy and contribution combinations that yield the policymaker the same level of welfare. It is, of course, not literally true that the SIG can choose the policy. But our proposed definition captures the idea that the SIG can always offer "just a little bit more" to break any ties. With this in mind, we first define the policymaker's *best-response set*. This is a set of policies (and corresponding contributions) that are equally desirable from the policymaker's perspective and more desirable than any others not in the set.

Definition 7.1   The policymaker's best-response set to a contribution function $C(\mathbf{p})$ consists of all feasible policy vectors $\mathbf{p}$ that maximize $G[\mathbf{p}, C(\mathbf{p})]$.

The best-response set includes all policy vectors that give the policymaker the greatest possible political welfare. Of course, if a unique policy vector maximizes $G[\mathbf{p}, C(\mathbf{p})]$, then the best-response set includes only this vector. Note that we restrict attention to so-called "feasible" policies. Infeasible policies might include those that violate an aggregate budget constraint. We also allow for the possibility that the choice set is limited for reasons outside the model, as for example when some policies are deemed to be "unconstitutional."

With the definition of the best-response set in hand, we next define an equilibrium for the two-stage game with a single policymaker and a single interest group.

Definition 7.2   A policy vector $\mathbf{p}^{\circ}$ and a contribution schedule $C^{\circ}(\mathbf{p})$ constitute an equilibrium in the contribution game with a single policymaker and a single SIG if

(i) $\mathbf{p}^{\circ}$ belongs to the policymaker's best-response set to $C^{\circ}(\mathbf{p})$;

(ii) there exists no other feasible contribution function $C^{a}(\mathbf{p})$ and policy vector $\mathbf{p}^{a}$ such that $\mathbf{p}^{a}$ is in the policymaker's best-response set to $C^{a}(\mathbf{p})$ and $U[\mathbf{p}^{a}, C^{a}(\mathbf{p}^{a})] > U[\mathbf{p}^{\circ}, C^{\circ}(\mathbf{p}^{\circ})]$.

By a feasible contribution schedule, we mean one that is everywhere non-negative. Moreover, further restrictions may apply, depending on the application. For example, campaign giving laws may limit the contribution offers in some institutional settings, while liquidity constraints may limit the group's offers in others. We will mention any feasibility constraints that are relevant in particular applications.

7.4   Regulation and Protection

At this point another example might be helpful. Our next example focuses on an industry that competes with foreign producers while being subject to domestic environmental regulation. The incumbent policymaker has two policy instruments at her disposal: an ad valorem tariff t that can be used to provide relief from imports, and an emissions tax τ that can be used to limit environmental damage.

Consider a competitive industry in a small, open economy. The industry uses two factors of production, labor—which is available in a perfectly elastic supply at a fixed wage w—and capital. This capital is in fixed supply and is specific to the industry in question; that is, it cannot be reallocated to other sectors of the economy. The owners of the industry capital comprise an organized interest group; their goal is to maximize the quasi-rents that derive from their factor ownership.

Let p^* be the international price of the industry's output. Domestic consumers pay the price $p_y = p^*(1 + t)$, in view of the tariff t imposed by the policymaker. Domestic production of the good generates pollution, with a fixed rate v of emissions per unit of output. The government taxes these emissions at rate τ, which means that the producers receive a net revenue of $p_x = p^*(1 + t) - v\tau$ for each unit they produce.

Assume that the owners of the capital also own and operate the firms in the industry. This is without loss of generality, because competitive firms earn no excess profits. The firms hire labor up to the point where the value of its marginal product equals the wage rate. This gives a return to capital equal to the difference between revenues and labor costs. We will denote these returns by $\Pi(p_x)$ and refer to them as the "profits" of the industry. In general, the profits depend also on the wage rate, w, but since we hold this constant throughout the analysis, we do not include it in the expression for $\Pi(\cdot)$.

The SIG's objective is to maximize the joint welfare of its members. If the capital owners are few in number, they will enjoy only a tiny share of the surplus generated by consumption of the good they produce. Moreover, their rightful share of any tax revenues also will be small. Finally, these individuals will bear only a tiny part of the environmental damages caused by their production activities. In this case of concentrated ownership, the objective of the SIG is simply to maximize $\Pi(p_x) - c$, where c represents the size of their political contribution. To maximize group welfare, the SIG offers contributions that are linked to the policymaker's choice of tariff and emissions tax.

The policymaker is concerned with contributions and aggregate welfare. Aggregate welfare is given by

$$W = \Pi(p_x) + S(p_y) + \tau vx + tp^*(y - x) - D(vx), \qquad (7.3)$$

which is the sum of producer surplus, consumer surplus, revenues from emissions taxes, revenues from the import tariff, and the cost of environmental damage. Here, $S(p_y)$ represents consumer surplus, achieved when each consumer equates marginal utility with the consumer price; τvx is the proceeds from the emissions tax, when x units of output are produced and each generates v units of pollution; $tp^*(y - x)$ is the tariff revenue collected on $y - x$ units of imports, where y is total consumption of the good; and $D(vx)$ is the social cost of the pollution, with $D'(\cdot) > 0$ and $D''(\cdot) > 0$. The politician's objective function is

$$G = \lambda W(t, \tau) + (1 - \lambda)C(t, \tau),$$

where $C(t, \tau)$ is the contribution schedule put forward by the interest group.

It is instructive to identify first the policies that would maximize aggregate welfare in the absence of political influence. For a small country a zero tariff rate is optimal, because such a country cannot affect its international terms of trade. The optimal emissions tax is one that forces the industry to internalize the cost of the environmental externality. The government could achieve this by equating the tax rate to the marginal social damage caused by the pollution. It is easy to check that $t = 0$ and $\tau = D'(vx)$ satisfy the first-order conditions for maximizing W.[9]

---

9. The first-order conditions are

$$\frac{\partial W}{\partial t} = p^*\left[\tau v\frac{\partial x}{\partial p_x} + tp^*\left(\frac{\partial y}{\partial p_y} - \frac{\partial x}{\partial p_x}\right) - vD'\frac{\partial x}{\partial p_x}\right] = 0$$

and

$$\frac{\partial W}{\partial \tau} = -\tau v^2 + tvp^*\frac{\partial x}{\partial p_x} + v^2D'\frac{\partial x}{\partial p_x} = 0.$$

In deriving these equations, we have used the fact that the derivative of the profit function, $\Pi'(p_x)$, gives the competitive output, and that the derivative of the consumer surplus function, $S'(p_y)$, gives minus the utility-maximizing quantity of consumption. If we divide the first condition by p^* and the second by v, and sum the resulting equations, we find $tp^*\partial y/\partial p_y = 0$, from which we conclude that the optimal tariff is zero. Substituting $t = 0$ into one of these equations gives the optimal emissions tax, $\tau = D'(vx)$.

Now consider the political equilibrium with campaign contributions. As we have seen, the equilibrium policies must be jointly efficient for the policymaker and the interest group. That is, they must maximize $\Pi - c$, subject to $G \geq \bar{G}$, for some constant $\bar{G}$. Equivalently, the equilibrium choices of tariff and emissions tax maximize $\lambda W + (1 - \lambda)\Pi$.[10] The resulting first-order conditions imply

$$(1 - \lambda)x + \lambda\left[\tau v \frac{\partial x}{\partial p_x} + tp^*\left(\frac{\partial y}{\partial p_y} - \frac{\partial x}{\partial p_x}\right) - vD'\frac{\partial x}{\partial p_x}\right] = 0, \qquad (7.4)$$

and

$$-(1 - \lambda)x + \lambda\left[-\tau v \frac{\partial x}{\partial p_x} + tp^*\frac{\partial x}{\partial p_x} + vD'\frac{\partial x}{\partial p_x}\right] = 0. \qquad (7.5)$$

Summing (7.4) and (7.5) gives $\lambda tp^*\partial y/\partial p_y = 0$. But this condition can be satisfied only if $t = 0$. Thus, the policymaker provides no import protection to the industry in the political equilibrium.

With $t^\circ = 0$, equation (7.5) becomes $(1 - \lambda)x + \lambda(\tau - D')v\partial x/\partial p_x = 0$, or

$$\tau^\circ = D' - \frac{(1 - \lambda)x}{\lambda v}\left(\frac{\partial x}{\partial p_x}\right)^{-1}. \qquad (7.6)$$

Here we see the influence of the interest group. The SIG tailors its contribution schedule to induce the policymaker to go easy on environmental protection. The resulting emissions tax is smaller than the one the policymaker would choose if she were only concerned with aggregate welfare. To exert this influence, the interest group must compensate the politician for the associated loss of political welfare. The group pays $\lambda/(1 - \lambda)$ times the loss in aggregate welfare that results from setting the emissions tax according to (7.6) rather than according to $\tau = D'$.

It may seem surprising that the SIG concentrates its political effort on reducing the emissions tax, while demanding no import relief whatsoever. But this pair of policies is, in fact, jointly efficient for the interest group and the policymaker. To understand why this is so, recall that industry profits depend only on p_x. Thus, the welfare of the capital owners is not affected by a reduction in the tariff rate

---

10. Note that $G \geq \bar{G}$ implies $c \geq (\bar{G} - \lambda W)/(1 - \lambda)$. Then $\Pi - c$ is maximized when $c = (\bar{G} - \lambda W)/(1 - \lambda)$. This is equivalent to the unconstrained maximization of $(1 - \lambda)\Pi + \lambda W - \lambda\bar{G}$, which is achieved when t and τ maximize $(1 - \lambda)\Pi + \lambda W$.

accompanied by a reduction in the emissions tax rate that leaves the net producer price unchanged. Such a change in the pair of tax rates also leaves output and pollution unchanged, while increasing consumer surplus by more than it reduces government revenue.[11] Thus, it raises aggregate welfare and thereby serves the policymaker's political interests. It follows that the tariff can be cut to zero, and the emissions tax rate reduced in parallel, in such a way that the policymaker's welfare is enhanced and the industry suffers no harm.

It is worth emphasizing how the jointly efficient outcome comes about. The interest group knows that it can exert influence over both the trade and regulatory policies. But it recognizes that it will cost more to induce a given positive tariff than to induce a cut in the emissions tax that effects the same increase in the net price. The two alternatives leave the industry with the same profits. So it chooses the less costly route. In other words, the interest group perceives a higher cost for policies that are more politically damaging to the policymaker, which gives the group an incentive to take the policymaker's preferences into account.

If the policymaker places relatively little weight on aggregate welfare (i.e., λ is small), the formula in (7.6) implies $\tau^{\circ} < 0$. Then the equilibrium policy is a negative tax on emissions or, in other words, a *subsidy* for pollution. It may seem strange that a policymaker would agree to subsidize pollution, or that any interest group would demand such a policy. But in fact, a subsidy to pollution is much like a subsidy to output when emissions are proportional to output. Clearly, the industry benefits from a subsidy to output, and if the policymaker puts a great enough weight on campaign contributions, the SIG may be able to induce such a subsidy in spite of the adverse effect on the environment.

Pollution subsidies may not be politically feasible, however. This could be true for several reasons. First, the policymaker might lack the authority to subsidize emissions. There would be no reason for the public to grant her such authority, inasmuch as subsidies could never serve the public interest. If the rules of the polity do not prohibit subsidies, the policymaker might nonetheless choose to avoid them if she believed that she would suffer an additional political cost

---

11. This statement is true so long as the tariff rate is positive; it reflects the social desirability of consumption up to the point where the marginal utility equals the opportunity cost of imports, p^*. Marginal utility exceeds p^* as long as $p_y > p^*$, or $t > 0$.

were she to implement such a policy. Pollution subsidies are such an obvious affront to the public interest that many voters might hold her in disdain if she were to pander to special interests so blatantly. Finally, firms in the industry might be able to add to their emissions intentionally, thereby polluting beyond the level that is an inevitable consequence of production. If this were the case, a pollution subsidy could not be contemplated, because it would induce emissions far in excess of vx.

Recall that our model allows for constraints on the set of feasible policies. It might be reasonable to restrict the set of environmental policies to exclude pollution subsidies. Then the political game would be one in which the SIG could bid for any import tariff and for any non-negative level of the emissions tax. There would be no reason for the group to bid for a pollution subsidy, because the policymaker could not deliver on such a policy.

Let us consider briefly the contribution game that results when there is a constraint that $\tau \geq 0$. If (7.6) implies that $\tau^\circ \geq 0$, the constraint does not bind. Then the outcome is the same as before. The SIG induces a pollution tax rate that is less than the socially optimal one, but nonetheless is positive. And the equilibrium tariff rate is zero. The constraint on τ does not matter in this case, because the price of a pollution subsidy is so high that the SIG would not choose to effect such an outcome even if it were feasible.

A more interesting situation arises when (7.6) implies that $\tau^\circ < 0$. Then the constraint does indeed bind. The equilibrium is a pair of policies t and τ that maximizes $\Pi(\cdot) - c$, subject to the constraints that $G(\cdot) \geq \bar{G}$ and $\tau \geq 0$. Hence, the equilibrium has $\tau^\circ = 0$ and[12]

$$ t^\circ = \frac{1}{p^*} \left(\frac{\partial x}{\partial p_x} - \frac{\partial y}{\partial p_y} \right)^{-1} \left(\frac{1-\lambda}{\lambda} x - vD' \frac{\partial x}{\partial p_x} \right). $$

Notice that the SIG uses its influence to ensure that there is no tax on emissions, and also to extract some protection from imports. The tariff rate is higher, the smaller is the weight that the policymaker places on aggregate welfare in her political objective function, the smaller is the marginal environmental damage caused by domestic production, and the less responsive are imports to changes in

---

12. The expression for the equilibrium tariff is found by substituting $\tau = 0$ into (7.4), which is the first-order condition for the jointly efficient tariff.

domestic price.[13] A smaller marginal loss from pollution means a smaller political cost to the politician from greater domestic output (hence pollution), and therefore a greater willingness on the politician's part to confer protection in exchange for campaign funding. Similarly, a smaller responsiveness of imports to price changes means a smaller deadweight loss from protection, and again a greater willingness on the part of the politician to cater to the SIG's demands.

7.5 Bargaining

In the preceding sections we allowed the interest group to take the initiative in its quest for influence. We assumed that the group moves first by designing a contribution schedule. The policymaker then must respond to a set of take-it-or-leave-it offers. Under these conditions, the group's contribution leaves the policymaker no better off than she would be without any financial support. In other words, the first-mover advantage puts the interest group in a position to extract all of the surplus in its relationship with the policymaker.

But there is no reason to think that the SIG can extract all of the surplus from this relationship. The policymaker might decline the group's offer and respond with a counterproposal. This could lead to a negotiation between the two sides over the size of the group's donation and the policymaker's willingness to grant its policy demands. Such a negotiation might be difficult to navigate in light of the reluctance of each side to be explicit about the exchange of money for influence. Still, it might be possible for the sides to use code words to generate a division of the surplus. We proceed now to consider how the policy outcome might differ if the deal between the SIG and the policymaker results from a bargaining process.

Bargaining can be modeled in many ways, depending on the cost of making offers and the protocol for doing so. Rather than choosing a particular model of the bargaining process, we observe that most models predict a jointly efficient outcome when both sides are fully informed.[14] Indeed, Nash (1950) considered efficiency to be a rea-

---

13. Note that $y - x$ equals imports; thus, $-\left(\dfrac{\partial x}{\partial p_x} - \dfrac{\partial y}{\partial p_y}\right)$ is the change in imports in response to a change in the domestic consumer and producer price of the same amount.

14. Osborne and Rubinstein (1990) provide a detailed treatment of bargaining theory.

sonable property of any bargaining "solution." So we might ask, How far can we get with only the assumption that the bargain is jointly efficient?

Joint efficiency means that the policy and contribution cannot be changed so as to benefit one side without harming the other. Formally, it requires that p and c maximize $U(p,c)$, subject to the constraint that $G(p,c) \geq \bar{G}$ for some value of $\bar{G}$.[15] The first-order conditions for this maximization imply that

$$\frac{\partial G(p,c)/\partial p}{\partial G(p,c)/\partial c} = \frac{\partial U(p,c)/\partial p}{\partial U(p,c)/\partial c}. \qquad (7.7)$$

This equation has a simple interpretation. In an efficient bargain, the marginal trade-off between changes in the policy and changes in income must be the same for the policymaker and the interest group.

Let us look first at the case in which $G(p,c) = \lambda W(p) + (1 - \lambda)c$ and $U(p,c) = W_s(p) - c$; that is, the politician maximizes a weighted average of aggregate welfare and campaign contributions and the SIG has a constant marginal utility of income. In this case, the policy that maximizes $U(p,c)$ subject to the constraint that $G(p,c) \geq \bar{G}$ is the same as the one that maximizes $\lambda W(p) + (1 - \lambda)W_s(p)$. But this means that the equilibrium policy is independent of the details of the negotiating process. The same policy emerges when the interest group has all of the bargaining power (as in the model of Section 7.1) as when the policymaker has all of the power, and for cases in between. The explanation for this finding is straightforward. When money enters the welfare function of each side additively, contributions can be used to effect a direct transfer of utility from the SIG to the policymaker. An efficient bargain selects the policy that maximizes the size of the joint pie, and the contributions are negotiated separately to achieve an agreed distribution of that pie.

This separate determination of policy and contributions does not hold for more general forms of the welfare function. Consider figure 7.4, which illustrates an efficient bargain for an arbitrary $G(p,c)$ and $U(p,c)$. For the preferences illustrated in the figure, the group's trade-off between policy and income is not independent of the level of contributions. This can be seen by comparing the slope of the indifference curve UU at point A with the slope of $U'U'$ at point B.

---

15. We illustrate the arguments with a single policy variable p. The same arguments apply when there are many policy instruments.

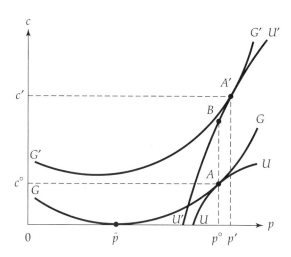

Figure 7.4
Bargaining Outcome

Both of these points involve a policy of p°. Clearly, the slopes of the curves are not the same, indicating a different SIG trade-off between policy and money at the two points. Similarly, the marginal trade-off between policy and contributions differs for the policymaker at different contribution levels.

As we have noted, an efficient bargain requires that the trade-off be the same for the two sides. The point labeled A is one point where this is so; it is the equilibrium identified in Section 7.1, corresponding to a bargaining situation in which the interest group has all of the bargaining power. But point A'—with a policy of p' and a contribution of c'—is another possible outcome of an efficient bargain. This outcome leaves both the policymaker and the SIG better off than they would be under a policy of $\hat{p}$ and a contribution of zero. Hence, it could arise if bargaining leads the two sides to share the surplus.

At point A', the policy level is greater than at point A. Notice that the SIG prefers p' to p° at any given level of contributions, whereas the policymaker has the opposite ranking of these two policies. Yet the bargaining outcome is p° when the SIG has all of the bargaining power, and it may be p' when each side has some power. In the case depicted in the figure, the better the bargaining position of the policymaker, the greater is the equilibrium contribution. But as the contribution rises from c°, the group's marginal willingness to trade money for policy becomes greater than that of the SIG. Thus, the efficient bargain with a higher level of contributions involves a higher level of the policy. It is not true, evidently, that as the bargaining power of one side grows, the policy must move in the direction preferred by that party.

In this chapter, we have examined how a SIG might use its campaign giving to influence the decisions of an incumbent policymaker. Our discussion has focused on the bilateral relationship between a single politician and a single interest group. In so doing, we have neglected the interaction between various organized groups that might have divergent policy interests, as well as the interaction between different politicians. We generalize the model in Chapter 8 in order to allow for competing interest groups, while postponing our discussion of multiple politicians until the last two chapters. In Chapter 9 we discuss how a group might act to influence decisions by a legislature, while in Chapter 10 we discuss groups' efforts to influence a pair of political parties that are engaged in an electoral contest.

8   Competing for Influence

Many policy decisions affect more than one interest group. For example, health care regulations concern doctors, hospitals, insurance companies, and the disabled. Changes in the minimum wage are important to hotel owners, fast-food restaurateurs, and members of certain labor unions. Environmentalists, the furniture industry, and chemical producers share an interest in rules for hazardous waste disposal. And many industry and labor groups have stakes in the outcome of multilateral trade negotiations.

In this chapter we study the competition for influence. Our setting is one in which several organized groups share an interest in one or more policy issues. The groups hold different views about the relative desirability of the different options, and each would like to use its campaign giving to influence the policy choice. We ask, How does the equilibrium policy reflect the preferences of the different SIGs and of the policymaker? Which groups are most successful in getting their way? And how much do the various groups contribute to exert their influence?

First we must consider how the interest groups go about offering their contributions in exchange for consideration. It would not be possible for the policymaker to hold separate negotiations with every interest group, because the bargain she would strike with any one of them has implications for the others. If she were to agree, for example, to enact a certain policy to satisfy the demands of SIG 1, there would be nothing left for her to negotiate with SIG 2, SIG 3, and so on. In other circumstances she might consider gathering the groups together to negotiate a decision and a distribution of the surplus. But such a grand negotiation would be impractical here, because the policymaker would not wish to be seen as openly peddling her influence. It might be more natural, then, for the interest groups to approach the policymaker and advise her of their preferences and willingness to contribute.

To gain insight into the relationship between the interest groups and the policymaker, we draw on analysis of similar relationships that arise in other contexts. In many economic environments, agents take actions that affect the well-being of several principals. For example, a real estate agent decides how to allocate her time and sales effort among her various listings. A distributor decides which products to push when meeting with customers. The economics literature refers to a situation in which an agent takes an action that simultaneously affects several principals as a relationship of "common agency." In such situations, the principals typically design payment schedules that give the agent an incentive to take their interests into account.

The relationship between a policymaker and the interest groups is much akin to common agency. The interest groups are like principals, because they lack the authority to set policies themselves and thus need the policymaker to act on their behalf. The policymaker is like an agent, because her actions directly affect the principals' well-being, as well as, perhaps, her own. So, each SIG must try to motivate the agent to act on its behalf, giving her incentives to heed its demands in addition to those of the others groups, while she also addresses her own concerns. Like the manufacturer who tries to motivate an agent by offering a commission schedule, so the interest group can design a contribution schedule in order to influence the policy choice. In other words, a group can inform the policymaker about its preferences among the policy options and make known its willingness to contribute to her campaign in accordance with her attentiveness to the members' concerns.

We model the interaction between SIGs as a competition in contribution schedules. That is, we imagine that each interest group meets privately with the policymaker and informs her of what contributions it is willing to make in consideration of the various policy options at her disposal. As before, the offers might be left implicit so as not to offend either side's sense of propriety. Once the politician has met with all of the organized groups, she selects the policy that maximizes her political welfare. The policy choice may invoke positive contributions from one, several, or many interest groups, depending on the promises that have been made. We discuss the general theory of common agency as applied to policy making in Section 8.1, and provide an application to the choice of a minimum wage rate in the following section. In Section 8.3 we describe a particular class of equilibria that arise when the shapes of the contribution schedules reflect the preferences of the interest groups. In such cases we can make stronger predictions about the size of contributions from different groups. The last two sections provide additional applications to the determination of trade policy and to redistributive taxation.

8.1   The Politician as Common Agent

We consider a policymaker who must choose the level of some policy or set of policies. Her decision will affect the well-being of several (or many) organized interest groups. The groups are ready to offer campaign contributions to influence her decision. Each group independently designs a contribution schedule that associates a gift to the politician's campaign fund with every policy option available to her. Contributions cannot be negative, but some policies may evoke a gift of zero, if for example they are ones that the SIG does not like. The groups communicate their schedules to the politician privately. After the policymaker has heard all of the offers, she selects the policy that maximizes her political welfare, and collects from each group the contribution it has promised for that choice.[1]

What we have described is a typical relationship of common agency. Here the interest groups are principals and the policymaker is the agent. The groups must design their schedules with an eye toward the incentives that others might be offering, while bearing in mind that the policymaker herself may have preferences over the alternative policy levels. Common agency relationships have been studied in depth by Bernheim and Whinston (1986a, 1986b), Stole (1991), and others. We apply their methods to the political setting at hand.

We begin by describing the maximization problem facing the policymaker. This is analogous to the problem that we solved in

---

1. Denzau and Munger (1986) study a precursor to the model developed here. In their analysis, each SIG cares only about a single dimension of policy, and no two SIGs are concerned with the same policy issues. However, the groups compete for influence, because the policy levels are related through an aggregate budget (or "effort") constraint. Denzau and Munger do not consider the strategic interaction between interest groups; rather, they treat each group as if it were solving an independent decision problem. Accordingly, they do not fully identify the equilibrium of their game, but only some properties that must hold in any equilibrium.

Chapter 7. We assume now that the welfare of the policymaker depends on the vector of policies, $\mathbf{p}$, and on the vector of contributions $\mathbf{c}$ from the various interest groups. In many applications, only the sum of the contributions will matter to the politician. But for now, we allow for the more general case in which she has preferences over the source of her gifts. We denote the policymaker's welfare function by $G(\mathbf{p}, \mathbf{c})$, and assume only that $\partial G / \partial c_i \geq 0$ for every i, that is, that the policymaker does not dislike (larger) gifts from any group.

The policymaker's optimal response to a collection of offers from the organized groups is to choose one of the set of policy vectors that yields the highest possible level of welfare.[2] Let $C_i(\mathbf{p})$ denote the contribution schedule of SIG i and let $\mathbf{C}(\mathbf{p})$ denote the complete list of contribution schedules. Then we can define the policymaker's *best-response set* much as we did in Chapter 7. The formal definition is as follows.

Definition 8.1 The policymaker's best-response set to a vector of contribution schedules $\mathbf{C}(\mathbf{p})$ consists of all feasible policy vectors that maximize $G[\mathbf{p}, \mathbf{C}(\mathbf{p})]$.

It will prove useful to define as well the set of best responses to a list of contribution offers from all groups but one. In so doing we take the contribution from the omitted group to be zero no matter what policies are chosen. We denote by $\mathbf{C}_{-i}(\mathbf{p})$ the vector of contributions that is identical to $\mathbf{C}(\mathbf{p})$ in all elements with the exception of element i, and that has a zero in place of the contribution from SIG i. Then the policymaker's set of best responses to the offers from interest groups other than SIG i includes all policies that maximize $G[\mathbf{p}, \mathbf{C}_{-i}(\mathbf{p})]$. The reason for extending the definition in this way will become apparent in a moment.

In Chapter 7, after we defined the policymaker's set of best responses, it was a simple matter to find the optimal strategy for the (single) interest group. Now the problem is a bit more difficult, because there are several groups, and what is optimal for any one of them depends on the behavior of the others. We seek a subgame perfect Nash equilibrium in the political competition between the groups, which means that the contribution schedule of each group

---

2. As before, if there is a unique policy vector that maximizes the policymaker's welfare, the best-response set consists of only this single vector.

must be an optimal response to the set of schedules of the others, when all groups correctly anticipate the policymaker's best response.

Consider the problem facing SIG i. This group has some expectations about the contribution schedules that its rivals will offer. Given these expectations, it seeks to design its bid to maximize $U_i(\mathbf{p}, c_i)$. We may solve this problem in a manner analogous to the one we used in Chapter 7. Imagine that the SIG (rather than the policymaker) chooses a policy vector $\mathbf{p}^i$ and a contribution level c_i, subject to a constraint. Clearly, the policymaker cannot be made to accept an offer that leaves her with a lower welfare level than she could achieve by selecting a best response to the set of offers from the groups other than i. The welfare level that she can achieve without group i is $G[\mathbf{p}^{-i}, \mathbf{C}_{-i}(\mathbf{p}^{-i})]$, where $\mathbf{p}^{-i}$ is any element of the policymaker's best-response set to $\mathbf{C}_{-i}(\mathbf{p})$. Then, $\mathbf{p}^i$ and c_i must be such that

$$G[\mathbf{p}^i, C_1(\mathbf{p}^i), \ldots, C_{i-1}(\mathbf{p}^i), c_i, C_{i+1}(\mathbf{p}^i), \ldots, C_K(\mathbf{p}^i)] \geq G[\mathbf{p}^{-i}, \mathbf{C}_{-i}(\mathbf{p}^{-i})],$$

where K is the total number of organized interest groups. Once it chooses $\mathbf{p}^i$ and c_i to maximize its utility subject to this constraint, it can design a contribution schedule to implement its choices. An optimal schedule has $C_i(\mathbf{p}^i) = c_i$ and has the property that the policymaker achieves less welfare than $G[\mathbf{p}^{-i}, \mathbf{C}_{-i}(\mathbf{p}^{-i})]$ for all other policy options available to her. We illustrated how such a schedule can be constructed in Chapter 7.

More formally, we define a best response by SIG i to a set of contribution schedules for the groups other than i, $\mathbf{C}_{-i}(\mathbf{p})$. This response consists of a contribution schedule and a policy vector, with the restriction that the policy must belong to the policymaker's set of best responses, but SIG i can select any vector in this set. By defining the group's best response in this way, we capture the idea that SIG i could always offer "a little bit more" than c_i to break any ties in the eyes of the policymaker.

Definition 8.2   The contribution schedule $C_i(\mathbf{p})$ and the policy vector $\mathbf{p}^i$ are a best response by SIG i to the list of contribution schedules $\mathbf{C}_{-i}(\mathbf{p})$ of the groups other than SIG i if and only if

(i) $\mathbf{p}^i$ belongs to the policymaker's best-response set to the list of contribution schedules $\mathbf{C}(\mathbf{p})$, which includes the given schedules of the groups other than i and $C_i(\mathbf{p})$;

(ii) there does not exist a contribution amount $\hat{c}_i \geq 0$ and a policy vector $\hat{\mathbf{p}}^i$ such that $U_i(\hat{\mathbf{p}}^i, \hat{c}_i) > U_i[\mathbf{p}^i, C_i(\mathbf{p}^i)]$ and $G[\hat{\mathbf{p}}^i, C_1(\hat{\mathbf{p}}^i), \ldots, C_{i-1}(\hat{\mathbf{p}}^i), \hat{c}_i, C_{i+1}(\hat{\mathbf{p}}^i), \ldots, C_K(\hat{\mathbf{p}}^i)] \geq G[\mathbf{p}^{-i}, \mathbf{C}_{-i}(\mathbf{p}^{-i})]$.

Now we are ready to define an equilibrium in the common agency game. An equilibrium must satisfy three requirements. First, the contribution schedule of any group must be a best response to the equilibrium schedules of all others. Second, the policy selected by each group in its best response must coincide with the selections of the others. If this condition is not satisfied, some group would have an incentive to offer a little bit more than its equilibrium contribution to induce a policy outcome different from the one anticipated by the other groups in their equilibrium behavior. But this would violate the mutual consistency requirement for equilibrium expectations. Finally, the equilibrium policy must belong to the policymaker's set of best responses to the list of contribution schedules. Formally, we have

Definition 8.3   A vector of feasible contribution schedules $C^\circ(\mathbf{p})$ and a policy vector $\mathbf{p}^\circ$ constitute an equilibrium in the common agency contribution game if and only if

(i) $\mathbf{p}^\circ$ is in the policymaker's best-response set to $\mathbf{C}^\circ(\mathbf{p})$;

(ii) for every SIG i, $C_i^\circ(\mathbf{p})$ and $\mathbf{p}^\circ$ are in the set of best responses to $\mathbf{C}_{-i}^\circ(\mathbf{p})$.

Taking definitions 8.2 and 8.3 together, we may think of each SIG i as choosing a policy vector and a contribution *level* to maximize its own welfare, taking the contribution *schedules* of the other groups as given, and subject to the constraint that the policymaker must fare at least as well in the equilibrium as she would in the absence of any contributions from SIG i. Each interest group can choose from among the many schedules that have the "right" size of contribution for the chosen policy and that offer the policymaker a lower welfare for all other policies. Clearly, each SIG will be indifferent among the various alternatives that have these properties, because all such schedules result in the same policy outcome and the same payment. But the choice that each group makes affects the incentives facing the others. This suggests the possibility of multiple equilibria, with the choices of contribution level and policy by each group justified by the shapes of the contribution schedules of the others. Indeed, common agency games typically feature a multiplicity of equilibria.

Fortunately, we are able to narrow the set of possible policy outcomes by placing a reasonable restriction on the type of contribution schedule that the groups use in equilibrium. To this end, we limit our attention to schedules that are continuous and differentiable; that is, they offer contributions that vary smoothly with changes in policy.[3] We offer no formal justification for this restriction, although one could perhaps be developed by introducing uncertainty on the part of the SIGs about the preferences of their rivals. In any case, the groups suffer no harm by restricting their attention to differentiable schedules. In fact, for any policy $\mathbf{p}^i$ and contribution c_i that solve a group's welfare maximization problem, there are many continuous and differentiable contribution schedules that can be used to implement its choices.

We observe that when interest groups choose among differentiable contribution schedules, their equilibrium choices will always have a certain shape in the neighborhood of an equilibrium. In particular, if an equilibrium contribution schedule is differentiable, any small change in a component of the policy vector near the equilibrium must induce a change in the group's contribution that matches exactly its marginal rate of substitution between the policy component and money. More formally, we shall see that for any SIG i that pays a positive contribution in an equilibrium in which all contribution schedules are differentiable, we must have

$$\frac{\partial C_i^\circ(\mathbf{p}^\circ)}{\partial p_j} = -\frac{\partial U_i(\mathbf{p}^\circ, c_i^\circ)/\partial p_j}{\partial U_i(\mathbf{p}^\circ, c_i^\circ)/\partial c_i} \tag{8.1}$$

for all elements p_j of the vector $\mathbf{p}$. We shall refer to a contribution schedule that obeys (10.23) as *locally compensating*. The term "compensating" refers to the fact that the change in contribution compensates the SIG for the change in policy, so that its welfare remains the same. The term "locally" means that this property need only hold for small (or local) changes in the policy near the equilibrium, $\mathbf{p}^\circ$.

To understand why differentiability implies that the groups' contribution schedules must be locally compensating, consider figure 8.1. This figure depicts the problem facing SIG i in regard to the

---

3. Actually, we only require that the schedules be differentiable when the contributions are strictly positive. We need a further (technical) assumption that contributions are bounded from above by some finite, maximum amount. This seems a reasonable restriction to impose, inasmuch as the total wealth of the members of any SIG is finite.

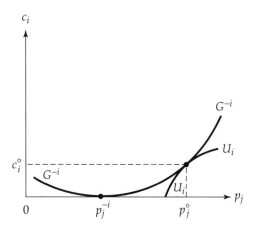

Figure 8.1
SIG i's Choice

choice of policy dimension j. On the horizontal axis is the policy variable p_j, and on the vertical axis is the group's contribution c_i. The group seeks to maximize its utility, which depends directly on p_j and on the size of its contribution. We can represent the group's preferences by a set of indifference curves, of which $U_i U_i$ is a typical example. According to our previous discussion, SIG i maximizes its welfare subject to the constraint that the policymaker can be no worse off when she accepts the group's offer than she would be if she were to decline it entirely. With $C_i(p) \equiv 0$, the policymaker would choose the policy component p_j^{-i}, which we have labeled in the figure. With this choice and a zero contribution from group i (together with optimal choices along the other policy dimensions), she attains a welfare level of $G[\mathbf{p}^{-i}, \mathbf{C}_{-i}(\mathbf{p}^{-i})]$. We have drawn an indifference curve, $G^{-i}G^{-i}$, that passes through this point. The constraint facing SIG i is to choose a policy-contribution pair that is on or above this curve.

The group solves its maximization problem by choosing the policy labeled p_j° and the contribution labeled c_i°, which together define a point where the two indifference curves are tangent. In order to achieve this outcome with a differentiable contribution schedule, the SIG must design the schedule so that it is tangent to $G^{-i}G^{-i}$ at p_j°, and lies everywhere below the curve for policies other than p_j°.[4] Only a

---

4. Of course, the contribution schedule would have to have similar characteristics along the other dimensions of the policy vector as well.

schedule with this property would induce a welfare-maximizing policymaker to set p_j equal to p_j^o. But note that any contribution schedule that is tangent to $G^{-i}G^{-i}$ at p_j^o is locally compensating; that is, it has the same slope at p_j^o as the indifference curve U_iU_i.[5]

When all the contribution schedules are locally compensating, the equilibrium policy has some notable properties. Recall that the policy vector maximizes the policymaker's welfare, given the contribution schedules that have been offered to her. The first-order condition for the policymaker's maximization problem takes the form

$$\frac{\partial G}{\partial p_j} + \sum_i \frac{\partial G}{\partial c_i}\frac{\partial C_i}{\partial p_j} = 0.$$

We can substitute for $\partial C_i/\partial p_j$ using (8.1), which describes a locally compensating schedule for SIG i. This gives

$$\frac{\partial G}{\partial p_j} - \sum_i \frac{\partial G}{\partial c_i}\frac{\partial U_i/\partial p_j}{\partial U_i/\partial c_i} = 0. \tag{8.2}$$

Now notice that (8.2) is a necessary condition for maximizing $G(\mathbf{p},\mathbf{c})$ subject to the constraints that $U_1(\mathbf{p},c_1) \geq \bar{U}_1$, $U_2(\mathbf{p},c_2) \geq \bar{U}_2$, etc., for an arbitrary set of constants, $\bar{U}_1,\ldots,\bar{U}_K$.[6] In other words, the equilibrium policy vector and associated contributions obey the necessary conditions for an outcome to be jointly efficient for the politician and the organized interest groups taken together. This means that joint efficiency—which necessarily is achieved when there is only one SIG—remains a possibility when many SIGs compete for influence. In fact, joint efficiency is ensured if $G(\cdot)$ and $U_i(\cdot)$ have certain commonly assumed curvature properties.

---

5. SIG i could implement its favorite policy with a differentiable contribution schedule even if the indifference curve $G^{-i}G^{-i}$ not differentiable, as would be the case, for example, if one of the other SIGs had proposed a contribution schedule that is not differentiable.

6. The first-order conditions for this problem are

$$\frac{\partial G}{\partial p_j} + \sum_i \chi_i \frac{\partial U_i}{\partial p_j} = 0$$

and

$$\frac{\partial G}{\partial c_k} + \chi_k \frac{\partial U_k}{\partial c_k} = 0, \quad \text{for all } k,$$

where χ_k is the Lagrange multiplier on the constraint $U_k(\mathbf{p},c_k) \geq \bar{U}_k$. Together these conditions imply (8.2) in the text.

An even stronger statement can be made when the policymaker's welfare is a function of aggregate welfare and the sum of campaign contributions, and when contributions enter the welfare functions of the politician and the interest groups linearly. With $G = \lambda W(\mathbf{p}) + (1 - \lambda) \sum_i c_i$, where $W(\mathbf{p})$ is aggregate welfare, and $U_k = W_k(\mathbf{p}) - c_k$, (8.2) becomes

$$\lambda \frac{\partial W}{\partial p_j} + (1 - \lambda) \sum_i \frac{\partial W_i}{\partial p_j} = 0. \tag{8.3}$$

Now the equilibrium policy satisfies the first-order condition for maximizing a weighted sum of the welfare of the interest groups and the general public. All interest groups receive the same weight. Moreover, if the objective function of every interest group is to maximize the aggregate welfare of its members, then (8.3) represents the first-order condition for maximizing a weighted sum of the welfare of individuals who are members of organized groups and those who are not. The group members receive a weight of one (since they appear in both the aggregate and in one of the groups), while the nonmembers receive a smaller weight of λ. If there is a unique policy vector that maximizes this weighted sum of utilities, it may be the unique outcome in the common agency game. We will see an example of this in the next section.

8.2   The Minimum Wage

We illustrate the competition for influence by means of an example. Our example concerns a policymaker's choice of a minimum wage.

Imagine an economy with two output sectors, textiles and pharmaceuticals, and workers with many different levels of skill. In each sector, producers use labor and capital as inputs. There are two distinct types of capital, one that is used only in the textiles sector and another that is used only in the pharmaceuticals sector.[7] We assume that all workers are perfectly substitutable after allowing for differences in their skills. That is, a worker of ability a provides a times as much "effective labor" as a worker of ability 1, but otherwise performs a similar role in the production process. The economy is small in relation to world markets and takes the world prices of the two (traded) goods as given.

---

7. In the parlance of the economics literature, the capital is "sector specific."

We consider initially the competition between two special interest groups. One group represents the owners of capital used in the textiles industry. We shall refer to this SIG as the textiles industry association. The other SIG is a union that represents a group of workers whose abilities are skewed toward the high end of the skill distribution. Initially, we assume that the owners of capital used in the pharmaceuticals sector and the remaining workers are politically unorganized. Later, we shall consider other possible configurations of political representation.

Suppose that skill levels in the work force range from $a_{\min}$ to $a_{\max}$. Let $\Phi(a)$ represent the fraction of workers whose ability is less than or equal to a. Similarly, let $\Phi_U(a)$ be the fraction of union members with skills less than or equal to a. With N total workers in the labor force and a fraction θ represented by the union, $\Phi'(a)N$ gives the total number of workers with skill level a, and $\Phi'_U(a)\theta N$ gives the number of union members with that level of ability. The ratio of $\theta\Phi'_U(a)$ to $\Phi'(a)$, which we will denote by $\phi(a)$, measures the relative prevalence of workers of ability a in the union compared to their prevalence in the labor force as a whole.

We assume that $\phi(a_{\min}) = 0$, $\phi(a_{\max}) = 1$, and $\phi'(a) > 0$ for all a between $a_{\min}$ and $a_{\max}$; that is, virtually none of the least skilled workers and virtually all of the most skilled workers are represented by the union, and the fraction of workers of a given ability who are union members rises monotonically with the skill level. This is the sense in which political representation is skewed toward the higher-ability workers.

We represent the technologies for producing textiles and pharmaceuticals by a pair of constant-returns-to-scale production functions. Output of textiles is given by $F_T(K_T, E_T)$, where K_T is the economy's endowment of capital that is useful in textile production and E_T is the total amount of effective (or skill-adjusted) labor hired by textile firms.[8] Similarly, output of pharmaceuticals is $F_P(K_P, E_P)$, where the variables are defined analogously. We choose units of output so that the world price of each good is equal to one.

Consider, for a moment, the equilibrium that would emerge in the absence of any legal floor on wages. With all workers being perfect

---

8. More formally, if $e_T(a)$ is the employment by textile firms of workers of ability a, then

$$E_T = \int_{a_{\min}}^{a_{\max}} a e_T(a)\, da.$$

substitutes after adjusting for ability, there would be a single market wage for a unit of effective labor. Let $\hat{w}_E$ denote this wage. Then a worker with skill level a would earn $a\hat{w}_E$ in the competitive equilibrium. With this pattern of wages, firms would be indifferent as to the composition of their work forces and would care only about the aggregate amount of effective labor they employed. With any other pattern of wages, there would be excess demand for some types of labor and no demand for others.

Firms in each sector choose their effective labor input to maximize their profits. Let us denote by $\Pi_T(w_E)$ the maximum level of profits that firms in the textiles sector can achieve when the cost of a unit of effective labor is w_E. Then, as is well known from microeconomic theory, the demand for labor is given by minus the derivative of this function; that is, $E_T(w_E) = -\Pi_T'(w_E)$. Similarly, the demand for labor by the pharmaceuticals sector is given by $E_P(w_E) = -\Pi_P'(w_E)$, where $\Pi_P(w_E)$ is the maximal profits of the industry when the wage rate is w_E. Demand for effective labor by both industries shrinks as the wage rate rises.

When wages are flexible, the labor market clears. In other words, the wage per unit of effective labor adjusts until all workers seeking employment can find jobs. The total demand for effective labor by the two sectors is given by $E(w_E) = E_T(w_E) + E_P(w_E)$. The available supply is $N \int_{a_{min}}^{a_{max}} a\Phi'(a)\,da$. Thus, full employment requires a wage per unit of effective labor such that

$$E(w_E) = N \int_{a_{min}}^{a_{max}} a\Phi'(a)\,da. \tag{8.4}$$

The unique solution to this equation gives the value of $\hat{w}_E$.

We are now ready to examine the political forces that determine the minimum wage. Suppose the policymaker's objective is to maximize a weighted average of aggregate welfare and political contributions. In particular, let $G = \lambda W + (1 - \lambda)(c_T + c_U)$, where W is aggregate welfare, c_T is contributions from the textiles industry association, and c_U is contributions from the union. Assuming that all citizens have identical and homothetic preferences, we can replace aggregate welfare in the politician's objective function by aggregate income, namely the sum of wage income and profits for each type of capital.[9]

9. When preferences are homothetic and prices are fixed, utility is proportional to income. Therefore, aggregate utility is proportional to aggregate income. We can always measure utility in a way that makes the constant of proportionality equal to one.

The union designs its contribution schedule to maximize the net-of-contributions income of its members. Similarly, the textiles industry association designs its schedule to maximize the net-of-contributions return to capital used in textiles. Both SIGs choose from among schedules that are differentiable when positive.

In order to understand the incentives facing the interest groups, we need to know how a minimum wage affects the economy. With a minimum wage in place, firms still hire effective labor so as to maximize their profits. Therefore, $E_T(w_E)$ and $E_P(w_E)$ remain the industry demands for effective labor as functions of the wage rate, w_E, and $E(w_E)$ is the aggregate demand. However, if the minimum wage binds, this demand falls short of the supply. In the equilibrium with full employment, the least skilled worker in the economy earns $\hat{w}_E a_{\min}$. Now suppose there is a minimum wage of $\bar{w} > a_{\min}\hat{w}_E$. With this floor on wages, firms would not be willing to hire the least skilled worker, because his marginal contribution to output is less than the amount he must be paid. In fact, when every worker must be paid at least $\bar{w}$, the least skilled employee will be a worker with skill level $\bar{a}$ such that

$$\bar{a} w_E = \bar{w}. \tag{8.5}$$

Since only workers with ability greater than or equal to $\bar{a}$ are employed in equilibrium, we must replace the full-employment condition (8.4) by

$$E(w_E) = N \int_{\bar{a}}^{a_{\max}} a\Phi'(a)\,da. \tag{8.6}$$

We now have two equations, (8.5) and (8.6), that jointly determine w_E and $\bar{a}$ as functions of $\bar{w}$. We denote the solutions by $w_E(\bar{w})$ and $\bar{a}(\bar{w})$, respectively. Since these functions determine, in turn, the income levels of all groups in the economy, we have all of the ingredients we need to find the political equilibrium.

Let us suppose, provisionally, that the contribution offers induce the politician to set a binding minimum wage, that is, one that is above the wage paid to the least skilled worker in an economy with flexible wages and full employment. The equilibrium policy maximizes the politician's objective function, so it satisfies

$$\lambda W'(\bar{w}) + (1 - \lambda)[C_T'(\bar{w}) + C_U'(\bar{w})] = 0, \tag{8.7}$$

where

$$W(\overline{w}) = w_E(\overline{w})E[w_E(\overline{w})] + \Pi_T[w_E(\overline{w})] + \Pi_P[w_E(\overline{w})]$$

is aggregate income with a minimum wage of $\overline{w}$, and $C_i(\overline{w})$ is the contribution schedule offered by SIG i. Using the properties of the profit functions, the fall in aggregate income that results from an increase in the minimum wage is $W' = w_E(E_T' + E_P')w_E'$. This is simply the value of the output that disappears as a result of the decline in employment. We can write this equation instead as

$$W' = -\varepsilon_E E w_E', \tag{8.8}$$

where ε_E is the absolute value of the elasticity of the demand for effective labor with respect to w_E. Henceforth, we shall assume that $\varepsilon_E > 1$.[10]

We asume that the contribution schedules are differentiable and therefore must be locally compensating near a political equilibrium. If $\overline{w} > a_{\min}\hat{w}_E$ is such an equilibrium, then we must have $C_T'(\overline{w}) = W_T'(\overline{w})$ and $C_U'(\overline{w}) = W_U'(\overline{w})$. We can use this property of the equilibrium contribution schedules to substitute for $C_T'(\overline{w})$ and $C_U'(\overline{w})$ in the policymaker's first-order condition (8.7). For the textiles industry association, an increase in the minimum wage increases the cost of effective labor, which in turn reduces industry profits. Since $W_T(\overline{w}) = \Pi_T[w_E(\overline{w})]$, we have

$$W_T' = -E_T w_E'. \tag{8.9}$$

For the union,

$$W_U(\overline{w}) = w_E(\overline{w})\theta N \int_{\tilde{a}(\overline{w})}^{a_{\max}} a\Phi_U'(a)\, da,$$

where $\theta N \int_{\tilde{a}(\overline{w})}^{a_{\max}} a\Phi_U'(a)\, da$ is the total units of effective labor among employed union members. A minimum wage hike affects the income of union members in two ways. Those with sufficient skills see their incomes rise, as the decline in total employment raises the marginal product of effective labor. But some union members lose their jobs, as the higher minimum wage makes them unprofitable to the firms.

---

10. This assumption is sufficient for our conclusions, but not necessary for any of them. The assumption is satisfied, for example, when the production function in each sector has a Cobb-Douglas form. Without the assumption that $\varepsilon_E > 1$ for E close to zero, it is possible that the union would push the minimum wage to infinity, thereby driving employment to zero. This might be desirable for the union, because the wage bill would remain positive, and indeed, workers would capture the entirety of national income.

The total impact on union income is the sum of these two effects, or

$$W'_U = E_U w'_E - \bar{a} w_E \theta N \Phi'_U(\bar{a}) \bar{a}'. \tag{8.10}$$

Substituting for $W'(\bar{w})$, $C'_T(\bar{w})$ and $C'_U(\bar{w})$ in the politician's first-order condition (8.7), we see that any binding minimum wage must satisfy the first-order condition for maximizing a weighted sum of the incomes of the different members of society. In forming this weighted sum, the wages of union members and the profits of textile firms receive a weight of one, while the wages of other workers and the profits of pharmaceutical firms receive a weight of λ. After rearranging terms, the first-order condition for maximizing this weighted sum becomes[11]

$$(1 - \lambda)[E_U - E_T - \phi(\bar{a})\varepsilon_E(E_T + E_P)] = \lambda \varepsilon_E (E_T + E_P). \tag{8.11}$$

The left-hand side of (8.11) is proportional to $1 - \lambda$ times the increase in the joint income of the two SIGs in response to an increase in the minimum wage, while the right-hand side is proportional (with the same factor of proportionality) to λ times the decline in aggregate income. We can use this equation to evaluate whether, in fact, the policymaker will impose a binding minimum wage, and if so, how its level reflects the various political and economic variables in the model.

Consider first an economy in which, at every conceivable minimum wage, demand for effective labor by the textiles industry would exceed the employment of effective labor among union members ($E_T > E_U$). This might be true, for example, if the textiles industry is large and the union is relatively small. In such an environment, there can be no binding minimum wage in the political equilibrium. To see that this is so, suppose to the contrary that $\bar{w}$ is an equilibrium minimum wage above $a_{\min}\hat{w}_E$ (the wage of the least skilled worker in an equilibrium with full employment). Then the contribution schedules of the two interest groups must be locally compensating near $\bar{w}$. But with $E_T > E_U$, a slight reduction in the minimum wage raises the joint welfare of the union members and the owners of capital in the textiles industry, and thus induces a larger combined contribution from the two SIGs.[12] It also raises aggregate welfare. It follows that

---

11. In deriving (8.11), we use the relationships $\bar{a}(\bar{w})$ and $w_E(\bar{w})$ implied by (8.5) and (8.6).

12. The marginal effect of an increase in $\bar{w}$ on the joint welfare of the two SIGs is given by the term in square brackets in equation (8.11). This term is negative when $E_T > E_U$.

the policymaker would benefit from such a policy change, which contradicts the assumption that $\overline{w}$ is an equilibrium policy choice.[13]

Now consider an economy in which the supply of effective labor by union members exceeds the demand for that labor by the textiles industry at the market-clearing wage $\hat{w}_E$. In such circumstances, there will exist a political equilibrium with a binding minimum wage if the policymaker values campaign contributions sufficiently. To see this, let us evaluate the left-hand side of (8.11) at $\overline{w} = a_{\min}\hat{w}_E$. At this minimum wage, all workers are able to find jobs, so $\bar{a}(\overline{w}) = a_{\min}$. Then $\phi(\bar{a}) = 0$, because there are virtually no members of the union with the minimum level of skill. It follows that the left-hand side of (8.11) equals $(1 - \lambda)(E_U - E_T)$, which is positive under our assumption that $E_U > E_T$ at $\overline{w} = a_{\min}\hat{w}_E$. Moreover, if λ is not too large (i.e., the weight on contributions is not too small), the left-hand side of (8.11) exceeds the right-hand side at this wage level. The left-hand side of (8.11) must, however, be *smaller* than the right-hand side for very high levels of the minimum wage.[14] Since both sides of the equation are continuous in $\overline{w}$, there must be some level of the minimum wage above $a_{\min}\hat{w}_E$ at which the two sides are equal. We can always find contribution schedules for the two SIGs that support this level of $\overline{w}$ as a political equilibrium.

Intuitively, when $E_U > E_T$ at $w_E = \hat{w}_E$, the benefit to the union from pushing the minimum wage somewhat above the market-clearing level exceeds the cost to the textiles industry. The union benefits from the introduction of a binding minimum wage, because the earnings of its employed workers increase and virtually none of the resulting job loss falls on its members. So the gain to the union from pushing $\overline{w}$ a bit above $a_{\min}\hat{w}_E$ is proportional to E_U. The loss in profits for textile producers, meanwhile, is proportional to E_T. Since the two SIGs together gain from the introduction of a slightly binding minimum wage (although the textiles industry alone loses), the net effect of their bids for influence is to push the policymaker in that direc-

---

13. Note that the left-hand side of (8.11) is negative when $E_T > E_U$, whereas the right-hand side is positive. Therefore, the equation can never be satisfied in the case under consideration.

14. Note that $\bar{a}$ approaches $a_{\max}$ as $\overline{w}$ grows large, and thus $\phi(\bar{a})$ approaches one. Also, $\varepsilon_E > 1$ by assumption. Bringing the term $(1 - \lambda)\phi(\bar{a})\varepsilon_E E$ to the right-hand side and combining it with $\lambda\varepsilon_E E$, we have something that exceeds E, the aggregate level of employment. Meanwhile, the remaining term on the left-hand side is $(1 - \lambda)(E_U - E_T)$, which is smaller than E_U and thus certainly smaller than the aggregate level of employment.

tion. The policymaker might be reluctant to submit to this pressure, because the minimum wage generates unemployment and thus reduces aggregate income. But if her need for campaign contributions is sufficiently great, she will yield to the pressure, at least to some extent.

There is no guarantee that equation (8.11) has a unique solution. So there may be multiple values of $\bar{w}$ that can emerge from the political process. Our earlier arguments do, however, suggest that political forces will never push the minimum wage beyond a certain level. The maximum possible level of the minimum wage is the rate above which the right-hand side of (8.11) must exceed the left-hand side. No minimum wage higher than this can emerge from the bids for influence, because in this range of wage rates both the joint interests of the SIGs and the interests of the general public are served by a reduction in $\bar{w}$. If the solution to (8.11) does happen to be unique—which certainly is not precluded by our assumptions—then the equilibrium policy outcome is unique as well. When the policy outcome is unique, it nonetheless can be supported by a myriad of different contribution schedules, some of which imply different levels of contributions by the two SIGs than others.

Equation (8.11) can also be used to examine the connection between the political equilibrium and the underlying economic conditions. Take, for example, the elasticity of labor demand. The larger is ε_E, the smaller is the benefit to the union from a marginal increase in the minimum wage (because a given increase in $\bar{w}$ causes a greater job loss among union members) and the larger is the associated decline in aggregate welfare (because a given increase in $\bar{w}$ causes more unemployment). This means that a rise in ε_E can be expected to reduce the minimum wage $\bar{w}$.[15] Or consider the composition of the union's membership. The more skewed is the distribution of union members toward high skill levels, the smaller will be the value of $\phi(a)$ for any given value of a. But the smaller is $\phi(a)$, the smaller is the share of the unemployment at a given minimum wage that falls on union members. This can be expected to raise the minimum wage.

---

15. We use cautious language in this argument, because to reach a precise conclusion it is necessary to specify precisely how the shift in the elasticity comes about. The reason is that, since this elasticity is related to properties of the production functions and the size of the two sectors, a change in the elasticity will normally also affect sectoral employment levels. For this reason the argument in the text is only suggestive.

So far we have focused on a particular pattern of political organization. Now let us consider some further possibilities. First, suppose that an organized SIG represents the interests of those with capital invested in the pharmaceuticals industry, and that this SIG and the other two offer contributions to influence the policymaker's decision. In this case, if there is a binding minimum wage in the political equilibrium, then $\bar{w}$ must satisfy the first-order condition for maximizing a weighted sum of aggregate welfare and the welfare of union members and of owners of both types of capital. In place of the term in square brackets on the left-hand side of equation (8.11), we will have a term that reflects the marginal effect of an increase in the minimum wage on the joint incomes of the members of the three organized interest groups.

Much as a marginal increase in the minimum wage causes a loss of profits for textile producers equal to $E_T w'_E$, it causes a loss of profits for pharmaceutical producers equal to $E_P w'_E$. Therefore, a binding minimum wage must satisfy

$$(1 - \lambda)[E_U - (E_T + E_P) - \phi(\bar{a})\varepsilon_E(E_T + E_P)] = \lambda\varepsilon_E(E_T + E_P). \qquad (8.12)$$

Here the first term in the square brackets is the gain in income for employed union members, the second is the loss in income for the two types of capital owners, and the third is the loss in union income due to the induced unemployment among members. But notice that $E_U < E_T + E_P$, because employment of (effective) union labor cannot exceed total demand for effective labor by the two sectors of the economy. In other words, the two types of capital owners lose more from a minimum wage increase than the employed union members gain. The unemployment created among union members only adds to the joint welfare loss. Thus, any increase in the minimum wage reduces the joint welfare of the organized SIGs even as it reduces aggregate welfare. It follows that a binding minimum wage cannot emerge in a political equilibrium.[16]

Now suppose that there are three organized SIGs, but that they are the textiles industry association and two different labor unions. We may think of the two unions as representing predominantly high-skill workers and predominantly low-skill workers, respectively, although the make-up of the unions does not matter for our argu-

16. Notice that the left-hand side of (8.12) must be negative, whereas the right-hand side is positive. Thus, the equation cannot be satisfied by any value of $\bar{w} > a_{\min}\hat{w}$.

ment. We do assume that every worker is a member of one union or the other.

With this pattern of political representation, a binding minimum wage would have to satisfy the first-order condition for maximizing a weighted sum of aggregate income and the income of owners of textile capital plus workers in both unions. Here, $E_{U1} + E_{U2}$ takes the place of E_U in equation (8.11), where E_{Ui} is employment of effective labor among workers in union i. Also, $E_{U1} + E_{U2} = E_T + E_P$, since all labor demand is satisfied by union workers of one type or the other. Finally, $\phi(a) = 1$ for all a, because the fraction of represented workers at every skill level is 100% of the total. Making all of these changes to (8.11), the equation for the equilibrium minimum wage becomes

$$(1 - \lambda)[(1 - \varepsilon_E)(E_T + E_P) - E_T] = \lambda \varepsilon_E (E_T + E_P). \tag{8.13}$$

But this equation cannot be satisfied for any $\bar{w} > a_{\min} \hat{w}_E$ when (as we have assumed) $\varepsilon_E > 1$. Since aggregate labor demand is elastic, the aggregate wage bill declines as the effective wage rises. This means that any increase in the minimum wage causes labor income to shrink. It also reduces the return to capital invested in the textiles sector, and thus reduces the joint welfare of the three SIGs. It follows that the equilibrium has a market-clearing wage. Here, the union for the unskilled workers joins the textiles industry association in opposing a binding floor on wages, and since these workers lose more than the skilled workers stand to gain, the opponents of the minimum wage are able to carry the day.

Our examples illustrate a lesson that has more general validity. In an equilibrium of the contribution game, the policy outcome need not differ from that which maximizes aggregate welfare, even if the policymaker puts positive weight on campaign contributions. Rather, a departure from welfare-maximizing policies requires that there be some feasible alternative that brings joint benefit to the members of the organized interest groups at the expense of those who are not members of any such group.

8.3 Compensating Equilibria

We have seen that a SIG has considerable latitude in designing an optimal contribution schedule, because the sizes of its offers for policies that are different from the ones chosen in equilibrium do not affect the group's welfare. Although a SIG does not care about the shape of its schedule away from the equilibrium, its choice of schedule does bear on the incentives facing other groups. It is possible, therefore, to have many equilibria in the contribution game, where in each one the arbitrary aspects of the decisions made by every group justify the meaningful actions taken by the others.

If we are willing to assume that, among their many best responses, the SIGs choose contribution schedules that are differentiable, we can significantly narrow the set of possible policy outcomes. We have seen that any differentiable schedule that is a best response to other differentiable schedules must be locally compensating in the neighborhood of an equilibrium policy. In some cases there is only one policy that can be supported by a set of locally compensating schedules. In other cases there are several possibilities, but all share similar properties. For example, any binding minimum wage that is chosen in response to differentiable contribution offers from a union and a textiles industry association must satisfy the strong conditions of equation (8.11). Even in this case, however, we can say little about the contributions that the interest groups make to achieve their influence.

In this section we go further in narrowing the set of possible outcomes. We continue to assume that the SIGs have unlimited freedom in choosing a best response to the schedules designed by others. But we focus on equilibria in which the chosen schedules are compensating not only for small changes in policies and contributions, but for larger changes as well. We define a *compensating contribution schedule* to be one that coincides with a group's indifference surface everywhere that contributions are positive.[17] When a contribution schedule is compensating according to this definition, the difference in two (positive) contributions for different policy options "compensates" the interest group for its different evaluations of these two options. A *compensating equilibrium* is an equilibrium of the contribution game in which all interest groups happen to use compensating contribution schedules.

17. As we noted in Chapter 7, a compensating contribution schedule is defined relative to a reference level of utility. For SIG i, the compensating contribution schedule relative to the constant utility level U_i is

$$H_i(\mathbf{p}, U_i) = \max[0, \mu_i(\mathbf{p}, U_i)],$$

where $\mu_i(\mathbf{p}, U_i)$ is the compensating variation in terms of money—that is, the sum that, when taken from group i, leaves it with utility U_i when the policy vector is $\mathbf{p}$.

We have already encountered compensating contribution schedules in Chapter 7. There we noted that a single interest group can
design a compensating contribution schedule to achieve any desired
outcome. In other words, a restriction to this type of schedule
imposes no burden on the interest group. We argue now that the
same conclusion applies in the presence of competing interest
groups.

Suppose group i contemplates a best response to the set of contri-
bution schedules $\mathbf{C}_{-i}(\mathbf{p})$. This can be an arbitrary set of schedules; in
particular, group i need not anticipate that other groups will set
compensating schedules themselves. Then, as we have previously
described, SIG i solves a constrained maximization problem. It
chooses a policy vector $\mathbf{p}$ and a contribution level c_i to maximize
$U_i(\mathbf{p}, c_i)$, subject to the constraint that $G[\mathbf{p}, C_1(\mathbf{p}), \ldots, C_{i-1}(\mathbf{p}), c_i,$
$C_{i+1}(\mathbf{p}), \ldots, C_K(\mathbf{p})] \geq G[\mathbf{p}^{-i}, \mathbf{C}_{-i}(\mathbf{p}^{-i})]$. The solution is found at a
point of tangency between one of the group's indifference curves and
an indifference curve for the policymaker, as we illustrated in figure
8.1. The relevant indifference curve for the policymaker passes
through the point $(\mathbf{p}^{-i}, 0)$ and reflects not only her personal policy
preferences (or concern for her constituents), but also the contribution schedules offered by groups other than i.

In figure 8.2 we have reproduced the solution from the previous
figure. The new figure shows how SIG i can achieve its desired outcome using a compensating contribution schedule. The compensat-

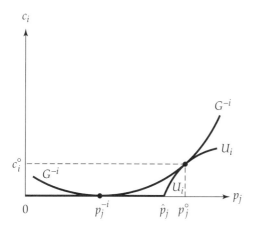

Figure 8.2
Compensating Contribution Schedule

ing schedule, depicted by the heavy solid line, coincides with the horizontal axis for policies $p_j \leq \hat{p}_j$ and with the indifference curve $U_i U_i$ for policies $p_j > \hat{p}_j$. It has the same shape as the indifference curve whenever contributions are positive. Faced with this schedule, it is a best response for the policymaker to choose p_j°. Evidently, the SIG can always design such a compensating contribution schedule to achieve its political objectives at no extra cost to itself.[18]

The fact that it is not costly for the interest groups to use compensating schedules is perhaps not reason enough to focus on cases in which they do. But the equilibria that arise when all contribution schedules are compensating have two appealing properties. First, these equilibria are always jointly efficient for the policymaker and the interest groups. That is, when all of the SIGs offer compensating schedules, the outcome is such that neither the policymaker nor any SIG could be made better off by a different policy choice and set of contribution levels without another SIG or the policymaker being harmed. Efficiency is not a property shared by all equilibria of common agency games. By using compensating schedules, the SIGs eliminate the possibility that there will be unexploited gains in their joint relationship with the policymaker.

Why is it that an equilibrium supported by compensating schedules from all interest groups must be efficient? Intuitively, when the contribution schedules are compensating, the SIGs confront the policymaker with offers that accurately reflect their own evaluations of the alternative policy options. Collectively, the offers give the policymaker the appropriate incentive to weigh the conflicting interests of the different interest groups.

More formally, we can prove that every compensating equilibrium must be jointly efficient as follows. Suppose that some such equilibrium is not efficient. Then an alternative policy vector and list of contributions exists, different from the equilibrium policy $\mathbf{p}^\circ$ and contributions $\mathbf{c}^\circ$, with the property that every interest group and the politician are at least as well off under the alternative as in the equilibrium, and at least one SIG or the politician is better off. Call the alternative policy vector $\hat{\mathbf{p}}$ and the alternative vector of contributions $\hat{\mathbf{c}}$. Since, by hypothesis, group i is not worse off with policy $\hat{\mathbf{p}}$ and

---

18. A formal proof of this claim is provided by Bernheim and Whinston (1986a) for the case of quasi-linear preferences, and extended by Dixit, Grossman, and Helpman (1997) to more general preferences.

payment $\hat{c}_i$ than it is with policy $\mathbf{p}^\circ$ and contribution c_i°, it must be that $\hat{c}_i \le H_i(\hat{\mathbf{p}}, U_i^\circ)$, where $H_i(\mathbf{p}, U_i^\circ)$ is the contribution schedule employed by SIG i in the compensating equilibrium and U_i° is its resulting welfare level.

The fact that the policymaker chooses $\mathbf{p}^\circ$ over the alternative $\hat{\mathbf{p}}$ in the compensating equilibrium implies that $G(\mathbf{p}^\circ, \mathbf{c}^\circ) \ge G[\hat{\mathbf{p}}, \mathbf{H}(\hat{\mathbf{p}}, \mathbf{U}^\circ)]$, where $\mathbf{U}^\circ$ is the vector of equilibrium utility levels and $\mathbf{H}(\cdot)$ is the vector of compensating contribution schedules. Since $\hat{c}_i \le H_i(\hat{\mathbf{p}}, U_i^\circ)$ for every SIG i, it follows that $G[\hat{\mathbf{p}}, \mathbf{H}(\hat{\mathbf{p}}, \mathbf{U}^\circ)] \ge G(\hat{\mathbf{p}}, \hat{\mathbf{c}})$. Finally, we know that $G(\hat{\mathbf{p}}, \hat{\mathbf{c}}) \ge G(\mathbf{p}^\circ, \mathbf{c}^\circ)$, because the policymaker is by assumption not worse off with policies $\hat{\mathbf{p}}$ and contributions $\hat{\mathbf{c}}$ than with policies $\mathbf{p}^\circ$ and contributions $\mathbf{c}^\circ$. These inequalities can be satisfied only if $G(\mathbf{p}^\circ, \mathbf{c}^\circ) = G[\hat{\mathbf{p}}, \mathbf{H}(\hat{\mathbf{p}}, \mathbf{U}^\circ)] = G(\hat{\mathbf{p}}, \hat{\mathbf{c}})$. But, if the policymaker is indifferent between $(\mathbf{p}^\circ, \mathbf{c}^\circ)$ and $(\hat{\mathbf{p}}, \hat{\mathbf{c}})$, then there must be some SIG i that strictly prefers $(\hat{\mathbf{p}}, \hat{c}_i)$ to $(\mathbf{p}^\circ, c_i^\circ)$. But SIG i could have induced the policy choice $\hat{\mathbf{p}}$ with the contribution $\hat{c}_i$ and an appropriately designed contribution schedule.[19] So it cannot prefer $(\hat{\mathbf{p}}, \hat{c}_i)$ to $(\mathbf{p}^\circ, c_i^\circ)$. This is a contradiction. We conclude that if $\mathbf{p}^\circ$ and $\mathbf{c}^\circ$ are outcomes in a compensating equilibrium, there are no alternative policies and contributions $\hat{\mathbf{p}}$ and $\hat{\mathbf{c}}$ that make group i better off and no group worse off.

The second reason why compensating equilibria may deserve special attention is that these equilibria, and only these equilibria, are what Bernheim and Whinston (1984) have termed "coalition proof."[20] Bernheim and Whinston proposed the notion of a coalition-proof Nash equilibrium as a refinement of the set of Nash equilibria. The idea is that, if the players have an opportunity to engage in private

---

19. To see this final point, note that the policymaker is no worse off with policy $\mathbf{p}^\circ$ and the vector of contributions $\mathbf{c}^\circ$ than she is with any other policy $\mathbf{p}'$ and contributions $\mathbf{H}_{-i}(\mathbf{p}', \mathbf{U}^\circ)$ from the groups other than i and zero from group i; otherwise she would not have chosen $\mathbf{p}^\circ$ in the compensating equilibrium. But the policymaker is indifferent between $(\hat{\mathbf{p}}, \hat{\mathbf{c}})$ and $(\mathbf{p}^\circ, \mathbf{c}^\circ)$, and $(\hat{\mathbf{p}}, \hat{\mathbf{c}})$ is no worse for her than to choose $\hat{\mathbf{p}}$ and receive $\mathbf{H}_{-i}(\hat{\mathbf{p}}, \mathbf{U}^\circ)$ from groups other than i and $\hat{c}_i$ from group i, because the contributions indicated by $\mathbf{H}_{-i}(\hat{\mathbf{p}}, \mathbf{U}^\circ)$ are no smaller than the corresponding elements of $\hat{\mathbf{c}}$. It follows that the policymaker also does not prefer any $\mathbf{p}'$ and contributions of $\mathbf{H}_{-i}(\mathbf{p}', \mathbf{U}^\circ)$ from the groups other than i and zero from i to $\hat{\mathbf{p}}$ and the contributions $\mathbf{H}_{-i}(\hat{\mathbf{p}}, \mathbf{U}^\circ)$ from the groups other than i and $\hat{c}_i$ from i. By appropriately designing the rest of its contribution schedule, SIG i could have induced $\hat{\mathbf{p}}$ while paying $\hat{c}_i$.

20. Peleg (1984) independently developed a similar concept, which he called a "quasi-coalitional equilibrium." The proof that compensating equilibria are coalition proof and that any coalition-proof equilibrium of a common agency game can be implemented with compensating strategies can be found in Bernheim and Whinston (1986a).

and costless communication before the play of a game, then a subset of them (the "coalition") might suggest to one another what strategies they ought to pursue. These suggestions carry no commitment, so they will be viable (if at all) only when it is indeed in the interest of each member of the coalition to carry out its assigned action when other members of the coalition do likewise. Bernheim and Whinston have argued that, if every member of a coalition can better its lot relative to some equilibrium by carrying out one such suggestion, then the original equilibrium should not be considered stable.

Compensating equilibria are easier to characterize than other equilibria of political contribution games. These equilibria involve the choice of only one item by each interest group. Each group might choose, for example, a positive contribution for some particular policy option. Then all other contribution levels are fixed by the joint requirement that gifts cannot be negative and that, if positive, they compensate for the difference in welfare under alternative options. Moreover, it is often possible to use the efficiency property of compensating equilibria to characterize what outcomes can occur.

In the remainder of this chapter we will examine the properties of compensating equilibria in two examples. The first example focuses on trade policy, the second on redistributive taxation. Together they demonstrate how compensating equilibrium can be calculated in particular applications while also providing insights into the properties of compensating equilibria that hold more generally.

8.4   Trade Policy

In this section we derive compensating equilibria of a game in which interest groups representing different factors of production compete for influence over a small country's trade policy.

Consider the familiar Heckscher-Ohlin model of international trade with two goods and two factors of production. Let the two goods be footwear and consumer electronics, and the factors be capital and labor. Each good is produced with constant returns to scale and sold on a competitive world market. The small home country faces a fixed world price of footwear equal to p_F^* and a fixed world price of consumer electronics equal to 1.

The home country has an abundance of capital. Therefore, it would import footwear (the labor-intensive good) in a free trade equilibrium. A SIG representing the interests of labor covets a tariff on imported footwear. Such a tariff would raise the relative domestic price of footwear and consequently the real wage paid to labor, the latter because labor is the factor used intensively in producing footwear.[21] A SIG representing the interests of capital would like a subsidy to exports of consumer electronics. This policy is one that would boost the real incomes of the capitalists. For the time being, we ignore the world trade rules that prevent countries from subsidizing their exports.

All individuals own either capital or labor, but not both. To make matters simple, we adopt a particular form for an individual's utility function. We assume that each person has a function of the form $u(y_E, y_F) = y_E + u_F(y_F)$, where y_E is his consumption of electronics and y_F is his consumption of footwear. With this utility function, an individual buys footwear up to the point where the marginal utility of shoe purchases, $u_F'(y_F)$, equals the domestic relative price of footwear, p_F, and spends all remaining income on consumer electronics. An individual who spends I achieves a utility level of $I + S(p_F)$, where $S(p_F)$ is the consumer surplus derived from footwear purchases.[22]

A worker has two sources of income. He earns a wage w that depends in equilibrium on the domestic price of footwear, p_F. He also receives a share of any tariff revenues. Tariff revenues are $t p_F^* m_F(p_F)$, where t is the ad valorem tariff rate and $m_F(p_F)$ is the volume of imports, and each individual is assumed to receive the same rebate. A typical worker also bears a per capita share of the cost of any export subsidy. The subsidy costs are $s e_E(p_F)$, where s is the subsidy rate and $e_E(p_F)$ denotes exports. Finally, the worker pays his share of any contributions made by his interest group. We can write the net income of a typical worker as

$$I_L = w(p_F) + \frac{t p_F^* m_F(p_F) - s e_E(p_F)}{N_L + N_K} - \frac{c_L}{N_L},$$

where N_L is the number of workers, N_K is the number of capitalists, and c_L is the contribution by the labor SIG to the policymaker. The goal of the labor SIG is to maximize $U_L = N_L[I_L + S(p_F)]$.

Similarly, a capitalist earns income from her capital endowment and she receives a share of any tariff proceeds. She helps to pay for

---

21. This is an implication of the well-known Stolper-Samuelson theorem: An increase in the price of a good increases the real income of the factor used intensively in producing that good, and decreases the real income of the factor used intensively in the other sector (see Stolper and Samuelson (1941)).

22. Formally, $S(p_F) = u_F(y_F^*) - p_F y_F^*$, when y_F^* satisfies $u_F'(y_F^*) = p_F$.

the export subsidy and for any contributions that her interest group makes. An individual who owns the average amount of capital, k, has a net income of

$$I_K = r(p_F)k + \frac{tp_F^* m_F(p_F) - se_E(p_F)}{N_L + N_K} - \frac{c_K}{N_K},$$

where $r(p_F)$ is the return on a unit of capital. The joint welfare of all capitalists is $U_K = N_K[I_K + S(p_F)]$.

The policymaker chooses the tariff rate t and the export subsidy rate s to maximize a weighted sum of aggregate welfare and campaign contributions. Aggregate welfare is $N_L I_L + N_K I_K + (N_L + N_K)S(p_F)$, while total contributions are $c_L + c_K$. The policymaker's objective is

$$G = \lambda[N_L I_L + N_K I_K + (N_L + N_K)S(p_F)] + (1 - \lambda)(c_L + c_K),$$

with $\lambda < \frac{1}{2}$.[23]

We denote the (compensating) contribution schedules by $H_L(t,s)$ and $H_K(t,s)$. The two trade policies, together with the fixed international prices, determine the domestic relative price of footwear,

$$p_F = \frac{(1+t)p_F^*}{1+s}, \tag{8.14}$$

which in turn determines the allocation of resources and the income levels.

Finding a Nash equilibrium in contribution schedules might seem a difficult task. However, we can use what we know about compensating equilibria to characterize these outcomes. First, we know that a compensating equilibrium must be jointly efficient for labor, capital, and the politician. Joint efficiency means that G is maximized subject to constraints on the levels of U_L and U_K. It is easy to see that this requires a policy that maximizes the sum of private sector income plus aggregate consumer surplus.[24] But private sector income plus

---

23. For values of $\lambda > 1/2$, the policymaker values the welfare of citizens higher than campaign contributions, and so never accepts any contributions from the interest groups.
24. Let $Y = N_L w(p_F) + N_K kr(p_F) + tp_F^* m_F(p_F) - se_E(p_F)$ be private-sector income. Then $G = \lambda[Y + (N_L + N_K)S(p_F)] + (1 - 2\lambda)(c_N + c_K)$.
If the labor and capital SIGs must achieve utility levels of $\bar{U}_L$ and $\bar{U}_K$, respectively, then
$$c_N + c_K = Y + (N_L + N_K)S(p_F) - \bar{U}_L - \bar{U}_K,$$
in which case maximizing G is the same as maximizing $Y + (N_L + N_K)S(p_F)$.

aggregate consumer surplus are maximized when $p_F = p_F^*$, that is, when the domestic relative price of footwear is equal to the world relative price. Therefore, $s^\circ = t^\circ$ in any compensating equilibrium (see (8.14)).

Whenever $s = t$, all resource allocations and (gross) income levels are the same as in free trade. Thus, the competition for influence results in a stalemate. The labor SIG wants a high tariff and a low export subsidy, whereas the business group wants a low tariff and a high subsidy. Since neither policy increases the total economic pie and there are no other groups in the economy to exploit, the equilibrium outcome favors neither group. What is worse for the groups is that they do not achieve this standoff costlessly. In fact, each group must contribute positively to secure the equivalent of a free trade outcome. If a group were to withhold its contributions, it would suffer yet a worse fate than it does with the neutral policies.

We derive the equilibrium contributions in two steps. First, we make use of the fact that a compensating schedule calls for a payment, if positive, that compensates for any differences in utility relative to the equilibrium utility level. In the equilibrium, the aggregate utility of labor equals $U_L^\circ = N_L[w(p_F^*) + S(p_F^*)] - c_L^\circ$. The contribution schedule of the labor SIG thus can be written as

$H_L(s, t)$

$$= \max\left\{ N_L[w(p_F) + S(p_F)] + \frac{N_L}{N_L + N_K}[tp_F^* m_F(p_F) - se_E(p_F)] - U_L^\circ, 0 \right\},$$

where $p_F = (1 + t)p_F^*/(1 + s)$. The contribution schedule of the capital SIG is analogous.

Now that we have the form of the contribution schedule, we can find the policy that the politician would choose in the absence of contributions from the capital SIG. In such circumstances, the policymaker would maximize

$$G^{-K} = \lambda[N_L I_L + N_K I_K + (N_L + N_K)S(p_F)] + (1 - \lambda)H_L(s, t),$$

a weighted sum of aggregate welfare and contributions from the labor group. This maximization results in policies that imply a relative price $p_F^{-K} > p_F^*$. Without contributions from capital, trade policy would favor the labor SIG, which means that the domestic relative price of footwear would be greater than the world price. This would give the workers a real income higher than under free trade. The

policymaker can induce a domestic price of p_F^{-K} by enacting either a
tariff $(t > 0)$, an export tax $(s < 0)$, or a combination of the two; see
equation (8.14).

Similarly, we can calculate the policies that the politician would
set in the absence of contributions from the labor group. These policies are the ones that maximize

$$G^{-L} = \lambda[N_L I_L + N_K I_K + (N_L + N_K)S(p_F)] + (1 - \lambda)H_K(s,t).$$

In this case, the policymaker would choose policies that result in the
domestic relative price $p_F^{-L} < p_F^*$. She could do so by enacting a subsidy to exports, a subsidy to imports, or a combination of the two.
Such policies would reduce the relative price of footwear, and so
boost the real income of capital.

It is these policies, leading to p_F^{-K} and p_F^{-L}, that the interest groups
must guard against. The labor SIG must give a sufficient contribution
to ensure that the policymaker chooses the equilibrium policies and
not ones that result in a domestic relative price of $p_F = p_F^{-L}$. This requirement pins down the size of c_L°. Similarly, the capital SIG must
contribute sufficiently so that the policymaker chooses the equilibrium policies and not ones that lead to $p_F = p_F^{-L}$. This determines c_K°.
In the equilibrium, the policymaker achieves an efficient allocation
of resources and collects political tributes from both interest groups.
This outcome is typical of situations in which the policymaker cares
about aggregate welfare and all members of society are represented
by some interest group or another.[25]

Let us briefly consider how our conclusions would change if we
introduce a prohibition on export subsidies. Such a prohibition was
incorporated into the original articles of the General Agreement on
Tariffs and Trade (GATT) and remains a part of the trading rules
today. As the formula for domestic prices reveals, the effects of an
export subsidy (with $s > 0$) can be mimicked by the use of a subsidy
to imports $(t < 0)$.[26] If a prohibition on export subsidies is to have
any real effects, it must be coupled with a rule preventing import
subsidies as well. So, suppose that the political competition plays out

25. Note that, in the compensating equilibrium, factor incomes are the same as in free
trade, there is no net government revenue to redistribute, and the citizens all share in
the cost of political contributions. Thus the competition for influence leaves everyone
(except the politician) worse off than in a world without influence payments.
26. The equivalence between export subsidies and import subsidies is known in the
international trade literature as the Lerner symmetry theorem.

subject to the constraints that $s \leq 0$ and $t \geq 0$. These constraints do not alter the conclusion that the policy outcomes must be jointly efficient for the interest groups and the policymaker. Recall that unconstrained joint efficiency required $p_F = p_F^*$, or $s = t$. The same outcome can be achieved subject to the policy constraints, but only if $s = t = 0$. Thus, we now have an unambiguous prediction about the trade policies, but of course the same resource allocation as we had without the constraints. The contributions that support the equilibrium are not, however, the same as before. In particular, in the absence of contributions from labor, the government could not choose policies that reduce the domestic relative price of footwear. Such domestic prices require an export subsidy or an import subsidy, both of which are not feasible. Accordingly, $p_F^{-L} = p_F^*$ under the new rules of the game; that is, the policy choices are the same whether the labor SIG contributes to the policymaker or not. In equilibrium, the labor SIG has nothing to fear from its rival interest group, and so it refrains from contributing.

To summarize, a rule prohibiting export subsidies and import subsidies has no effect on the equilibrium allocation of resources and (essentially) no effect on the policy choice. Such a rule does, however, have distributional implications for the policymaker and the interest groups. Since the threat of export subsidies no longer exists, the position of the policymaker has been weakened vis-à-vis the labor group. The labor SIG achieves higher utility, and the politician lower welfare, when export subsidies are prohibited than when they are allowed.

8.5 Redistributive Taxation

In this section we study the political economy of income redistribution. We assume that the policymaker's objective function includes as arguments the utility levels of all members of society and the total amount of her campaign contributions. This objective function could reflect her personal aversion to inequality—she might prefer, for example, a situation in which all individuals have roughly the same level of utility to one in which some individuals are very well off and others are not—or it might be that individuals base their voting decisions on their personal levels of well-being and the politician is concerned about her chances of being reelected. In the latter case, the politician's objective function might give greater weight to certain individuals, if for example some of them are more likely to turn out to vote than others or if their voting behavior is more responsive to their level of personal well-being. We write $G = \hat{G}(\mathbf{U}, c)$, where $\mathbf{U} = (U_1, \ldots, U_N)$ is the vector of utility levels of the N members of society and $c = \sum c_i$. Here, an individual may belong to one interest group, several, or none. The individual i has a utility function $U_i(\mathbf{p}, c_i)$, where $\mathbf{p}$ is a vector of policy outcomes and c_i is the total amount of her payments to the various SIGs of which she is a member, which in turn contribute to the policymaker.

Interest groups are arbitrary collections of individuals. SIG 1 might have individuals 1, 7, 12, 16, and others as members, while SIG 2 has individuals 2, 7, 13, 15, and so on as members. Notice that in this example, individual 7 is a member of both groups. All that we insist on is that each SIG maximize an objective function that includes the utility levels of all of its members as arguments. The groups offer compensating contribution schedules to the policymaker and allocate the burden of their contributions to their members in whatever manner they choose.

This formulation has one distinguishing feature. Economic policies affect the welfare of the citizenry, which in turn affects the policymaker's welfare. But the policymaker has no personal preferences about policy outcomes beyond their impact on her constituents. In other words, the vector $\mathbf{p}$ enters $\hat{G}(\cdot)$ only indirectly through $U_1(\mathbf{p}, c_1)$, $U_2(\mathbf{p}, c_2)$, and so on; it does not appear as a separate argument in this function.[27] For now, we take $\mathbf{p}$ to be an arbitrary set of feasible policies. It might include, for example, subsidies to production, regulations on the use of certain factors, taxes or subsidies on trade, and other policies. We assume that $\hat{G}(\cdot)$ is strictly increasing in all of its arguments.

We are now ready to describe an important property of compensating equilibria in this rather general setting. It can be shown that all compensating equilibria are constrained Pareto efficient. That is, in any compensating equilibrium, there exists no alternative vector of policies among those that are feasible and no alternative vector of contributions yielding the same total contribution with the property that all individuals (including those who are members of SIGs and those who are not) are at least as well off under the alternative poli-

---

27. Similarly, the policymaker cares about the sources of her contributions only insofar as the distribution of payments affects the utility levels of her various constituents.

cies and contributions as in the compensating equilibrium, and at least one individual is better off.[28]

This property of a compensating equilibrium is stronger than the one we identified earlier. Here the outcome must be efficient not only for the policymaker and the organized special interests, but also for the polity as a whole. The key to the strengthening of our earlier result is the assumption that $\hat{G}(\cdot)$ is increasing in each U_i. Pareto efficiency is achieved now, because the policymaker values an increase in the welfare of each and every citizen. Were the equilibrium not efficient, it would be possible to raise the policymaker's objective function without harming any of the interest groups. But this would violate the joint efficiency property of a compensating equilibrium.

Armed with this result, we can make many predictions about economic policy. In fact, we can draw on the large literature on economic policy that takes a normative approach. The normative literature is meant to be prescriptive, not predictive of the outcome of any political process. But now we can apply its findings to characterize equilibria of a well-specified game of political influence.

Take, for example, a pure case of redistributive taxation. Suppose that an individual's utility depends on his own consumption of a vector of goods and on his labor supply. Let goods be produced by profit-maximizing firms that operate under constant or decreasing returns to scale. Let there be perfect competition in all goods and factor markets, and no externalities or other rigidities in the economy. The economy is either closed to international trade or small in world markets. In this setting, if lump-sum taxes and transfers are feasible, Pareto efficiency is achieved by an appropriate set of such taxes and transfers and without any other government intervention of any sort.[29] The absence of distortionary taxes, subsidies, and regulations ensures economic efficiency. Only the lump-sum transfers and subsidies are used in response to the groups' political pressures, which are reflected in their compensating contribution schedules. They give rise to an equilibrium distribution of income.

---

28. This property of compensating equilibria follows almost immediately from our earlier result that all compensating equilibria are jointly efficient for the group of SIGs and the policymaker. A formal proof of the constrained efficiency result can be found in Dixit, Grossman, and Helpman (1997).

29. The closed-economy version of this result is a corollary of the second theorem of welfare economics; see Samuelson (1947). Dixit (1987) extended the result to a small open economy. In a large economy that engages in trade, the lump-sum taxes and transfers must be supplemented by a set of "optimal" tariffs and export taxes.

Many economists have noted that lump-sum taxes and transfers are difficult to implement. They require that the policymaker have perfect information about individuals' preference and abilities. In practice, the policymaker is not born with such information but needs to gather it by surveying the population or by observing its behavior. But if the individuals know that their tax liabilities will depend on their verbal responses or their economic behavior, they will have incentive to distort their words and actions in order to reduce their burden. Accordingly, lump-sum taxes and transfers may not be feasible. In the event, we can apply the findings of Diamond and Mirrlees (1971) to characterize the compensating equilibria. They have shown that when the government of a closed economy is constrained not to use lump-sum taxes or transfers, a Pareto efficient equilibrium requires the use of only taxes and subsidies on consumption and factor supplies, with no taxes or subsidies to output by particular industries, and no taxes or subsidies for the use of particular factors of production.[30] Once again, the normative prescriptions of an earlier literature become predictions about the equilibrium outcome in an influence game.

Finally, let us say a few words about the contributions that support a compensating equilibrium in a political game of income redistribution. Here we report the findings of Dixit, Grossman, and Helpman (1997). They show, first, that if lump-sum taxes and transfers are feasible as policy instruments, then the competition for influence will be very intense. Specifically, if no individual belongs to every interest group and if there are at least two such organized groups, then a member of a SIG will fare no better in the equilibrium than she would if her group were to unilaterally renounce its political activities. In other words, the policymaker captures all of the surplus in her relationship with the various interest groups. The policymaker achieves the same level of political welfare in the compensating equilibrium as she would in a setting where she could dictate not only the allocation of resources to various economic uses, but also the levels of campaign contributions by every group!

When the policymaker has complete freedom to fashion lump-sum taxes and transfers, she enjoys enormous political power. This power

---

30. Dixit (1987) provides the extension of this result to the open economy. He shows that efficiency requires free trade in a small economy, but a set of optimal tariffs and export taxes in an economy that is large enough to affect its international terms of trade.

emanates from the ability she has to cease her dealings with any SIG at no cost to herself. For, suppose that a deviant SIG were to demand some positive surplus from the policymaker in exchange for its contribution. The policymaker could reduce the transfer to this group (or increase the tax) by the amount of its equilibrium contribution and redirect the funds to the members of some other SIG. Since the SIGs all have compensating payment schedules, the policymaker would receive back from the recipients the entire amount of the redirected transfers as additional contributions. So the policymaker would not lose any contributions by this change, nor would the welfare of any individual be altered. Thus, the policymaker is indifferent between dealing with the deviant group or not. For this reason, the group cannot succeed in its attempts to share in the surplus.

When lump-sum taxes and transfers are not feasible, the SIGs may fare better in their relationship with the policymaker. Typically, none of them is willing to renounce its political activity in such circumstances, because all enjoy some surplus in the political equilibrium. In the absence of lump-sum tools for redistribution, if any SIG were to withhold its promised contribution, the policymaker would be forced to resort to distortionary taxes or subsidies if she wished to make up for the potential loss of campaign funds with greater gifts from other groups. But this would exacerbate economic inefficiencies, with resultant costs to society and the policymaker. Since the policymaker could not costlessly replace the gifts from a SIG with gifts from the others, each group can extract surplus by the implicit threat to withdraw from the deal. In fact, the less economically efficient are the tools of redistributive politics, the better is the bargaining position of the organized interest groups vis-à-vis the policymaker.

8.6   Competition for Influence: Good Thing or Bad Thing?

Our analysis sheds light on a controversy in the literature on interest-group competition. Some authors, following Becker (1983), believe that competition between interest groups is beneficial to society. Using a reduced-form model in which the government responds to "pressures" from special interests, Becker showed that competition can lead to Pareto efficient policies as the groups attempt to generate the greatest benefit for themselves, given the cost imposed on others. Tullock (1980) and others have argued differently. They see the rents created by policy being dissipated by socially wasteful expenditures.

In a simple model with risk-neutral groups in which each SIG has a probability of capturing a given rent that is proportional to the size of its investment in "rent-seeking activities," the fraction of the rent that is dissipated increases with the number of competitors. In this sense, competition among groups is harmful to society. Our more complete model of intergroup competition reveals that there is some element of truth in both of these positions.

In Dixit, Grossman, and Helpman (1997), the authors identify circumstances under which the equilibrium policies are bound to be efficient. If the SIGs all use compensating contribution schedules, the policymaker has no direct preferences over the policies except insofar as they affect her constituents' welfare, and if the objective function of the policymaker increases, however slightly, with an increase in the well-being of any constituent, then the competing bids for influence must result in a choice that is Pareto efficient among the set of feasible policies.[31] This means that, given the initial set of contribution levels—positive for members of some interests groups and zero for those who are not in any SIG—there is no feasible, alternative policy vector that could make some individual better off without making someone else worse off.

This, however, does not mean that competition between interest groups serves the SIG members well. As we have seen, the equilibrium outcome is supported by a set of political contributions. Some may regard the campaign spending funded by SIG contributions as a waste of resources. In any case, the contributions represent a dissipation of rents from the groups' perspective, as predicted by Tullock and others. When a fixed quantity of rents is up for grabs, it takes a large number of competitors to generate full dissipation. But when, as here, the quantity of rents is determined in the political equilibrium, the outcome can be even more dire. As mentioned previously, Dixit et al. consider a situation in which income can be transferred between groups without the creation of any deadweight loss. In such circumstances, competition between two interest groups is enough to dissipate fully the benefits from political activity. That is, each SIG fares no better in the political equilibrium than it would if it were to renounce entirely its efforts to curry favor.

31. Alternatively, efficiency will result even if the policymaker does not care about the welfare of her constituents, if each citizen belongs to an interest group and none is a member of more than one group.

The highly adverse effects of competition do, however, require some special conditions. Rents are fully dissipated only if utility can be transferred costlessly between groups, so that the recipient's gain from a change in policy exactly matches the payor's loss. If instead there are institutional constraints or feasibility constraints that force the policymaker to resort to redistributive instruments that generate deadweight loss, the interest groups will be able to capture some of the surplus in their political relationship with the policymaker. Whether the addition of more groups to compete with an initial set of SIGs will benefit or harm the typical group member, and whether it will benefit or harm those who are not represented by any SIG, depends on how the various interests align on the issues and on the nature of the policy decisions that are subject to influence.

In this chapter, we have studied the competition among SIGs for political influence. We modeled this competition as one in which each of several (or many) SIGs confronts the policymaker with offers of campaign contributions in exchange for various policies. An equilibrium is a set of contribution schedules that are mutual best responses, considering the anticipated behavior by the policymaker.

Typically there are many equilibria of such influence games. But the set of possible outcomes is narrowed considerably when we place reasonable restrictions on the form of the equilibrium contribution schedules. Using an assumption that the schedules are differentiable when positive, we are able to characterize the set of possible policy outcomes. With a further assumption that the schedules are compensating, we are also able to characterize the equilibrium contributions. We illustrated the general theory in several applications.

Throughout this chapter and the last, we have assumed that a unitary policymaker has unilateral authority to enact policies. Interpreted literally, this assumption renders the policymaker an omnipotent executive. But our analysis may also apply to settings with legislative decision making, provided that a single political party controls a majority of votes and that the delegates succumb to strict party discipline. When a legislature comprises members who vote independently and pursue their own objectives, the problem of buying influence is likely to be more complex. We turn to this problem in the next chapter.

9   Influencing a Legislature

In the last two chapters we assumed that policies are set by a single individual or by a cohesive, well-disciplined political party. In reality, of course, most policy decisions are made not by one person but by a group of elected representatives acting as a legislative body. Even when the legislature is controlled by a single party, the delegation members do not always follow the instructions of their party leaders. In situations with multiple, independent legislators, interest groups face a subtle problem in deciding how best to use their resources to influence policy choices. A SIG must decide where to concentrate its bid for influence and what actions it should try to affect. Should the group seek to solidify support among those legislators who would be inclined to support its positions anyway, or should it seek to win over those who might otherwise be hostile to its views? Should it focus mostly on buying votes for bills that it likes, or on influencing the legislators who might be deciding the bills' contents? Is it necessary to influence those who are drafting the bills initially, or is it enough to curry favor among those who will be in a position to offer amendments? The answers to these questions and others like them surely depend on the rules of the legislative process —for example, on how the agenda is determined and on what procedures are used for introducing and dispensing with amendments. In other words, the optimal strategy for wielding influence will vary with the institutional setting.

Beginning with Gilligan and Krehbiel (1987, 1989) and Baron and Ferejohn (1989), social scientists have developed formal models of the legislative process. These models emphasize how policy outcomes may vary with differences in procedures and differences in the structure of the political system. Procedural variation might include, for example, a comparison of "open rules," which allow members of the legislature to offer amendments to bills proposed to the body, and "closed rules," which prohibit such amendments. Structural variation might entail a comparison of congressional systems, in which members represent geographic regions and have relatively weak party loyalty, and parliamentary systems, where parties compete nationally and party loyalty is strong.[1] In most of this research, attention has been focused on the interaction between a group of legislators who have conflicting preferences. The question has rarely been raised of how these preferences relate to those of voters, on the one hand, and to the actions of SIGs on the other.[2]

This chapter aims to include both influence activities and legislative procedures in a single model, to see how the two interact in determining policy. Our approach will be to think of contribution offers as inducing preferences for the legislators, who then must interact in the parliament according to the rules of the legislative game. By taking this approach, we hope to shed light on what strategies interest groups might pursue to exert their influence over a legislature, and how the conflicts between interest groups might be resolved. Since this analysis is considerably more complex than what we have seen until now, we will present only a brief introduction to some of the issues that can arise. We begin with the case of a single interest group and then proceed to the case of competing interests.

9.1 Buying Votes

Consider a situation in which a legislature will decide a policy issue. An organized interest group seeks to influence the decision. The group's preferences are represented by $U(p,c) = W(p) - c$, where c now denotes the total of its campaign contributions. The group can contribute to one or more of the members of the legislature.

The legislature has three members. We choose the number three because it is the smallest number that allows for both legislative

---

1. Persson, Roland, and Tabellini (2000) have examined the budgetary process under these alternative systems. See also Baron (1991, 1993) and Diermeier and Feddersen (1998).

2. Austen-Smith and Banks (1988) and Chari, Jones, and Marimon (1997) are exceptions. These authors have incorporated both electoral competition and legislative bargaining in a single model.

deliberations and majority rule. We will refer to the legislators as $L1$, $L2$, and $L3$. Legislator Li seeks to maximize $G_{Li}(p, c_i) = \lambda W_{Li}(p) + (1 - \lambda)c_i$, which is a weighted average of his subjective evaluation of the policy outcome and his campaign receipts. Preferences like these may arise, for example, if legislator Li represents a district whose aggregate welfare is $W_{Li}(\cdot)$ and he cares about the well-being of his constituents as well as his campaign finances. In Chapter 10 we will see how an objective function like this can be derived from purely political objectives, such as a candidate's desire to win an election or a party's wish to maximize its patronage.

In this section we follow Snyder (1991) in assuming that the SIG has the ability to set the political agenda. That is, the SIG can propose a bill and offer contributions to some or all of the legislators in order to encourage their support.[3] The sole job of the legislature is to ratify or reject the group's proposal. This modeling of the legislative process is, of course, unrealistic. But it does provide for a simple analysis with several useful insights. In the next section we will designate one of the legislators to be the agenda setter; in such a setting both the policy outcome and the structure of contributions may be somewhat different from what we observe here.

The contribution-cum-legislative game plays out as follows. First, the interest group proposes a policy level p and makes a separate contribution offer to each legislator. It promises to contribute c_i to legislator Li if the legislator votes in favor of the bill. The voting pits the proposed legislation against a status quo policy, which we denote by q. If at least two of the legislators vote for the bill, then p is implemented as policy. Otherwise, the outcome is q. Finally, the SIG contributes to the various campaigns in accordance with its promises.[4]

We begin the analysis with the second stage, which arises after the bill has been drafted and the SIG has tendered its offers to the members of the legislature. Consider a legislator who expects not to

---

3. Snyder (1991), who developed a model with many legislators, also studied the case in which the SIG must offer the same payment to any supporter of its proposed legislation. This constraint on SIG contributions seems artificial to us, so we will not consider it here.

4. In principle, the SIG might also offer a contribution $\bar{c}_i$ to legislator Li if Li votes against the proposal. However, it is fairly obvious that the SIG has no reason to pay the legislator to oppose its own proposal. We avoid the unnecessary notation and simply observe that contributions to nonsupporters are optimally set to zero.

be pivotal: he expects the bill surely to pass or surely to fail no matter
how he votes. Such a legislator will vote in favor of the proposal if he
is offered any positive inducement to do so, and he will be indifferent
about his vote if no contribution is offered. We assume that the legislator responds to such indifference by voting for whichever policy
option he prefers.

Now consider a legislator Li who anticipates that his vote will be
decisive. If Li votes in favor of the bill, it passes, and he attains utility
$\lambda W_{Li}(p) + (1 - \lambda)c_i$. If he votes against the bill, it fails, and the legislator's utility is $\lambda W_{Li}(q)$. Clearly, Li will vote for the bill when he
expects to be pivotal if and only if $\lambda W_{Li}(p) + (1 - \lambda)c_i \geq \lambda W_{Li}(q)$.[5]

We turn next to the problem facing the interest group. Anticipating the behavior of the legislators, the SIG must decide what bill to
propose and what contributions to offer. For simplicity, suppose that
$W(p)$ and all $W_{Li}(p)$ are single-peaked functions and that the policy
must be chosen from a range of feasible policies. Under these conditions, each legislator has a unique favorite policy among those that
are feasible, and so does the SIG. Denote by π the ideal policy for the
SIG and by π_{Li} the ideal policy for legislator Li.

If at least two of the legislators prefer π to q, the solution to the
SIG's problem is simple. In such circumstances, the group should
propose its favorite policy and offer nothing to the legislators. The
two (or three) legislators who prefer π to q will vote in favor of the
bill, which thus becomes law. In the resulting equilibrium, the SIG
attains its optimal combination of $p = \pi$ and $c = 0$.

When at least two of the legislators prefer q to π, the situation
is different. Then the group must either compromise on its policy
demands or offer contributions in exchange for support. We proceed
now to consider which legislators are targeted, how much they
receive, and what policy is proposed.

Clearly, the SIG would like to buy support for any bill p at the
minimum total cost. If a legislator Li prefers p to q, then his vote
comes for free. Otherwise a payment must be made, the size of which
depends on whether Li expects to be pivotal or not. One possibility is
that none of the legislators who prefer q to p expects to be pivotal in

---

5. Technically, the legislator is indifferent between the options when $\lambda W_{Li}(p) +
(1 - \lambda)c_i = \lambda W_{Li}(q)$. Since the SIG could always resolve this indifference by offering a
bit more for the legislator's support, a legislator who expects to be pivotal breaks any
ties in favor of the proposal.

the voting. Then the SIG can get off cheaply. It can offer each of the legislators a tiny positive amount, which then would be enough to win his support.[6] Alternatively, each legislator who prefers q to p might expect his similarly inclined colleagues to vote their policy preferences unless they are adequately compensated. Then all legislators who receive positive offers will see themselves as pivotal voters. In the event, the SIG must offer substantial contributions that are large enough to overcome the legislature's resistance to its proposal.

We will focus here on the latter type of equilibria, in which all legislators who receive positive contributions perceive themselves to be pivotal.[7] In such circumstances the SIG must first calculate what it would take to induce each legislator to cast his vote in favor of p when the legislator knows himself to be decisive. We know that Li will vote in favor of the bill when he expects to be pivotal if and only if $\lambda W_{Li}(p) + (1 - \lambda)c_i \geq \lambda W_{Li}(q)$. It follows that the SIG must offer $c_i(p) = \max\{0, \hat{c}_i(p)\}$ to garner support for the policy p from legislator Li, where

$$\hat{c}_i(p) = \frac{\lambda}{1 - \lambda}[W_{Li}(q) - W_{Li}(p)] \tag{9.1}$$

is the contribution that leaves this legislator with the same utility under policy p as he would achieve with no contribution under the status quo.

The SIG needs the support of two legislators in order to pass a bill that implements p. Therefore, the group can enact the policy p at a minimum cost of

$$c(p) = \sum_{i=1}^{3} c_i(p) - \max_j c_j(p). \tag{9.2}$$

---

6. If a legislator expects the other two to vote in favor of a bill, then his best response is to accept any positive amount ε in exchange for his own vote. Since this argument does not depend on the size of ε, the SIG can reduce its positive offers to an arbitrarily small amount.

7. The equilibrium in which the SIG offers only a tiny amount to the legislators who favor q to p appears to be fragile. Each of these legislators knows that he would have company in opposing the bill if only the other(s) could count on his own vote. Thus, the equilibrium with tiny payments requires a coordination failure among the opponents to the bill. Such an equilibrium might not survive in an extended game with nonbinding communication between legislators.

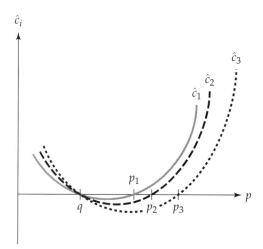

Figure 9.1
Compensation Functions for Legislators

As suggested by Riker's "size principle," the SIG achieves the lowest cost by forming a "minimum winning coalition" among those members of the legislature who are most sympathetic to p relative to the status quo.[8]

We can now use the function $c(p)$ to solve the broader problem facing the interest group. The SIG seeks the feasible policy that maximizes its utility net of contributions. Formally, the equilibrium policy p° solves

$$p^\circ = \arg \max \ U[p, c(p)] \qquad\qquad (9.3)$$

for p between $p_{\min}$ and $p_{\max}$. In equilibrium, the SIG pays $c_i^\circ = c_i(p^\circ)$ to the legislators who are induced to support the bill.

Figure 9.1 depicts the functions $\hat{c}_i(p)$ for a case in which $q < \pi_{L1} < \pi_{L2} < \pi_{L3}$. In the figure, a legislator's favorite policy π_{Li} can be found at the value of p for which $\hat{c}_i(p)$ attains a minimum. In drawing the figure, we have also assumed that $\hat{c}_1(p) < \hat{c}_2(p) < \hat{c}_3(p)$ for all $p < q$, while $\hat{c}_1(p) > \hat{c}_2(p) > \hat{c}_3(p)$ for all $p > q$. In other words, not only is the favorite policy of $L3$ greater than that of $L2$, which in turn is greater than that of $L1$, but $L3$ has the relatively strongest preference for all policies p greater than the status quo, and $L1$ has the

---

8. See Riker (1962) for the original statement. Riker and Ordeshook (1973, Chapter 7) provide a formal discussion and some empirical evidence.

relatively strongest preference for all policies less than the status quo.[9]

Using figure 9.1, we can construct the function $c(p)$. Consider first a policy $p < q$. Since all legislators prefer the status quo to any such policy, the SIG must buy two votes to effect such an outcome. To do so, it is least costly for the group to procure the support of legislators $L1$ and $L2$. These two have the least distaste for policies with a small value of p, so the cost of influencing them is less than for $L3$. For all policies $p < q$, then, $c(p) = \hat{c}_1(p) + \hat{c}_2(p)$.

Next consider a policy p between q and p_2. For all such values of p, at least two (and sometimes three) of the legislators prefer the proposal to the status quo. Thus, the SIG can effect any such policy at zero cost.

For policies to the right of p_2, the SIG must offer contributions to at least one legislator. The vote of legislator $L2$ is available to the SIG at a lower cost than that of $L1$. Accordingly, for policies between p_2 and p_3, the SIG pays $\hat{c}_2(p)$ to $L2$, and gains the support of $L3$ without cost. Finally, for policies $p > p_3$, the SIG must contribute to two legislators in order to enact its proposal. It chooses $L2$ and $L3$ as the least costly to influence, so that $c(p) = \hat{c}_2(p) + \hat{c}_3(p)$. We have thus completed the construction of $c(p)$, which is shown as the bold curve in figure 9.2.

We can now identify the equilibrium policy for different preferences of the interest group. The SIG achieves highest utility for any given c when $p = \pi$. Thus, its indifference curves are a set of inverted U-shaped curves, each with a peak at $p = \pi$. First consider a case where the group's ideal policy π is far to the left of q. Then the SIG achieves its highest utility for some policy p° between π and q, as shown in Panel a of figure 9.3, in which UU is the SIG's indifference curve. Here the SIG pays contributions to legislators $L1$ and $L2$, but it also compromises its policy goals. The policy outcome falls somewhere between the status quo and the group's ideal policy. Panel b of figure 9.3 illustrates a different case, where the SIG's favorite policy is only slightly smaller than the status quo q. Here the group contents itself with the status quo policy. Evidently, the benefit to the group from achieving a policy smaller than q in this situation is not worth the cost.

Now consider the case in which the group's ideal policy lies to the right of the status quo. We have already noted that, when π lies

9. The situation depicted in the figure applies, for example, when the utility functions are quadratic; that is, $W_{Li}(p) = -(p - \pi_{Li})^2$, in which case $\hat{c}_i(p) = [\lambda/(1 - \lambda)] \cdot (p - q)(p + q - 2\pi_{Li})$. Snyder analyzes this case of quadratic utility functions in his 1991 paper.

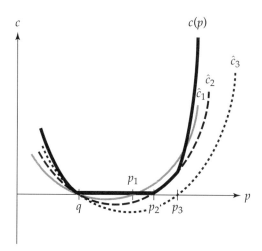

Figure 9.2
The Cost of Legislation

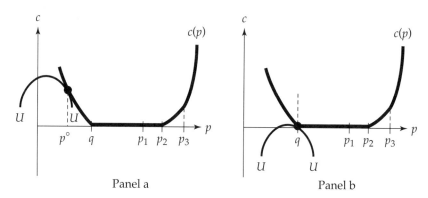

Figure 9.3
Equilibrium Policy without an Agenda Setter

between q and p_2, the SIG can attain its favorite outcome at zero cost. The group simply proposes its ideal policy and watches as (at least) two of the legislators vote in favor of the bill. When the SIG's ideal policy exceeds p_2, this strategy will not work. Then the reasoning is similar to the case of $\pi < q$. When $\pi > p_2$ by only a small amount, the group contents itself with the policy $p = p_2$, which it can achieve at zero cost. As the group become more extreme in its preferences, it eventually wishes to implement a policy greater than p_2. To do so, it contributes to the campaign of legislator $L2$ and possibly to that of legislator $L3$ as well.

Notice who are the recipients of the group's contributions in each case. A legislator with preferences very different from the SIG does not receive any contributions, because the group only needs a majority of votes, and these unsympathetic legislators are too costly to win over. Only the most sympathetic legislators are included in the minimum winning coalition. But a legislator with preferences very similar to those of the group does not receive contributions either. Such a legislator is ready to support the group's bill without any added inducement. Rather, it is the legislators whose preferences differ from the group by an intermediate amount who capture the largest donations.

We can use a similar approach to analyze a situation in which one of the legislators has an ideal policy on the opposite side of the status quo from the favorite policies of the other two; for example, $\pi_{L1} < q < \pi_{L2} < \pi_{L3}$. In such circumstances, the function $c(p)$ has a flat portion to the right of q, just as in figure 9.2. In other words, there again is a range of proposals $p > q$ that will receive the support of legislators $L2$ and $L3$ without any positive contributions. But now there is a range of policies to the left of the status quo that the SIG can implement with contributions only to $L2$. In any case, the main conclusions still apply. The SIG builds a minimum winning coalition among the legislators whose preferences are most similar to its own, and contributes the most to the legislator whose preferences are neither the most similar nor the most different.

9.2   A Legislature with an Agenda Setter

The Snyder model, while analytically convenient, gives too much power to the interest group. Not only can the SIG use its resources to influence the legislators' voting behavior, but it can also dictate the provisions of the law that stands as an alternative to the status quo. In reality, interest groups have no such authority to introduce bills to the legislature. But they can use their resources to influence those who do have this authority.

In order to understand how this might work, we need a more complete description of the legislative process. A useful starting point is the elegant model of legislative bargaining formulated by Baron and Ferejohn (1989). In this model, an "agenda setter" occupies center stage. The agenda setter—who might be the chair of the relevant committee of the U.S. Congress, or the relevant minister in a parliamentary system—has the sole authority to propose new legislation. Once the agenda setter drafts a bill, it comes to the floor for deliberation and a vote. At this stage the parliamentary rules dictate whether representatives can amend the proposal and, if so, by what means. Then the legislators vote on the bill (amended or not) to determine whether it will replace the status quo.

We introduce an interest group into the Baron-Ferejohn framework. The SIG can seek to influence the agenda setter but cannot usurp his authority. We imagine that the SIG can offer campaign contributions both to the agenda setter and to other members of the legislature. First the SIG meets with the agenda setter and confronts him with a contribution schedule. This schedule associates a donation with each bill that the agenda setter might sponsor. The agenda setter receives the specified contribution $c_a(p)$ if he proposes a bill that implements p and continues to support it when it comes to a vote. After the agenda setter has drafted a bill, the SIG can meet privately with the remaining legislators. At these meetings, the SIG can offer a contribution in return for a vote in favor of the proposed legislation, or it can offer one to encourage a vote against. To keep matters simple, we assume a closed parliamentary rule that excludes the possibility of amendments. Thus, after all of the offers are tendered, the legislators vote on the bill as originally proposed.

It is easy to see that the equilibrium of this legislative game need not be the same as in the Snyder model. For example, suppose the legislators' preferences give rise to compensation functions such as those depicted in figure 9.1, and suppose that the SIG's ideal point π lies well to the left of the status quo. Recall the equilibrium (illustrated in Panel a of figure 9.3) that arises when the SIG dictates the content of legislation. The group chooses a policy $p°$ to the left of q and makes contributions to $L1$ and $L2$ to win their support. The equilibrium policy is the one that maximizes $W(p) - \hat{c}_1(p) - \hat{c}_2(p)$, which, in view of (9.1), is the one that maximizes a weighted sum of the welfare levels of the interest group and legislators $L1$ and $L2$.[10] But now suppose that the SIG lacks agenda-setting authority and that in fact this authority rests with legislator $L3$. Then clearly the SIG cannot induce p° with contributions to $L1$ and $L2$ alone. The agenda setter prefers the status quo to p°, and so would never propose p° unless he were given some incentive to do so. Moreover, once the SIG recognizes that $L3$ must be included in the winning coalition, it no longer has reason to seek the support of both $L1$ and $L2$. Accordingly, the preferences of at least one of these legislators play no role in determining the outcome.

Let us analyze more fully the game that arises when $L3$ is the agenda setter. We begin with a case in which $\pi < q$, and continue to assume that $q < \pi_{L1} < \pi_{L2} < \pi_{L3}$. Our first task is to identify what policy the agenda setter would propose without any influence from the interest group. By identifying this policy, we learn how well the agenda setter would fare should he choose to decline the offers he receives from the SIG. This in turn tells us how costly it will be for the group to convince him to make a proposal more to its liking.

Were the agenda setter to receive no contributions from the SIG, he would opt for the policy closest to π_{L3} that would not be defeated by the legislature. In thinking about what bills would command a majority, the agenda setter must consider not only the preferences of his colleagues, but also the incentives the SIG might have to exert pressure once a particular bill has been proposed. Surely the agenda setter would not introduce any bill calling for a policy $p > p_2$. Both $L1$ and $L2$ prefer the status quo to all policies greater than p_2, so both would be inclined to vote against such a bill. Moreover, the SIG also prefers the status quo to any such policy, so it would have no reason to discourage the legislators' opposition. In short, any bill with $p > p_2$ is bound to be defeated.

In contrast, some bills calling for a policy between q and p_2 might succeed in the legislature. Notice that legislator $L2$ prefers all such policies to the status quo, and he would be inclined to join the agenda setter in voting in favor of such proposals unless the SIG were to offer a sufficient inducement to convince him otherwise. To convince $L2$ to vote against a bill with a p between q and p_2, the SIG must offer him a contribution of at least $-\hat{c}_2(p)$. As for legislator $L1$, he will vote against proposals calling for any policy p between p_1 and p_2 even without a contribution from the SIG, because he prefers the status quo to policies in this range. But for policies p between q and p_1, the SIG must also contribute to $L1$ an amount of at least $-\hat{c}_1(p)$, if the group wishes to have this legislator join in opposing the agenda setter's proposal. In view of these voting strategies of $L1$ and $L2$, it would cost the SIG at least $-\hat{c}_2(p) + \max\{0, -\hat{c}_1(p)\}$ to block the agenda setter's proposal of a p between q and p_2. The interest group will let pass all those proposals for which the cost of exercising its influence exceeds its comparative preference for the status quo; in other words, a bill will succeed if and only if $W(q) - W(p) \leq -\hat{c}_2(p) + \max\{0, -\hat{c}_1(p)\}$.

We can now identify the "best-alternative policy" for the agenda setter, which we denote by $\bar{p}$. Without contributions, he would choose the policy between q and p_2 that maximizes his own utility, $W_{L3}(p)$, subject to the constraint that

$$W(p) \geq W(q) + \hat{c}_2(p) + \min\{0, \hat{c}_1(p)\}. \tag{9.4}$$

The constraint limits the choice to policies that actually would become law. If the agenda setter's favorite policy π_{L3} is among these, then of course, $\bar{p} = \pi_{L3}$. Otherwise, he would be forced to settle for a more moderate policy choice.

In figure 9.4 we illustrate the determination of $\bar{p}$ for a case where π_{L3} would be defeated by the opposing forces. The bold line in the figure represents the sum $\hat{c}_2(p) + \min\{0, \hat{c}_1(p)\}$, while the curve UU shows combinations of p and c that give the SIG the same utility as under the status quo policy with contributions of zero. The constraint (9.4) is satisfied for policies at which the UU curve lies on or above the bold line. In the figure, these are the policies between q and the one marked $\bar{p}$. Since the agenda setter's ideal exceeds all policies in this range, he prefers $\bar{p}$ among those that could pass.

Next we consider the initial stage of the influence game. At this stage the SIG approaches the agenda setter with a contribution offer. We may think of the agenda setter as targeting a specific policy and finding a contribution to go along with that policy.[11] Of course, the

---

11. As in Chapter 7, the SIG can readily design a (continuous) contribution schedule to implement any targeted policy. Such a schedule would provide the indicated contribution for the intended policy and would rapidly shrink to zero for policies different from the intended one.

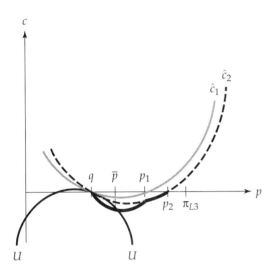

Figure 9.4
The Agenda Setter's Best Alternative

agenda setter can decline any offer, which would lead him to $\bar{p}$ as his best alternative. Clearly, the SIG must compensate $L3$ for any loss of political welfare relative to what he could attain by pursuing $\bar{p}$. Thus, the agenda setter receives $c_3 = \max\{\hat{c}_3(p) - \hat{c}_3(\bar{p}), 0\}$, which compensates him for the difference between $W_{L3}(\bar{p})$ and $W_{L3}(p)$, whenever the difference is positive. In addition, the SIG may need to contribute to one of the other legislators to generate additional support for the targeted proposal. If such a contribution proves to be necessary, it will be paid to legislator $L1$ for policies smaller than q, and to legislator $L2$ for policies larger than q. Taking all of this into account, the minimum cost to the SIG of inducing an outcome p is

$$c(p) = \max\{\hat{c}_3(p) - \hat{c}_3(\bar{p}), 0\} + \min\{\max\{\hat{c}_1(p), 0\}, \max\{\hat{c}_2(p), 0\}\}.$$

The interest group targets the policy p that maximizes $U[p, c(p)]$. Figure 9.5 illustrates the solution to the group's problem for a particular set of preferences. In the figure, the group's indifference curves again are inverted U-shaped curves that peak at its ideal policy. The cost curve $c(p)$ has several segments. For policies smaller than q, the agenda setter receives positive compensation and the SIG must also secure the support of legislator $L1$; so $c(p) = \hat{c}_1(p) + \hat{c}_3(p)$ $- \hat{c}_3(\bar{p})$. For policies between q and $\bar{p}$, the agenda setter must be compensated, but $L2$ votes in favor without any inducement; thus

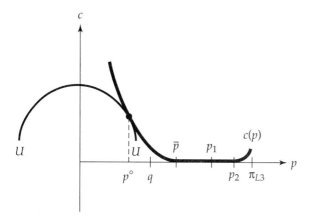

Figure 9.5
Equilibrium Policy with an Agenda Setter

$c(p) = \hat{c}_3(p) - \hat{c}_3(\bar{p})$. For policies between $\bar{p}$ and p_2, the agenda setter requires no compensation and neither does legislator $L2$. So, the SIG can induce policies in this range at virtually no cost to itself. Finally, for policies between p_2 and π_{L3}, $c(p) = \hat{c}_2(p)$, because $L2$ must be induced to support the agenda setter's proposal, or else he and $L1$ would collaborate to defeat the bill.[12]

The solution to the SIG's problem is found at p°. This policy maximizes the group's welfare, considering what it must pay to effect the different outcomes. In general, the equilibrium will be found somewhere along the downward-sloping portion of $c(p)$ to the right of π, or possibly at the corner where $p = \bar{p}$. Thus, the equilibrium must fall in the range between π and $\bar{p}$.

Several observations are in order. First, the agenda setter may receive a contribution from the interest group even if his policy preferences differ greatly from the SIG's. Moreover, the group's contribution to the agenda setter might well exceed that to a legislator whose policy preferences are more similar to its own, or to a legislator with intermediate preferences. In this respect, the model's predictions are consistent with the evidence for the United States, which shows that congressional committee members receive especially

---

12. Note that $c(p)$ would look somewhat different if $\bar{p}$ were larger than p_2 (which requires $\pi > p_2$). For example, if $\bar{p}$ were located between p_2 and π_{L3}, $c(p) = \hat{c}_3(p) - \hat{c}_3(\bar{p})$ for $p \in [q, p_2]$, $c(p) = \hat{c}_3(p) - \hat{c}_3(\bar{p}) + \hat{c}_2(p)$ for $p \in [p_2, \bar{p}]$, and $c(p) = \hat{c}_2(p)$ for $p \in [\bar{p}, \pi_{L3}]$.

large contributions from interest groups that have stakes in the policies under their control.[13] Second, the equilibrium policy, if it is to the left of the status quo, now maximizes a weighted sum of the welfare (net of contributions) of the interest group, the agenda setter, and the friendliest legislator, while the preferences of legislator $L2$ are neglected in the policy choice. This implies an outcome farther from the SIG's ideal than the equilibrium in the Snyder model. Third, the interest group may pay positive contributions even though the status quo prevails in equilibrium. If the group's preferences are such that $p^\circ = q$, the SIG must still pay the agenda setter $c_3 = -\hat{c}_3(\bar{p})$, or else he would propose the bill $\bar{p}$ that is even less to the group's liking.

Fourth, the equilibrium policy may occur to the right of q when the SIG's ideal policy is to the left of the status quo. For example, if $\bar{p} < p_2$, as in figure 9.5, the $c(p)$ curve has a downward-sloping segment between q and $\bar{p}$. For a SIG favorite of π that is close enough to the status quo, the tangency between UU and $c(p)$ will fall in the range between q and $\bar{p}$, and contributions will go only to the agenda setter. Alternatively, when $\bar{p} > p_2$, the $c(p)$ curve has a downward-sloping segment along which $c(p) = \hat{c}_2(p) + \hat{c}_3(p) - \hat{c}_3(\bar{p})$. Then the equilibrium could occur between p_2 and $\bar{p}$, with contributions paid to $L2$ and $L3$. In either of these cases, the best the SIG can do is to moderate the tendencies of the agenda setter, even though the result will be a policy that the group likes less well than the status quo. Of course, the equilibrium policy will never exceed π_{L3}, because all legislators and the SIG would prefer π_{L3} to any such policy.

Notice that when the equilibrium policy falls between p_2 and $\bar{p}$, it is the two legislators who are least sympathetic to the group's concerns that receive its financial support. Notice too that the group's total contributions depend on its preferences not only because they affect the targeted choice, but also through a more subtle channel. The further to the left is the group's ideal policy, the more credible will be its threats to block alternative legislation that the agenda setter might be tempted to propose. Since $-\hat{c}_3(\bar{p})$ falls as π moves to the left, so too does the cost of inducing a given p.

We can also examine cases where the SIG's ideal policy lies to the right of the status quo. Again, we need to calculate the policy $\bar{p}$ that

13. See, for example, Munger (1989), Stratmann (1992), Loucks (1996), and Thompson (2000a).

the agenda setter would propose in the absence of contributions from the interest group. This calculation will differ depending on whether p_{SIG} is greater or less than p_2, where p_{SIG} is the policy greater than π that the interest group likes just as much (or as little) as the status quo. We will describe the determination of $\bar{p}$ for the case where $p_{SIG} < p_2$, and leave the other case as an exercise for the interested reader.

In this setting, like the earlier one, the agenda setter should ignore policies greater than p_2. Legislators $L1$ and $L2$ both prefer the status quo to all such policies and, with $p_{SIG} < p_2$, so does the interest group. It follows that any such proposal would meet sure defeat. In contrast, a proposal of any policy between q and p_{SIG} is sure to pass. Legislator $L2$ prefers these policies to the status quo and the SIG has no reason to dissuade him from this view. Thus, $L2$ would join the agenda setter in voting in favor of any such proposal. In the middle range, where the policy lies between p_{SIG} and p_2, a proposal will pass if the SIG has insufficient incentive to block it, but will fail otherwise. The SIG is willing to pay up to $W(q) - W(p)$ to block a proposal p in this range. But it would cost the group at least $-\hat{c}_2(p) + \max\{0, -\hat{c}_1(p)\}$ to convince legislators $L2$ and $L1$ to vote against a proposal that the former surely prefers to the status quo and that the latter may prefer as well. Thus, for policies p between p_{SIG} and p_2, the agenda setter can consider only those that satisfy $W(q) - W(p) \leq -\hat{c}_2(p) + \max\{0, -\hat{c}_1(p)\}$, which is the same constraint as in (9.4).

Figure 9.6 illustrates how $\bar{p}$ now is determined. The figure shows in boldface the sum $-\hat{c}_2(p) + \max\{0, -\hat{c}_1(p)\}$, which is the total contribution that would be needed for the SIG to defeat a proposal p. This is the same curve as in figure 9.4. Here, however, the SIG's ideal policy exceeds the status quo. Therefore, the peak of the indifference curve UU falls to the right of q. The agenda setter can choose from among policies at which UU lies on or above the bold line. In the figure, the constraint is satisfied for policies between q and $\bar{p}$, including the end points. Since the agenda setter's favorite policy exceeds all of these, he chooses $\bar{p}$ when he receives no contributions.

We can now introduce the cost-of-influence curve $c(p)$ and use it to find the equilibrium policy. The $c(p)$ curve has similar features to the one depicted in figure 9.5; it is downward sloping for policies smaller than $\bar{p}$, equal to zero for policies between $\bar{p}$ and p_2, and upward sloping for policies greater than p_2. This means that here, too, the

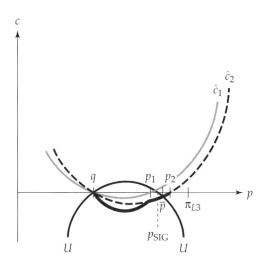

Figure 9.6
The Agenda Setter's Best Alternative $\bar{p}$ When $\pi > q$

equilibrium policy p° falls between π and $\bar{p}$, and that the SIG contributes only to the agenda setter. The only other possibility that can arise is that $p^\circ = \bar{p}$. Then the interest group makes no contributions at all, and the agenda setter proposes the largest policy that the SIG will not block.

We emphasize one implication of the model that applies no matter what the configuration of ideal points. That is, as the legislators' taste for campaign contributions grows, so too does the influence of the SIG, while the amounts contributed become smaller. In the limit, as the relative weight that the legislators put on campaign contributions approaches one, the equilibrium outcome approaches the group's ideal point, π, and the cost of influence approaches zero. While this point may be fairly obvious, it is nonetheless important, because it implies that influence cannot be gauged simply by comparing the size of a group's stake in a policy decision to the total amount that it actually contributes.

9.3 Multiple Interest Groups

Now we suppose that there are two interest groups that wish to influence the legislature. These groups may share the same bias in their policy preferences relative to the status quo, or they may wish to push the policy in opposite directions. We represent the groups' preferences by $U_i(p, c_i) = W_i(p) - c_i$, where $c_i = \sum_{j=1}^{3} c_{ij}$ is the aggregate contribution by SIG i to the three legislators for $i = 1, 2$, and c_{ij} is the contribution of SIG i to legislator Lj. We assume that $W_1(\cdot)$ and $W_2(\cdot)$ are single-peaked functions with peaks at π_1 and π_2, respectively.

The influence game is played as before. First, each SIG offers a contribution schedule to the agenda setter, whom we take to be legislator L3. Each such schedule associates a contribution pledge with every policy the agenda setter might propose. To receive the promised contributions, the agenda setter must support his own bill when it comes to the floor for a vote. After a bill has been drafted, the two SIGs approach the remaining legislators. At this stage a SIG may offer a legislator something to vote in favor of the bill or something to oppose it. The proposed legislation is implemented if and only if it captures majority support.[14]

Consider first the subgame that arises after a proposal has been made. An important observation about this subgame is that, when the groups disagree about the desirability of the proposed legislation, an equilibrium with pure strategies may fail to exist. To see why this is so, let SIG 1 be the group that favors the proposal p, and let SIG 2 be the one that prefers the status quo. Now define $\Delta_1 = W_1(p) - W_1(q)$ to be the maximum amount that SIG 1 would be willing to pay to induce an outcome of p rather than q. Similarly, define $\bar{\Delta}_2 = W_2(q) - W_2(p) = -\Delta_2$ to be the most that SIG 2 would pay for the status quo. For the purposes of this example, we assume that $\Delta_1 > \bar{\Delta}_2 > 0$ and also that legislators L1 and L2 care much more about their campaign finances than the policy issue at hand.[15]

Let us entertain the possibility that SIG 1 offers a contribution only to L1. It promises some $c_{11} > 0$ to L1 if he votes in favor of the bill, but leaves L2 to vote as he wishes. In the event, SIG 2 can defeat the proposal by offering a tiny gift to L2 plus a contribution to L1 that slightly exceeds the bid of SIG 1. The most that SIG 2 is willing to

---

14. Helpman and Persson (1998) have studied an alternative model of SIG influence on legislatures. In their model, each of three interest groups is allied with a different legislator, and the groups may contribute only to their allies. Each legislator shares the policy preferences of its allied group. The campaign contributions can be conditioned on a legislator's vote of yea or nay, but not on the details of the agenda setter's proposal.

15. Formally, we take $\lambda = 0$, so that $G_{L1} = c_{11} + c_{21}$ and $G_{L2} = c_{12} + c_{22}$.

offer to $L1$ to vote against p is $\bar{\Delta}_2$. So SIG 1 must offer at least this amount to secure the bill's passage. But if $c_{11} = \bar{\Delta}_2$ and $c_{12} = 0$, SIG 2 has no reason to make a positive offer to legislator $L2$. Although such an offer will win the legislator's vote, that single vote would not be enough to defeat the proposal. Accordingly, SIG 2 does better by accepting defeat and conserving its resources. Now, if $c_{22} = 0$, SIG 1 would be tempted to buy the vote of $L2$ rather than that of $L1$. Thus, there can be no pure-strategy equilibrium in which SIG 1 contributes only to $L1$.

But it is also impossible that SIG 1 contributes to both legislators in a pure-strategy equilibrium. If $c_{11} > 0$ and $c_{12} > 0$, and if one of the legislators votes against the bill, it means that SIG 2 has promised him something more than what SIG 1 has offered. But SIG 2 has no reason to contribute anything, because it cannot engineer the defeat of the bill. Alternatively, if $c_{11} > 0$ and $c_{12} > 0$, and both legislators vote in favor of the bill, then SIG 1 should eliminate its contribution to one of the legislators. The bill would still pass, and the total cost to the group would be reduced. We conclude that there are no pairs of offers (c_{11}, c_{12}) and (c_{21}, c_{22}) that constitute a Nash equilibrium.

The nonexistence of a pure-strategy equilibrium reflects the interplay of two conflicting forces. On the one hand, if SIG 1 surely will contribute to only one legislator, then the rival group can buy the support of the other relatively cheaply. This makes the competition for the sympathies of the contested legislator quite intense. On the other hand, if SIG 1 contributes to both legislators, it purchases more influence than it needs.

One way to resolve the existence problem is to assume that the efforts to buy influence occur sequentially. Groseclose and Snyder (1996) have considered one possible sequence of moves. They assume that the interest group favoring change has the opportunity to move first. Only after this group has tendered its offers does the one that prefers the status quo have a chance to respond. With this sequencing of offers, a pure-strategy equilibrium exists, and it has an intriguing property. In particular, the SIG that moves first will often buy more votes than it needs to ensure passage of the bill. Suppose, for example, that $\bar{\Delta}_2 = 3$, $\Delta_1 > 6$, and that (contrary to what we have assumed here) the legislature has five members. If SIG 1 buys only two votes in addition to the agenda setter, it must offer at least three to each of its prospective allies. Otherwise SIG 2 can offer a small amount to each of the legislators that does not receive an offer from

SIG 1 and a bit more than SIG 1 does for a third and deciding vote. The total cost to SIG 1 of buying exactly two votes besides the agenda setter is 6. But SIG 1 can limit its outlay to four by instead offering a contribution of one to each of the four legislators. Its rival would have no incentive to respond, because it would need to buy at least three votes to block the legislation, and the cost of doing so would exceed its willingness to pay. Groseclose and Snyder offer their model as a reason for "buying supermajorities."[16]

An equilibrium with pure strategies also exists in our model with a different sequence of moves. Suppose, for example, that the SIGs first make simultaneous offers to legislator $L1$ and only later make simultaneous offers to $L2$. Then, in our example with $\Delta_1 > \bar{\Delta}_2 > 0$, the equilibrium has all contributions by SIG 1 close to zero. SIG 2 has no reason to offer anything to $L1$, because it anticipates that it will be outbid anyway for the support of $L2$. And given that $c_{21} = 0$, it is a best response for SIG 1 to offer only a tiny amount to $L1$ to ensure that he votes in favor of the bill. Then, with the issue already decided, neither group contributes anything to $L2$.

However, to impose a sequence of moves seems artificial here. Why should one SIG have the ability to preempt the other in making offers to the legislators? What is to stop the other group from approaching the legislators at the same time? And what forces the groups to approach some particular legislator first, rather than another? Why wouldn't a group approach $L2$ first, if by doing so it could achieve a better outcome? Inevitably, the sequencing of offers in a model of legislative influence introduces unjustifiable restrictions on the groups' political efforts.

9.3.1 Randomized Offers

We prefer an alternative resolution of the existence problem, one that allows the groups to randomize their contribution offers. When each side makes random offers, neither knows for sure what bids its rival will make. So each must imagine a set of possible offers by its rival and attach a probability to each one. In an equilibrium, each side makes an offer that maximizes its expected utility. It follows that a group will randomize only among strategies that yield the same

---

16. See also Diermeier and Myerson (1999) for an application of this approach to the internal organization of legislatures.

expected utility. A mixed-strategy equilibrium arises when each SIG randomizes among equally attractive offers, and it is these alternatives that its rival regards as the set of possibilities. By introducing uncertainty about the rival's intentions, we are able to resolve the problem of nonexistence of a pure-strategy equilibrium without having to resort to arbitrary restrictions on the sequence of offers.

Let us consider anew the voting stage of the legislative game. At this stage, the agenda setter has already proposed a bill p, which he intends to support in order to collect his promised contributions. The bill will become law if either legislator $L1$ or $L2$ joins the agenda setter in voting for the bill, but it will be defeated if both vote against. For simplicity, we continue to assume that $L1$ and $L2$ care overwhelmingly about campaign contributions and place only a negligible weight on the particular policy issue at hand.[17] Each SIG bids for the support of the two undecided legislators, but formulates its strategy while being uncertain about how its rival will respond.

For concreteness, we suppose that SIG 1 favors the proposed legislation, while SIG 2 may feel similarly or prefer the status quo.[18] It is convenient to distinguish three situations, which are: (i) $\Delta_1 > \bar{\Delta}_2/2 > 0$; (ii) $\bar{\Delta}_2/2 > \Delta_1 > 0$; and (iii) $\Delta_1 > 0 > \bar{\Delta}_2$. In (i), the amount that SIG 1 is willing to pay for the bill exceeds one-half of what SIG 2 is willing to pay to block it. In (ii), the opposite is true. Finally, in (iii), the groups are united in their support for the proposed bill. We consider each of these possibilities in turn.

Case (i): $\Delta_1 > \bar{\Delta}_2/2 > 0$

In this case, SIG 1 offers a contribution to either $L1$ or $L2$, but never to both. It randomizes its offer so that the probability of a bid smaller than or equal to c_1 is given by

$$F_1(c_1) = \frac{c_1}{\bar{\Delta}_2 - c_1}. \tag{9.5}$$

---

17. This simplifying assumption makes the analysis more transparent. While it is important for us to allow the agenda setter to have policy preferences, the assumption that other legislators have little direct concern for the outcome may be a good approximation for many issues. Many legislators serve on committees that have jurisdiction in the areas of greatest interest to them. Accordingly, they play a role in formulating legislation in these areas, while they act only as floor voters on issues that concern them less.

18. The scenarios that may arise when SIG 1 prefers the status quo are analogous to those described here.

The group targets its offer to either $L1$ or $L2$ with equal probability, and, of course, it links the gift to a vote in favor of the proposal. SIG 1 bids for only one vote, because that is all it needs (in addition to the agenda setter's vote) to ensure passage of the bill.

SIG 2, in contrast, needs two votes to defeat the proposal. With probability $1 - \bar{\Delta}_2/2\Delta_1$ it offers nothing to either legislator, thereby conceding the issue to its rival. Otherwise, it offers equal positive sums to $L1$ and $L2$. The probability that its common offer to $L1$ and $L2$ is less than or equal to c_2 is given by

$$F_2(c_2) = \frac{\Delta_1 - \frac{1}{2}\bar{\Delta}_2}{\Delta_1 - c_2}, \tag{9.6}$$

for $c_2 \leq \bar{\Delta}_2/2$.

To show that these are equilibrium strategies, we must establish that they are best responses. That is, there can be no opportunity for either group to benefit from acting differently, when the other behaves according to the equilibrium prescription.

Consider first the choice by SIG 1, when it anticipates the indicated response by SIG 2. If SIG 1 were to make a positive offer to both $L1$ and $L2$, the lesser of these offers conceivably would be accepted but would never improve the prospects for the bill. This is because SIG 2 tenders equal bids to $L1$ and $L2$, so the smaller offer by SIG 1 can only succeed in buying a vote when the larger one does so as well. Thus, SIG 1 will not deviate to a pair of positive offers. Moreover, SIG 1 does not wish to offer either legislator anything more than $\bar{\Delta}_2/2$, because any such offer would exceed the maximum amount that SIG 2 might bid. It remains to show only that SIG 1 is willing to randomize among positive bids between 0 and $\bar{\Delta}_2/2$. For this to be true, the group must not prefer to take a specific one of these actions; that is, it must be indifferent among all of the alternatives.

Let x be one of its possible bids. For argument's sake, let it be $L1$ who receives the offer. If $x > c_2$, $L1$ will vote in favor of the bill, and the bill will pass. If $x < c_2$, he will vote against it, and the bill will fail.[19] Accordingly, when SIG 1 bids x, the bill passes with probability $(\Delta_1 - \frac{1}{2}\bar{\Delta}_2)/(\Delta_1 - x)$, in view of the distribution of offers that is

---

19. Note that SIG 2 chooses from a continuous distribution that has no finite probability attached to any positive offer. Since SIG 1 does not bid zero, the chance that the offer from SIG 2 will be exactly the same as the offer from SIG 1 is virtually zero, and thus this outcome can safely be ignored.

given in (9.6). When the proposed legislation passes, SIG 1 achieves utility net of contributions of $W_1(p) - x$. When it fails, the group's utility is $W_1(q)$, since no contributions are paid to $L1$ in this case. All told, the group's expected utility amounts to

$$E[U_1|x, 0] = \left(\frac{\Delta_1 - \frac{1}{2}\bar{\Delta}_2}{\Delta_1 - x}\right)[W_1(p) - x] + \left[1 - \frac{\Delta_1 - \frac{1}{2}\bar{\Delta}_2}{\Delta_1 - x}\right]W_1(q)$$

$$= W_1(q) + \Delta_1 - \tfrac{1}{2}\bar{\Delta}_2, \tag{9.7}$$

where $E[U_1|x, 0]$ denotes the expected utility of SIG 1 when it offers x to $L1$ and zero to $L2$. In deriving the second line of (9.7), we have made use of the definition of $\Delta_1 = W_1(p) - W_1(q)$.

Notice that $E[U_1|x, 0]$ does not depend on x. Given the equilibrium strategy of SIG 2, SIG 1 achieves the same expected utility for any positive contribution level less than or equal to $\bar{\Delta}_2/2$. Moreover, $E[U_1|x, 0] = E[U_1|0, x]$, so the group also is indifferent between making an offer to $L1$ and making one to $L2$. Therefore, the SIG is willing to randomize in the manner indicated.[20]

Now consider the problem facing SIG 2 when it anticipates the equilibrium behavior of SIG 1. This group, too, has no reason to offer either legislator anything more than $\bar{\Delta}_2/2$, given that its rival has no intention of doing so. Since the group expects SIG 1 to target only one legislator, its own offer to the other legislator is bound to be the highest. But SIG 2 does not know which legislator its rival intends to target, so it cannot concentrate its effort on winning the vote of the single, contested legislator.

Suppose SIG 2 contemplates offers of y_{21} to $L1$ and y_{22} to $L2$. With a probability of one-half, $L1$ will also receive an offer from SIG 1. If this happens, the group's own offer to this legislator will exceed that from SIG 1 with probability $y_{21}/(\bar{\Delta}_2 - y_{21})$, in view of (9.5). In the event, SIG 2 will succeed in defeating the bill and will achieve a utility of $W_2(q) - y_{21} - y_{22}$. If instead $L1$ receives an offer from SIG 1 that exceeds the offer from SIG 2, the bill will pass by a vote of two to

---

20. We must also check that SIG 1 does not wish to offer zero with some positive probability. If it were to offer zero, there would be a positive probability that the competing offers would be the same. We need to specify how the (indifferent) legislator $L1$ would vote under such circumstances. However, as long as there is some small chance that an indifferent legislator would vote against the proposal, SIG 1 realizes strictly lower expected utility with this action than it does by making a strictly positive bid.

one. Then SIG 2 still must make good on its pledge to $L2$, so its utility level will be $W_2(p) - y_{22}$.

Similarly, with a probability of one-half, only $L2$ will receive an offer from SIG 1. If this occurs, we must compare the size of the offer to the bid of y_{22} from SIG 2. If y_{22} is greater than the offer from SIG 1, which happens with probability $y_{22}/(\bar{\Delta}_2 - y_{22})$, the bill is defeated. Otherwise, it succeeds. The utility of SIG 2 is $W_2(q) - y_{21} - y_{22}$ when the proposed legislation passes, and $W_2(p) - y_{21}$ when it fails.

Considering the likelihood of each of these outcomes, we can calculate the expected utility of SIG 2 when it offers y_{21} to $L1$ and y_{22} to $L2$. We find that

$$
\begin{aligned}
E[U_2|y_{21}, y_{22}] = {} & \frac{1}{2}\left(\frac{y_{21}}{\bar{\Delta}_2 - y_{21}}\right)[W_2(q) - y_{21} - y_{22}] \\
& + \frac{1}{2}\left(1 - \frac{y_{21}}{\bar{\Delta}_2 - y_{21}}\right)[W_2(p) - y_{22}] \\
& + \frac{1}{2}\left(\frac{y_{22}}{\bar{\Delta}_2 - y_{22}}\right)[W_2(q) - y_{21} - y_{22}] \\
& + \frac{1}{2}\left(1 - \frac{y_{22}}{\bar{\Delta}_2 - y_{22}}\right)[W_2(p) - y_{21}] \\
= {} & W_2(p), \quad\quad\quad\quad\quad\quad\quad\quad\quad\quad\quad (9.8)
\end{aligned}
$$

where the derivation of the second equality makes use of the definition of $\bar{\Delta}_2 = W_2(q) - W_2(p)$. Observe that $E[U_2|y_{21}, y_{22}]$ does not depend on y_{21} or y_{22}. Thus, given the equilibrium strategy of SIG 1, SIG 2 achieves the same expected utility for any pair of offers to the two legislators with the property that each bid is less than or equal to $\bar{\Delta}_2/2$. SIG 2, like its counterpart, is willing to randomize in the manner indicated.

In the resulting equilibrium, the expected utility of SIG 2 is the same as if it had no opportunity to bid for votes. In competing for influence, the group raises its bids to the point where it leaves itself with no political surplus. SIG 1, in contrast, does realize a surplus. Its expected utility of $EU_1 = W_1(q) + \Delta_1 - \frac{1}{2}\bar{\Delta}_2$ exceeds what it would be if the group were not involved in the influence game.

Notice that the policy outcome is random. The deliberative process yields the policy p when the bid by SIG 1 for the contested legislator happens to be the largest. Otherwise, the outcome is q. The probability of each outcome is readily calculated, and depends on the stake that each interest group has in the policy decision.[21]

Case (ii): $\bar{\Delta}_2/2 > \Delta_1 > 0$
Next consider the case where $\bar{\Delta}_2/2 > \Delta_1 > 0$; that is, the proposal p is such that what SIG 2 is willing to pay to preserve the status quo exceeds twice what SIG 1 is willing to pay for the proposed policy. Under these conditions, SIG 1 offers Δ_1 to $L1$ and nothing to $L2$ with probability ζ, and nothing to $L1$ and Δ_1 to $L2$ with probability $1 - \zeta$. The value of ζ is not uniquely determined; it can take any value between $1 - \Delta_1/\bar{\Delta}_2$ and $\Delta_1/\bar{\Delta}_2$. But, no matter what the value of ζ is, the outcome is the same. SIG 2 offers a bit more than Δ_1 to each of $L1$ and $L2$ and the legislature rejects the proposed legislation with probability one.

Again, let us verify that these are equilibrium strategies. For SIG 1 the matter is simple. A larger offer would ensure the bill's passage, but at a cost that exceeds its value to the group. A smaller offer would make no difference at all. Thus, SIG 1 can find no alternative strategy that yields a better outcome than the indicated strategy.

The problem facing SIG 2 is that it does not know which legislator will be targeted by its rival. By pursuing the indicated strategy, it defeats the bill for sure. An alternative would be to offer something less to one of the legislators, and accept a risk that the bill might pass. If the group were to offer something less than Δ_1 to $L1$, it should offer that legislator only a tiny amount. Such a bid would suffice if the offer from SIG 1 happened to go to $L2$, and would be no worse than any other losing offer, otherwise. By offering Δ_1 to $L2$ and virtually nothing to $L1$, SIG 2 achieves an expected utility of $\zeta[W_2(p) - \Delta_1] + (1 - \zeta)[W_2(q) - \Delta_1]$. But when $\zeta \geq \Delta_1/\bar{\Delta}_2$, this is less than the expected utility of $W_2(q) - 2\Delta_1$ that it achieves by pursuing the indicated strategy. Similarly, it might offer Δ_1 to $L1$ and a tiny amount to $L2$, thereby achieving expected welfare of $\zeta[W_2(q) - \Delta_1] +$

---

21. When SIG 1 bids x, the probability that its bid exceeds that by SIG 2 is $F_2(x)$. Considering the distribution of bids by SIG 1, we can calculate the unconditional probability of the bill's passage. We find, using (9.5) and (9.6), that

$$\Pr[p \text{ succeeds}] = \begin{cases} \dfrac{\Delta_1 - \frac{1}{2}\bar{\Delta}_2}{\Delta_1 - \bar{\Delta}_2}\left[1 + \dfrac{\bar{\Delta}_2}{\Delta_1 - \bar{\Delta}_2}\ \log\left(\dfrac{\Delta_1}{2\Delta_1 - \bar{\Delta}_2}\right)\right] & \text{if } \Delta_1 \neq \bar{\Delta}_2 \\ \frac{3}{4} & \text{if } \Delta_1 = \bar{\Delta}_2 \end{cases}.$$

$(1 - \zeta)[W_2(p) - \Delta_1]$. Again, this is less than the expected utility associated with its equilibrium strategy when $\zeta \leq 1 - \Delta_1/\bar{\Delta}_2$.

With $\bar{\Delta}_2/2 > \Delta_1 > 0$, the bill is doomed to fail. The group that prefers the status quo buys influence from each of the uncommitted legislators and does so at a price that leaves the group favoring the bill with no room to respond.[22]

Case (iii): $\Delta_1 > 0 > \bar{\Delta}_2$

The final case arises when both SIGs stand behind the proposed legislation. In such circumstances, it would take only a tiny bid from one of the groups to convince an indifferent legislator to vote in favor of the bill. And neither group wishes to promote a different outcome. In this case the proposal passes for sure, and does so at virtually no cost to the SIGs.[23]

Let us pause to recapitulate. We have seen that when the agenda setter proposes a policy that both groups prefer to the status quo, the bill passes for sure and the groups contribute (virtually) nothing to the uncommitted legislators. When the agenda setter instead proposes a policy that one group favors and the other does not, the outcome depends on the intensities of their conflicting preferences. If the group that favors the bill stands to gain more than one-half of what the other stands to lose, the groups randomize their offers and the bill passes with some positive probability. The probability that the bill will pass is close to zero when $\bar{\Delta}_2$ is near $2\Delta_1$, and close to one when $\bar{\Delta}_2$ is small. If the agenda setter proposes a policy that would harm a group by more than twice what the other stands to gain, the influence game spells sure defeat for the bill. The group that opposes the legislation offers each legislator a bit more than the other's maximum willingness to pay, thereby guaranteeing that its rival cannot profitably buy the needed vote.

---

22. In case (ii), there also exists a pure-strategy equilibrium. In this equilibrium, SIG 1 offers Δ_1 to both legislators and SIG 2 offers a bit more than this to each one. This equilibrium is discussed in Prat and Rustichini (1999), who consider, more generally, conditions for the existence of efficient, pure-strategy equilibria in games with several principals and several agents. The pure-strategy equilibrium has the same outcome (the bill is defeated) and the same ex post contributions (SIG 2 pays Δ_1 to $L1$ and $L2$) as the mixed-strategy equilibrium, so it is not necessary for us to choose between them.

23. Actually, a free-rider problem exists here, because each group prefers that the other pay the contribution. But the required bid is so small that we may as well overlook this technical problem.

9.3.2 *Competing for Influence at the Proposal Stage*

Now we return to the initial stage of the game, when the interest groups seek to influence the agenda setter's decision. The important thing to notice is that this game has exactly the same form as the one we studied in Chapter 8. In particular, there are two interest groups that wish to influence a politician's decision in a setting where the politician has preferences over the policy outcomes but also values contributions. We can use the results from Chapter 8 to analyze the proposal stage of the legislative game.

In the previous section we described how events would unfold following any proposal by the agenda setter. We know from there the chance that any bill has of becoming law and the expected contributions that each SIG will pay in the run-up to the floor vote. Let $\hat{W}_i(p)$ be the expected utility for SIG i, net of expected contributions to $L1$ and $L2$, that results when the agenda setter proposes the policy p. The problem facing SIG 1 is to design a contribution schedule $c_{13}(p)$ that maximizes $U_1 = \hat{W}_1(p) - c_{13}(p)$. The group pledges a contribution $c_{13}(p)$ to the agenda setter when he proposes a bill p and later supports it in the roll-call vote. Similarly, SIG 2 designs a contribution schedule $c_{23}(p)$ in order to maximize $U_2 = \hat{W}_2(p) - c_{23}(p)$. An equilibrium consists as usual of a pair of schedules, each of which is a best response to the other when the groups correctly anticipate the behavior of the agenda setter and the competition for votes that would ensue after any proposal.

Recall that the agenda setter seeks to maximize the expectation of $G_{L3}(p, c_{L3}) = \lambda_3 W_{L3}(p) + (1 - \lambda_3)(c_{13} + c_{23})$. The agenda setter is likely to care about the policy outcome ($\lambda_3 > 0$), because legislators typically serve on committees that have jurisdiction over issues of direct concern to their constituents. Still, it is easiest to understand the competitive process if we begin with the opposite assumption. That is, we take $\lambda_3 = 0$ for now, so that the agenda setter focuses only on maximizing his total contributions. We will return to the more realistic case with $\lambda_3 > 0$ later in the section.

Let us review the net expected welfare that each group achieves under the various policy proposals. Figure 9.7 proves useful for this purpose. The figure depicts a situation in which the interest groups have favorite policies that lie on the same side of the status quo. The curve labeled Δ_1 shows the amount that SIG 1 would be willing to pay to have the policy p instead of the status quo, q. This curve

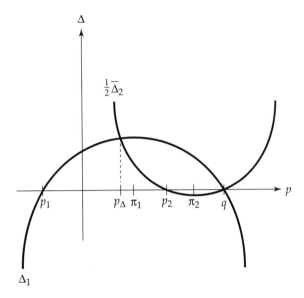

Figure 9.7
Regions of Conflict and Nonconflict between the SIGs

reaches a peak at π_1, the group's ideal policy. It returns to zero at p_1, which is the policy that gives SIG 1 the same utility as the status quo. For $p < p_1$, $\Delta_1 < 0$.

The curve labeled $\frac{1}{2}\bar{\Delta}_2$ plots one-half of the amount that SIG 2 would be willing to pay to preserve the status quo. This amount is negative for policies that the group prefers to the status quo, that is, those between p_2 and q. Among these is π_2, the group's favorite policy. We have identified the policy p_Δ for which $\Delta_1 = \frac{1}{2}\bar{\Delta}_2$. Recall that SIG 2 will engineer the defeat of any legislation that has $\bar{\Delta}_2 > 0$ and $\frac{1}{2}\bar{\Delta}_2 > \Delta_1$. Thus, bills calling for $p < p_\Delta$ have no chance of legislative success.

The figure allows us to identify five ranges of policies. (i) For $p < p_1$, both groups oppose the bill, which is defeated at virtually no cost to either one. Then $\hat{W}_1(p) = W_1(q)$ and $\hat{W}_2(p) = W_2(q)$. (ii) For $p_1 \leq p \leq p_\Delta$, the bill is defeated, but SIG 2 must pay $2\Delta_1 = 2[W_1(p) - W_1(q)]$ to engineer its defeat. Then $\hat{W}_1(p) = W_1(q)$ and $\hat{W}_2(p) = W_2(q) - 2[W_1(p) - W_1(q)]$. (iii) For $p_\Delta \leq p \leq p_2$, the SIGs contest the bill, which passes with some positive probability. From (9.7), $\hat{W}_1(p) = W_1(p) - \frac{1}{2}[W_2(q) - W_2(p)]$, while from (9.8), $\hat{W}_2(p) = W_2(p)$. (iv) For $p_2 \leq p \leq q$, both groups favor the bill, which passes at virtually no cost to the groups. Then $\hat{W}_1(p) = W_1(p)$ and $\hat{W}_2(p) = W_2(p)$.

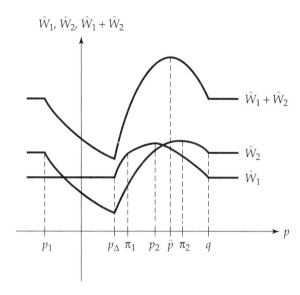

Figure 9.8
Joint Welfare of SIG 1 and SIG 2

(v) Finally, for $p \geq q$, both groups oppose the bill, and influence costs again are negligible. Then $\hat{W}_1(p) = W_1(q)$ and $\hat{W}_2(p) = W_2(q)$.

Next we construct figure 9.8. It shows $\hat{W}_1(p)$, $\hat{W}_2(p)$, and the sum of the two. The figure illustrates one possible configuration. In the figure the peak of the $\hat{W}_1(p)$ curve occurs at $p = p_2$. It is possible, though, that this curve is already falling by the time it reaches p_2, in which case the peak would occur somewhere between π_1 and p_2.[24] In either case the joint welfare of the groups, $\hat{W}_1(p) + \hat{W}_2(p)$, is maximized for some p between π_1 and π_2. We denote the proposal that maximizes $\hat{W}_1(p) + \hat{W}_2(p)$ by $\hat{p}$.

Now consider the competition to influence the agenda setter. Recall from Chapter 8 that, if the contribution schedules are differentiable, they must be locally compensating near any equilibrium. That is, $dc_{13}(p)/dp = \hat{W}_1'(p)$ and $dc_{23}(p)/dp = \hat{W}_2'(p)$ when evaluated at an equilibrium proposal, p°. Also, when $\lambda_3 = 0$, the agenda setter selects a proposal to maximize contributions. This maximization requires $d[c_{13}(p) + dc_{23}(p)]/dp = 0$, or, if the total contribution has a

---

24. In the range between π_1 and p_2, $\hat{W}_1(p) = W_1(p) - \frac{1}{2}[W_2(q) - W_2(p)]$. The slope of this curve is $W_1'(p_2) + \frac{1}{2}W_2'(p_2)$ as p_2 is approached from the left. Since p_2 lies to the left of π_2, but perhaps to the right of π_1, we might have that $W_1'(p_2) < 0$ and $W_2'(p_2) > 0$. Then the slope of $\hat{W}_1(p)$ at p_2 will depend on the relative magnitudes of these two derivatives.

kink at some p, then $d[c_{13}(p) + dc_{23}(p)]/dp > 0$ to the left of the kink and $d[c_{13}(p) + dc_{23}(p)]/dp < 0$ to the right of the kink.[25] Together, these observations imply that an equilibrium proposal must occur where $\hat{W}_1'(p) + \hat{W}_2'(p) = 0$ or where $\hat{W}_1(p) + \hat{W}_2(p)$ has an upward kink. In other words, an equilibrium proposal achieves a local maximum of the joint welfare of the two groups.

In figure 9.8 the joint welfare of SIG 1 and SIG 2 has local maxima at $p \le p_1$, at $p \ge q$, and at $p = \hat{p}$. However, no proposal of a policy $p \le p_1$ or $p \ge q$ can emerge as an equilibrium of the influence game. To see this, suppose to the contrary that $\bar{p}$ is an equilibrium proposal for some $\bar{p} \le p_1$ or $\bar{p} \ge q$. Since neither group prefers any such $\bar{p}$ to the status quo policy, the policy outcome would be the status quo. Then SIG 1 achieves expected welfare of $W_1(q)$, which is the worst possible outcome for this group. It follows that SIG 1 would not contribute positively to encourage the agenda setter to make such a proposal. But if $c_{13}^\circ(\bar{p}) = 0$, SIG 2 could offer the agenda setter a tiny amount to propose its favorite policy π_2, and the agenda setter would readily oblige. Since SIG 2 prefers this outcome to the status quo, it would never design a contribution schedule to induce the proposal $\bar{p}$.

The unique equilibrium proposal is $\hat{p}$, the proposal that maximizes $\hat{W}_1 + \hat{W}_2$. For the example illustrated in figure 9.8, neither interest group contributes anything to $L1$ or to $L2$ when the agenda setter proposes $\hat{p}$. This is because $p_2 < \hat{p} < \pi_2$, so both groups prefer the proposed policy to the status quo. The proposal $\hat{p}$, which passes the legislature with probability one, maximizes the sum of the groups' ex ante utilities.[26] The agenda setter is the only legislator who receives campaign contributions in this case.[27]

25. Such a kink might occur at p_2, if $\hat{W}_1(p)$ slopes sharply downward to the right of that point.
26. This statement presumes that $W_1(p) + W_2(p)$ has a unique local maximum, as it must when both functions are concave. This is true of the functions that underlie figure 9.8.
27. If we further assume that both groups use compensating contribution schedules, we can calculate their equilibrium contributions. Were SIG 1 to be inactive at the proposal stage, SIG 2 would induce the agenda setter to set $p^{-1} = \pi_2$, and would pay virtually nothing to $L3$. This would yield SIG 2 a utility of $W_2(\pi_2)$. Therefore, according to the analysis presented in Chapter 8, SIG 1 pays $c_{13}^\circ = W_2(\pi_2) - W_2(\hat{p})$ to the agenda setter in a compensating equilibrium. Similarly, if SIG 2 were to be inactive at the proposal stage, SIG 1 would induce the agenda setter to set $p^{-2} = p_2$ for the case illustrated in figure 9.8. The group prefers this policy to its overall ideal, because the latter would require greater contributions in the second stage and its legislative prospects would remain dim. The contributions from SIG 2 to the agenda setter must compensate for the surplus that SIG 1 otherwise could achieve. Therefore, $c_{23}^\circ = W_1(p_2) - W_1(\hat{p})$.

As we have indicated, it is also possible that $\hat{W}_1(\cdot)$ peaks at a proposal between π_1 and p_2. Then the joint-welfare-maximizing proposal $\hat{p}$ may fall between π_1 and p_2. Such a $\hat{p}$ again would be the unique equilibrium proposal when the agenda setter seeks to maximize contributions. In such a case, $\hat{W}_1'(p) + \hat{W}_2'(p) = 0$ implies $W_1'(p) + \frac{3}{2}W_2'(p) = 0$, considering that $\hat{W}_1(p) = W_1(p) - \frac{1}{2}[W_2(q) - W_2(p)]$ and $\hat{W}_2(p) = W_2(p)$ for proposals in this range. So the equilibrium proposal in this case is not the one that maximizes the sum $W_1(p) + W_2(p)$, but rather one that puts more weight on the policy preferences of SIG 2. Of course, SIG 2 pays for this privilege, not only to the agenda setter but also to the remaining legislators. In fact, at the voting stage, SIG 2 opposes the proposed legislation, and offers a random amount to $L1$ and $L2$ in an effort to engineer its defeat. The bill's fate remains uncertain, which means that there is a positive probability that the status quo will persist. Because the inefficient status quo prevails with positive probability, and because the proposed alternative does not maximize $W_1(p) + W_2(p)$, the equilibrium outcome is not jointly efficient for the interest groups and the legislators.

Now that we understand the political pressures on the agenda setter, we can allow for his policy preferences. The agenda setter chooses the proposal that maximizes $G_{L3} = \lambda_3 \hat{W}_{L3}(p) + (1 - \lambda_3) \cdot [c_{13}(p) + c_{23}(p)]$ where $\hat{W}_{L3}(p)$ is his expected welfare in the voting stage. Observe that the agenda setter must consider not only whether a policy meets his political objectives, but also whether it has a reasonable chance to succeed. Thus,

$$\hat{W}_{L3}(p) = \Pr[p \text{ succeeds}] \cdot W_{L3}(p) + \Pr[p \text{ fails}] \cdot W_{L3}(q).$$

When the contribution schedules are locally compensating, the candidates for equilibrium are those proposals that achieve a local maximum of $\lambda_3 \hat{W}_{L3}(p) + (1 - \lambda_3)[\hat{W}_1(p) + \hat{W}_2(p)]$.

Take, for example, a case where the agenda setter has a favorite policy of π_{L3} and single-peaked policy preferences. Consider the proposal $\hat{p}$ that maximizes $\hat{W}_1(p) + \hat{W}_2(p)$. If $p_2 < \hat{p} < \pi_2$, as in figure 9.8, then the proposal $\hat{p}$ and others close to it would succeed in the legislature with probability one. Then, if $\pi_{L3} < \hat{p}$, there is an equilibrium in which the agenda setter proposes a policy to the left of $\hat{p}$, whereas if $\pi_{L3} > \hat{p}$, there is an equilibrium in which the agenda setter proposes a policy to the right of $\hat{p}$. Alternatively, $\hat{p}$ might fall between π_1 and p_2. Then the success of $\hat{p}$ and other similar proposals is not ensured. Proposals to the right of $\hat{p}$ stand a better chance of success than $\hat{p}$ itself, whereas those to the left of $\hat{p}$ are more likely to fail. If $\pi_{L3} > \hat{p}$, both the agenda setter's preferences and the legislative realities point to his choosing something to the right of $\hat{p}$. But if $\pi_{L3} < \hat{p}$, these forces push in opposite directions, and it is not clear which one is stronger.

All of this may be clearer in the following example.

9.3.3 The Scale of a Public Project

Imagine a legislature that must decide whether to proceed with an important public project, and if so, at what scale. There are two interest groups in society. One stands much to gain from the project, while the other would also benefit from the undertaking but to a lesser extent. For SIG 1, $W_1(p) = 36p - \frac{1}{2}p^2$, where $W_1(p)$ represents the group's utility from a project of size p net of its share of the construction cost. As for SIG 2, $W_2(p) = 6p - \frac{1}{2}p^2$. With these preferences, $\pi_1 = 36$ and $\pi_2 = 6$. Of course, the groups seek to maximize their welfare net of any contributions, which are c_1 and c_2, respectively. The project has no other sources of funding, so the status quo is $q = 0$.

Both groups prefer small projects to the status quo. Since legislators $L1$ and $L2$ care only about contributions, any bill calling for $p < 12$ would be passed in the legislature at virtually no cost to the groups. But SIG 2 would oppose any project with $p > p_2 = 12$, as can be seen in figure 9.9. Thus, for any $p < p_1 = 72$, there would be conflict between the groups. The conflict would be resolved in favor of SIG 2, if $\bar{\Delta}_2 > 2\bar{\Delta}_1$. This spells sure defeat for any bill calling for $p > p_\Delta = 52$. For proposed projects with scales between 12 and 52, the groups would randomize their offers, leaving the legislative prospects for any such bill uncertain. The probability of passage declines as the proposed scale grows larger in this range.

Now consider the groups' efforts to influence the agenda setter. Suppose first that the agenda setter cares only about campaign contributions. For $12 \leq p \leq 52$, the expected welfare for SIG 1 net of contributions is $\hat{W}_1(p) = W_1(p) - \frac{1}{2}[W_2(q) - W_2(p)]$. In this range, $\hat{W}_2(p) = W_2(p)$. Thus, $\hat{W}_1(p) + \hat{W}_2(p) = W_1(p) + \frac{3}{2}W_2(p) = 45p - \frac{5}{4}p^2$, in view of the fact that $q = 0$ implies $W_2(q) = 0$. This function—which represents the joint welfare of the SIGs at the voting stage—reaches a maximum at $p = 18$. So this is the equilibrium proposal as we saw in

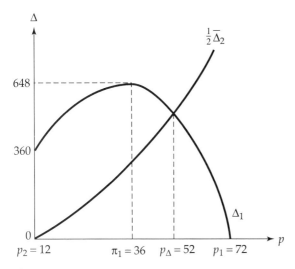

Figure 9.9
Conflicting SIG Tastes for a Public Project

the previous section. The agenda setter determines his proposal in response to the opposing incentives provided by the two interest groups. The agenda setter could obtain more contributions from SIG 1 by increasing the scale of the project, and more from SIG 2 by scaling it back. On the margin, the offsetting incentives balance, and the agenda setter maximizes his contributions by proposing $p = 18$.

Once the equilibrium bill has been drafted, the objectives of the two SIGs conflict. SIG 1 would like to see the bill passed by the legislature, whereas SIG 2 prefers the status quo. In the equilibrium, the groups randomize their contribution offers to $L1$ and $L2$. SIG 1 offers a contribution to only one of these legislators, hoping to encourage a single additional positive vote. The group targets $L1$ and $L2$ with equal probability, and offers a positive contribution that is no more than $\bar{\Delta}_2/2 = 27$. SIG 2 offers the same contribution to both legislators, but the offers may be zero. In fact, the group makes no (positive) offers with probability $1 - \bar{\Delta}_2/2\Delta_1 = 17/18$. Using the equation in footnote 21, we can calculate the probability that the bill will pass. We find that it does so with a probability of almost 98 percent.

If we further assume that the two groups design compensating contribution schedules, we can calculate the (actual or expected) contribution that each makes to the three legislators. In a compensating equilibrium, SIG 1 pays the agenda setter $c_{13} = 261$. This is the difference between the group's expected welfare of $\hat{W}_1(18) = 459$ at the start of the voting phase and the expected welfare of $\hat{W}_1(6) = 198$ that it would achieve if the proposal were instead $p^{-1} = 6$. A project of size 6 maximizes $\hat{W}_2(p)$ and therefore is the one that SIG 2 would pick if SIG 1 did not participate in the first-stage game. Similarly, SIG 2 pays the agenda setter $c_{23} = 128$ in the compensating equilibrium. This is the difference between its expected welfare of $\hat{W}_2(18) = -54$ and the lower expected welfare of $\hat{W}_2(26) = -182$ it would suffer if SIG 1 were to induce a proposal of $p^{-2} = 26$.

At the voting stage, SIG 1 pays an expected contribution of 382, which goes to either $L1$ or $L2$ with equal probability. SIG 2 pays expected contributions totaling approximately 1.2. Half of this sum goes to each of $L1$ and $L2$.[28]

Now suppose the agenda setter has policy preferences of his own. We take $W_{L3}(p) = 24p - \frac{1}{2}p^2$, so that the agenda setter has an ideal project of $\pi_{L3} = 24$. Let the agenda setter place equal weight on the policy outcome and campaign contributions, that is, $\lambda_3 = \frac{1}{2}$.

Without contributions, the agenda setter would propose $p \simeq 22.5$, which is the policy that maximizes $\hat{W}_{L3}(p)$. This proposal is a bit less than his personal favorite of $p = 24$, because he recognizes that the smaller project has a better chance of succeeding in the legislature. But the joint influence of SIG 1 and SIG 2 causes the agenda setter to propose a project even smaller than this. The equilibrium proposal is the one that maximizes $\lambda_3 \hat{W}_{L3}(p) + (1 - \lambda_3)[\hat{W}_1(p) + \hat{W}_2(p)]$. We calculate that $p^\circ \simeq 19.3$ and that this proposal passes in the legislature with a probability of approximately 97 percent.

In this example, the equilibrium proposal by an agenda setter who himself covets a project of $p = 24$ is larger than the proposal that would be made by an agenda setter who does not care about the size of the project at all. This is not surprising, because the agenda setter's ideal scale exceeds the size of the project that would be proposed by an agenda setter who sought only contributions. It is worth emphasizing, though, that the equilibrium proposal need not fall between the agenda setter's own ideal policy and the proposal that would result were the agenda setter not to care about the policy outcome. Take, for example, a case where the agenda setter's policy preferences are given by $W_{L3}(p) = 18.1p - \frac{1}{2}p^2$. In this case, his favorite project is

---

28. These expected contributions can be calculated using the distribution functions of the offers, (9.5) and (9.6), recognizing that the contributions are paid only when a group's offer to $L1$ or $L2$ is the largest.

$\pi_{L3} = 18.1$, which exceeds the size of the equilibrium proposal that results when $\lambda_{L3} = 0$. But the equilibrium proposal is $p^\circ = 17.8$. The equilibrium proposal does not lie between 18 and 18.1, but it does lie between 18 and the proposal that the agenda setter would make if he encountered no bids for influence. The proposal that maximizes $\hat{W}_{L3}(p)$ has $p \simeq 17.4$, a scale that is smaller than the agenda setter's ideal, because he factors in the legislative realities. The contribution offers cause him to propose a project slightly bigger than this, but not so big as the one that would result were his own preferences to play no role.

In this chapter, we have extended the analysis of influence seeking by SIGs to settings in which policy decisions are made by groups of policymakers acting as a legislature. If party discipline is strong, so that individual legislators invariably vote with their party leaders, then a legislature can be regarded as a single actor, and the analysis presented in Chapters 7 and 8 applies. But in many polities, party dictums are not inviolable. Then a SIG that wishes to influence policy must consider the legislative process. It may wish, for example, to curry favor with those who will decide the contents of a bill, instead of or in addition to those who will determine its fate.

We have illustrated how a legislature may be influenced by special interests, using one particularly simple specification of the legislative process. In this specification, an agenda setter determines the content of a bill, which then stands in opposition to a given status quo. This example mostly is meant to point the way forward. Different legislatures follow a variety of rules for determining what bills are reported to the floor, how amendments are offered, and how the voting proceeds. Further research is needed to understand how these different rules affect the influence of special interests and to identify which rules best serve the general public.

10   Contributions and Elections

The previous three chapters focused on campaign contributions. We have tried to capture the tension that many elected officials feel between serving their constituents and raising vitally needed campaign funds. Our approach has been to include policy outcomes and campaign contributions as separate arguments in the policymaker's objective function. In so doing, we have treated the politicians' motivations in reduced form, with an allusion to electoral considerations but without a full-fledged model of voting behavior and rival candidates.

While useful for highlighting the interaction between politicians and interest groups, the reduced-form approach has several shortcomings. It does not allow one to say anything about how policy outcomes matter to a politician who is driven by a desire to be reelected. Nor can it shed any light on what determines the perceived trade-off between policies and money. Moreover, it is not at all clear that a policymaker's concern for policies or her taste for contributions is invariant to the electoral context. Voters may be more forgiving of a politician who advocates certain policies if they expect her rival would do the same or worse. Campaign resources may be more valuable to an unknown or unpopular candidate than to one who is already well liked or one who faces a weak opponent. None of these considerations can be addressed in a model that puts voting behavior off to the side.

There is another reason why we may wish to study campaign giving and voting together. Until now, we have considered only one of the possible motivations that interest groups have for contributing to political campaigns.[1] We have focused exclusively on the *influence*

---

1. Actually, in Chapter 5 we also discussed the use of campaign giving as a means to gain access to a less than perfectly informed policymaker and as a way for a group to signal its private information.

motive, according to which groups give to candidates or parties in the hope of influencing their positions and the policies they enact. Some political scientists question the importance of this explanation for campaign giving, attributing instead an *electoral motive* to virtually all contributors.[2] According to this view, SIGs regard the positions and intentions of most politicians as inviable. They contribute to the candidates whose positions they like so as to enhance their prospects for winning the election. In order to understand the conditions under which each of the motives for campaign giving is operative, and to assess whether they work in tandem or in conflict, we need a model in which the relationship between campaign spending and election outcomes is made explicit.

In this chapter we will modify our earlier modeling of electoral competition to allow a role for campaign spending. As before, we examine a single electoral contest between two political parties. The election will determine the outcome of some fixed and some pliable policy issues. The parties' stances on the fixed issues are given from the outset, but the parties take positions on the pliable issues to further their electoral objectives. By adopting a certain position, a party commits to carry out the indicated policies if it should win the election. *Strategic voters*, as before, consider only the pair of platforms when deciding how to cast their ballots. But we introduce a second category of *impressionable voters* who pay heed to campaign advertising. These voters are the targets of the campaign spending, which is funded by donations from interest groups. A group may tie its donation to the positions that a party takes or grant the donation unconditionally. In this sense, a SIG may be guided by either an influence motive or an electoral motive (or both) in determining the size of its campaign gift.

The analysis in this chapter serves several purposes. It provides a rigorous underpinning for the reduced-form approach that we used

---

2. As we have noted before, many SIGs contribute primarily to politicians who are predisposed to their own positions. Some take this observation as evidence that campaign gifts are not meant to curry favor. But other evidence—of especially large contributions by certain industries to members of certain committees, of contributions by the same PAC to opposing candidates and parties, and of changes in giving when a representatitive is transferred to a new committee—points in the opposite direction. Moreover, gifts to like-minded politicians may have influence as their motive, if they are intended not to buy a vote but rather to encourage the recipient to play an active role in drafting or amending a bill, or perhaps to engage in log-rolling with other representatives who are not similarly inclined.

in Chapters 7 through 9, and it allows us to examine the determinants of a politician's willingness to trade off welfare for contributions. The expanded framework also enables us to weigh the different motives that interest groups have for engaging in campaign giving. Finally, it provides explanations for two common observations about political giving: namely, many SIGs contribute to both contestants in the same election, and patterns of giving are heavily skewed toward favorites relative to underdogs.[3]

10.1   Electoral Competition with Campaign Spending

Recall the electoral model of Chapters 2 and 3.[4] There are two political parties, each with fixed positions on some set of issues. The parties choose their positions on the remaining issues so as to maximize their chances of winning a majority of the votes. The parties are committed to carry out their platforms in the event they emerge victorious. Voters belong to identifiable groups, indexed by j. The members of group j share a common interest in the pliable issues but hold different views on the fixed issues.

10.1.1   The Voters

We extend the earlier model to include two categories of voters. *Strategic voters* understand the political environment and the implications of their votes. Each such voter recognizes that his vote will increase slightly the subjective probability that the party he has named will be victorious. A voter's uncertainty reflects his imperfect information about the aggregate popularity of the two parties. By voting for the party whose platform he prefers, a strategic voter slightly raises his expected welfare. This is a dominant strategy for him.

Impressionable voters, in contrast, are receptive to the messages of the political campaign. Perhaps these voters do not deem it worth-

3. Snyder (1990) has presented evidence that, in open-seat races for the U.S. Congress, campaign spending varies in proportion to a candidate's probability of being elected. The often noted bias in contributions toward incumbent candidates can also be understood in these terms, once we recognize that most incumbents are heavily favored in their bids for reelection.
4. We used a similar model in Chapter 6, except that there we assumed voters are unsure of the connection between the policy variable and their own welfare.

while to make the calculations necessary for strategic voting. Or perhaps the campaign ads provide them with bits of credible evidence about a party's competence or its rival's incompetence. In any case, we assume that impressionable voters respond to campaign spending.[5] The more a party spends (holding constant the spending of its rival), the greater is its share of the impressionable votes.[6]

Let us focus first on the behavior of strategic voters. This discussion should be familiar by now.[7] The strategic voter i in group j has the utility function $u_j(\mathbf{p}^k) + v_{ij}^k$, where $\mathbf{p}^k$ is the vector of pliable policy outcomes and v_{ij}^k is the voter's utility from the fixed positions of party k, $k = A, B$. Note that the first component depends only on the group to which the individual belongs, whereas the second component varies across individuals in the same group. We again let $v_{ij} = v_{ij}^B - v_{ij}^A$ denote the relative preference of voter i in group j for the fixed positions of party B. We assume that v_{ij} has the same uniform distribution in all interest groups, with a mean of b/f and a density of f. The mean of the distribution indicates which party's ideology is more popular among strategic voters and by how much. Specifically, the greater is b, the greater is the fraction of strategic voters that prefer the fixed policy positions of party B.

The strategic voter i in group j votes for party A if and only if $v_{ij} \leq u_j(\mathbf{p}^A) - u_j(\mathbf{p}^B)$. Considering that v_{ij} is distributed uniformly

---

5. The available evidence supports the view that campaign spending wins votes. Jacobson (1980, 1985) has argued that in U.S. congressional elections, campaign spending is effective only for challengers, not for incumbents. But after controlling for the quality of challengers and the endogeneity of various regressors, Green and Krasno (1988) found significant marginal vote gains from spending for both challengers and incumbents. More recently, Gerber (1998) has produced additional evidence for U.S. senatorial races that supports the Green-Krasno position.

6. We follow Baron (1994) in treating the productivity of campaign spending in reduced form. In contrast, Austen-Smith (1987) has modeled informative advertising that reduces voters' uncertainty about the candidates' positions. Potters, Sloof, and van Winden (1997) and Prat (2001) study models in which campaign spending is indirectly informative. In Prat's model, for example, the SIGs have better information than voters about the competence of the incumbent candidate. The level of his campaign spending signals his competence, because the SIGs are more willing to contribute to the incumbent the better they regard his chances of being reelected. Prat does not allow for contributions to the challenger, but a suitably extended version of his model could be used to justify our treatment of the effectiveness of campaign spending in a setting with only strategic voters.

7. We highlight one difference from Chapters 3 and 6. There we assumed that a voter's utility from the pliable policy declines with the square of the difference between that policy and the voter's ideal policy level. Here, as in Chapter 2, we allow for a vector of pliable policies and do not impose any functional form on the utility function.

with mean b/f and density f, this implies that a fraction

$$s_j^S = \tfrac{1}{2} - b + f[u_j(\mathbf{p}^A) - u_j(\mathbf{p}^B)]$$

of the strategic voters in group j vote for party A. Notice that if $\mathbf{p}^A = \mathbf{p}^B$, then $s_j^S = \tfrac{1}{2} - b$; when pliable platforms are the same, the votes divide according to the popularity of the parties. We assume that f is small enough that s_j^S falls between zero and one for all feasible policy options.

We can take a weighted sum of the vote shares in the various groups to compute the fraction of all strategic votes that go to party A. The appropriate weights are the shares of each group in the total number of strategic voters. Let N_j be the number (measure) of voters in group j and let $N = \sum_j N_j$ be the total size of the electorate. We treat the fraction of strategic voters in each group as exogenous and common to the groups; for future reference, we denote it by μ.[8] Forming the weighted sum, we find that the fraction of the strategic votes cast for party A is

$$s^S = \tfrac{1}{2} - b + f[u(\mathbf{p}^A) - u(\mathbf{p}^B)], \tag{10.1}$$

where $u(\mathbf{p}^k) = \sum_j N_j u_j(\mathbf{p}^k)/N$ is the average utility component associated with the pliable policies of party k in the population of all strategic voters.

Now consider the impressionable voters. These individuals account for a fraction $1 - \mu$ of the members of each group. For simplicity, we do not derive the voting behavior of these individuals from first principles. Rather, we assume that the fraction of them who vote for each party reflects the popularity of the fixed positions of each party and the difference in campaign spending. A fraction

$$s_j^I = \tfrac{1}{2} - b + e(c^A - c^B)$$

of the impressionable voters in group j votes for party A when this party spends c^A on the campaign and its rival spends c^B. Implicit in this specification is the assumption that, all else being equal, the parties enjoy the same popularity among impressionable voters as they do among strategic voters. Since the same fraction of impres-

---

8. It would be straightforward to allow the fraction of strategic voters to vary by group. This would introduce an additional bias in policies that is similar to the bias caused by differential turnout, as discussed in Chapter 3, Section 3.1. Here we wish to emphasize the role of competing campaign contributions, which is easier to see when the fraction of impressionable voters is the same in every group.

sionable voters votes for party A in every group, we have that

$$s^I = \tfrac{1}{2} - b + e(c^A - c^B), \tag{10.2}$$

where s^I is party A's vote share among all impressionable voters.

Finally, we can weight s^S and s^I respectively by the shares of strategic and impressionable voters in the voting population, and sum the two terms. This gives the overall share of the votes that goes to party A. Using (10.1) and (10.2), we have

$$s = \tfrac{1}{2} - b + \mu f[u(\mathbf{p}^A) - u(\mathbf{p}^B)] + (1 - \mu)e(c^A - c^B), \tag{10.3}$$

where s is the total vote share for party A.

10.1.2 The Parties

Each party must announce its positions on the pliable issues before it learns the relative popularity of its fixed positions. That is, at the time that $\mathbf{p}^A$ and $\mathbf{p}^B$ are chosen, each party regards b as the future realization of a random variable $\tilde{b}$. Ex ante, b can be positive or negative, so that even if the pliable platforms converge, each party has a chance to win a majority. We again use $F_b(\cdot)$ to denote the distribution of $\tilde{b}$ as perceived by the parties at the time they adopt their positions. Each party sets its platform to maximize its chance of winning a majority, in light of its prior beliefs about the distribution of $\tilde{b}$.

To establish a benchmark, let us first consider a setting with $\mu = 1$, so that all voters are strategic. In this case the parties have no productive use for campaign funds. Party A chooses $\mathbf{p}^A$ to maximize the probability that $s > \tfrac{1}{2}$, which is $F_b\{f[u(\mathbf{p}^A) - u(\mathbf{p}^B)]\}$. Since $F_b(\cdot)$ is an increasing function, the party maximizes its prospects for a victory by choosing the platform that maximizes $u(\mathbf{p})$. Similarly, party B chooses $\mathbf{p}^B$ to maximize the probability that $s < \tfrac{1}{2}$, which is $1 - F_b\{f[u(\mathbf{p}^A) - u(\mathbf{p}^B)]\}$. This party too sets its pliable platform to maximize the welfare of the average voter. Thus, the pliable policies that emerge are the same no matter which party wins the election. Without impressionable voters, our model predicts a pliable policy outcome that is not biased toward the preferences of any group.

When $\mu < 1$, campaign spending produces votes. Therefore, the parties do not ignore their campaign finances when choosing their pliable positions. Recall that the SIGs may link their contributions to the policy platforms. Let $C_j^A(\mathbf{p}^A)$ be the contribution schedule offered by SIG j to party A as a function of that party's campaign announce-ments. Similarly, let $C_j^B(\mathbf{p}^B)$ be the offer by SIG j to party B. The party's total contributions are

$$c^A = \sum_j C_j^A(\mathbf{p}^A) \tag{10.4}$$

and

$$c^B = \sum_j C_j^B(\mathbf{p}^B), \tag{10.5}$$

respectively. Substituting (10.4) and (10.5) into (10.3), we can compute the objective of each party. For party A, the probability that $s > \frac{1}{2}$ is greatest when the party adopts the pliable platform that maximizes

$$G^A = \mu f u(\mathbf{p}^A) + (1 - \mu)e \sum_j C_j^A(\mathbf{p}^A). \tag{10.6}$$

For party B, the optimal platform is the one that maximizes the probability that $s < \frac{1}{2}$, which implies that the party should maximize

$$G^B = \mu f u(\mathbf{p}^B) + (1 - \mu)e \sum_j C_j^B(\mathbf{p}^B). \tag{10.7}$$

Notice that the parties have similar objectives, namely, to maxi-mize a weighted sum of campaign contributions and the welfare of strategic voters. Of course, this objective is exactly what we took to be the policymaker's welfare function in Chapters 7 and 8. Here the incentives in the electoral contest determine the relative weights. The parties attach a greater weight to welfare, the greater is the fraction of strategic voters (the larger is μ) and the more narrow is the range of their views on the ideological issue (the larger is f). This is intuitive. The strategic voters are the ones who compare the pliable positions when deciding how to vote. The more numerous they are, the more attention their preferences will receive from the competing parties. Also, when their ideological perspectives are diverse, there are rela-tively few of them who will change their votes in response to a given change in a party's position. Then the parties have relatively little incentive to cater to their interests in setting their platforms. The weight on campaign contributions increases with the fraction of impressionable voters and with the effectiveness of campaign spend-ing. When e is large, a small increase in spending can be used to win over a large number of impressionable voters. In such circumstances, campaign finances weigh heavily in the strategies of the two parties.

10.1.3   The Interest Groups

The organized interest groups promote the policy objectives of their members. As in Chapter 6, the leaders of a SIG might have either a narrow mandate to pursue only their members' common objectives in regard to the pliable policies or a broader mandate to pursue total welfare from both the fixed and pliable policies. Here, to keep matters simple, we suppose that the mandate is narrow. We take the objective function for the leaders of an organized SIG j to be $E[N_j u_j(\tilde{\mathbf{p}})] - c_j$, where $c_j = c_j^A + c_j^B$ is the sum total of the group's campaign contributions and $\tilde{\mathbf{p}}$ is the vector of policies enacted by the party that wins. The expectation reflects the group's uncertainty about who will win the election.

The SIGs formulate their contribution offers before the policy positions have been chosen. This means that the contribution schedules are designed before the relative popularity of the parties is known. Each SIG takes the contribution schedules of its rivals as given. It forms an expectation of the probability that each party will win the election and calculates its optimal contributions accordingly.

The SIGs anticipate the pliable positions that the parties will choose in response to any contribution schedule they might design, and given the schedules they expect their rivals to offer. With this anticipation, a group can calculate the implied probabilities of a victory by each side. Specifically, the SIG knows that party A will win a majority if and only if the realization of $\tilde{b}$ is such that $s > \frac{1}{2}$. This happens with probability $F_b(\Delta)$, where from (10.6) and (10.7),

$$\Delta = G^A - G^B = \mu f[u(\mathbf{p}^A) - u(\mathbf{p}^B)] + (1 - \mu)e(c^A - c^B). \tag{10.8}$$

So, in evaluating its objective function, the group attaches a probability $F_b(\Delta)$ to the event that $\mathbf{p} = \mathbf{p}^A$, and a probability $1 - F_b(\Delta)$ to the event that $\mathbf{p} = \mathbf{p}^B$. Accordingly, we can rewrite its objective function as

$$U_j = F_b(\Delta)N_j u_j(\mathbf{p}^A) + [1 - F_b(\Delta)]N_j u_j(\mathbf{p}^B) - c_j^A - c_j^B. \tag{10.9}$$

We can approach the problem facing SIG j as we did in Chapter 8. First, the leaders of a SIG contemplate what pliable platforms would be best for their members, considering the incentives facing the political parties. Then they consider what platforms would result in the absence of any contributions of their own. Finally, they design a pair of contribution schedules to implement their preferred positions, bearing in mind the constraints imposed by the fact that a party need not accept the group's offer of support. Notice that a SIG may well choose to contribute to both sides in the election. Since there is a positive probability that either platform will be enacted, the SIG has reason to try to influence the positions taken by both parties.

In order to proceed, we need some additional notation. Let $\mathbf{p}_{-j}^A$ and $\mathbf{p}_{-j}^B$ be the platforms that the two parties would adopt in the absence of any contributions from SIG j. These are the platforms that maximize G^A and G^B respectively, but with $C_j^A(\mathbf{p}^A)$ and $C_j^B(\mathbf{p}^B)$ set identically equal to zero. Now let G_{-j}^A and G_{-j}^B denote the levels of G^A and G^B that the parties would achieve under these circumstances.[9] The problem facing SIG j is to select policies $\mathbf{p}_j^A$ and $\mathbf{p}_j^B$ and contribution levels c_j^A and c_j^B to maximize its objective in (10.9), subject to the constraints that $G^A \geq G_{-j}^A$ and $G^B \geq G_{-j}^B$.

We will be interested in whether the constraints $G^A \geq G_{-j}^A$ and $G^B \geq G_{-j}^B$ are binding in equilibrium. If $G^A = G_{-j}^A$, it means that party A is just indifferent between announcing the platform $\mathbf{p}_j^A$ preferred by SIG j (preferred, that is, in light of the offers to party A by other interest groups) and ignoring the group's offer altogether. The party's indifference implies that it has the same probability of victory when the offer is accepted as when it is declined. Accordingly, the gift from SIG j does not improve the party's electoral prospects under such circumstances. Then the motivation for SIG j in giving to party A could only be to influence its policy positions. If $G^A = G_{-j}^A$ in the equilibrium, we will say that SIG j has exercised only an *influence motive* for contributing to party A.

In contrast, when $G^A > G_{-j}^A$ in equilibrium, it means that SIG j is giving to party A more than the minimal amount needed to influence

---

9. More formally,

$$\mathbf{p}_{-j}^k = \arg \max_{\mathbf{p}} \ \mu f u(\mathbf{p}) + (1-\mu)e \sum_{l | l \neq j} C_l^k(\mathbf{p})$$

and

$$G_{-j}^k = \mu f u(\mathbf{p}_{-j}^k) + (1-\mu)f \sum_{l | l \neq j} C_l^k(\mathbf{p}_{-j}^k)$$

for $k = A, B$.

its platform. The only reason the group could have for such generosity is to enhance the party's prospects for electoral success. In case of a nonbinding constraint, we will say that the interest group has exercised an *electoral motive* for campaign giving.

An equilibrium arises when the pair of contribution schedules for each organized SIG are mutual best responses in light of the anticipated outcome at the platform-setting stage. The platform choices must also be best responses to the contribution schedules.

10.2   One Interest Group

In this section we examine electoral competition in a setting in which only a single interest group is politically organized. First, we hypothesize that the group gives only to influence the parties' positions and derive some of the implications that follow from this assumption. Then we alter the game so that the group has no chance to exert influence. This allows us to examine a pure electoral motive for campaign giving. Finally, we study the general case in which a group may contribute for either or both reasons. We ask, When does each motive operate, and what effect do the optimal contributions have on the policy positions and the election odds?

10.2.1   The Influence Motive

Suppose there is only one active interest group, denoted by j. The group can contribute to one or both of the political parties. In this section, we hypothesize that only the influence motive operates. That is, the SIG gives to each party, if anything, exactly what is needed to induce the party to choose the prescribed platform. We will examine the validity of this hypothesis in Section 10.2.3 below.

When only one SIG contributes to the political parties, they have no alternative sources of campaign funding. This makes it easy to compute $\mathbf{p}_{-j}^A$ and $\mathbf{p}_{-j}^B$, the positions that each would take in the absence of contributions from the group. If SIG j were to offer nothing to party A, the party would maximize its probability of winning by choosing $\mathbf{p}^A$ to maximize $u(\mathbf{p})$. Party B would likewise announce the platform that maximizes $u(\mathbf{p})$. So $\mathbf{p}_{-j}^A = \mathbf{p}_{-j}^B = \mathbf{p}^*$, where $\mathbf{p}^*$ denotes the policy vector that maximizes the welfare of the average strategic voter. These best alternatives give the parties reservation utility levels of $G_{-j}^A = G_{-j}^B = \mu f u(\mathbf{p}^*)$.

If the interest group wishes to have a party take a position different from $\mathbf{p}^*$, it must compensate the party for the loss of votes that such an announcement would imply. To make party A indifferent between announcing $\mathbf{p}^*$ and some other platform $\mathbf{p}^A$, the group must contribute

$$c_j^A = \frac{\mu f}{(1-\mu)e}[u(\mathbf{p}^*) - u(\mathbf{p}^A)]. \tag{10.10}$$

Similarly, an announcement of $\mathbf{p}^B$ by party B would cost the group

$$c_j^B = \frac{\mu f}{(1-\mu)e}[u(\mathbf{p}^*) - u(\mathbf{p}^B)]. \tag{10.11}$$

In each case, the contribution leaves the party with the same chance of winning the election as it would have without any campaign spending. But if spending by both parties were zero, they would choose identical pliable platforms of $\mathbf{p}^*$, and party A would win the election with probability $F_b(0)$. It follows that this too is the probability of an electoral victory by party A no matter what pair of platforms the SIG decides to pursue.

The problem facing the leaders of the SIG is to choose $\mathbf{p}^A$ and $\mathbf{p}^B$ to maximize the members' expected welfare from the pliable policy outcome net of campaign contributions. Using (10.10) and (10.11), we can rewrite the organization's objective function, (10.9), as

$$F_b(0)N_j u_j(\mathbf{p}^A) + [1 - F_b(0)]N_j u_j(\mathbf{p}^B) - \frac{\mu f}{(1-\mu)e}[2u(\mathbf{p}^*) - u(\mathbf{p}^A) - u(\mathbf{p}^B)].$$

Then the solution implies

$$\mathbf{p}^A = \arg\max_{\mathbf{p}}\left\{F_b(0)N_j u_j(\mathbf{p}) + \frac{\mu f}{(1-\mu)e}u(\mathbf{p})\right\} \tag{10.12}$$

and

$$\mathbf{p}^B = \arg\max_{\mathbf{p}}\left\{[1 - F_b(0)]N_j u_j(\mathbf{p}) + \frac{\mu f}{(1-\mu)e}u(\mathbf{p})\right\}. \tag{10.13}$$

The SIG induces each party to announce a platform that maximizes a weighted sum of the members' aggregate welfare from the pliable policies, $N_j u_j(\mathbf{p})$, and the utility component for the average strategic voter, $u(\mathbf{p})$. The relative weight that either party attaches to SIG members depends on the ex ante probability that the party will prove to be the more popular, $F_b(0)$ for party A and $1 - F_b(0)$ for party B. The more popular a party is likely to be, the greater is the bias in its pliable platform.

The influence motive inclines the SIG to give to both political parties. Since even the underdog may emerge as the winner of the election, the SIG has reason to guard itself against the possibility that this party's platform will become the law. The group must pay to influence each platform. But the cost to the group of inducing a small departure from a party's best alternative is quite small. This follows from the fact that the best alternative positions maximize $u(\mathbf{p})$. By the properties of a maximum, a small departure from $\mathbf{p}^*$ does not reduce $u(\mathbf{p})$ by very much and so does not cost a party many votes. Therefore, the compensation that is needed for the SIG to buy the first bit of influence is negligible.

Although the SIG exerts its influence on both platforms, it does not contribute equally to the two parties. Rather, it gives more to the party that is more likely to win the election. This can be seen by comparing (10.12) and (10.13). The comparison shows that the front-runner ultimately gives relatively more weight to SIG members and less weight to strategic voters. In order to induce the front-runner to pay less attention to the interests of strategic voters, the SIG must give more to this party by way of compensation (see equations (10.10) and (10.11)).

It is easy to understand why an influence-motivated SIG would give more generously to the electoral favorite. Political contributions are an investment that pays off for the SIG only if the recipient wins the election. Since the electoral favorite has a better chance of winning, an investment in this party is more likely to yield a positive return. Accordingly, the SIG invests more to influence the favorite than the underdog. This prediction of the model is consistent with the evidence on campaign giving presented by Snyder (1990). It also helps to explain why incumbents, who typically are heavily favored in their bids for reelection, often raise more in contributions from interest groups than their opponents do.

Let us conclude this section with some observations about the extent of the bias in the pliable policies. If only an influence motive operates, then with probability $F_b(0)$ the realized policy outcome is $\mathbf{p}^A$ and with probability $1 - F_b(0)$ it is $\mathbf{p}^B$, where $\mathbf{p}^A$ and $\mathbf{p}^B$ are given in (10.12) and (10.13), respectively. In either case the size of the policy bias is larger, the greater is the effectiveness of campaign spending, the greater is the fraction of impressionable voters, and the

greater is the dispersion of views on the ideological issues. When
campaign spending is more effective, the parties are more willing
to trade off popular positions on the pliable policies for increased
campaign funding. This makes influence cheaper to buy. Similarly,
an increase in the fraction of impressionable voters raises the party's
demands for campaign funds and lowers the price of influence. A
large spread of views on the fixed issues means a low sensitivity
of the vote totals to a change in the pliable policies, and thus a low
political cost to the parties of departing from $\mathbf{p}^*$. Again, this reduces
the price of influence.

10.2.2   *A Pure Electoral Motive*

In this section, we begin to investigate the electoral motive for campaign giving. In order to best understand what is different about this
alternative reason for contributing, we make a temporary modifica-
tion to our model. For the time being, we assume that the SIG can
offer contributions to the parties only after they have announced
their positions on the pliable issues. With this timing, there is no
possibility for the SIG to influence the parties' platforms. Rather, the
SIG can only hope to alter the probabilities that either side will win
the election.[10]

Consider first the incentives facing the leaders of the interest
group. By the time they must decide on their contributions, they will
know the parties' positions on the pliable issues. The leaders will
know that if they contribute c_j^A to party A and c_j^B to party B, then
party A will win a majority of the votes if and only if $b < \Delta$, where Δ
is given in (10.8). This will happen with probability $F_b(\Delta)$. The leaders
choose the group's contributions to maximize the members' expected
welfare from the pliable policies net of the payments; that is, they
maximize U_j given in (10.9).

It is obvious that, unlike the influence-motivated SIG, the electorally motivated SIG contributes to at most one party. If it contributes
to party A, it increases Δ and thus the probability that party A will
win the election. If it contributes to party B, it does just the opposite.
But the leaders will only wish to further the electoral prospects of

---

10. Austen-Smith (1987) and Magee, Brock, and Young (1989) have studied models of
electorally motivated campaign contributions in which the order of moves is as specified here. Austen-Smith investigated the provision of public goods, whereas Magee
et al. focused on the determination of trade policies.

one party, namely the one whose pliable positions the members prefer. Therefore, only this party is a candidate to receive the group's electorally motivated gifts.

Suppose, for concreteness, that $u_j(\mathbf{p}^A) > u_j(\mathbf{p}^B)$. Will SIG j necessarily contribute to party A? The answer is no. The group perceives a marginal benefit from its first dollar of contribution equal to $F_b'(\Delta_0)(1 - \mu)eN_j[u_j(\mathbf{p}^A) - u_j(\mathbf{p}^B)]$, where $\Delta_0 = \mu f[u(\mathbf{p}^A) - u(\mathbf{p}^B)]$. This benefit reflects the marginal effectiveness of the first bit of campaign spending by party A in improving its chances of victory, and also the extent of the members' preference for $\mathbf{p}^A$ over $\mathbf{p}^B$. The cost of the dollar of contributions is, of course, one. The group will make a positive contribution if the marginal benefit exceeds the marginal cost, or if[11]

$$F_b'(\Delta_0)(1 - \mu)eN_j[u_j(\mathbf{p}^A) - u_j(\mathbf{p}^B)] > 1. \tag{10.14}$$

But there is no guarantee that this condition will be satisfied. Moreover, it can never be satisfied if the parties' pliable positions are the same. An electoral motive is more likely to operate the greater is the difference in the group's evaluation of the parties' positions and the more productive is campaign spending in generating votes.

If inequality (10.14) is satisfied, SIG j will contribute to party A. The size of its gift will be such that the marginal benefit of the last dollar of contribution matches the marginal cost, or

$$F_b'(\Delta)(1 - \mu)eN_j[u_j(\mathbf{p}^A) - u_j(\mathbf{p}^B)] = 1. \tag{10.15}$$

Similarly, if $F_b'(\Delta_0)(1 - \mu)eN_j[u_j(\mathbf{p}^B) - u_j(\mathbf{p}^A)] > 1$, the group will contribute to party B, and c_j^B will be chosen so that

$$F_b'(\Delta)(1 - \mu)eN_j[u_j(\mathbf{p}^B) - u_j(\mathbf{p}^A)] = 1.$$

To summarize, there are two important lessons to take from the discussion up to this point. First, when an electoral motive operates, it generates giving to only one political party. Second, such a motive

---

11. This is a sufficient condition for positive contribution by SIG j, but it is not a necessary condition. It is possible that SIG j would not benefit from a small contribution to party A but would benefit from a larger one. However, if $F_b'(\cdot)$ is single-peaked and the value of Δ_0 lies to the right of that peak, then (10.14) will be necessary and sufficient for a positive contribution. Our discussion focuses on this case and also assumes that the contribution does not bring a party's probability of election to one. But the main result discussed in this section—that equilibrium platforms converge and equilibrium contributions are zero—holds for all distribution functions $F_b(\cdot)$ and all parameter values.

is more likely to operate the greater is the group's relative preference for the pliable positions of one party over those of the other.

Now we consider the competition between the two parties. Each party sets a platform in anticipation of the possible gift it might receive from the interest group and that which its rival might get. That is, the parties understand how the SIG will respond to any pair of platform announcements. We seek a pair of pliable platforms that are mutual best responses.

A first observation follows from the fact that the parties are engaged in a zero-sum game. Party A knows that, if it adopts the same pliable positions as those of its rival, the SIG will have no incentive to give to either party. In the event, party A will win the election with probability $F_b(0)$. Since the party can assure itself of at least this chance of winning by mimicking the positions of its rival, it would never accept a smaller probability than this in any equilibrium. By the same token, party B knows that it, too, can mimic the positions of its rival, and thereby eliminate the group's incentive for electoral giving. Then its probability of a victory would be $1 - F_b(0)$. This party will not accept a probability of its own victory smaller than this. Putting these observations together, it follows that the probability of a victory by party A must be exactly equal to $F_b(0)$ in any pure-strategy equilibrium.

The fact that the probability of a victory by party A must equal $F_b(0)$ limits the possible configurations of platforms and contributions in any equilibrium. One possibility is that pliable platforms are the same ($\mathbf{p}^A = \mathbf{p}^B$) and the interest group contributes to neither party. The other possibility is that the platforms differ, but the contributions by the SIG are of just the right size to ensure that $\Delta = 0$.

Let us hypothesize that $\mathbf{p}^A$ and $\mathbf{p}^B$ are equilibrium platforms with $\mathbf{p}^A \neq \mathbf{p}^B$, and that SIG j contributes to party A. The first-order condition (10.15) gives the size of the group's contribution. The second-order condition—which ensures that the group's giving achieves a maximum of its objective function and not a minimum—implies that $F_b''(\Delta) < 0$. We will now show that, under these conditions, party B can increase its probability of victory by shifting its pliable platform in a direction favorable to the members of the interest group. Of course, this contradicts the assumption that $\mathbf{p}^A$ and $\mathbf{p}^B$ are equilibrium platforms.

Any change in $\mathbf{p}^B$ that increases $u_j(\mathbf{p}^B)$ reduces the size of the gap, $u_j(\mathbf{p}^A) - u_j(\mathbf{p}^B)$, that motivates the SIG's giving. From the first-order condition (10.15) and the fact that $F_b''(\Delta) < 0$, this implies a fall in Δ. But the probability of victory by party B is $1 - F_b(\Delta)$, and $F_b(\cdot)$ is an increasing function, so the deviation improves the party's electoral prospects. Since this contradicts the hypothesis that $\mathbf{p}^A$ and $\mathbf{p}^B$ are equilibrium platforms, we conclude that there can be no equilibrium with $\mathbf{p}^A \neq \mathbf{p}^B$ and $c_j^A > 0$. We can similarly rule out any equilibrium with $\mathbf{p}^A \neq \mathbf{p}^B$ and $c_j^B > 0$ by considering deviations by party A. The only remaining possibility, given that Δ must equal zero, is that $\mathbf{p}^A = \mathbf{p}^B$ and $c_j^A = c_j^B = 0$. In other words, the equilibrium must have convergence of the parties' pliable positions and no electorally motivated campaign contributions.

We note in passing that the equilibrium platforms may or may not coincide with the policies that maximize the welfare of the average strategic voter. Consider, for example, a situation in which campaign advertising is very ineffective (e is small) and the fraction of impressionable voters is small (μ is close to one). Then the interest group may not be willing to contribute to a party even if it takes as its pliable position the group's favorite policies. In this case the equilibrium will have $\mathbf{p}^A = \mathbf{p}^B = \mathbf{p}^*$. Now consider the opposite situation in which campaign spending is very effective (e is large) and the fraction of impressionable voters is large (μ is close to zero). Then, if party A were to announce the welfare-maximizing policies $\mathbf{p}^*$ as its pliable platform, the best response by party B would be to announce a platform that caters more to the interest group. Such a platform would induce positive contributions from SIG j. The combined effect of the different positions and the positive contributions would be such as to improve the party's electoral odds.[12] In this case, the equilibrium still has $\mathbf{p}^A = \mathbf{p}^B$, but the common platforms are biased toward the interests of the SIG members as compared to the benchmark outcome.

10.2.3 A Choice of Motives

Now we return to the timing previously described. The SIG once again may contribute to the parties before they announce their pli-

---

12. For example, if

$$F_b'(0)(1 - \mu)eN_j[u_j(\mathbf{p}_j^*) - u_j(\mathbf{p}^*)] > 1$$

where $\mathbf{p}_j^*$ is the vector of pliable policies that maximizes $u_j(\cdot)$, then party B could announce the platform $\mathbf{p}_j^*$ in response to party A's announcement of $\mathbf{p}^*$, and thereby induce contributions from SIG j that would increase its probability of a victory above $1 - F_b(0)$.

able positions. This time, however, we do not insist that they give only what is needed to influence the platform choices. The group may choose to give more than this amount to affect the election odds, and it may even elect to provide its support with no strings attached. In short, we leave the size and nature of the contributions entirely up to the interest group.

Before we begin the formal analysis, let us indicate how the influence motive and the electoral motive might interact. If only the influence motive operates, the group contributes equally to the two parties unless one of them has a better ex ante chance of winning the election. Any ex ante advantage that a party has must reflect the greater (expected) popularity of its fixed positions. When such an advantage does exist, the group gives more generously to the ex ante favorite and, in return, it induces the party to take pliable positions more to its liking. Now recall that the electoral motive can operate only when the parties' pliable positions differ. If the competitive forces in an election cause convergence in the parties' pliable platforms, they eradicate this motive for giving. Influence-motivated contributions can create the difference in positions needed for the electoral motive to operate. And the electorally motivated contributions can tilt the election odds further in the front-runner's direction, so that it becomes an even more attractive target for the group's influence-motivated giving. In short, we will find that the two motives for campaign giving can reinforce one another.

Let us turn to the formal analysis. Consider the problem facing the leaders of the SIG, who must design a pair of contribution schedules to maximize their members' expected utility from the pliable policies net of the political payoffs. Recall how we solved such problems before. We imagined that the SIG chooses the policies and level of contributions, but subject to constraints. Here we can envision the group choosing $\mathbf{p}^A$, $\mathbf{p}^B$, c_j^A, and c_j^B, subject to the constraints that each party must be left with at least as good a chance of victory as it would have if its contribution was zero and its pliable position was $\mathbf{p}^*$. We can write the leaders' problem as

$$\max_{\mathbf{p}^A, \mathbf{p}^B, c_j^A, c_j^B} F_b(\Delta)N_j u_j(\mathbf{p}^A) + [1 - F_b(\Delta)]N_j u_j(\mathbf{p}^B) - c_j^A - c_j^B$$

subject to

$$c_j^A \geq \frac{\mu f}{(1-\mu)e}[u(\mathbf{p}^*) - u(\mathbf{p}^A)]$$

and

$$c_j^B \geq \frac{\mu f}{(1-\mu)e}[u(\mathbf{p}^*) - u(\mathbf{p}^B)],$$

where $\Delta = \mu f[u_j(\mathbf{p}^A) - u_j(\mathbf{p}^B)] + (1-\mu)e(c_j^A - c_j^B)$.

Suppose, for concreteness, that $F_b(0) > \frac{1}{2}$. In other words, if the parties were to adopt the same pliable positions and spend similarly on their campaigns, then party A would have the better chance of winning the election. In this sense, party A is the ex ante favorite. We will now show that, under certain mild restrictions on the distribution of $\tilde{b}$, only party A is a candidate to receive electorally motivated contributions.

We restrict the distribution of $\tilde{b}$ by assuming that, for all values of b, $F_b(b) + F_b(-b) > 1$.[13] This restriction is satisfied, for example, by all single-peaked distribution functions that are symmetric about their means. The restriction implies that, were party A to gain a further electoral advantage from the combined effects of the contributions and positions (i.e., $\Delta = \delta > 0$), it would have a better chance of victory than party B would have were that party to capture the same net advantage due to contributions and positions (i.e., $\Delta = -\delta < 0$).

To see that party B can never receive electorally motivated contributions, first observe that the group never gives extra contributions to both parties. Were it the case that $c_j^A > \mu f[u_j(\mathbf{p}^*) - u_j(\mathbf{p}^A)]/(1-\mu)e$ and $c_j^B > \mu f[u_j(\mathbf{p}^*) - u_j(\mathbf{p}^B)]/(1-\mu)e$, the SIG could cut both c_j^A and c_j^B by the same amount while leaving the positions unchanged. This would not change the probability of a victory for either side and thus is bound to increase the expected welfare of the group's members. It follows that at least one of the constraints must hold as an equality.

Now suppose that the leaders of the SIG were to contemplate giving an extra contribution only to party B. We will argue that they could design a different strategy that yields a higher value of their objective function. To this end, let $c_j^B > \mu f[u_j(\mathbf{p}^*) - u_j(\mathbf{p}^B)]/(1-\mu)e$ be the contribution the group contemplates giving to party B, and let $c_j^A = \mu f[u_j(\mathbf{p}^*) - u_j(\mathbf{p}^A)]/(1-\mu)e$ be the one intended for party A, with $\mathbf{p}^B$ and $\mathbf{p}^A$ as the associated positions. Since the group would only wish to help party B if it expected that party to announce a

---

13. If we were to assume that $F_b(0) < \frac{1}{2}$, so that party B was the ex ante favorite, then our restriction on the distribution of $\tilde{b}$ would be that $F_b(b) + F_b(-b) < 1$. The interpretation of the restriction would be the same as that given in the text.

position more to its liking, it must be that $u_j(\mathbf{p}^B) > u_j(\mathbf{p}^A)$. Now consider the following change in strategy. Let the group contribute to party A what it had contemplated giving to party B, while inducing that party to take position $\mathbf{p}^B$ instead of $\mathbf{p}^A$. At the same time, let it contribute to party B what it had contemplated giving to party A, so that it induces party B to announce position $\mathbf{p}^A$ instead of $\mathbf{p}^B$. In other words, let the group swap the contemplated contribution schedules, offering to party A what it had thought to offer to party B, and vice versa. The new contribution levels and positions do not violate either of the constraints on the minimum sizes of the contributions. The total amount of contributions is the same as the group had contemplated. And, because $F_b(\Delta) > 1 - F_b(-\Delta)$, the group would increase the probability of attaining its more preferred outcome ($\mathbf{p}^B$) while reducing the probability of attaining its less preferred outcome ($\mathbf{p}^A$). Thus, the proposed change in strategy would improve the value of the leaders' objective function. It follows that the contemplated offer of an extra contribution to party B could not have been optimal.

Now that we know that only party A is a candidate to receive electorally motivated contributions, two questions remain. First, when does the party actually receive such contributions? Second, in cases where the SIG contributes to party A to further its electoral prospects, does it also contribute to party B for purposes of influence?

To answer these questions, it is helpful to reformulate the SIG's problem. We define c_j^{AI} as the size of the contribution that is needed to induce party A to adopt the position p^A, and c_j^{AE} as the residual contribution.[14] Using this new notation, we can write the probability of a victory for party A as $F_b[(1-\mu)ec_j^{AE}]$, because the combined effect of the influence-motivated contributions to both parties and the induced platform announcements leaves the election odds the same as they would be without any contributions. Only the electorally motivated contributions improve the prospects for party A. The problem facing the SIG can now be written as

$$\max_{\mathbf{p}^A, \mathbf{p}^B, c_j^{AE}} F_b[(1-\mu)ec_j^{AE}]N_j u_j(\mathbf{p}^A) + \{1 - F_b[(1-\mu)ec_j^{AE}]\}N_j u_j(\mathbf{p}^B)$$

$$- \frac{\mu f}{(1-\mu)e}[2u(\mathbf{p}^*) - u_j(\mathbf{p}^A) - u_j(\mathbf{p}^B)] - c_j^{AE}.$$

---

14. More formally, $c_j^{AI}(\mathbf{p}^A) = \mu f[u(\mathbf{p}^*) - u(\mathbf{p}^A)]/(1-\mu)e$ and $c_j^{AE} = c_j^A - c_j^{AI}$.

Our questions become: When does the SIG choose $c_j^{AE} > 0$? And when is the optimal $\mathbf{p}^B$ different from $\mathbf{p}^*$?

For $c_j^{AE} > 0$, it is sufficient that the expected benefit from the first dollar of extra contributions exceeds the cost. The marginal benefit of the first bit of electorally motivated giving is

$$(1 - \mu)eF_b'(0)N_j[u_j(\hat{\mathbf{p}}^A) - u_j(\hat{\mathbf{p}}^B)],$$

where $\hat{\mathbf{p}}^A$ and $\hat{\mathbf{p}}^B$ are the platforms defined by (10.12) and (10.13), or the platforms that would be chosen in the absence of any electorally motivated contributions. The marginal cost of the extra gift is one. Thus, the SIG will give to party A to further its electoral prospects if its gift would have a sufficiently large impact on the likely election outcome and if the platforms that resulted from its influence activities were sufficiently different. The SIG is more likely to pursue an electoral motive the larger is the fraction of impressionable voters and the greater is the efficacy of campaign spending. The larger is $(1 - \mu)e$, the greater is the impact that extra contributions from the SIG have on the election odds, and the more different is $\hat{\mathbf{p}}^A$ from $\hat{\mathbf{p}}^B$. It is not clear, however, whether we are more likely to observe electorally motivated contributions in a close election race or in a lopsided contest. The more lopsided is the election, the greater will be the induced difference between the platforms of the two parties. But if the election odds are already quite uneven, it may be difficult for the SIG to add much to the chances of a victory by the front-runner.

Even if the SIG contributes something extra to party A to help its bid for election, it will still contribute to party B unless a victory by party A becomes a virtual certainty. To see that $c_j^B > 0$ even when $c_j^{AE} > 0$, note that the SIG chooses $\mathbf{p}^B$ to maximize

$$\{1 - F_b[(1 - \mu)ec_j^{AE})]\}N_ju_j(\mathbf{p}) + \frac{\mu f}{(1 - \mu)e}u(\mathbf{p}).$$

As long as $F_b[(1 - \mu)ec_j^{AE}] < 1$, the solution does not have $\mathbf{p}^B = \mathbf{p}^*$. Since $\mathbf{p}^B \neq \mathbf{p}^*$, it must be that $c_j^B > 0$, because a positive contribution is needed to induce party B to take pliable positions different from the ones that maximize the welfare of the average strategic voter.

We conclude that the pattern of giving is qualitatively the same no matter whether an electoral motive is present or not. In either case, the SIG contributes to both contestants, but it reserves its larger contribution for the party whose fixed positions are expected to be more popular. With the larger contribution, the group buys greater influence from the electoral favorite. Its electorally motivated contributions, if any, add to the party's initial advantage. Overall, the contributions bias the policy outcome away from the public interest, both by influencing the parties' positions and perhaps by tilting the election odds.

10.3   Multiple Interest Groups

Now we consider an election with many potential contributors. We will find that the greater the number of contributing interest groups, the weaker is the incentive any one of them has to pursue an electoral motive for giving. In fact, when the number of SIGs grows sufficiently large, the electoral motive vanishes entirely. The SIGs do, however, continue to contribute to influence the parties' platforms. When there are many interest groups, there is no clear-cut connection between a party's ex ante prospects of victory and the extent of its catering to special interests. In equilibrium, the SIGs collectively purchase greater influence from the party that they view as more likely to win the election. But the ultimate electoral favorite need not be the party that had an initial advantage in popularity. Rather, a party may become the favorite due to the size of its campaign war chest. The expectation that some party will prove a better fund raiser than its rival can become a self-fulfilling prophecy in a game with many independent contributors.

We consider the problem facing a SIG j, which is one of several (or many) different organized interest groups. The group's objective function is given by equation (10.9). It chooses platforms, $\mathbf{p}_j^A$ and $\mathbf{p}_j^B$, and contribution levels, c_j^A and c_j^B, to maximize this function, subject to the constraints that $G^A \geq G_{-j}^A$ and $G^B \geq G_{-j}^B$. In so doing, the group takes the contribution schedules of all other SIGs as given. In an equilibrium, the choices by each group are best responses to the schedules put forth by the others, and the platforms selected by the different SIGs coincide.

If an electoral motive operates for SIG j, then $G^A > G_{-j}^A$ or $G^B > G_{-j}^B$ (but not both). Suppose that SIG j does happen to give to party A beyond what is needed to curry favor. Then its contribution to this party will be governed by a first-order condition, namely

$$F_b'(\Delta)e(1 - \mu)N_j[u_j(\mathbf{p}^A) - u_j(\mathbf{p}^B)] = 1, \tag{10.16}$$

where

$$\Delta = \mu f[u_j(\mathbf{p}^A) - u_j(\mathbf{p}^B)] + (1 - \mu)e\left[\sum_k (c_k^A - c_k^B)\right].$$

This condition equates the expected marginal benefit from the last dollar given to party A with the marginal cost. The marginal benefit reflects the effectiveness of the dollar in improving the party's chance of winning, and also the SIG's relative preference for the pliable platform of party A relative to that of party B. The marginal cost is one.

Now suppose that some other SIG, say SIG m, also makes electorally motivated contributions to party A. Then its contribution too must satisfy a first-order condition of the form

$$F_b'(\Delta)e(1 - \mu)N_m[u_m(\mathbf{p}^A) - u_m(\mathbf{p}^B)] = 1. \tag{10.17}$$

But notice that (10.16) and (10.17) together imply

$$N_j[u_j(\mathbf{p}^A) - u_j(\mathbf{p}^B)] = N_m[u_m(\mathbf{p}^A) - u_m(\mathbf{p}^B)]. \tag{10.18}$$

That is, if two interest groups make electorally motivated contributions to the same political party, they must share exactly the same relative preference for the party's pliable positions. It would be quite a coincidence for equation (10.18) to be satisfied for two groups with different preferences. We conclude that it is unlikely that an electoral motive will operate for more than one interest group contributing to a given party.

The reason why multiple groups are unlikely to make electorally motivated contributions to the same party has to do with the opportunity that each group has to take a free ride. All of the SIGs that prefer $\mathbf{p}^A$ to $\mathbf{p}^B$ would like to see the probability of a victory by party A increased. But all would also like to see others pay for any improvement in the election odds, rather than having to pay for it themselves. In equilibrium, only the group that stands to gain the most from the victory by party A (if any) purchases the public good that benefits them all.

The first-order condition (10.16) also suggests why it is unlikely that a small interest group would pursue an electoral motive for campaign giving. For given values of e, μ, and $F_b'(\Delta)$, this condition cannot be satisfied as N_j becomes small unless the difference in the group's evaluation of the two platforms grows large. A small interest group has relatively little to gain from boosting the electoral success of its preferred party. When all groups are small, none of them will have a sufficient incentive to pursue an electoral motive for giving.

Next we examine the behavior of a SIG j whose only motivation for giving is to influence the parties' platforms. Such a group satisfies the pair of constraints on its contributions and platform choices with equality. Therefore, each party has the same chance of winning the election when it accepts a gift from SIG j as it would without the contribution. The SIG takes the probability of a victory by each party as given, because it knows that its own contribution makes no difference to the electoral odds. For SIG j, the perceived probability of victory by party A is $F_b(G^A_{-j} - G^B_{-j})$. The problem facing the leaders of the group is to choose a pair of platforms, $\mathbf{p}^A_j$ and $\mathbf{p}^B_j$, and a pair of contributions, c^A_j and c^B_j, to maximize

$$F_b(G^A_{-j} - G^B_{-j})N_j u_j(\mathbf{p}^A) + [1 - F_b(G^A_{-j} - G^B_{-j})]N_j u_j(\mathbf{p}^B) - c^A_j - c^B_j$$

subject to the constraints that

$$\mu f u(\mathbf{p}^A) + (1 - \mu)e\left[c^A_j + \sum_{m \neq j} C^A_m(\mathbf{p}^A)\right] = G^A_{-j}$$

and

$$\mu f u(\mathbf{p}^B) + (1 - \mu)e\left[c^B_j + \sum_{m \neq j} C^B_m(\mathbf{p}^B)\right] = G^B_{-j}.$$

The solution to this problem implies

$$\mathbf{p}^A_j = \arg\max_{\mathbf{p}^A} F_b(G^A_{-j} - G^B_{-j})N_j u_j(\mathbf{p}^A)$$

$$- \frac{1}{(1-\mu)e}[G^A_{-j} - \mu f u(\mathbf{p}^A)] + \sum_{m|m \neq j} C^A_m(\mathbf{p}^A) \qquad (10.19)$$

and

$$\mathbf{p}^B_j = \arg\max_{\mathbf{p}^B} [1 - F_b(G^A_{-j} - G^B_{-j})]N_j u_j(\mathbf{p}^B)$$

$$- \frac{1}{(1-\mu)e}[G^B_{-j} - \mu f u(\mathbf{p}^A)] + \sum_{m|m \neq j} C^B_m(\mathbf{p}^B). \qquad (10.20)$$

Notice that we cannot conclude from these equations, as we did in discussing the case of a single SIG, that SIG j buys more influence from the party that is the ex ante favorite to win the election. To draw such a conclusion, we would need to be able to argue that party A puts relatively more weight on the group's preferences if and only if $F_b(0) > \frac{1}{2}$. But this argument cannot be made, for two reasons. First, the contribution schedules offered by groups other than SIG j affect the incentives facing this interest group. Notice the terms following the summation signs in (10.19) and (10.20). These terms need not be identical, and they can have different impacts on the group's choice of $\mathbf{p}_j^A$ and $\mathbf{p}_j^B$. Second, the party that is more popular ex ante need not be the one that ultimately has the better chance of winning the election. If, for example, $F_b(0) > \frac{1}{2}$, this does not imply that $F_b(G_{-j}^A - G_{-j}^B) > \frac{1}{2}$. If SIG j expects that the other SIGs would give more generously to party B than to party A in the absence of its own contributions, this could outweigh the initial advantage that it sees for party A as a result of its greater ex ante popularity.[15]

Of course, a similar argument applies for every interest group. In equilibrium, all groups must share the same expectations about the election odds, and their incentives must be such that all "choose" the same pair of pliable platforms. If the groups all regard party B as more likely to win the election, they may collectively contribute more to this party than to party A, thereby making party B the electoral favorite. In other words, the uncoordinated contribution decisions of all the interest groups can create a self-fulfilling prophecy.

In fact, there is nothing to pin down the groups' equilibrium expectations about which party is more likely to win the election and how much better its chances are. In one equilibrium, the groups' contribution schedules justify a common belief that party A is quite likely to prove victorious. In another equilibrium, a different set of schedules justifies a belief that a victory by party A is only slightly more likely than one by party B. In still another equilibrium, it is party B that is regarded as the likely winner. Indeed, there are many equilibria, each with different election odds and a different pair of pliable policy platforms.

Despite the multiplicity of equilibria, there are remarks we can make about the equilibrium platforms for the case in which all in-

---

15. From the definitions of G_{-j}^A and G_{-j}^B, we have

$$G_{-j}^A - G_{-j}^B = \mu f[u(\mathbf{p}_{-j}^A) - u(\mathbf{p}_{-j}^B)] + (1 - \mu)e \sum_{m \neq j} [C_m^A(\mathbf{p}_{-j}^A) - C_m^B(\mathbf{p}_{-j}^B)].$$

It is possible to have $F_b(G_{-j}^A - G_{-j}^B) < \frac{1}{2}$ with $F_b(0) > \frac{1}{2}$ if, for example, $\sum_{m \neq j} C_m^B(\mathbf{p}_{-j}^B)$ is much larger than $\sum_{m \neq j} C_m^A(\mathbf{p}_{-j}^A)$.

fluence groups give only to influence the parties' positions. Suppose that all of the groups employ differentiable contribution schedules and that their welfare levels are concave functions of the pliable policy vector. With concavity, the platforms described by (10.19) and (10.20) are ones that satisfy a set of first-order conditions with equality. Using, for example, the first-order condition that determines p_{jk}^A, the kth component of the vector of positions that SIG j selects for party A, we have

$$F_b(G_{-j}^A - G_{-j}^B)N_j \frac{\partial u_j(\mathbf{p}_j^A)}{\partial p_{jk}^A} + \frac{\mu f}{(1-\mu)e} \frac{\partial u(\mathbf{p}^A)}{\partial p_{jk}^A} + \sum_{m|m \neq j} \frac{\partial C_m^A(\mathbf{p}_j^A)}{\partial p_{jk}^A} = 0.$$

(10.21)

Moreover, in equilibrium, the platform that SIG j induces party A to choose must coincide with the one that every other SIG chooses, and it must be among those in the party's best-response set. The optimal choice of platform by party A maximizes its probability of winning the election. From this, we know that p_k^A (the kth element of the party's platform $\mathbf{p}^A$) satisfies

$$\mu f \frac{\partial u(\mathbf{p}^A)}{\partial p_k^A} + (1-\mu)e \sum_m \frac{\partial C_m^A(\mathbf{p}^A)}{\partial p_k^A} = 0.$$

(10.22)

Combining (10.21) and (10.22), and using the fact that in equilibrium $p_k^A = p_{jk}^A$ and $G_{-j}^A - G_{-j}^B = G^A - G^B$, we find that

$$\frac{\partial C_j^A(\mathbf{p}^A)}{\partial p_k^A} = F_b(G^A - G^B)N_j \frac{\partial u_j(\mathbf{p}^A)}{\partial p_{jk}^A}.$$

(10.23)

Equation (10.23) implies that the contribution schedule that SIG j offers to party A is locally compensating in light of the equilibrium election odds. It says that the change in the group's contribution for a small change in the party's position matches the effect of that change on the group members' expected welfare from the pliable policies. It has a similar interpretation as equation (8.1) in Chapter 8, except that here the utility change must be multiplied by the probability that party A will win the election. Of course, the group's contribution offer to party B also is locally compensating in the same sense.

When all groups employ differentiable contribution schedules and pursue only an influence motive for giving, all of the equilibrium bids must be locally compensating. We can use this fact and (10.23) to rewrite equation (10.22) as

$$\mu f \frac{\partial u(\mathbf{p}^A)}{\partial p_k^A} + (1 - \mu)eF_b(G^A - G^B) \sum_m \frac{\partial N_m u_m(\mathbf{p}^A)}{\partial p_k^A} = 0.$$

Evidently, party A then chooses the pliable platform that maximizes a weighted sum of the aggregate welfare of strategic voters and the combined welfare of interest-group members. The platform for party B maximizes a similar weighted sum, except that it is the likelihood of an electoral victory for this party, $1 - F_b(G^A - G^B)$, that enters the weight on the second term. Thus, the real indeterminacy of equilibrium concerns only the likelihood of an electoral victory by each side. Once we posit expectations about the electoral odds, the model predicts a unique pair of equilibrium platforms.

In this chapter, we have incorporated campaign contributions in a model of electoral competition. Competing political parties face a fundamental trade-off. They can adopt pliable positions to maximize their appeal to strategic voters or they can cater to special interests so as to attract campaign funding. In equilibrium, the parties act as if they were intending to maximize a weighted average of campaign contributions and the aggregate welfare of strategic voters. Thus, the analysis provides the underpinnings for the reduced-form approach that we used in the earlier chapters.

In the framework of this chapter, it is possible to distinguish two distinct motives that SIGs may have for their campaign contributions. An interest group might contribute in order to influence a party's positions or to improve a party's chances of winning the election. Whereas the influence motive will operate in almost all settings, an active electoral motive requires special conditions. Typically, the electoral motive will operate for at most one group that gives to a given party. And if there are many different interest groups, each with a relatively small stake in the policy outcome, then no group will perceive it worthwhile to give to a party so as to improve its electoral prospects.

Groups that are after influence have reason to contribute to both political parties. But their incentive is to curry more favor with the party that they believe has the better chance of winning the election. Thus, good prospects attract contributions. At the same time, the spending financed by the contributions improves a party's prospects. As in other contexts, this positive feedback mechanism creates the possibility of a self-fulfilling prophecy and implies the existence of multiple equilibria. A party that is expected to win may attract the contributions that make its victory more likely. Collectively, the interest groups induce the electoral favorite to cater more heavily to special interests.

References

Aldrich, John H. (1993). Rational choice and turnout. *American Journal of Political Science*, 37, 246–278.

Alesina, Alberto (1988). Credibility and policy convergence in a two-party system with rational voters. *American Economic Review*, 78, 796–805.

Ansolabehere, Stephen D., and James M. Snyder, Jr. (1996). Party platform choice in single-member-district and party-list systems. Mimeo.

Austen-Smith, David (1984). Two-party competition with many constituencies. *Mathematical Social Sciences*, 7, 177–198.

Austen-Smith, David (1987). Interest groups, campaign contributions and probabilistic voting. *Public Choice*, 54, 123–139.

Austen-Smith, David (1995). Campaign contributions and access. *American Political Science Review*, 89, 566–581.

Austen-Smith, David, and Jeffrey S. Banks (1988). Elections, coalitions, and legislative outcomes. *American Political Science Review*, 82, 405–422.

Austen-Smith, David, and John R. Wright (1994). Counteractive lobbying. *American Journal of Political Science*, 38, 25–44.

Baldwin, Robert E., and Christopher S. Magee (2000). *Explaining Congressional Voting on Trade Bills in the 1990's: From NAFTA Approval to Fast-Track Defeat*. Washington, D.C.: Institute for International Economics.

Ball, Richard J. (1995). Interest groups, influence and welfare. *Economics and Politics*, 7, 119–146.

Banerjee, Abhijit, and Rohini Somanathan (2001). A simple model of voice. *Quarterly Journal of Economics*, 116, 189–228.

Baron, David P. (1991). A spatial bargaining theory of government formation in parliamentary systems. *American Political Science Review*, 85, 137–164.

Baron, David P. (1993). Government formation and endogenous parties. *American Political Science Review*, 87, 34–47.

Baron, David P. (1994). Electoral competition with informed and uninformed voters. *American Political Science Review*, 88, 33–47.

Baron, David P., and John A. Ferejohn (1989). Bargaining in legislatures. *American Political Science Review*, 83, 1181–1206.

Battaglini, Marco (2000). Multiple referrals and multidimensional cheap talk. Discussion Paper No. 1295. Evanston, Ill.: Northwestern University, Center for Mathematical Studies in Economics and Management Science.

Bauer, Raymond, Ithiel de Sola Pool, and Lewis A. Dexter (1963). *American Business and Public Policy*. New York: Atherton Press.

Baumgartner, Frank R., and Beth L. Leech (1998). *Basic Interests: The Importance of Groups in Politics and in Political Science*. Princeton, N.J.: Princeton University Press.

Becker, Gary S. (1983). A theory of competition among pressure groups for political influence. *Quarterly Journal of Economics*, 98, 371–400.

Bernheim, B. Douglas, and Michael D. Whinston (1984). Coalition-proof Nash equilibrium. Discussion Paper No. 1075. Cambridge, Mass.: Harvard University, Harvard Institute of Economic Research.

Bernheim, B. Douglas, and Michael D. Whinston (1986a). Menu auctions, resource allocation, and economic influence. *Quarterly Journal of Economics*, 101, 1–31.

Bernheim, B. Douglas, and Michael D. Whinston (1986b). Common agency. *Econometrica*, 54, 923–942.

Berry, Jeffrey (1977). *Lobbying for the People: The Political Behavior of Public Interest Groups*. Princeton, N.J.: Princeton University Press.

Besley, Timothy, and Stephen Coate (1997). An economic model of representative democracy. *Quarterly Journal of Economics*, 112, 85–114.

Binmore, Kenneth G., Ariel Rubinstein, and Asher Wolinski (1986). The Nash bargaining solution in economic modelling. *Rand Journal of Economics*, 17, 176–188.

Birnbaum, Jeffrey H. (1992). *The Lobbyists: How Influence Peddlers Get Their Way in Washington*. New York: Times Books.

Birnbaum, Jeffrey H., and Alan S. Murray (1987). *Showdown at Gucci Gulch: Lawmakers, Lobbyists and the Unlikely Triumph of Tax Reform*. New York: Random House.

Bronars, Stephen G., and John R. Lott Jr. (1997). Do campaign donations alter how a politician votes? Or, do donors support candidates who value the same things they do? *Journal of Law and Economics*, 40, 317–350.

Calvert, Randall L. (1986). *Models of Imperfect Information in Politics*. Chur, Switzerland: Harwood Academic Publishers.

Center for Responsive Politics (1999). *Influence, Inc.* Washington, D.C.: Center for Responsive Politics.

Chappell, Henry W., Jr. (1981). Campaign contributions and voting on the cargo preference bill: A comparison of simultaneous models. *Public Choice*, 36, 301–312.

Chari, V. V., Larry E. Jones, and Ramon Marimon (1997). The economics of split ticket voting in representative democracies. *American Economic Review*, 87, 957–976.

Cho, In-Koo, and David Kreps (1987). Signaling games and stable equilibria. *Quarterly Journal of Economics*, 102, 179–221.

Coleman, James S. (1990). *Foundations of Social Theory*. Cambridge, Mass.: Harvard University Press.

Corrado, Anthony, Thomas E. Mann, Daniel R. Ortiz, Trevor Potter, and Frank J. Sorauf (eds.) (1997). *Campaign Finance Reform*. Washington, D.C.: Brookings Institution.

Coughlin, Peter J. (1990). Majority rule and election models. *Journal of Economic Surveys*, 3, 157–188.

Coughlin, Peter J., Dennis C. Mueller, and Peter Murrell (1990). A model of electoral competition with interest groups. *Economics Letters*, 32, 307–311.

Cox, Gary W. (1997). *Making Votes Count*. Cambridge, England: Cambridge University Press.

Crawford, Vincent P., and Joel Sobel (1982). Strategic information transmission. *Econometrica*, 50, 1431–1451.

Denzau, Arthur T., and Michael C. Munger (1986). Legislators and interest groups: How unorganized interests get represented. *American Political Science Review*, 80, 89–106.

Dexter, Lewis A. (1969). *How Organizations Are Represented in Washington*. Indianapolis: Bobbs-Merrill.

Diamond, Peter A., and James A. Mirrlees (1971). Optimal taxation and public production: I. Production efficiency. *American Economic Review*, 61, 8–27.

Diermeier, Daniel, and Timothy J. Feddersen (1998). Comparing constitutions: Cohesion and distribution in legislatures. *European Economic Review*, 42 (Papers and Proceedings), 665–672.

Diermeier, Daniel, and Roger B. Myerson (1999). Bicameralism and its consequences for the internal organization of legislatures. *American Economic Review*, 89, 1182–1196.

Dixit, Avinash (1987). Strategic aspects of trade policy, in Truman Bewly (ed.), *Advances in Economic Theory: Fifth World Congress*. Cambridge, England: Cambridge University Press.

Dixit, Avinash, Gene M. Grossman, and Elhanan Helpman (1997). Common agency and coordination: General theory and application to government policymaking. *Journal of Political Economy*, 105, 752–769.

Dixit, Avinash, and John Londregan (1996). The determinants of success of special interests in redistributive politics. *Journal of Politics*, 58, 1132–1155.

Downs, Anthony (1957). *An Economic Theory of Democracy*. New York: Harper and Row.

Drazen, Allan (2000). *Political Economy in Macroeconomics*. Princeton, N.J.: Princeton University Press.

Durden, Garey C., Jason F. Shogren, and Jonathan I. Silberman (1991). The effects of interest group pressure on coal strip-mining legislation. *Social Science Quarterly*, 72, 237–250.

Elster, Jon (1989). Social norms and economic theory. *Journal of Economic Perspectives*, 4, 99–117.

Epstein, David, and Sharyn O'Halloran (1994). Administrative procedures, information and agency discretion. *American Journal of Political Science*, 38, 697–722.

Evans, Diana M. (1986). PAC contributions and roll-call voting: Conditional power, in A. J. Cigler and B. A. Loomis (eds.), *Interest Group Politics*, 2nd ed. Washington, D.C.: Congressional Quarterly.

Fair, Ray C. (1978). The effect of economic events on votes for president. *Review of Economics and Statistics*, 60, 159–173.

Fallows, Susan E. (1980). Technical staffing for congress: The myth of expertise. Ph.D. Dissertation, Cornell University.

Farrell, Joseph (1993). Meaning and credibility in cheap talk games. *Games and Economic Behavior*, 5, 514–531.

Farrell, Joseph, and Matthew Rabin (1996). Cheap talk. *Journal of Economic Perspectives*, 10, 103–118.

Feddersen, Timothy J., and Wolfgang Pesendorfer (1996). The swing voter's curse. *American Economic Review*, 86, 408–424.

Feddersen, Timothy J., Itai Sened, and Stephen G. Wright (1990). Rational voting and candidate entry under plurality rule. *American Journal of Political Science*, 34, 1005–1016.

Feldstein, Paul J., and Glenn Melnick (1984). Congressional voting behavior on hospital legislation: An exploratory study. *Journal of Health Politics, Policy and Law*, 8, 686–701.

Filer, John, Lawrence Kenny, and Rebecca B. Morton (1993). Redistribution, income and voting. *American Journal of Political Science*, 37, 63–87.

Fleisher, Richard (1993). PAC contributions and congressional voting on national defense. *Legislative Studies Quarterly*, 18, 391–409.

Fudenberg, Drew, and Jean Tirole (1991). *Game Theory*. Cambridge, Mass.: MIT Press.

Gawande, Kishore, and Usree Bandyopadhyay (2000). Is protection for sale? Evidence on the Grossman-Helpman theory of endogenous protection. *Reveiw of Economcs and Statistics*, 82, 139–152.

Gerber, Alan (1998). Estimating the effect of campaign spending on Senate election outcomes using instrumental variables. *American Political Science Review*, 92, 401–411.

Gilligan, Thomas W., and Keith Krehbiel (1987). Collective decision-making and standing committees: An informational rationale for restrictive amendment procedures. *Journal of Law, Economics, and Organization*, 3, 145–193.

Gilligan, Thomas W., and Keith Krehbiel (1989). Asymmetric information and legislative rules with a heterogeneous committee. *American Journal of Political Science*, 33, 459–490.

Goldberg, Pinelopi K., and Giovanni Maggi (1999). Protection for sale: An empirical investigation. *American Economic Review*, 89, 1135–1155.

Green, Donald P., and Jonathan S. Krasno (1988). Salvation for the spendthrift incumbent: Reestimating the effects of campaign spending in House elections. *American Journal of Political Science*, 32, 884–907.

Groseclose, Tim, and James M. Snyder (1996). Buying supermajorities. *American Political Science Review*, 90, 303–315.

Grossman, Gene M., and Elhanan Helpman (1996a). Competing for endorsements. Discussion Paper in Economics No. 182. Princeton, N.J.: Princeton University, Woodrow Wilson School.

Grossman, Gene M., and Elhanan Helpman (1996b). Electoral competition and special interest politics. *Review of Economic Studies*, 63, 265–286.

Grossman, Gene M., and Elhanan Helpman (1999). Competing for endorsements. *American Economic Review*, 89, 501–524.

Hansen, John M. (1991). *Gaining Access: Congress and the Farm Lobby*, 1919–1981. Chicago: University of Chicago Press.

Hayes, Michael T. (1981). *Lobbyists and Legislators*. New Brunswick, N.J.: Rutgers University Press.

Heinz, John P., Edward O. Laumann, Robert L. Nelson, and Robert H. Salisbury (1993). *The Hollow Core: Private Interests in National Policymaking*. Cambridge, Mass.: Harvard University Press.

Helpman, Elhanan, and Torsten Persson (1998). Lobbying and legislative bargaining. NBER Working Paper No. 6589.

Hinich, Melvin J., and Michel C. Munger (1997). *Analytical Politics*. Cambridge, England: Cambridge University Press.

Hinich, Melvin J., and Peter C. Ordeshook (1974). The electoral college: A spatial analysis. *Political Methodology*, 1, 1–29.

Hotelling, Harold (1929). Stability in competition. *Economic Journal*, 39, 41–57.

Jacobson, Gary C. (1980). *Money in Congressional Elections*. New Haven, Conn.: Yale University Press.

Jacobson, Gary C. (1985). Money and votes reconsidered: Congressional elections, 1972–1982. *Public Choice*, 47, 7–62.

Johnson, Linda L. (1985). The effectiveness of savings and loan political action committees. *Public Choice*, 46, 289–304.

Kandori, Michihiro (1992). Social norms and community enforcement. *Review of Economic Studies*, 59, 63–80.

Kau, James B., Donald Keenan, and Paul H. Rubin (1982). A general equilibrium model of congressional voting. *Quarterly Journal of Economics*, 97, 271–293.

Knack, Stephen (1992). Civic norms, social sanctions, and voter turnout. *Rationality and Society*, 4, 133–156.

Kramer, Gerald H. (1978). Existence of electoral equilibrium, in Peter C. Ordeshook (ed.), *Game Theory and Political Science*. New York: New York University Press.

Krishna, Vijay, and John Morgan (2001). A model of expertise. *Quarterly Journal of Economics*, 116, 747–775.

Krozner, Randall S., and Thomas Stratmann (1998). Interest group competition and the organization of Congress: Theory and evidence from financial services' political action committees. *American Economic Review*, 88, 1163–1187.

Langbein, Laura I., and Mark A. Lotwis (1990). The political efficacy of lobbying and money: Gun control in the U.S. House, 1986. *Legislative Studies Quarterly*, 15, 413–440.

Ledyard, John D. (1982). The paradox of voting and candidate competition, in G. Horwich and J. Quirk (eds.), *Essays in Contemporary Fields of Economics*. West Lafayette, Ind.: Purdue University Press.

Ledyard, John D. (1984). The pure theory of large two candidate elections. *Public Choice*, 44, 7–41.

Leighley, Jan E., and Jonathan Nagler (1992). Individual and systematic influence on turnout: Who votes? 1984. *Journal of Politics*, 54, 718–740.

Lindbeck, Assar, and Jörgen W. Weibull (1987). Balanced-budget redistribution as the outcome of political competition. *Public Choice*, 52, 273–297.

Lipman, Barton L., and Duane J. Seppi (1995). Robust inference in communication games with partial provability. *Journal of Economic Theory*, 66, 370–405.

Lohmann, Suzanne (1993). A signaling model of informative and manipulative political action. *American Political Science Review*, 87, 319–333.

Lohmann, Suzanne (1994). Information aggregation through costly political action. *American Economic Review*, 84, 518–530.

Lohmann, Suzanne (1995). Information, access, and contributions: A signaling model of lobbying. *Public Choice*, 85, 267–284.

Lohmann, Suzanne (1998). An information rationale for the power of special interests. *American Political Science Review*, 92, 809–827.

Loucks, Christine (1996). Finance industry PAC contributions to U.S. senators. *Public Choice*, 89, 210–219.

Magee, Stephen P., William A. Brock, and Leslie Young (1989). *Black Hole Tariffs and Endogenous Policy Theory: Political Economy in General Equilibrium*. Cambridge, England: Cambridge University Press.

Magelby, David B., and Candice J. Nelson (1990). *The Money Chase: Congressional Campaign Finance Reform*. Washington, D.C.: Brookings Institution.

McCarty, Nolan M., and Keith T. Poole (1998). An empirical spatial model of congressional campaigns. *Political Analysis*, 7, 1–30.

McKelvey, Richard D., and Richard Wendell (1976). Voting equilibria in multidimensional choice spaces. *Mathematics in Operations Research*, 1, 144–158.

Milbrath, Lester M. (1963). *The Washington Lobbyists*. Chicago: Rand McNally.

Milgrom, Paul, and John Roberts (1986). Relying on the information of interested parties. *Rand Journal of Economics*, 17, 18–32.

Morton, Rebecca B. (1991). Groups in rational turnout models. *American Journal of Political Science*, 35, 758–776.

Morton, Rebecca B. (1993). A group majority voting model of public good provision. *Social Choice and Welfare*, 4, 117–131.

Morton, Rebecca B., and Roger Myerson (1992). Campaign spending with impressionable voters. CMSEMS Working Paper No. 1023. Evanston, Ill.: Northwestern University.

Munger, Michael C. (1989). A simple test of the thesis that committee jurisdictions shape corporate PAC contributions. *Public Choice*, 62, 181–186.

Nash, John F. (1950). The bargaining problem. *Econometrica*, 18, 155–162.

Nownes, Anthony J., and Patricia Freeman (1998). Interest group activity in the States. *Journal of Politics*, 60, 86–112.

Olson, Mancur (1965). *The Logic of Collective Action*. Cambridge, Mass.: Harvard University Press.

Osborne, Martin J. (1995). Spacial models of political competition under plurality rule: A survey of some explanations of the number of candidates and the positions they take. *Canadian Journal of Economics*, 28, 261–301.

Osborne, Martin J., and Ariel Rubinstein (1990). *Bargaining and Markets*. New York: Academic Press.

Osborne, Martin J., and Al Slivinski (1996). A model of political competition with citizen candidates. *Quarterly Journal of Economics*, 111, 65–96.

Owens, John E. (1986). The impact of campaign contributions on legislative outcomes in Congress: Evidence from a House committee. *Political Studies*, 34, 285–295.

Palfrey, Thomas R., and Howard Rosenthal (1983). A strategic calculus of voting. *Public Choice*, 41, 7–53.

Palfrey, Thomas R., and Howard Rosenthal (1985). Voter participation and strategic uncertainty. *American Political Science Review*, 79, 62–78.

Peleg, Bezalel (1984). Quasi-coalition equilibria. Part I. Definitions and preliminary results. Research Memorandum No. 59. Jerusalem: Hebrew University of Jerusalem, Center for Research in Mathematics and Game Theory.

Persson, Torsten, Gerard Roland, and Guido Tabellini (2000). Comparative politics and public finance. *Journal of Political Economy*, 108, 1121–1161.

Persson, Torsten, and Guido Tabellini (2000). *Political Economics: Explaining Economic Policy*. Cambridge, Mass.: MIT Press.

Plott, Charles R. (1967). A notion of equilibrium and its possibility under majority rule. *American Economic Review*, 57, 787–806.

Poole, Keith T., and Thomas Romer (1985). Patterns of PAC contributions to the 1980 campaigns for the U.S. House of Representatives. *Public Choice*, 47, 63–111.

Potters, Jan, Randolph Sloof, and Frans van Winden (1997). Campaign expenditures, contributions and direct endorsements. *European Journal of Political Economy*, 13, 1–31.

Potters, Jan, and Frans van Winden (1992). Lobbying and asymmetric information. *Public Choice*, 74, 269–292.

Prat, Andrea (2001). Campaign spending with office-seeking politicians, rational voters and multiple lobbies. *Journal of Economic Theory* (forthcoming).

Prat, Andrea, and Aldo Rustichini (1999). Games played through agents. Tilburg, the Netherlands: Tilburg University, Center for Economic Research.

Riker, H. William (1962). *A Theory of Political Coalitions*. New Haven, Conn.: Yale University Press.

Riker, H. William, and Peter C. Ordeshook (1968). A theory of the calculus of voting. *American Political Science Review*, 62, 25–42.

Riker, H. William, and Peter C. Ordeshook (1973). *An Introduction to Positive Political Theory*. Englewood Cliffs, N.J.: Prentice-Hall.

Roemer, John E. (1994). A theory of policy differentiation in single issue electoral politics. *Social Choice and Welfare*, 11, 355–380.

Romer, Thomas, and Howard Rosenthal (1979). Political resource allocation, controlled agendas, and the status quo. *Public Choice*, 33, 27–44.

Sabato, Larry J. (1981). *The Rise of the Political Consultants*. New York: Basic Books.

Saltzman, Gregory M. (1987). Congressional voting on labor issues: The role of PACs. *Industrial and Labor Relations Review*, 40, 163–179.

Samuelson, Paul A. (1947). *Foundations of Economic Analysis*. Cambridge, Mass.: Harvard University Press.

Schlozman, Kay L., and John T. Tierney (1986). *Organized Interests and American Democracy*. New York: Harper and Row.

Schram, Martin (1995). *Speaking Freely*. Washington, D.C.: Center for Responsive Politics.

Shachar, Ron, and Barry Nalebuff (1999). Follow the leader: Theory and evidence on political participation. *American Economic Review*, 89, 525–547.

Sheets, Tara E., ed. (2000). *Encyclopedia of Associations, 36th edition: Volume 1, National Organizations of the U.S.* Detroit: The Gale Group.

Shepsle, Kenneth A. (1979). Institutional arrangements and equilibrium in multidimensional voting models. *American Journal of Political Science*, 23, 27–60.

Shepsle, Kenneth A. (1991). *Models of Multiparty Electoral Competition*. Chur, Switzerland: Harwood Academic Publishers.

Shepsle, Kenneth A., and Barry Weingast (1981). Structure-induced equilibrium and legislative choice. *Public Choice*, 37, 503–519.

Smith, Hedrick (1988). *The Power Game: How Washington Works*. New York: Random House.

Smith, Richard A. (1995). Interest group influence in the U.S. Congress. *Legislative Studies Quarterly*, 20, 89–139.

Snyder, James M., Jr. (1990). Campaign contributions as investments: The U.S. House of Representatives, 1980–1986. *Journal of Political Economy*, 98, 1195–1227.

Snyder, James M., Jr. (1991). On buying legislatures. *Economics and Politics*, 3, 93–109.

Stern, Philip M. (1992). *Still the Best Congress Money Can Buy*. Washington, D.C.: Regnery Publishing, Inc.

References   355

Stole, Lars (1991). *Essays on the Economics of Contracts*. Ph.D. diss., Massachusetts Institute of Technology, Cambridge, Mass.

Stolper, Wolfgang F., and Paul A. Samuelson (1941). Protection and real wages. *Review of Economic Studies*, 9, 58–73.

Stratmann, Thomas (1992). Are contributors rational? Untangling strategies of political action committees. *Journal of Political Economy*, 100, 647–664.

Stratmann, Thomas (1998). The market for congressional votes: Is timing of contributions everything? *Journal of Law and Economics*, 41, 85–113.

Stratmann, Thomas, and Randall S. Krozner (1998). Interest group competition and the organization of congress: Theory and evidence from financial services political action committees. *American Economic Review*, 88, 1163–1187.

Strömberg, David (1998). Mass-media competition, political competition, and public policy. Mimeo. Department of Economics, Princeton University.

Sutton, John (1998). *Technology and Market Structure: Theory and History*. Cambridge, Mass.: MIT Press.

Thompson, Caroline (2000a). Self-selection or cultivation? Industry loyalties and congressional committees. Unpublished paper, Department of Economics, Princeton University.

Thompson, Caroline (2000b). Paying tribute: Candidate giving to political parties. Unpublished paper, Department of Economics, Princeton University.

Truman, David B. (1951). *The Governmental Process: Political Interests and Public Opinion*. New York: Knopf.

Tullock, Gordon (1967). *Towards a Mathematics of Politics*. Ann Arbor: University of Michigan Press.

Tullock, Gordon (1980). Efficient rent seeking, in J. M. Buchanan, R. D. Tollison, and G. Tullock (eds.), *Toward a Theory of the Rent-Seeking Society*. College Station: Texas A&M Press.

Uhlaner, Carole J. (1989). Rational turnout: The neglected role of groups. *American Journal of Political Science*, 33, 390–422.

Vesenka, Mary H. (1989). Economic interests and ideological conviction: A note on PACs and agriculture acts. *Journal of Economic Behavior and Organization*, 12, 259–263.

Walker, Jack L., Jr. (1991). *Mobilizing Interest Groups in America*. Ann Arbor: University of Michigan Press.

Welch, William P. (1980). Allocation of political monies: Economic interest groups. *Public Choice*, 20, 83–97.

Welch, William P. (1982). Campaign contributions and legislative voting: Milk money and dairy price supports. *Western Political Quarterly*, 35, 478–495.

Wittman, Donald A. (1983). Candidate motivations: A synthesis of alternatives. *American Political Science Review*, 77, 142–157.

Wolfinger, Raymond E., and Steven J. Rosenstone (1980). *Who Votes?* New Haven, Conn.: Yale University Press.

Index

Access costs, 11, 26, 144, 171–183
  bias and, 28, 172–183
  for groups with known bias, 172–175
  for groups with unknown bias, 176–183
  as signals of interest group preferences, 180–184
Advertising. *See* Issue advertising; Voter education
Advocacy lobbying, 157–161. *See also* Lobbying
Agency, common, 248–256. *See also* Principal-agent relationship
Agenda setters, 18, 35, 43
  in legislative bargaining, 291–299
Aldrich, J. H., 76n
Alesina, A., 59
Altruism, 14
Annenberg Public Policy Center, 7
Ansolabehere, S., 66, 71n
Austen-Smith, D., 66, 180, 183, 284n, 322n, 331n

Babbling equilibrium, 109–110, 113, 117, 118, 141, 151
  for voter education, 198, 204
Baldwin, R. E., 12, 13n
Ball, R., 166n, 229n
Bandyopadhyay, U., 16
Banerjee, A., 148n
Banks, J., 284n
Bargaining
  in influence buying, 243–246
  legislative. *See* Legislative bargaining
Baron, D. P., 43n, 188n, 283, 292, 322n
Battaglini, M., 133, 134n, 137–138
Bauer, R., 171n

Baumgartner, F. R., 3, 4n
Bayesian equilibrium, 15n, 108n
Bayes' rule, 108n, 139n, 197
Becker, G. S., 279n
Bernheim, B. D., 232n, 249, 268n, 269, 270
Berry, J., 4, 8
Besley, T., 61, 62
Best-response set, 250–251
  in influence buying, 237
Bias, 23–26
  access costs and, 28, 172–183
  credibility and, 23–26
  like, 25, 121–130, 153–155
  with multiple lobbies, 120–138
  opposite, 25, 121, 130–133, 155–156
  in pliable party platforms, 330–331
  with single lobby, 106–113
  unknown, 156–161
Birnbaum, J. H., 5
Broad mandates
  by interest groups, 193–194
  voter education and, 202, 216–223
Brock, W. A., 331n
Bronars, S. G., 13n
Budget allocation, 233–235

Calculus of voting, 77, 84–85
Calvert, R. L., 41
Campaign contributions, 8–13, 30–38, 319–345
  for access, 11, 144, 171–183. *See also* Access costs
  for credibility, 11–12
  effects of, 11–13
  electoral motive for, 37–38, 319–320, 328, 331–339, 340–341

Campaign contributions (cont.)
  growth in, 9
  impressionable voters and, 320, 321–
    324, 325–326
  influence motive for, 12–13, 31, 37–38,
    319–320, 327, 328–331, 334–339, 341–
    345
  from multiple interest groups, 339–345
  pliable party platforms and, 324–327
  regulation of, 9–11
  soft money, 10
  to state party organizations, 9–10
  strategic voters and, 320, 321, 322–323,
    325
Candidates. *See* Politicians
Center for Responsive Politics, 6
Chappell, H. W., Jr., 13n
Chari, V., 284n
Cheap-talk game, 109–110, 138
Cho, I.-K., 163n
Coalition-proof equilibrium, 269–270
Coate, S., 61, 62
Coelho, Tony, 6
Common agency, 248–256
  contribution schedules for, 251–252,
    253–256
  equilibrium for, 252
Compensating contribution function,
    232, 232n
  in influence buying, 232
Compensating contribution schedules
  for competing interest groups, 266–
    270
  definition of, 266
  local, 253–256
  for single interest group, 232
Compensating equilibrium, 33–34, 266–
    270
  coalition-proof, 269–270
  definition of, 266
  in influence buying, 236–237
  joint efficiency of, 244, 268–269
  Pareto-efficient, 276–278
  in redistributive taxation, 275–279
  in trade policy, 270–275
Condorcet winner, 43, 49, 56, 66
Congressional representatives. *See*
    Politicians
Constrained Pareto efficiency, 276–278
Contribution function, 228–229, 237
  compensating, 232, 232n

Contribution schedules
  in common agency game, 251–256
  compensating, 232, 232n, 266–270. *See
    also* Compensating contribution
    schedules
  differentiable, 253–256, 266
  for interest group competition, 248–
    249
  locally compensating, 253–256
  Nash equilibrium in, 272–274
  for one-dimensional policy choice, 229–
    232
Corrado, A., 9n, 10
Coughlin, P. J., 41, 97n
Cox, G. W., 68
Crawford, V. P., 24, 112, 141, 142, 197,
    199
Credibility
  buying of, 11–12
  endorsements and, 210–212
  lobbying costs and, 161–170
  of lobbyists, 105–118
  voter assessment of, 186
  voter education and, 186–194, 195–199,
    202–204
Democracy
  direct, 42–53. *See also* Direct democracy
  Downsian model of, 18
  representative, 53–64. *See also*
    Representative democracy
Demonstrations, protest, 8
Denzau, A. T., 188n, 249n
de Sola Pool, I., 171n
Dexter, L. A., 171n
Diermeier, D., 284n, 302n
Differentiable contribution schedules,
    253–256, 266
Direct democracy, 42–53
  with agenda setters, 42–45
  median voter in, 42–45
  multidimensional policy in, 50–52
  sincere voting in, 45, 46–48, 49
  strategic voting in, 45, 46, 48, 49
  structure-induced equilibrium for, 52
  without agenda setters, 45–48
Dixit, A., 96, 98, 268n, 277n, 278, 280
Downey, Thomas, 11
Downs, A., 18, 54, 76
Downsian model, 18, 54–58
Durden, G. C., 13n

Education. *See* Voter education
Election-oriented politicians, 66–67
Elections
    campaign contributions in. *See*
        Campaign contributions
    of endogenous candidates, 59–64
    legislative, 64–73. *See also* Legislative
        elections
    runoff, 46
    turnout in, 19–20, 76–87. *See also* Voter
        participation
Electoral motive, for campaign
    contributions, 37–38, 319–320, 328,
    331–339, 340–341
Elster, J., 82
Emissions tax problem, 238–243
Encyclopedia of Associations, 2, 3
Endogenous lobbying costs, 26, 144,
    161–170
    credibility and, 161–170
    with dichotomous information, 161–164
    with multiple states of nature, 164–168
Endorsement equilibrium, 211–212
Endorsements, 7, 30, 187, 210–212
    credibility and, 210–212
    by interest groups, 187
Epstein, D., 229n
Equilibrium
    babbling, 109–110, 113, 117, 118, 141,
        151, 198, 204
    Bayesian, 15n, 108n
    coalition-proof, 269–270
    common agency, 252–256
    compensating, 33–34, 266–270. *See also*
        Compensating equilibrium
    contribution, 236–237
    definition of, 15
    efficiency of, 31
    with endogenous entry, 59–61
    endorsement, 211–212
    ex ante welfare and, 113n, 118–120, 142
    full-revelation, 124–125, 134n, 137–138,
        139–141, 162–163
    information and, 20–21
    mixed-strategy, 56n, 78–81, 149–150
    Nash, 44n, 45, 55, 65, 66, 78, 269–270,
        272–274
    partial-revelation, 133
    partition, 24–25, 29, 113, 118, 119, 126–
        130, 141–142, 197, 198, 203–204
    properties of, 140–142

pure-strategy, 56, 62–64, 78, 308n
separating, 163
structure-induced, 52
symmetric, 78–81
2-partition, 117, 118, 123, 126–130, 131,
    141, 151–152, 198, 203–204, 218–220
3-partition, 118, 126, 128–129, 132–133,
    152
uniqueness of, 142
Equilibrium policy
    with agenda setter, 291–299
    without agenda setter, 289–291
Evans, D. M., 13n
Exogenous lobbying costs, 26, 143–144
    with like biases, 153–155
    with opposite biases, 155–156
    for single lobby, 145–152
        with continuous information, 150–152
        with dichotomous information, 145–150
    for two lobbies, 152–161

Fair, R. C., 70n
Farrell, J., 110
Feddersen, T., 59, 61, 190n, 217n, 284n
Federal Election Campaign Act of 1974,
    2, 8, 10
Federal Election Committee, 9–10
Federalist Papers, The, 4
Feldstein, P. J., 13n
Ferejohn, J. A., 43n, 283, 292
Filer, J., 86n
Fixed positions, 19, 69–73, 89–95
    knowledge asymmetries and, 89–95
    partisanship and, 21–22, 95–99
Fleisher, R., 13n
Freeman, P., 4, 5, 8
Free riders, 103, 308n
Fudenberg, D., 108n
Full-revelation equilibrium, 124–125,
    134n, 137–138, 139–141, 162–163

Gawande, K., 16
Gerber, A., 322n
Gilligan, T. W., 283
Goldberg, P. K., 16
Green, D. P., 322n
Groseclose, T., 301
Grossman, G. M., 188n, 211, 268n, 277n,
    278, 280
Group norms, voting and, 20
Group-participation models, 84

Hansen, J. M., 11
Heckscher-Ohlin model, of international
    trade, 270
Heinz, J. P., 4, 5
Helpman, E., 188n, 211, 268n, 277n, 278,
    280, 300n
Hinich, M. J., 49, 66
Hotelling, H., 54

Impressionable voters, 320, 321–324,
    325–326
Income redistribution, 275–279
  compensating equilibria for, 278
Industry regulation and protection,
    influence buying for, 238–243
Influence, competition for, 32, 247–281.
    See also Interest group competition
Influence, Inc., 6
Influence buying, 12–13, 31, 37–38, 225–
    246
  bargaining in, 243–246
  best-response set in, 237
  for budget allocation, 233–235
  compensating contribution function in,
    232, 232n
  implicit vs. explicit, 228
  with incumbent politician, 225–246
  for industry regulation and protection,
    238–243
  legislative, 283–317. *See also* Legislative
    bargaining
  with multiple policy instruments, 235–
    237
  with one-dimensional policy choice,
    226–232
  policy vector in, 235, 237
Influence motive, for campaign
    contributions, 12–13, 31, 37–38, 319–
    320, 327, 328–331, 334–339, 341–345
Information
  bias and, 18–30, 23–26
  continuous, 113–118
  costs of, 26–28. *See also* Lobbying costs
  credibility of, 23–26, 105–118
  dissemination of, 20–21, 28–30, 104,
    107–118. *See also* Lobbying
  fixed vs. pliable positions and, 89–95
  multidimensional policy and, 133–138
Information asymmetries
  in principal-agent relationships, 229n
  voter participation and, 88–95

Informative lobbying, 107–118, 185–222.
    See also Lobbying; Voter education
Interest group competition
  advantages and disadvantages of, 279–
    281
  for income redistribution policy, 275–279
  for legislative influence, 299–317. *See
    also* Legislative bargaining
  for minimum wage policy, 256–265
  for trade policy, 270–275
Issue advertising, 7. *See also* Voter
    education
  credibility of, 195–199. *See also*
    Credibility
  for interest group members, 212
  timing of, 194–209

Jacobson, G. C., 322n
Johnson, L. L., 13n
Jones, L. E., 284n

Kandori, M., 82, 83, 84
Kau, J. B., 13n
Keenan, D., 13n
Kenney, L., 86n
Knack, S., 83
Knowledge asymmetries
  in principal-agent relationships, 229n
  voter participation and, 88–95
Kramer, G. H., 56n
Krasno, J. S., 322n
Krehbiel, K., 283
Kreps, D., 163n
Krishna, V., 120–121, 125, 126n, 129, 130,
    133
Krozner, R., 13n

Langbein, L. I., 13n
Ledyard, J., 77, 78
Leech, B., 3, 4n
Legislative bargaining, 283–317
  with agenda setter, 291–299
  Baron-Ferejohn model of, 292–299
  best-alternative policy in, 294–295
  minimum winning coalition in, 288–291
  by multiple groups, 299–317
  project scale and, 314–317
  at proposal stage, 309–314
  randomized, 301–302
  sequential, 301–302
  by single group, 284–291

Snyder model of, 285–291
without agenda setter, 284–291
Legislative elections, 64–73. *See also*
  Elections
campaign contributions for. *See*
  Campaign contributions
for proportional representation, 68–73
for single-member districts, 65–68
Legislative process, models of, 283–284
Legislators. *See* Politicians
Leighley, J. E., 86n
Lerner symmetry theorem, 274n
Like bias, 25, 121–130
lobbying costs and, 153–155
Lindbeck, A., 72n
Lipman, B. L., 120n
Lobbying, 4–13, 103–142
advocacy, 157–161
bias in, 106–113. *See also* Bias
as cheap talk, 109–110, 138
definition of, 104
ex ante welfare and, 113n, 118–120
expenditures on, 6–7
informative, 107–118, 185–222. *See also*
  Voter education
of legislative bodies, 34–36
multi-group, 120–138
persuasiveness of, 105–118
private messages in, 123–125
public messages in, 125–130
scale of, 6
secret messages in, 122–123
single-group, 105–120
for voter education, 185–222. *See also*
  Voter education
Lobbying costs, 26–28, 143–184
access, 11, 26, 28, 144, 171–183. *See also*
  Access costs
endogenous, 26, 144, 161–170. *See also*
  Endogenous lobbying costs
exogenous, 26, 143–161. *See also*
  Exogenous lobbying costs
minimum, 166–168
with multiple interest groups, 168–
  170
partition equilibrium and, 150–152
with unknown biases, 156–161
Lobbying Disclosure Act of 1995, 6
Lobbying equilibria. *See* Equilibrium
Lobbyists
credibility of, 105–118. *See also*
  Credibility

as information sources
for legislators, 5–6
for organization members, 7–8
for public, 6–7
numbers of, 6
Locally compensating contribution
  schedule, 253–256
Logic of collective action, 103
Lohmann, S., 95n, 156, 168, 170, 172n
Londregan, J., 96, 98
Lott, J. R., Jr., 13n
Lotwis, M. A., 13n
Loucks, C., 13n, 297n

Madison, James, 4
Magee, C., 12, 13n, 331n
Maggi, G., 16
Mandates, narrow vs. broad, 193–194
Marimon, R., 284n
McCarty, N. M., 174n
McKelvey, R., 51
Media, issue advertising in. *See* Issue
  advertising
Median voter theorem, 17–18, 42–44
Melnick, G., 13n
Milbrath, L. M., 4, 11
Milgrom, P., 120n
Minimum wage issue, 32–33, 256–265
Minimum winning coalition, 35, 288–
  291
Mitchell, George, 11
Mixed-strategy equilibrium, 56n, 78–81,
  149–150
Monotonic equilibrium, 126n
access costs and, 180
Morgan, J., 120–121, 125, 126n, 129, 130,
  133
Morton, R. B., 84, 85, 86n
Mueller, D. C., 97n
Multidimensional policy, 50–52, 133–
  138
Multipeaked preferences, 48–49
Munger, M. C., 13n, 49, 188n, 249n, 297n
Murray, A., 5
Murrell, P., 97n
Myerson, R. B., 302n

Nagler, J., 86n
Nalebuff, B., 84, 85n
Narrow mandates
by interest groups, 193–194
voter education and, 193–215

Nash, J. F., 243
Nash equilibrium, 44n, 45, 55, 65, 78
  coalition-proof, 269–270
  in contribution schedules, 272–274
Nonconnected political action
    committees, 9
Non-single-peaked preferences, 48–49
Nownes, A. J., 4, 5, 8

O'Halloran, S., 229n
Olson, M., 103
Opposite bias, 25, 121, 130–133
  lobbying costs and, 155–156
Ordeshook, P. C., 66, 76, 82, 288n
Osborne, M. J., 41, 44n, 61, 67, 243n
Owens, J. E., 13n

Palfrey, T., 78, 79, 81, 82
Paradox of voting, 77–82
Pareto efficiency, 276–278
Partial-revelation equilibrium, 133, 141
Partisanship, 21–22
  voter turnout and, 95–99
Partition equilibrium, 24–25, 29, 113,
    118, 119, 126–130, 141–142, 197
  lobbying costs and, 150–152
  monotonic, 126n
  for voter education, 198, 203–204
Party-list system, 68
Party platforms
  election- vs. policy-motivated
    politicians and, 65–68
  fixed vs. pliable, 19, 69–73, 89–95, 97–
    99. See also Fixed positions; Pliable
    positions
Peleg, B., 269n
Penny, Tim, 13
Persson, T., 284n, 300n
Pesendorfer, W., 190n, 217n
Pliable positions, 19, 21, 22, 69–73
  bias in, 330–331
  campaign contributions and, 324–327
  knowledge asymmetries and, 89–95
  partisanship and, 22, 95–99
  voter turnout and, 89–95
Plott, C. R., 51
Plurality rule, 43
Policy, multidimensional, 50–52, 133–
    138
Policy issues. See also Party platforms
  voter understanding of, 88–95
Policy-motivated politicians, 67

Policy preferences
  non-single-peaked, 48–49
  single-peaked, 17, 48–49, 56
Policy vector
  in common agency game, 251–256
  in influence buying, 235, 237
Political action committees, 2, 8–13
  campaign contributions by, 9–13. See
    also Campaign contributions
  corporate, 9
  definition of, 2
  nonconnected, 9
  numbers of, 2
Political influence, buying of. See
    Influence buying
Political moderates, 98
Political parties
  campaign contributions to. See
    Campaign contributions
  platforms of. See Party platforms
Politicians
  access fees of, 11, 28, 144, 171–183. See
    also Access costs
  as common agents, 248–256. See also
    Common agency
  contributions to. See Campaign
    contributions
  election-oriented, 66–67
  endogenous, 59–64
  endorsements of. See Endorsements
  with policy commitments, 59–61
  without policy commitments, 61–64
  policy-motivated, 67
Pollution tax problem, 238–243
Poole, K. T., 174n
Potters, J., 148, 322n
Prat, A., 322n
Presidential candidates. See Politicians
Principal-agent relationship, 229, 248–
    256. See also Common agency
Private messages, 123–125
Proportional representation, legislative
    elections for, 68–73
Protests and demonstrations, 8
Proxmire, William, 12
Public messages, 125–130
Public spending, allocation of, 233–235
Pure-strategy equilibrium, 56, 62–64, 78,
    308n

Rabin, M., 110n
Rational ignorance, of voters, 185

Redistributive taxation, 275–279
Repeated-game theory, 82–83
Representative democracy, 53–64
  Downsian model of, 18, 54–56, 57–58
  endogenous candidates in, 59–64
  legislative bargaining in, 283–317. *See
  also* Legislative bargaining
Riker, H. W., 76, 82, 288n
Riker's size principle, 288
Roberts, J., 120n
Roemer, J. E., 58n
Roland, G., 284n
Romer, T., 43n, 174n
Rosenthal, H., 43n, 78, 79, 81, 82
Rubin, P. H., 13n
Rubinstein, A., 243n
Runoff elections, in direct democracy, 46

Sabato, L. J., 171n
Saltzman, G. M., 13n
Samuelson, P. A., 271n, 277n
Scholzman, K. L., 3, 4, 7, 8, 23n
Schram, M., 11, 13
Secret messages, 122–123
Self-interest, as motivation, 14
Senators. *See* Politicians
Separating equilibria, 163
Seppi, D. J., 120n
Shachar, R., 84, 85n
Shepsle, K. A., 52, 53
Shogren, J. F., 13n
Silberman, J. I., 13n
Sincere voting, 18, 45
  in direct democracy, 45, 46–48, 49
Single-member districts, legislative
  elections in, 65–68
Single-peaked preferences, 17, 42, 48–
  49
Slivinski, A., 61
Sloof, R., 322n
Smith, H., 5, 6n
Snyder, J. M., 66, 71n, 285, 289n, 292,
  301, 321n
Snyder model, of legislative bargaining,
  285–291
Sobel, J., 24, 112, 141, 142, 197, 199
Social norm(s)
  definition of, 20, 82
  enforcement of, 83–84
  voting as, 20, 82–86
Soft money, 10
Somanathan, R., 148n

State party organizations, contributions
  to, 9–10. *See also* Campaign
  contributions
Stern, P., 12
Stole, L., 249
Stolper, W., 271n
Stolper-Samuelson theorem, 271n
Strategic information transmission, 112
Strategic interaction, equilibrium with,
  15
Strategic voting, 18, 45–46
  in direct democracy, 45–49
Stratmann, T., 13n, 297n
Strömberg, D., 88n
Structure-induced equilibrium, 52
Sutton, J., 56n
Swing voters, 18, 98
Symmetric equilibrium, 78–81
Systemic mistakes, avoidance of, 14–15

Tabellini, G., 284n
Taxation, redistributive, 275–279
Thompson, C., 13n, 227n, 297n
3-partition equilibrium, 118, 126, 128–
  129, 132–133, 152
Tierney, J. T., 3, 4, 7, 8, 23n
Tirole, J., 108n
Trade associations, 3
Trade policy, 270–275
Truman, D. B., 11
Tullock, G., 52, 76, 279n
Turnout, 19–20, 76–78. *See also* Voter
  participation
2-partition equilibrium, 117, 123, 126–
  130, 131, 141
  lobbying costs and, 151–152
  for voter education, 198, 203–204, 218–
  220

Uhlaner, C. J., 84
Unique equilibrium outcome, 43–44
Unknown biases, lobbying costs and,
  156–161

van Winden, F., 148, 322n
Vesenka, M. H., 13n
Vote buying. *See* Campaign
  contributions; Influence buying
Voter(s), 41–73
  in direct democracy, 42–53
  impressionable, 320, 321–324, 325–326
  median, 17–18, 42–44

Voter(s)
  rational ignorance of, 185–186
  swing, 22, 98
Voter education, 7, 185–222
  beneficiaries of, 199–201
  broad mandates and, 216–223
  credibility and, 186–194, 195–199, 202–
    204
  endorsements and, 187, 210–212
  for interest group members, 7–8, 186–
    187, 188–191, 191, 193–194, 212–215
  interparty competition and, 204–208,
    214–215
  narrow mandates and, 193–215
  timing of, 187, 194–209
Voter knowledge, 88–95
Voter participation, 19–20, 76–87
  calculus of voting and, 77
  consumption benefits of, 28
  group-participation models of, 84–86
  knowledge asymmetries and, 88–95
  paradox of voting and, 77–82
  partisanship and, 95–99
  policy consequences of, 86–87
  rates of, 76
  as social norm, 20, 82–86
Voting. *See also* Voter participation
  calculus of, 77, 84–85
  paradox of, 77–82
  sincere, 18, 45, 46–48, 49
  single- vs. non-single-peaked
    preferences in, 48–49
  strategic, 18, 45–49, 320, 321, 322–323,
    325
Voting behavior, models of, 17–19
Voting groups, 75–99

Walker, J. L., 4
Washington Representatives, 2
Weibull, J. W., 72n
Weingast, B., 52, 53
Welch, W. P., 13n, 174n
Welfare
  aggregate, 239, 256
  ex ante, 106, 113n, 118–120, 142, 163–
    164
  voter education and, 200–201
Wendell, R., 51
Whinston, M., 232n, 249, 268n, 269, 270
Wittman, D., 58n

Young, L., 331n